Management Consulting Today and Tomorrow Casebook

D1260354

This casebook complements the text *Management Consulting Today and Tomorrow*. The book consists of 19 cases, including those from Harvard and Stanford and the University of Southern California. The cases cover a broad range of topics and practice areas that are pertinent to current management consulting. The six parts parallel the six parts in the text, including an introduction to the cases by the editors, delineating topics and issues that are critical for today's consultants. Several cases offer new insights into the practice areas of Strategy, IT, Operations Management, Change Management and more on Data Gathering and the Future of Consulting. This casebook, together with the text, will help to increase awareness among consultants and students about skill requirements, as well as make clients sensitive to what is demanded of them in a highly competitive consulting environment.

Larry Greiner is Professor of Management and Organization at the University of Southern California.

Thomas H. Olson is Professor of Clinical Management and Organization at the University of Southern California.

Flemming Poulfelt is Professor of Management and Strategy, Vice Dean at Copenhagen Business School, and Director of the CBS Leadership Lab.

Teaching notes for the cases in this book are available on the companion website **www.routledge.com/textbooks/9780415803564**.

Management Consulting Today and Tomorrow Casebook

Enhancing Skills to Become Better Professionals

Edited by

Larry Greiner, Thomas H. Olson, and Flemming Poulfelt

Routledge
Taylor & Francis Group

NEW YORK AND LONDON

First published 2005
by South-Western, part of the Thomson Corporation

This edition published in its original form
by Routledge
270 Madison Ave, New York, NY 10016

Simultaneously published in the UK
by Routledge
2 Park Square, Milton Park, Abingdon, Oxon OX14 4RN

Routledge is an imprint of the Taylor & Francis Group, an informa business

© 2005 South-Western, part of the Thomson Corporation

© 2010 Taylor & Francis

Typeset in Minion by
Swales & Willis Ltd, Exeter, Devon
Printed and bound in the United States of America on acid-free paper by
Sheridan Books, Inc.

Library of Congress Cataloging-in-Publication Data
Management consulting today and tomorrow casebook : enhancing skills to become better professionals / edited by Larry E. Greiner, Thomas H. Olson, and Flemming Poulfelt.
    p. cm.
    Includes bibliographical references and index.
    1. Business consultants—Case studies.   2. Consulting firms—Case studies.   I. Greiner, Larry E.   II. Olson, Thomas H.   III. Poulfelt, Flemming.
    HD69.C6G734 2010
    001—dc22   2009005999

ISBN10: 0–415–80357–8 (hbk)
ISBN10: 0–415–80356–X (pbk)

ISBN13: 978–0–415–80357–1 (hbk)
ISBN13: 978–0–415–80356–4 (pbk)

CONTENTS

Part 6.   The Future of Consulting

PREFACE

Management consulting is a fast changing industry. Any "student" of consulting, whether neophyte or experienced professional, needs constant updating about the profession and its varied skills. This process of updating occurs not just from reading, such as gained from this casebook's companion book, *Management Consulting Today and Tomorrow*, but also from engaging in experiential exercises that focus on the practice and skills of consulting. This casebook (and its surrounding course if the reader is currently in a training program or university setting) provides a major learning step in this broadening direction of advanced consultant development.

By going through this casebook, the reader and student of consulting will become more aware of how different clients view their problems, how consulting firms analyze and even redefine these problems, and how they intervene with proposed solutions. You will also learn how all the major practice areas are marketed, sold and managed, from information systems to strategic studies, as well as observing how these different projects evolve in a variety of client situations, including the global context. There are also several cases focused on how consulting firms manage themselves as they seek to grow and perform better. Finally, there is a concluding section and case on the future of the consulting industry.

The case method of teaching adds more than new knowledge about consulting; it also provides an intensive experience in sharpening one's analytical abilities, discovering the different opinions of others, and attempting to change the views of others through dialog. Under an experienced teacher, this method of teaching can make a major difference in learning.

But even cases and discussion are not enough. The cases in this book should also be supplemented by readings (see *Management Consulting Today and Tomorrow*), exercises, and a field consulting project. The use of several educational methods is more likely to develop the full range of necessary skills for performing the profession more effectively. For this purpose, we have provided a detailed syllabus in the *Teachers Manual* outlining an "ideal" course that employs all these learning methods.

We are especially indebted to the authors of the cases in this casebook. We conducted a broad search to find the best teaching cases, and they are included here. While all the cases are recent, their dates are less important than the underlying learning about the enduring issues in them. Cases are a form of research, and we need more research of all kinds to document what *actually* takes place in consulting and in consulting firms. Writing an informative case about consulting is not easy, since many consulting firms are private and the industry's credibility depends on confidentiality with clients. We hope this collection and its use in an exciting learning environment helps to advance the profession and the skills of the students involved.

Teaching notes for the cases in this book are available on the companion website **www.routledge.com/textbooks/9780415803564**.

Larry Greiner, Thomas Olson, Flemming Poulfelt

Part 1

Consulting Industry, Skills and Marketing

Introduction

Case 1.1

McKinsey & Company: An Institution at a Crossroads
(Ashish Nanda and Kelley Morrell)

Case 1.2

Marketing at Bain & Company
(Robert Pedrero and Miklos Sarvary)

INTRODUCTION

Consulting is a profession, and it requires a high degree of skill and ethical conduct. It is also an exciting business to study because of its wide influence on management practice throughout the world. All students of consulting need to understand the industry for the broader context it provides to their own work and career plans. In addition to studying the cases, a student can gain greater depth in understanding the industry, its related skills and marketing implications from reading Chapters 1 to 3 in Greiner and Poulfelt's book, *Management Consulting Today and Tomorrow*.[1]

The case on *McKinsey & Company* not only provides insight into this outstanding consulting firm but also tells us how it has established its successful niche in the industry over many years while adapting to a changing market. The case on *Marketing at Bain & Company*, which is another well-positioned strategy consulting firm, describes its various marketing activities. This case raises questions about how the firm can further develop its position relative to other consulting firms. In both of these cases, the class will be able to infer and discuss much about the required skills and professional values of effective consultants.

Management consulting is a high-growth industry, achieving an annual expansion rate of approximately 20% over many years, which is exceptional in comparison with other industries. However, in late 2001, the consulting industry experienced more than a normal wake-up call after the tragedies of 9/11, the Enron and Arthur Andersen scandals, and a worldwide economic recession. Consolidation of the industry is accelerating, moving toward fewer mega global firms performing a variety of consulting and nonconsulting services. At the same time, there remains an abundance of small- and medium-sized national, regional, and local niche players offering specialized and personalized services.

Looking at the industry from the demand side, this is where meeting a client's needs becomes the acid test for a consultant's relevance and value. Being able to help clients to create more value is the *raison d'être* for management consultants. The legitimacy and success of the industry to date is more evident as attested by the number of organizations that continue to engage consultants and by the high rate of repeat business.

The profile of service offerings, whether it be in strategy or operations consulting, is rooted in the intellectual capital business, which causes consulting firms to be highly innovative in developing new models and methods for improving business practice. Conversely, the industry has sometimes been accused of spreading fads when they have little value. In the press, the consulting industry has frequently been criticized for its high fees, occasional failures, secrecy, and mystery. Nevertheless, for new graduates, the consulting business continues to be extremely attractive for those seeking challenging work and hoping for a shortcut to senior executive positions in the corporate world.

Today the consulting industry is at a crossroads, given the many changes that are taking place. The challenges are numerous: Can firms still compete if they are not actively involved in providing web-based services and outsourcing management? Which firms will grow from acquisitions to become mega firms? What will be the impact of new ownership structures? Will the industry still be attractive for new recruits? How can firms enforce strong ethical codes? What issues will be most on the minds of clients in coming years? And can the value of consulting be measured by research, so that the business is further legitimized? For each firm, these questions will be answered differently. That is the value in analyzing and discussing each case in this book.

This initial section in the book contains cases that focus on the dynamics of the consulting industry, its required skills, and the importance of marketing by consulting firms in selling their services.

NOTE

1.   Greiner, L. & Poulfelt, F. 2009. *Management Consulting Today and Tomorrow*, Taylor & Francis.

Case 1.1

McKINSEY & COMPANY: AN INSTITUTION AT A CROSSROADS

(Ashish Nanda and Kelley Morrell)

ABOUT THE AUTHORS

Professor Ashish Nanda and Research Associate Kelley Morrell prepared this case. This case was developed from published sources. The case draws upon the following earlier HBS cases: Christopher A. Bartlett, "McKinsey & Company: Managing Knowledge and Learning," HBS Case No. 396-357; Amar V. Bhide, "McKinsey & Company (A): 1956," HBS Case No. 393-066; Amar V. Bhide, "McKinsey & Company (B): 1966," HBS Case No. 393-067; and Jay W. Lorsch and Katharina Pick, "McKinsey & Co.," HBS Case No. 402-014. HBS cases are developed solely as the basis for class discussion. Cases are not intended to serve as endorsements, sources of primary data, or illustrations of effective or ineffective management.

Nearing the end of his three-term tenure as managing director of McKinsey & Company in July 2002, 54-year-old Rajat Gupta could look back at his legacy with considerable satisfaction. "In every generation, there are issues that define the firm," observed Gupta. "We've had our share in the last decade. But I feel very proud of where we've come out."[1] The firm had experienced tremendous growth under his leadership, opening 26 new offices across the globe and doubling the number of its partners. Noted an industry observer:

> The firm remains the high priest of high-level consulting, with the most formidable intellectual firepower, the classiest client portfolio, and the greatest global reach of any adviser to management in the world. Most of the firm's top clients pay $10 million a year and up in fees. . . . McKinsey serves 147 of the world's 200 largest corporations, including 80 of the top 120 financial-services firms, 9 of the 11 largest chemical companies, and 15 of the 22 biggest healthcare and pharmaceutical concerns.[2]

And yet, the 74-year-old management consulting giant with revenues of $1.8 billion in 2001 was facing new challenges, as it was mired in the midst of a long and deep worldwide recession. As Gupta's final term came to a close and McKinsey began the many-month process of selecting a new managing director, questions were raised as to whether McKinsey's rapid expansion was a sustainable source of strength or a burdensome mistake.

FIRM HERITAGE: 1926–1966[3]

The Formative Years: 1926–1934

In 1926, James O. McKinsey ("Mac"), a University of Chicago professor, founded James O. McKinsey & Company in Chicago to provide accounting and consulting services to clients. Mac's inspiration to help corporate management improve its performance stemmed from a series of frustrating experiences with inefficient and disorganized suppliers during his stint in the Army Ordinance Department during World War I. From its inception, McKinsey dealt with big clients such as Armour and Company, one of the country's largest meat packers. Mac focused on analyzing clients' upper-management problems and produced detailed reports suggesting alternatives and solutions for the clients' executives. McKinsey & Company expanded rapidly over the next five years, adding several partners, including Andrew Thomas (Tom) Kearney, and opening a tiny new office in New York City.

In 1932, Mac recruited Marvin Bower, a lawyer with both a JD and an MBA from Harvard. Born in August 1903 in Cincinnati, Ohio,

Bower had graduated from Brown University in 1925 with a degree in economics and psychology and, unsure of his career path, had entered Harvard Law School that fall. Upon graduation from law school in 1928, Bower had applied to the leading Cleveland corporate law firm of Jones Day but had been turned down. Determined to work for Jones Day, Bower decided to get an MBA from Harvard Business School and then reapply to the law firm. Two years later, MBA in hand, he reapplied to Jones Day and accepted its offer.

During his employment with Jones Day, Bower realized that his professional understanding of company business and management problems was "amateurish and superficial." While working with Frank Ginn, the firm's senior partner, Bower developed the view that business problems, like legal problems, could be handled in a superior manner by an independent professional firm. When he met Mac in 1932, he was "amazed" to learn that Mac's accounting and consulting services firm was trying to do just that. Bower joined the firm with "a program in mind and a determination to do as much as I could to help McKinsey develop into the kind of firm that I had envisioned."[4] Bower admired Mac's intelligence, self-criticism, and especially his independence from clients. He saw how important training was to Mac, who ran the Saturday afternoon company meetings like a class. He noticed how Mac's deep analytical approach, candor, and understanding of people allowed him to quickly gain a client's confidence. However, he was not comfortable with offering both audit and management services to clients. "In the New York office, we had several small audits on which I spent some time," recalled Bower.

> The work did not interest me; it was dull and boring. Also, I felt that there was an inherent conflict of interest in a corporation's retaining its auditors to study management problems. The actual or perceived lack of independence of an auditor who seeks income from a client was most troublesome for me. I discussed this point with Mac, but could not convince him to change his thinking.[5]

After being promoted to manager of the New York office in 1934, Bower proposed to Mac that the accounting practice be dropped there because there were no certified public accountants (CPAs) in the New York office. Without hesitation, Mac gave Bower the go-ahead. Throughout his 60-year tenure at McKinsey, Bower insisted that independence was the only way to offer impartial, thoughtful, and valuable advice to clients. As Bower began to take on increased responsibility, he was determined to develop an active client base on the East Coast to lessen the dependence on the Chicago office for clients. He began networking and making contacts but found that few people understood the field of management consulting, let alone the firm. Many saw McKinsey as a group of "efficiency experts" or "business doctors" and felt that hiring them was an admission of corporate "sickness."[6] Bower decided that the best way to counter this notion was to simply serve clients so well that their executives would recommend McKinsey to others.

Building the "Top Management Consulting Firm": 1934–1943

As McKinsey's reputation grew, so did its client base. In 1934, the firm was hired by Marshall Field and Company, the largest department store in the Midwest. Impressed by McKinsey's recommendations, Marshall Field hired Mac as its new chairman and CEO to implement them. Seeing both a growth opportunity for his small firm and the chance to free more of his time for his new responsibilities at Marshall Field, Mac, in 1935, merged McKinsey & Company with the accounting and management engineering firm of Scovell, Wellington & Company, which had offices in a number of U.S. cities. Two partnerships were formed: Scovell, Wellington & Company (SW), accountants; and McKinsey, Wellington & Company (MW), management engineers. McKinsey partner Kearney, along with Scovell, Wellington & Company head C. Oliver Wellington, directed the MW Chicago office. Bower remained in the MW New York office, which was run by Horace "Guy" Crockett, a 55-year-old CPA and the former manager of Scovell, Wellington's New York consulting practice. (See Exhibit 1.1.)

The McKinsey-Scovell merger initially brought in more business from bigger clients, including a major study for U.S. Steel Corporation, and gradually established "management engineers" as professionals. However, a lack of harmony and a clash of cultures beneath the surface continued to trouble the merged firms. Tragedy struck in 1937 when Mac died unexpectedly. Simultaneously, U.S. Steel Corporation, which accounted for 55% of MW's total billings, terminated its contract.

Faced with the crisis, Bower proposed a reorganization of the firm that called for formally separating MW from SW. Bower planned to keep the New York and Chicago offices together and bring new personnel and money into MW. Kearney and the other Chicago partners supported the split but were not fully satisfied with some parts of Bower's plan. Kearney, questioning the wisdom of operating the then-sagging New York office, believed that there was more than enough

Exhibit 1.2 Timeline of McKinsey/s Early History (1926–1946) and its Evolution (1935–1939)

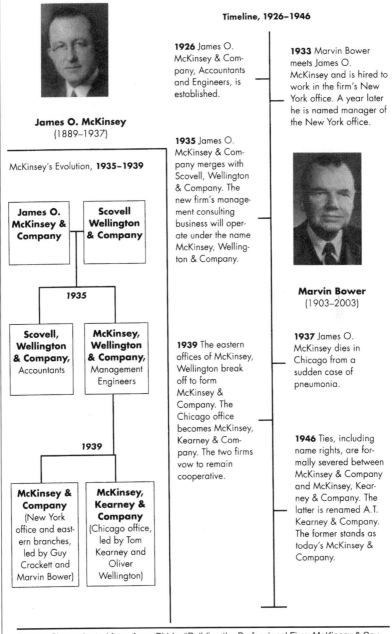

Timeline, 1926–1946

1926 James O. McKinsey & Company, Accountants and Engineers, is established.

1933 Marvin Bower meets James O. McKinsey and is hired to work in the firm's New York office. A year later he is named manager of the New York office.

James O. McKinsey
(1889–1937)

McKinsey's Evolution, **1935–1939**

1935 James O. McKinsey & Company merges with Scovell, Wellington & Company. The new firm's management consulting business will operate under the name McKinsey, Wellington & Company.

James O. McKinsey & Company	Scovell Wellington & Company

1935

Marvin Bower
(1903–2003)

Scovell, Wellington & Company, Accountants	McKinsey, Wellington & Company, Management Engineers

1939 The eastern offices of McKinsey, Wellington break off to form McKinsey & Company. The Chicago office becomes McKinsey, Kearney & Company. The two firms vow to remain cooperative.

1937 James O. McKinsey dies in Chicago from a sudden case of pneumonia.

1939

McKinsey & Company (New York office and eastern branches, led by Guy Crockett and Marvin Bower)	McKinsey, Kearney & Company (Chicago office, led by Tom Kearney and Oliver Wellington)

1946 Ties, including name rights, are formally severed between McKinsey & Company and McKinsey, Kearney & Company. The latter is renamed A.T. Kearney & Company. The former stands as today's McKinsey & Company.

Source: Chart adapted from Amar Bhide, "Building the Professional Firm: McKinsey & Co.: 1939–1968," Harvard Business School Working Paper 95–010; and Jack Sweeney, "The Last Lion: Marvin Bower and his Quest for Professional Independence," *Consulting Magazine*, February/March 2003, pp. 12–21. Photos used by permission from http://www. mckinsey.com/firm/history, accessed on August 15, 2003.

local work if the firm operated solely out of the Chicago office. So, Bower modified his reorganization plan to allow MW to split into two new partnerships that would be contractually affiliated. The plan, accepted by all sides in 1939, led to the Chicago office of MW led by Kearney forming McKinsey, Kearney & Company and the New York office, including Bower and Crockett, forming McKinsey & Company.

With a staff of 22 consulting professionals, including Crockett and Bower, and its own capital supplemented with $10,000 that Bower had raised from one of his acquaintances at the HBS Club of New York, the new McKinsey set a seemingly audacious goal of becoming the top management consulting firm in the United States.[7] "Crockett was the head [of the firm], but Bower was the drive and the idea person," recalled McKinsey partner Ron Daniel.[8] When some consultants suggested that the firm develop a printed description to give to prospective clients, Bower initially rejected the idea, deeming it unprofessional. However, recognizing later that development of such a document would unify internal views of the firm's strategy, Bower gave the go-ahead, stipulating that before publishing each McKinsey partner had to agree to every word of the document. After a year of going through several drafts, a 42-page book was published. Bower recalled:

> We had established, in our minds, the goal of becoming the leading management-consulting firm in the United States. We agreed that meant being a large firm—with multiple offices—but not necessarily the largest, and being known as favorably as any other firm in our field for the quality of our work, the prestige of our clientele, our professional standing, and the caliber and competence of our consulting staff. We agreed also that in order to attract, hold, and motivate high-caliber consultants, we must be an economically stable firm. Achieving economic stability required, in turn, charging higher fees than we and other firms were charging. We wanted to build a firm that would continue in perpetuity. This goal required every individual to protect and build the firm's future and reputation so that each generation of partners would pass the firm along to the next generation stronger than they had found it.[9]

During its first year, McKinsey lost money. However, in 1940, the firm earned profits of $57,000 on revenues of $284,000. The firm grew significantly over the next two years, generating revenues of $323,000 and $420,000 and earning profits of $73,000 and $135,000 in 1941 and 1942, respectively.[10]

Establishing an Institution: 1943–1956

In response to a growing West Coast client base, McKinsey opened an office in San Francisco in 1943 to be close to one of its most important patrons. In 1946, the Chicago-based McKinsey, Kearney & Company formally separated from the New York-based McKinsey & Company and, to avoid client confusion, chose the name A.T. Kearney & Company. Although the two firms agreed to cooperate closely, Bower recalled, "We adhered to the letter but not the spirit of the affiliation contract. Each firm competed with the other from the outset."[11] Over the next decade, offices sprang up across the country. By 1951, McKinsey had offices in New York, San Francisco, Boston (closed in 1953 and later reopened in 1981), Chicago, Los Angeles, and Washington, D.C. (See Exhibit 1.2 for an historical listing of all offices.)

As the company opened new offices, Bower, named McKinsey's managing partner in 1950, was determined not to let distance divide the company. The partnership followed a "one-firm" policy. "We almost instinctively treated all consultants as firm members, not office members," Bower remarked. "All earnings were put in a common pool, and all firm members who shared in them drew from *firm*, not office, earnings."[12]

Client-Service Philosophy

McKinsey stuck to the "integrated, top-management" approach established by Mac. The firm did not want to be labeled as specializing in one area of expertise but, instead, wanted to be recognized for its ability to apply appropriately a set of broad, general, well-known techniques to a variety of top-management problems. Moreover, McKinsey would accept work only with the approval and liaison of its client's CEO.

However, in a departure from Mac's approach of simply leaving clients with excellent reports, McKinsey partners began emphasizing that clients would not get the most value for their money without implementing their recommendations effectively. Besides, McKinsey had moved from billing clients for time spent to billing them prearranged fees based on the perceived value of the studies.

Bower believed that clients' trust in McKinsey's professionalism and concern for them differentiated McKinsey from its competitors. Recognizing that cooperation, trust, and support from clients was essential for success, Bower declared that the client's interests must be put ahead of the firm's own interests. He emphasized that McKinsey must adhere

Exhibit 1.2 McKinsey's Worldwide Office Locations

Year Founded	Location	Year Founded	Location
1939	New York	1990	Berlin
1944	San Francisco	1991	Buenos Aires
1947	Chicago	1991	Gothenburg
1949	Los Angeles	1991	Monterrey
1951	Washington, D.C.	1991	Montréal
1959	London	1991	Seoul
1963	Cleveland	1992	New Jersey
1963	Melbourne	1992	Taipei
1964	Amsterdam	1993	Cologne
1964	Düsseldorf	1993	Delhi
1964	Paris	1993	Warsaw
1966	Zurich	1993	Progue
1968	Toronto	1993	Shanghai
1969	Milan	1994	Auckland
1970	Mexico City	1994	Bogotá
1971	Sydney	1994	Dublin
1971	Tokyo	1994	Istanbul
1973	Stamford	1995	Jakarta
1974	Caracas	1995	Moscow
1974	Dallas	1995	Pacific Northwest
1975	Houston	1995	Beijing
1975	Munich	1996	Charlotte
1975	Saõ Paulo	1996	Orange County
1977	Hamburg	1996	Santiago
1977	Madrid	1997	Bangkok
1978	Atlanta	1997	Detroit
1979	Brussels	1997	Kuala Lumpur
1979	Frankfurt	1997	Miami
1981	Boston	1997	Singapore
1983	Pittsburgh	1999	Dubai
1984	Lisbon	1999	Manila
1984	Oslo	1999	Rio de Janeiro
1985	Hong Kong	2000	Tel Aviv
1986	Stüttgart	2001	Verona
1987	Geneva	[a]	Budapest
1988	Helsinki	[a]	Copenhagen
1988	Minneapolis	[a]	Athens
1988	Rome	[a]	Johannesburg
1989	Barcelona	[a]	Silicon Valley
1989	Vienna		

Source: Adapted from http://www.mckinsey.com/locations, accessed November 25, 2002, and internal McKinsey document.

[a] Data not available.

to high ethical standards, preserve confidence, and maintain an independent position. Bower noted:

> The older, or classical, professions learned long ago that the only way to meet the basic requirements for success was to adopt and enforce self-imposed standards of competence, ethics, responsibility, and independence. By "professing" and adhering to their self-imposed standards, the practitioners found that they were able to serve patients and clients well, gain their trust and confidence, and build reputations that attracted others—in short, serve themselves most effectively. Professionalism is thus both an idealistic concept and, in the long run, a self-serving concept.[13]

By 1956, McKinsey was able to be selective about the clients that it took on. The firm decided that it would not serve a prospective client that was unwilling to deal with a tough problem, lacked prestige, did not need or appreciate McKinsey's experience, or otherwise provided the firm with nothing but income. The firm was looking to build long-lasting relationships with clients that would simultaneously boost McKinsey's reputation. Although attracting prestigious clients during these years was sometimes a struggle, McKinsey stood fast in its refusal to advertise its services, citing that "leading law and accounting firms did not solicit clients, and that as a professional firm, [we] would not either."[14] As a way of increasing professional exposure, the firm did, however, create a program of "clinic dinners" where prospective client executives would have dinner with firm members and a guest of honor.

McKinsey's Professionals

McKinsey also changed its approach to selecting and developing consultants. Whereas Mac believed that McKinsey should hire people with several years of business experience and interesting-sounding titles to impress clients, McKinsey partners began to feel that the firm could not become the leading management consulting firm by hiring only this type of individual. Bower found that people of proven business and executive ability were generally neither qualified nor interested in the "professional work" undertaken by McKinsey. Many of the lateral hires that joined the firm lacked the personality, self-confidence, and superior intellect sought by McKinsey, and it was too difficult and ineffective to try and change them.

Bower decided to follow the lead of successful law and accounting firms that directly recruited candidates from professional schools. In 1953, McKinsey became the first management consulting firm to recruit directly from graduate business schools. The partners recognized that the tough requirements for admission to business school would yield the firm a "ready-made pool of good candidates." They believed that McKinsey had by then established a sufficiently good reputation to attract high-caliber graduates to the firm before they went into and settled in other jobs. The young consultants would be placed in an apprenticeship program where they would be given training, coaching from partners, and on-the-job experience serving clients.

Bower also developed a promotion system for McKinsey consultants. Associates (entry-level consultants) were promoted first to principals (midlevel consultants able to direct studies effectively and play leadership roles) and then to partners (who financed the firm, developed and maintained client relationships, and oversaw promotions). "The main difference between the criteria for election to principal and to partner is the greater emphasis on economic self-sufficiency," remarked a McKinsey partner. "Both principal and partner candidates have to demonstrate the ability to direct studies effectively and play a leadership role; partners also have to demonstrate their ability to develop and maintain clients."[15]

The firm's partners took on one of three roles: engagement director, office manager, or managing partner. Engagement directors led individual studies. They were the final judges of the quality of work done and were responsible for maintaining client relations, negotiating client fees, and using staff effectively. Office managers had considerable autonomy in managing individual offices. They were in charge of all decisions at the local level except for the selection of partners, which was done firmwide. The managing partner (later renamed managing director) was elected annually by the other partners and was charged with keeping the firm true to its principles. This individual was responsible for shaping and enforcing the firm's ethical and professional standards, enforcing the one-firm policy, and effecting needed changes in strategy and major policies. As one partner put it, "He must exercise strong leadership . . . in crystallizing thinking, and in bringing about action."[16] Additionally, partners contributed as members on three key committees. The executive committee made decisions for all partners on matters that did not involve basic policy. The planning committee was responsible for making recommendations about partnership and other major management questions to the rest of the partnership. The profit-sharing committee was in charge of distribution of profits.

Since 1936, when McKinsey was part of MW, associates had received bonus compensation. Even in the loss-making year of 1939 the practice continued. "Our partners held the concept that, as the founders and long-term believers in the firm, we should take the basic risks," noted Bower. "In fact, that was the best and perhaps the only way to attract the exceptional people we needed for success."[17] By 1956, the firm distributed roughly half of its profits to partners on the basis of the shares they owned and the other half as bonuses to associates, principals, and partners on the basis of their performance during the year.

Retention at partner level was excellent. Between 1939 and 1956, only one partner resigned. In 1954, McKinsey adopted a formal "up-or-out" policy for promotions from associates to principals, instituting a system requiring "that an associate be separated as soon as his performance demonstrates that he does not have the qualities to become a principal; that all associates be reviewed annually against that standard; and that associates not elected principal by age 40 be separated."[18] "Up-or-out is as great a benefit to the individual as it is to our firm," observed Bower. "We mustn't have people who think they are second-class citizens. We hire only exceptional people, and, if they don't work out here, they should be working somewhere else where their exceptional talents can be better used. If we've made a mistake, or they've made a mistake, we should correct it quickly."[19]

The Decade of International Expansion: 1956–1966

The firm's early experiences helped to develop and shape its management philosophy. By 1956, this philosophy had evolved into a concrete document. (See Exhibit 1.3 for a listing of these guiding principles.) Only then were skeptics, who had thus far resisted McKinsey's changing from a partnership to a corporation for fear of loss of firm values, sufficiently convinced that all McKinsey partners "would make determined efforts to maintain the firm's professional character"[20] to allow the firm to become a corporation.

After McKinsey's incorporation in 1956, partners were called directors and the managing partner was called the managing director. However, the firm had been careful to include provisions in the incorporation documents—restricting shareholders from selling to one another or to the firm and requiring them to sell at book value as they approached retirement—that kept ownership of all shares "exclusively in the hands of persons active in the firm." Rather than distribute corporate shares in proportion to partnership interests, McKinsey partners decided that "no individual should hold more than 25% of the total stock" and that "control be spread over as many individuals as is possible consistent with their contributions to the firm." The role

Exhibit 1.3 McKinsey's Guiding Principles, 1956

Fact-Based and Fair Personnel Decisions We try to base all decisions on facts—that is, we seek to determine what is right, not who is right. We have developed such a strong aversion to politics that a number of "politicians"—including partners—have been forced out of the firm. Performance is the central fact on which we base personnel decisions.

Responsibility for Dissent Every firm member has a responsibility for disagreeing with any firm decision that he cannot accept.

Spirit of Partnership The spirit of partnership requires every firm member to take a one-for-all, all-for-one attitude; meet high standards of integrity, openness, trustworthiness, and helpfulness in our dealings with one another; avoid divisive rivalries among offices and individuals; and refrain from backbiting, undercutting, and unfairness.

Consideration for Others Since we must work as teams on assignments and in our offices, we must show consideration for others—not just for other consultants, but for members of our operations staffs as well.

De-emphasis of Hierarchy We have tried to avoid a hierarchical structure, and we have not stressed position or titles either inside or outside the firm. In all successful professional groups, regard for the individual is based not on title but on competence, stature, and leadership.

Leadership by Consultants All non-consulting leadership positions are held by individuals who became partners because of their performance as consultants. Not only do professionals want leadership from other professionals, but only the respected professional can provide the example necessary for leadership. This policy has some disadvantages, however. The leader trained as a consultant may have shortcomings as an office manager, for example. Even more serious, the natural tendency to select the best consultants saps the primary strength of the firm and may divert from its real purpose of serving clients.

Source: Amar Bhide, "McKinsey & Company (A): 1956."

of principals, the junior partners, was diminished as they too became subject to the up-or-out rule.[21] Although a temporary senior consultant position was tried for associates who were not yet prepared for the role of principal but were too valuable to the firm to be separated permanently, the position never took hold and was abandoned quickly. "We tried the concept on an experimental basis," recalled Bower, "but it proved to be a bad thing for the firm and a bad thing for the four people we made senior consultants. They were quickly seen as second-class citizens."[22]

Incorporation allowed McKinsey to accumulate capital, which fueled the firm's international growth in the following decade. Between 1956 and 1966, McKinsey expanded abroad, primarily in Europe. Several McKinsey competitors had opened offices in Europe and South America. But McKinsey was more cautious, waiting until it had gained significant multinational experience through its consulting for Royal Dutch Shell before opening its first foreign office, in London, in 1959. The London office was followed by offices in Melbourne in 1963 and in Amsterdam, Paris, and Düsseldorf in 1964. McKinsey partners had come to believe that international expansion not only would help their domestic clients expand their own international businesses but would also expand McKinsey's total clientele. During this decade, only one U.S. office was opened (Cleveland in 1963). By the end of 1966, McKinsey was operating six offices in the United States and six abroad.

CONFRONTING BUSINESS SLOWDOWN AND COMPETITIVE CHALLENGES: 1967–1994[23]

Reorienting the Firm's Direction: 1967–1976

In October 1967, Bower stepped down after having served as McKinsey's managing director for 17 years. By the time that Bower stepped down, McKinsey was a well-established and respected international consulting powerhouse. However, many McKinsey partners were concerned about the transition, fearing derailment of the firm's principles, firm mismanagement, or a reversal of success. Although he pledged to remain active in the firm, Bower insisted resolutely that "for McKinsey to continue in perpetuity, we must have continuity of management and leadership as well as ownership."[24] He and the other directors voted to create an executive group, which would consist of the current managing director and the three most likely candidates for the next managing director. The next managing director would be elected by secret ballots, and the results would be tallied by the firm's auditors. A managing director could serve multiple three-year terms until the age of 60. However, each time the managing director was up for reelection, he would have to face a larger slate of candidates to reduce incumbency advantage.

After Bower stepped down in 1967, three managing directors served McKinsey over the next decade for single three-year terms each. The firm's growth faltered soon after Bower's retirement. Economic shocks such as the oil crisis and an economic downturn played a large role in McKinsey's slowed growth. But the partners were concerned that this slowdown was caused by more than just cyclical market fluctuations. McKinsey had gone through a period of rapid growth in Europe. The partners were wondering if the firm had grown too rapidly, opened too many offices, and pursued too many of the wrong kind of clients.

In 1971, the McKinsey partners enlisted some of their most respected peers to study the problem and make a recommendation. This committee, dubbed the "Commission on Firm Aims and Goals," concluded that McKinsey had been too fixated on geographic expansion and developing new areas of practice expertise. The quality of McKinsey's consulting work had become inconsistent, and McKinsey consultants lacked the deep industry knowledge that clients were demanding. The commission declared that McKinsey had been neglecting the technical and professional development of its consultants by accepting routine assignments from marginal clients. The commission proposed that the firm scale back the associate-to-management ratio from 7:1 to 5:1 and develop "T-shaped" consultants who supplemented a broad generalist perspective with an in-depth understanding of some industry specialty. (See Exhibit 1.4 for a characterization of "T-shaped" consultants.)

Throughout this period of self-assessment, McKinsey firmly adhered to the notion of independence staunchly championed by Bower. In 1969, a proposal to jump-start growth by establishing a joint venture

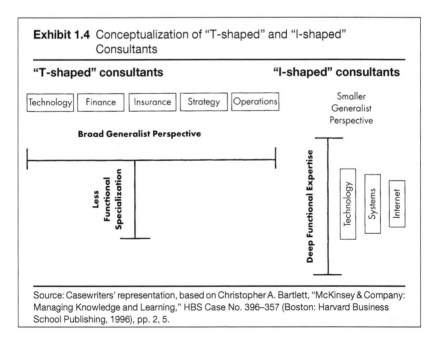

Exhibit 1.4 Conceptualization of "T-shaped" and "I-shaped" Consultants

"T-shaped" consultants

Technology | Finance | Insurance | Strategy | Operations

Broad Generalist Perspective

Less Functional Specialization

"I-shaped" consultants

Smaller Generalist Perspective

Deep Functional Expertise

Technology | Systems | Internet

Source: Casewriters' representation, based on Christopher A. Bartlett, "McKinsey & Company: Managing Knowledge and Learning," HBS Case No. 396–357 (Boston: Harvard Business School Publishing, 1996), pp. 2, 5.

with investment bank Donaldson Lufkin & Jenrette aimed toward serving small companies was shelved because of the strenuous opposition of several partners, including Bower, on the grounds that such an alliance would compromise the firm's independence. In 1973, when the Association of Management Consulting Firms opened its membership to publicly held consulting firms and accounting giants, McKinsey, citing threats to independence, withdrew from the association.

Confronting the BCG Challenge Under Daniel's Stewardship: 1976–1988

When Daniel became McKinsey's managing director in 1976, the fourth since Bower had stepped down, the firm was still struggling to implement the commission's recommendations. New concerns were also emerging. As clients became more and more sophisticated, so did their expectations of and demands for the types of service they needed. Additionally, McKinsey was confronting a new breed of competitors such as the Boston Consulting Group (BCG). Whereas McKinsey had stuck to the local office-based model of developing lasting client relationships in cities throughout the world, BCG operated out of a concentrated Boston office and flew consultants out to client sites for extended stays. Unlike McKinsey, which offered generalist advice tailored to client needs, BCG competed on the basis of "thought leadership," leveraging simple but powerful tools such as the "experience curve" and the "growth-share matrix" to make inroads into the strategy consulting market.[25] As it began to lose both clients and potential recruits to BCG, McKinsey's leadership decided that something had to be done (see Exhibit 1.5 for a snapshot of the evolving industry).

Besides encouraging formal development of practice areas, such as strategy, organization, and operations, Daniel created industry-focused clientele sectors in fields such as banking, health care, chemicals, industrial goods, and consumer products. Several McKinsey partners expressed the concern that increased specialization would lead to an attitude within McKinsey that selling service was more important than serving top-notch clients in the best possible way. Among those skeptical about this new product-driven approach was Bower, who had continued to be a major voice despite his nearing retirement.[a]

However, Daniel continued to press ahead with his initiative to build functional expertise. He assembled working groups to develop knowledge in the two areas that were at the heart of the firm's practice—strategy and organization. To head up the first group, he appointed

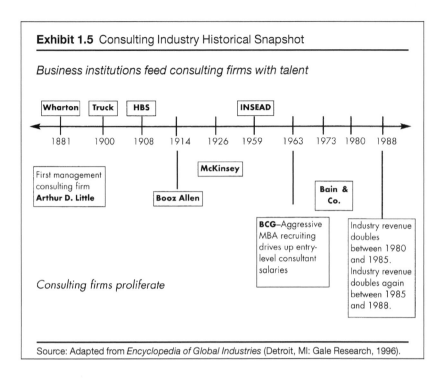

Exhibit 1.5 Consulting Industry Historical Snapshot

Business institutions feed consulting firms with talent

Source: Adapted from *Encyclopedia of Global Industries* (Detroit, MI: Gale Research, 1996).

Fred Gluck, an innovative partner who had been outspoken in urging the firm to move beyond its generalist approach ("Knowing what you're talking about is not necessarily a client service handicap," and "Would you want your brain surgery done by a general practitioner?" were just two of his oft-quoted barbs.) Senior partners Bob Waterman and Jim Bennett headed the second group. Among its first recruits was a young organizational theory Ph.D., Tom Peters.[26]

Daniel asked Gluck to help develop consultant training, knowledge, and expertise. Gluck shared Daniel's belief that knowledge development had to become a core, institutionalized, permanent firm activity and not some temporary, half-forgotten project. Gluck established 15 new specialty categories called "centers of competence" (virtual centers, not locations) and identified motivated and recognized experts to head these emerging practice areas. (See Exhibit 1.6 for a listing of McKinsey's practice areas, circa 1983.) In an attempt to shake an internal status hierarchy that was based largely on the size and importance of one's client base, Gluck actively encouraged consultants to publish their key findings in *The McKinsey Quarterly*, which McKinsey had begun publishing in 1964; the McKinsey staff paper series; and two-page practice bulletins. He suggested that the firm expand its

---

Exhibit 1.6 McKinsey's Practice Areas: Centers of Competence and
Industry Sectors, 1983

Centers of Competence	Clientele Sectors
Building Institutional Skills	Automotive
Business Management Unit	Banking
Change Management	Chemicals
Corporate Leadership	Communications and Information
Corporate Finance	Consumer Products
Diagnostic Scan	Electronics
International Management	Energy
Integrated Logistics	Health Care
Manufacturing	Industrial Goods
Marketing	Insurance
Microeconomics	Steel
Sourcing	
Strategic Management	
Systems	
Technology	

Source: Adapted from Christopher Bartlett, "McKinsey & Company: Managing Knowledge
and Learning," p. 16.

---

hiring practices and promotion policies to create a career path for specialists whose narrow expertise would make them more "I-shaped" than "T-shaped."

In 1987, Daniel launched a knowledge management project that led to the implementation of three interconnected systems—a firm practice information system (a computerized data base of client engagements), a practice development network (which captured the knowledge that had accumulated in the various practice areas), and a knowledge resource directory (a listing of firm experts and key document titles, which quickly became McKinsey's Yellow Pages).

Encouraged by Daniel's focus on building competencies, several McKinsey consultants published highly respected articles and books, including the bestsellers *In Search of Excellence* by Tom Peters and Bob Waterman (New York: Harper & Row, 1982) and *Triad Power* by Kenichi Ohmae (New York: Free Press, 1985), reestablishing the firm's preeminent position in thought leadership. In 1978, continuing a tradition established by Mac and followed by several senior McKinsey partners since, McKinsey partner Louis Gerstner departed the firm for American Express. He later became the CEO of RJR Nabisco and then IBM. Several other alumni left the firm during the following two decades to head some of the world's biggest and most respected companies—Harvey Golub as American Express's CEO, Leo Mullin as Delta Airlines's CEO, Jeff Skilling as Enron's CEO, Andrall Pearson as Pepsico's COO, Lukas Mühlemann as Credit Suisse's CEO, and Klaus Zumwinkel as Deutsche Post's CEO.

Growth resumed by the 1980s, and a guarded confidence returned to McKinsey for the first time in almost a decade. By the end of Daniel's tenure in 1988, the firm was rapidly expanding again. New offices were opened in Rome, Helsinki, São Paulo, and Minneapolis, bringing the total number of offices to 40.

Innovation Under Gluck's Leadership: 1988–1994

In 1988, Gluck assumed the role of managing director. Gluck continued to emphasize that enhancing McKinsey's reputation as a leader in new ideas was just as important as attracting new business. He also began to focus on ways to ensure that clients were receiving the maximum value for their services and that McKinsey was creating positive results. In 1992, the firm created a new path to partnership for specialists, requiring them to build credibility with clients through their specialized knowledge and expert application.

Despite the announcement of the new criteria and promotion process, confusion and skepticism abounded about the viability of the specialist track to partnership. Over the years, the evaluation and promotion criteria for specialists had gradually converged with those of the mainstream generalist. For example, instead of being judged by their level of "world-class expertise," specialist consultants began to be judged by their level of client impact under the expectation that, because they were "specialized," they should be able to serve at the same level of expertise as a generalist even if they did not enjoy the same degree of experience, respect from clients, or compensation. Although these changes reduced the confusion about the specialist's role because the specialist became more "T-shaped," it also missed the original point of allowing specialists to develop.

Over the years, Gluck's approach "to let a thousand flowers bloom" had resulted in the original group of 11 sectors and 15 centers expanding to "72 islands of activity" (sectors, centers, working groups, and special projects). To prevent excessive fragmentation, these diverse groups were integrated into seven sectors and seven functional capabilities. (See Exhibit 1.7 for a listing of these sectors and centers.)

During the mid-1980s, waves of reengineering swept large firms as they sought to redesign and optimize their business processes. McKinsey was faced with intensifying competition from information technology (IT) consulting firms that began offering clients a combination of strategy and IT advice, arguing that IT had become too critical for firms to not be closely integrated with strategy. In 1989, in a departure from its long-cherished approach of organic growth, McKinsey acquired Information Consulting Group (ICG) as "a massive recruitment effort" to speed up the building of its own IT capability.[27] Despite senior management support from both sides, the integration of ICG into McKinsey was less than successful. By late 1993, more than half of ICG's partner-level consultants had left and only 94 of the original 245 professionals remained.[28]

In 1994, after leading the firm for six years, doubling revenues to an estimated $1.5 billion annually, Gluck stepped down as managing director. His successor was 45-year-old Rajat Gupta, the first foreign-born managing partner of the consulting giant.

GUPTA'S TENURE: 1994–2002

Gupta was born in New Delhi, India, in 1948. After receiving his bachelor of technology degree in mechanical engineering from the Indian Institute of Technology in 1971, he received his MBA from Harvard Business School (HBS) in 1973. After graduation from HBS, he interviewed with McKinsey but was rejected due to a lack of work experience. An HBS professor intervened on his behalf and, vouching for his enthusiasm and intelligence, helped Gupta obtain an associate position at the firm's New York office. Gupta became the head of the Scandinavian offices in 1981 and the head of the Chicago office in 1990. In 1994, he was elected managing director.[29] When he took the position, McKinsey comprised 3,300 consultants, including 425 partners, in 58 offices in 24 countries and generated $1.5 billion in revenue.

Gupta's Initiatives

When he took charge, Gupta concurred with Gluck that continued global expansion was the correct path for the firm to follow in the near future. Over the next seven years, Gupta aggressively expanded the company's reach, opening offices around the world. Offices were

Exhibit 1.7 Gluck's Framework for Sectors and Centers, 1994

Functional Capability Groups	Clientele Industry Sectors
Corporate Governance and Leadership • Corporate organization • Corporate management processes • Corporate strategy development • Corporate relationship design and management • Corporate finance • Post-merger management **Marketing** • Market research • Sales force management • Channel management • Global marketing • Pricing • Process and sector support **Operations Effectiveness** • Integrated logistics • Manufacturing • Purchasing and supply management	**Organization** • Leadership and teams • Organization design and development • Energizing approaches • Corporate transformation design and leadership • Engaging teams **Cross-Functional Management** • Innovation • Customer satisfaction • Product /technology development and commercialization • Core process redesign **Strategy** • Strategy • Microeconomics • Business dynamics • Business planning processes **IT/Systems** • To be determined	**Financial Institutions** • Banking • Health care payer/provider • Insurance **Consumer** • Retailing • Consumer industries • Media • Pharmaceuticals **Aerospace, Electronics, & Telecom** • Telecom • Electronics • Aerospace **Transportation**	**Basic Materials** • Steel • Pulp and paper • Chemicals • Other basic materials **Energy** • Electrical utilities • Petroleum • Natural gas • Other energy **Automotive, Assembly, and Machinery** • Automotive assembly

Source: Adapted from Christopher Bartlett, "McKinsey & Company: Managing Knowledge and Learning," p. 17.

opened in Shanghai, Bogotá, Moscow, Beijing, Bangkok, Kuala Lumpur, and Singapore. By 2001, McKinsey had more than doubled in size—revenue had increased to more than $3.4 billion, and the firm had 7,700 consultants, including 891 partners, in 81 offices in 44 countries.[30] The firm's alumni directory contained over 8,000 names (see Exhibit 1.8 for distribution of McKinsey revenue across major practice areas.)

In following its expansion strategy, McKinsey stayed true to its long-term approach to individual office profitability, its one-firm philosophy, and an emphasis on preserving firm culture and identity. "The firm is one firm," Gupta stressed. "It is one profit pool. We are not looking at short-term performance of any particular unit. In fact, the only discussion I have with officers in emerging markets is how well they are doing developing people and what is the quality of our work and reputation."[31] New offices were opened only by McKinsey partners, not through acquisitions or hiring local professionals. In opening new offices, "what we want to do," said Gupta, "[is to have] a small number of people going there, hiring the best talent they can, and developing them in the image of McKinsey. No acquisitions, no senior hires, just building from the ground up. It takes a longer time to do it, but we have a very long time horizon for most of these developments."[32] (See Exhibit 1.9 for a statement of McKinsey's mission and values, circa 2002.)

Gupta wanted to ensure that McKinsey continued to remain in the forefront of knowledge development and knowledge application. In addition to focusing on its traditional areas of strategy and organization, McKinsey created a manufacturing institute in the late 1990s to conduct research and train consultants in principles of lean manufacturing

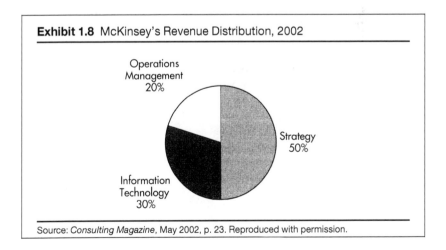

Exhibit 1.8 McKinsey's Revenue Distribution, 2002

Operations Management 20%

Strategy 50%

Information Technology 30%

Source: *Consulting Magazine*, May 2002, p. 23. Reproduced with permission.

Exhibit 1.9 McKinsey's Mission and Values, 2002

Mission
- Serve our clients as primary counselors on overall performance
- Deliver the best of the firm to every client
- Create an unrivaled environment for superior talent
- Govern ourselves through a values-driven partnership

Values
Impact-driven professional approach "It's very important to us to combine the notions of impact and professional approach, because we could each be impeccable in our approaches yet not necessarily achieve the impact to which we aspire. We want to make a difference in the institutions so as to have broader impact on the business community and society."

Being and delivering the best "This is rooted in our drive to develop knowledge and to convey that knowledge to every client, every time. I would argue that, in a professional services firm, if knowledge and being the best aren't part of our core values, then we're missing something."

Caring meritocracy, committed to people "There's an interesting tension between those words. Without a true meritocracy, we won't be able to maintain our quality standards or attract the kind of people we want to attract. But at the same time, I think everybody here feels this is a collegial community, and one that is very committed to caring about our people. Dedication to people development is essential to maintaining our long-term competitiveness. If you come here, we make the implicit promise that we're going to provide you with developmental opportunities you cannot equal anywhere else."

Self-governing, one-firm partnership "This is about how we manage ourselves and what kind of organization we want to be. This is not a firm of leaders and followers; it is a firm of leaders who want to have the freedom to do what they think is right for the institution. From your very first day with us, you're not only expected to do your assigned task, you're expected to step forward and do something about the issues and opportunities you care about. The only way we can keep such a large collection of outstanding leaders is through self-governance—so that people feel that they can control their own destiny and that they can make a difference in this place. 'One firm' simply means that we're all in this together and that all our incentives, evaluation processes, and the like apply firm-wide."

Source: Adapted from http://www.mckinsey.com/firm/values, accessed November 25, 2002.

and design of manufacturing systems. "We have easily doubled our investment in knowledge over these past couple of years," Gupta remarked in 1996.[33] In 2001, he reflected on the actions he had taken early in his tenure:

In my first couple of years, I remember a strong level of personal involvement and investment, to make sure that we took on knowledge development efforts in all fields, in functions and industries, in cross-cutting teams. We even launched seven special initiatives on topics that at the time were very, very important to our clients—things like the impact of rapidly falling interaction costs, the Internet, and e-commerce, which evolved as one topic. Another topic was globalization, and then there were the whole new developments in finance and valuation.[34]

These initiatives, in addition to the seven major functional areas and seven "centers of competence" established by previous managing directors, were supplemented with 16 industry groups (see Exhibit 1.10 for a listing of McKinsey's industry groups, circa 2002) formed by Gupta. These industry groups became, Gupta recalled, "performance cells within the firm, to understand what were the structural changes happening in each of these industries, what were the issues being faced."[35] In addition, several committees were operating: personnel committees to evaluate, elect, and compensate directors as well as to evaluate and elect principals (principals' compensation and associates' evaluation and compensation were determined by partner groups in

---

Exhibit 1.10 McKinsey's Functional and Industry Practices, 2002

Automotive & Assembly	Media & Entertainment
Banking & Securities	Metals & Mining
Business Building	Nonprofit
Business Technology Office	Operations Strategy & Effectiveness
Chemicals	Organization & Leadership
Consumer Packaged Goods	Payer / Provider
Corporate Finance & Strategy	Petroleum
Electric Power & Natural Gas	Pharmaceuticals & Medical Products
Global Strategy	Private Equity
High Tech	Pulp & Paper
Insurance	Retail
Marketing	Telecommunications

Source: Adapted from http://www.mckinsey.com/practices, accessed November 25, 2002.

individual offices); a 31-member shareholder committee (earlier called an executive committee) with the traditional board responsibilities; and four policy committees focused on people, clients, finance, and knowledge.[36]

With growing scale and scope, McKinsey's market footprint became considerably bigger. The firm continued to invest in long-term client relationships and as of 2002 had a roster of more than 400 active clients that it had been serving for 15 years or longer.[37] However, some partners looked back nostalgically at the days when the firm was smaller and much more informal. "It's a less personal place than it used to be," remarked a senior partner. "In the old days, you knew everybody. That's not possible anymore."[38] Another departing partner claimed that in its urge to rapidly expand, McKinsey had "lost its way."[39]

Partly to address this growing feeling of alienation, McKinsey conducted, between 1996 and 1998, a "firm strategy initiative": an 18-month process of defining and developing firm strategy designed and managed by a 70-partner task force and involving all the partners as well as firm alumni and clients. The initiative, Gupta believed, would engage the partnership in a dialogue on firm strategy and result in "a much greater understanding, tolerance, even appreciation of the diversity of the firm."[40] Gupta wanted the firm to strive to be "100% cubed," committed to delivering 100% of the firm, 100% of the time, to 100% of the world.[41] "There are lots more people involved in many more initiatives," remarked Gupta in 1996. "If that means we do 5% to 10% less client work today, we are willing to pay that price to invest in the future."[42]

The Promise and Challenge of the Technology Boom

The Internet boom of the late 1990s radically altered the competitive landscape of the consulting industry. Buffeted by competition both in the service market from the new e-consulting firms and in the labor market by high-tech entrepreneurial start-ups, the traditional management consulting firms began to change their own offerings in both the markets for services and for professionals.

Demand for e-consulting soared from both start-ups and large corporate clients, many of which had grown fearful that they were falling behind the Internet curve. Combining strategy with IT was clearly on many CEOs' agendas, and they were increasingly demanding advice on the interface of technology and strategy. PricewaterhouseCoopers management consulting services partner Scott Hart observed:

E-business has changed the rules about strategic plans, operations, supplies, production, sales, distribution, and customer
service. E-business has stolen time from every player in the marketplace, and it is forcing companies to transform their businesses
and to act faster with more agility, flexibility, and anticipation.
While the consulting industry has to help companies through this
transformation, they must also become e-businesses.[43]

Clients had earlier viewed technology-focused consulting firms as
inferior to pure-strategy consulting firms in the quality of their strategy
offerings. But increasingly peopled by alumni from the strategy-focused
firms promising close integration of strategy and technology consulting and offering strategy services at discount prices, the technology-
focused firms began to be seen as powerful competitors. The traditional
consulting firms, McKinsey included, were fighting, and often losing,
competitive battles with the technology firms on two fronts—clients
and consultants. McKinsey, for example, lost the heads of its technology
and insurance practices, as well as leaders in retail, consumer goods, and
media businesses, to technology-focused competitors.[b]

In 1996, McKinsey began building a business-technology practice (a
virtual office with five physical locations working as one office) that had
grown to 460 consultants by 2002. Significant new business opportunities opened up as the firm strengthened its technology-strategy interface. During the peak two years of the dot-com boom from 1998–2000,
McKinsey alone executed more than 1,000 e-commerce assignments.

Several management consulting firms molded their governance and
operations to better succeed in this "new economy." Gupta resisted the
urgings from various sources to start McKinsey's own venture capital
fund, create dot-com offshoots of its consulting practice, or go public,
even at the expense of the firm's being called "not 'with it,' not aggressive and progressive enough."[44] "Fundamentally, we are a client-service
firm," he asserted. "We're not going to become a principal investing
firm, a fund, or run our own venture fund."[45] Another important decision was to remain a private partnership and not go public. "We believe
the best form of ownership is a private partnership, a one-firm partnership," remarked Gupta. "That's what we will stay. . . . We want to be
able to serve our clients' interests first. One of the things we don't want
is to be exposed to external pressures." Nor did the firm need investment from the outside. "This is a knowledge-intensive business, not a
capital-intensive one," noted Gupta.[c, 46]

The dot-com boom had created a plethora of entrepreneurial

opportunities in high technology for bright, young professionals. Lucrative positions with dot-com start-ups or venture capital funds became the jobs of choice for the top MBA graduates, gobbling up McKinsey's potential recruits. Turnover of its professionals increased from 16% to 18% per annum, where it had been for several decades, to 21% to 22% per annum.[47] "[T]he new economy, very much the Internet and the entrepreneurial opportunities it created, intensified the competition for outstanding people," remarked Gupta. "[T]he emphasis shifted toward making value propositions [to our consultants] that were the absolute best they could be."[48] The "war for talent" was being waged in full intensity.[d]

McKinsey launched its "People First Initiative," which included a global staffing system detailing ongoing projects and openings worldwide, raising consultants' salaries, and shortening the time to partnership. The firm also diversified its hiring sources, recruiting from 20 schools in 2000 instead of the six or seven it had recruited from in 1978 and increasing the recruiting of non-MBAs, primarily Ph.D.s. Partly as a result of McKinsey's aggressive fight for people, the firm consistently remained the top employer for MBAs during the dot-com boom. (See Exhibits 1.11a–1.11e for employment, revenue, and recruiting data.) Some McKinsey partners questioned, however, whether, in placing people first, the firm was sliding back from its long-held value, "Client first, firm second, professionals third." Others worried that the firm had "made a lot of decisions about how to promote people, how to advance people, how to compensate people" that were "just wrong."[49]

Facing the Economic Slowdown

In April 2001, the dot-com market collapsed. The demand for e-consulting projects evaporated virtually overnight. The difficult market conditions pushed a number of e-businesses into bankruptcy. Although less impacted than consulting firms whose primary focus had been e-consulting, larger strategy firms, including McKinsey, also suffered a revenue decline. Besides, equity payments in return for services had lost most of their economic value. For example, in early 2000, McKinsey had helped EB2B Commerce develop its strategy after a merger in return for stock consideration. The client's stock, valued at $190 per share when McKinsey started working with it, had dropped to $0.11 per share by July 2002.[50]

The bursting of the technology stock bubble was followed by an economywide downturn in late 2001. Exacerbating the industrywide

Exhibit 1.11a McKinsey and its Competitors. 25 Largest Management Consulting Firms in the World

Rank	Firm Name	FY01 Global Consulting Revenue ($ m)	Global Consulting 1-Year Growth	2001 Global Consultants	FY01 U.S. Consulting Revenue ($ m)	U.S. Consulting 1-Year Growth	2001 U.S. Consultants
1	IBM	$10,800.0	4%	50,000	$2,600.0	0%	12,600
2	Accenture	$9,460.0	17%	63,000	$5,900.0	17%	39,540
3	Cap Gemini Ernst & Young	$5,875.3	0%	31,537	$1,988.2	-6%	5,356
4	Deloitte Consulting/DTT	$5,635.0	0%	26,000	$3,045.0	-6%	10,970
5	PricewaterhouseCoopers Consulting	$5,547.1	-1%	32,000	$2,898.2	-8%	16,719
6	CSC	$3,562.0	-5%	15,500	$2,493.0	1%	10,848
7	**McKinsey & Company**	**$3,293.0**	**-3%**	**8,423**	**$1,045.0**	**-5%**	**3,369**
8	EDS	$2,903.0	11%	8,936	$1,655.0	9%	5,094
9	KPMG Consulting	$2,700.0	-4%	7,500	$2,600.0	-4%	7,125
10	Mercer Consulting Group	$2,160.0	1%	11,719	$1,191.0	0%	4,408
11	Andersen	$1,710.0	6%	7,000	$960.0	5%	3,365
12	Booz-Allen & Hamilton	$1,600.0	4%	8,994	$1,200.0	4%	8,000
13	Atos Origin	$1,590.0	3%	14,310	$89.5	-25%	764
14	KPMG International	$1,500.0	19%	9,532	NA	NA	NA
15	T-Systems	$1,188.0	8%	5,500	$42.0	7%	194
16	Towers Perrin	$1,104.1	3%	7,000	$770.0	3%	4,900
17	The Boston Consulting Group	$1,050.0	-5%	2,790	$316.2	-7%	631
18	AMS	$1,020.0	-7%	6,000	$845.0	-9%	7,970
19	SchlumbergerSema	$1,001.0	-3%	8,303	$39.8	-3%	330
20	Watson Wyatt Worldwide	$953.0	7%	4,650	$576.0	7%	2,138
21	Aon Consulting Worldwide	$938.0	22%	7,400	$628.0	29%	4,200
22	Tata Consultancy Services	$875.0	28%	4,051	$637.0	29%	4,000
23	Bain & Company	$810.0	1%	2,100	$324.0	1%	840
24	CMG	$807.0	-6%	7,085	$21.0	-9%	190
25	Fujitsu Consulting	$700.0	-16%	7,000	$350.0	-15%	3,500

Source: *Consultants News*, June 2002. Reproduced with permission.

Exhibit 1.11b McKinsey and its Competitors: MBAs Prestige Rankings 2001

Rank	Firm Name	Rating
1	**McKinsey & Company**	**4.84**
2	Boston Consulting Group	4.78
3	Bain & Co.	4.53
4	Booz-Allen & Hamilton	4.22
5	Monitor	3.71
6	A.T. Kearney	3.67
7	Accenture	3.60
8	Mercer Management Consulting	3.56
9	Deloitte Consulting	3.55
10	DiamondCluster International	3.51
11	PricewaterhouseCoopers Consulting	3.24
12	Arthur D. Little	3.16
13	Marakon	3.14
14	Cap Gemini Ernst & Young	3.13
15	IBM	3.12
16	Andersen	3.11
17	Roland Berger & Partner	3.06
18	KPMG	3.05
19	Parthenon Group	2.97
20	L.E.K. Consulting	2.94
21	Towers Perrin	2.86
22	PRTM	2.83
23	Mars & Company	2.81
24	Kurt Salmon Associates	2.80
25	Hewitt	2.74
26	Dean & Company	2.73
27	Watson Wyatt	2.70
28	Sapient	2.69
29	Hay Group	2.68
30	Navigant	2.65
31	RSM McGladrey	2.65

Ratings based on scale 1 (lowest) to 5 (highest).

Source: *Consultants News*, November 2001. Reproduced with permission.

decline in demand for strategy consulting, few clients could afford McKinsey's hefty fees, resulting in a substantial drop in McKinsey's consulting business. After months of resisting downward price pressure, in the late summer of 2001, McKinsey was forced to begin offering discounts or cutting deals with clients (such as agreeing to finish

Exhibit 1.11c McKinsey and its Competitors. Where MBAs Perceive Long-Term Career Opportunities, Despite Layoffs November 2001

Rank	Firm Name	Rating
1	**McKinsey & Company**	**4.50**
2	Boston Consulting Group	4.32
3	Bain & Company	4.17
4	Booz-Allen & Hamilton	4.06
5	Deloitte Consulting	3.62
6	A.T. Kearney	3.62
7	Accenture	3.52
8	Mercer Management Consulting	3.48
9	Monitor	3.48
10	DiamondCluster International	3.48
11	PricewaterhouseCoopers Consulting	3.26
12	IBM	3.19
13	Cap Gemini Ernst & Young	3.19
14	Marakon	3.09
15	Andersen	3.07
16	KPMG	3.06
17	L.E.K. Consulting	3.03
18	Arthur D. Little	3.03
19	Parthenon Group	2.98
20	Towers Perrin	2.90
21	PRTM	2.88
22	Mars & Company	2.82
23	Kurt Salmon Associates	2.82
24	Navigant	2.73
25	Hewitt	2.71
26	Dean & Company	2.71
27	Sapient	2.70
28	Watson Wyatt	2.69
29	First Consulting Group	2.65
30	Keane	2.65
31	RSM McGladrey	2.64

Ratings based on scale 1 (lowest) to 5 (highest).

Source: *Consultants News*, November 2001. Reproduced with permission.

advisory projects in less time for the same price).[51] In July 2001, an industry researcher remarked, "[Y]ou can hire McKinsey for what it would have cost you to hire A.T. Kearney a year ago."[52]

Exhibit 1.11d McKinsey and its Competitors: Historical Revenue Growth ($ m)

Firm	FY93	FY94	FY95	FY96	FY97	FY98	FY99	FY00	FY01
McKinsey & Co.	**1,300.0**	**1,500.0**	**1,800.0**	**2,100.0**	**2,200.0**	**2,500.0**	**2,900.0**	**3,400.0**	**3,400.0**
Accenture	–	–	–	4,942.0	6,275.0	8,214.8	9,549.9	9,752.1	13,061.9
Bain & Co.	213.0	300.0	375.0	450.0	480.0	498.7	700.0	810.0	–
Booz-Allen & Hamilton	700.0	804.0	989.0	1,100.0	1,300.0	1,400.0	1,600.0	1,800.0	2,100.0
Boston Consulting Group	340.0	430.0	550.0	600.0	655.0	730.0	948.0	1,100.0	1,050.0
Towers Perrin	709.0	766.8	822.0	855.0	1,000.0	1,125.0	1,338.0	1,448.0	1,469.0
Watson Wyatt & Co.	410.1	433.4	474.5	492.5	511.0	512.7	556.9	624.6	700.2

Source: Adapted from data on Hoover's Online, accessed November 25, 2002.

Exhibit 1.11e McKinsey and its Competitors: Historical Employee Growth

Firm	FY93	FY94	FY95	FY96	FY97	FY98	FY99	FY00	FY01
McKinsey & Co.	**5,560**	**6,000**	**6,050**	**7,100**	**8,500**	**10,000**	**10,500**	**13,000**	**13,000**
Accenture	–	–	–	44,801	53,426	62,000	65,496	70,000	75,000
Bain & Co.	900	1,000	1,200	1,500	1,700	2,100	2,400	2,700	–
Booz-Allen & Hamilton	5,000	5,481	6,000	6,700	7,500	8,000	9,000	9,800	11,045
Boston Consulting Group	–	1,246	1,320	1,500	2,000	3,000	4,334	4,300	4,450
Towers Perrin	5,000	5,000	5,050	6,361	6,350	6,314	8,600	8,919	9,009
Watson Wyatt & Co.	3,400	3,500	4,700	4,980	4,500	5,100	5,300	5,800	4,200

Source: Adapted from data on Hoover's Online, accessed November 25, 2002.

Overcapacity in the firm was worsened by developments in the labor market. McKinsey, along with other strategy consulting firms, had experienced several years of double-digit revenue growth. Its professional recruitment and retention processes had been tuned to this growth rate, as the tech boom of the late 1990s had intensified the drive to recruit and retain skilled professionals. The economic slowdown caught most strategic consulting firms by surprise. Suddenly, as revenues plummeted, firms found themselves considerably overstaffed. McKinsey's turnover rate fell steeply, to 12% per annum.[53] In addition, yield rates on fresh recruits jumped dramatically. In an average year, McKinsey would offer consulting jobs to 3,100 MBAs, expecting to get roughly 2,000 acceptances. In 2000, however, more than 2,700 people accepted offers to join the firm. Not surprisingly, average utilization (percentage of total employee time on projects) fell to 52% in 2001 from 64% in the dot-com years. Some of the offices were reported to be working at 40% of capacity, well below the 80% generally considered optimal.[54]

Several consulting firms, caught in this vise of declining demand and declining attrition, began to take the "painful but necessary steps" of laying off professionals and reneging on job offers. "We honored every offer and didn't push people out," observed Gupta, with pride, "and we had no professional layoffs other than our traditional up-or-out stuff."[55] Instead, hiring of professionals was scaled down considerably, and the firm became tougher in implementing its up-or-out policy (in fall 2001, 9% of associates and analysts were counseled out, compared with 3% in fall 2000).[56] Associates spent more time on internal and *pro bono* work. Cost-cutting measures were initiated, including cutting travel costs and scaling back training retreats.

As the economic slowdown lengthened (revenues were flat in 2001, and partners' compensation was reported to have fallen, on average, by one-third[57]), in June 2001, all 891 partners were asked to contribute significant sums of money to firm capital. The amounts contributed varied by partner; some senior directors contributed more than $200,000 each.[58] Although the firm stated that the capital call was a routine way to generate capital, some long-time firm veterans described such a large call as very rare and saw the action as a response to the economic downturn. "While some firms choose to lay off people," remarked a retired McKinsey partner, "McKinsey cares about continuing to serve their clients and build their people."[59]

Complicating matters, many of McKinsey's largest and most well-known clients collapsed during 2001 and 2002. Enron, a multibillion-dollar energy giant that melted down in the winter of 2001 and entered bankruptcy amidst accusations of mismanagement, self-dealing, and fraud, had been one of McKinsey's biggest and longest-standing clients, paying nearly $10 million in annual fees for almost 18 years. Enron CEO Jeffrey Skilling had been a McKinsey partner and was a close and loyal alumnus. "They infiltrated Enron with Jeff, and he was just the tip of the iceberg," remarked a former McKinsey consultant who worked at Enron in an interview with *BusinessWeek*. "There were all sorts of McKinsey people who went in over the years. They were so happy they had Enron locked up."[60] Enron's securitization of debt, "asset-light" strategy, and "loose-tight" culture were reported to have been developed in consultation with McKinsey. Although it was not the subject of any investigations, its close involvement with Enron raised the question of whether McKinsey, like other professional firms related to the Enron debacle, had ignored the warning flags just to retain an important account. "In all the work we did with Enron," maintained Gupta, "we did not do anything that is related to financial structuring or disclosure or any of the issues that got them into trouble. We stand by all the work we did."[61] Enron's failure did lead to "a little egg on their [McKinsey's] face,"[62] remarked an industry expert, "because they had been touting that as one of their great success stories." A former McKinsey consultant who worked at Enron observed: "The problem for McKinsey with Enron isn't [Arthur] Andersen-type issues. Rather, it's 'Could they have seen the organization malfunctioning and spoken up?' The answer is yes. When you have a mega-client, 'This is what the client should hear' is twisted into, 'This is what is going to let us stay at the boardroom level.' "[63]

Several other large McKinsey clients also filed for bankruptcy during 2001, including Swissair, Kmart, and Global Crossing. Skeptics began speculating whether an era of McKinsey knowledge, expertise, and helping its clients achieve superior performance was nearing an end. A partner at another consulting firm remarked: "McKinsey seems to have partners who develop academic theories and then run clinical trials on their clients."[64]

LOOKING TO THE FUTURE

As it had in 1971 with its "Commission on Firm Aims and Goals," in 2002, the firm initiated a broad review of how it advised clients, the kind of advice it provided, and the clients it served. "We historically, from time to time, have looked at how we serve clients," remarked a McKinsey professional. "It's generally in response to changes in the market."[65] Commented an industry observer: "There's a redefinition going on within McKinsey and other strategy firms as to how they will be structured and perceived in the future."[66]

Soon after taking charge as McKinsey's managing director, Gupta had introduced a three-term limit for managing director. His final three-year term was slated to end in 2003. In 2002, McKinsey began the process of electing a new managing director. Gupta's successor would need to chart the way ahead for the firm. Importantly, McKinsey's new leader would have to do so without the advice and presence of Bower.

On January 22, 2003, Bower, who had been McKinsey's guiding influence for more than six decades, died at the age of 99. McKinsey's impact, reach, power, and influence was directly traceable, according to Ron Daniel, "to Marvin—to his vision, his energy, his relentless determination, and his selfless commitment to making his firm—our firm—the preeminent institution it has become."[67] Reflected former IBM CEO and McKinsey alumnus Lou Gerstner:

> There were two things remarkable and memorable about Marvin. First, there were his principles that gave him a very clear sense of what McKinsey should do—how it should behave, how it should perform, how it should relate to clients. He adhered to those principles without ever moving an inch from them. Second, he was an extraordinary leader. He was a powerful communicator, and this had to do with his clarity of thinking and his ability to communicate those principles and make everyone believe there was a right way for a consultant to behave. Even after he retired, McKinsey was driven by Marvin's principles and what he viewed as right and the correct thing to do. . . . [I]t wasn't as though there was this guru who sat in the corner and gave off messages. Instead, there was a very large and successful enterprise that he invented that embodied those messages every day through hundreds if not thousands of people.
>
> I was about 26 years old when Marvin walked into my office one day and asked, "What are you doing to give something back?" I said, "Well, I'm working to pay off all my student loans as fast as I can." And he said, "No, that's not good enough. How about coming over and helping me with a pro-bono effort I am leading related to public education?" And that was—let's see—36 years ago, and I'm still at it.[68]

Four months before he had died, reflecting on the challenges facing his firm and the consulting industry, Bower had remarked, "Today is not very different from then [1937, when Mac's death had placed McKinsey at a crossroads]."[69] Several issues weighed on the minds of McKinsey partners as they reflected on choosing their next leader. What were the strengths that the firm needed to build on? Should the firm continue on its growth trajectory or slow down? Were the values developed under Bower's stewardship still valid? What needed to change, and what needed to remain unchanged?

NOTES

a. Bower officially retired from McKinsey in 1992.
b. For more information on the e-consulting industry, refer to Ashish Nanda and M. Julia Prats, "The Rise and Decline of e-Consulting," HBS Case No. 1-902-175 (Boston: Harvard Business School Publishing, 2002).
c. The firm did set up facilitators to help entrepreneurs launch new dot-coms and even accepted payment in stock from 150 start-up companies that sought McKinsey's advice but did not have the cash to pay the approximately $300,000 per month fees. The equity was placed in a blind trust and liquidated as soon as possible into a profit pool for McKinsey partners.
d. In 1998, *The McKinsey Quarterly* published an article by McKinsey consultants Elizabeth Chambers, Mark Foulon, Helen Handfeld-Jones, Steven Hankin, and Edward Michaels on "The War for Talent" (number 3, pp. 44–57). Reflecting the reality of the times, the article argued that supply of 25- to 44-year-olds was in demographic decline in America and Europe, economic growth was strong, labor markets were tight, and growing numbers of skilled youths were being absorbed into the emerging dot-com economy. The article cautioned that besides competing in the product market by offering customer value propositions, employers should compete aggressively in the labor market by offering employee value propositions.

NOTES TO CASE

1. John A. Byrne, "Inside McKinsey," *BusinessWeek*, July 8, 2002, p. 66.
2. Ibid.
3. This section draws primarily from Amar V. Bhide, "McKinsey & Company (A): 1956," HBS Case No. 393-066; and Amar V. Bhide, "Building the Professional Firm: McKinsey & Co.: 1939–1968," HBS Working Paper 95-010.
4. Ibid., p. 6.
5. Bhide, "McKinsey & Company (A)," p. 5.
6. Bhide, "Building the Professional Firm," p. 6.

7. Bhide, "McKinsey & Company (A)," p. 5.
8. Jack Sweeney, "The Last Lion," *Consulting Magazine*, February/March 2003, pp. 12–21.
9. Bhide, "McKinsey & Company (A)," p. 9.
10. Ibid., p. 10.
11. Ibid., p. 11.
12. Ibid., p. 12.
13. Ibid., p. 14.
14. Ibid., p. 16.
15. Ibid., p. 20.
16. Ibid., p. 22.
17. Ibid., p. 19.
18. Ibid., p. 20.
19. Bhide, "Building the Professional Firm," p. 20.
20. Amar V. Bhide, "McKinsey & Company (B): 1966," HBS Case No. 393-067, p. 4.
21. Bhide, "Building the Professional Firm," p. 23.
22. Bhide, "McKinsey & Company (B)," p. 5.
23. This section draws upon Christopher A. Bartlett, "McKinsey & Company: Managing Knowledge and Learning," HBS Case No. 396-357.
24. Bhide, "McKinsey & Company (B)," p. 13.
25. Bartlett, p. 3.
26. Ibid., p. 3.
27. Alison Leigh Cowan, "McKinsey May Buy Consultants," *The New York Times*, October 2, 1989.
28. John Byrne, "The McKinsey Mystique," *BusinessWeek*, September 20, 1993.
29. Tony Jackson, "Quality Controller in a Culture Club," *The Financial Times* (London Edition), September 27, 1999, p. 18.
30. John Byrne, "Inside McKinsey," *BusinessWeek*, July 8, 2002, pp. 66–76.
31. Jay W. Lorsch and Katharina Pick, "McKinsey & Co.," HBS Case No. 402-014, p. 11.
32. Ibid., p. 11.
33. Bartlett, p. 13.
34. Jitendra V. Singh, "McKinsey's Managing Director Rajat Gupta on Leading a Knowledge-based Global Consulting Organization," *Academy of Management Executive*, vol. 15, no. 2, May 2001, pp. 34–44.
35. Ibid., pp. 34–44.
36. Bartlett, p. 14.
37. Byrne.
38. Ibid.
39. "Challenge at McKinsey," *The Economist*, March 4, 2000.
40. Lorsch and Pick, p. 12.
41. Ibid., p. 13.
42. Bartlett, p. 13.

43. Ashish Nanda and M. Julia Prats, "The Rise and Decline of e-Consulting," HBS Case No. 902–175, p. 9.
44. Vikram Khanna, "The McKinsey Take on Business—and Itself," *Business Times* (Singapore), June 28, 2001, p. 10.
45. Singh.
46. Michael Skapinker, "Happy to Pursue its Own Brand of Strategic Thinking," *The Financial Times* (London Edition), March 30, 2001, p. 3.
47. Skapinker.
48. Singh.
49. Jonathan D. Glater, "Hurt by Slump, a Consulting Giant Looks Inward," *The New York Times*, June 30, 2002, p. 4.
50. Byrne, EB2B Commerce, Inc. Securities and Exchange Commission Form 8-K, filed on June 16, 2002, http://globalbb.onesource.com/Shared-Scripts/Functions/OTFR/Misc/GetQuotes.asp?Ticker=EBTB&KeyID= 44098332, accessed July 25, 2002.
51. Glater.
52. Alden Cushman, quoted in "Winners' Curse," *The Economist*, July 21, 2001.
53. Jackson.
54. Byrne; Glater.
55. Byrne.
56. Glater.
57. Ibid.
58. Rachel Emma Silverman, "McKinsey Partners Get Request to Fill Company's Coffers," *The Wall Street Journal*, July 16, 2001; "McKinsey's Capital Call Does not Signal Firm Crisis," *Consultants News*, July 2001.
59. David Acorn, quoted in Silverman.
60. Byrne.
61. Ibid.
62. Wayne Cooper, quoted in Glater.
63. Ibid.
64. Glater.
65. Glater.
66. Tom Rodenhauser, quoted in Glater.
67. "Marvin Bower – The Soul of McKinsey," http://www.mckinsey.com/ firm/history/marvinbower/marvin_bower.asp, accessed August 18, 2003.
68. Sweeney.
69. Ibid.

Case 1.2

MARKETING AT BAIN & COMPANY

(Robert Pedrero and Miklos Sarvary)

David Bechhofer, a director at Bain & Company had a dilemma. He sat in his office at the consulting firm's headquarters in Boston's Back Bay and pondered what to do. A year ago the firm's Chairman of the Board, Orit Gadiesh, and Tom Tierney, Bain's Worldwide Managing Director, had informed David his next client would be Bain itself, rather than one of America's Fortune 500 companies. Instead of developing a new corporate strategy for a multinational corporation, David was to create and implement an integrated marketing communication strategy for the firm itself. The dynamics of marketing in the consulting industry were changing dramatically and the subtle, indirect approach of the past was increasingly giving way to mainstream "consumer-product" style marketing. The firm's management committee felt that the time had come to revisit Bain's marketing strategy.

During the past year David had researched Bain's perception and position in the industry and undertaken an extensive study of the marketing tools currently being used. Now, with this information, David needed to decide what course of action, if any, should be taken. This was no small task. Marketing was something Bain & Company until now had considered anathema and any sweeping recommendations would require the consent of the partner group at-large. While David gazed out his window upon the city's South End he considered how Bain, a firm famous for its disdain of marketing, should compete with other companies—companies that used everything from TV commercials to golf tournaments to promote their services.

MANAGEMENT CONSULTING INDUSTRY

The origins of the management consulting industry can be traced to the work done by Frederick Taylor at the turn of the century. Perhaps the first management guru, Taylor authored the book *Principles and Methods of Scientific Management*, which promoted the theory of workers as machines, and advocated using time and motion studies to better understand production and improve efficiency. These concepts were quickly adopted by many leading businessmen (Henry Ford among them) and spread rapidly around the world. Taylor, capitalizing upon this success, built a business offering personal instruction in his theories—for the price of $35 a day ($630 in today's dollars).

From these humble origins, management consulting evolved into a global industry employing more than 100,000 individuals. In particular, the 15 years prior to 1996 had seen astounding growth. The rapid rate of change in many industries, the ongoing downsizing of most organizations, and the ceaseless march of technology put the skills and objectivity of consulting firms at a premium. Many corporations considered outside advice essential to the resolution of key business issues. AT&T, for example, spent $1 billion on consulting services in 1996, three times what it spent in 1993.

Throughout the decade prior to 1996, the industry had been growing at twice the rate of the world economy. In 1995 alone, the consulting business generated more than $40 billion in revenues worldwide. The United States was predictably the major consumer of these services and accounted for $21 billion of those revenues. The industry itself was driven by a handful of large firms. The top 40 firms generated 58% of U.S. revenues and approximately 50% of worldwide billings (Exhibit 1.12). Despite this large firm prevalence, more than half of the leading consulting firms did not exist five years prior and only 1% existed fifty years ago.

Exhibit 1.12 Consultants News

40 Largest Management Consulting Firms	1996 MC Revenues* World	Consultants† World	1996 MC Revenues† U.S.	Consultants† U.S.	Worldwide Growth†† low—average—high
1. Andersen Consulting (a)	$3,115.3	43,808	$1,590.0	20,831	
2. McKinsey & Co.	$2,100.0	3,944	$800.0	1,600	
3. Ernst & Young (b)	$2,100.0	11,200	$1,400.0	6,900	
4. Coopers & Lybrand Consulting (c)	$1,918.0	9,000	$1,005.0	4,615	
5. KPMG Peat Marwick (c,d)	$1,380.0	10,764	$770.0	5,126	
6. Arthur Andersen (a,e)	$1,379.6	15,000	$766.2	8,000	
7. Deloitte & Touche (f)	$1,303.0	10,000	$821.0	4,700	
8. Mercer Consulting Group (g)	$1,159.0	9,241	$707.0	5,133	
9. Towers Perrin	$903.0	6,262	$659.0	4,321	
10. A.T. Kearney (h)	$870.0	2,300	$530.0	1,265	
11. Pricewaterhouse (i)	$840.2	6,230	$480.9	2,940	
12. IBM Consulting Group (j)	$730.0	3,970	$530.0	2,500	
13. Booz-Allen & Hamilton (k)	$720.0	5,685	$540.0	4,550	
14. Watson Wyatt Worldwide	$656.0	3,730	$417.0	2,310	
15. The Boston Consulting Group	$600.0	1,550	$180.0	450	
16. Gemini Consulting	$600.0	1,470	$218.0	600	
17. Arthur D. Little, Inc.	$574.0	1,939	$299.0	951	
18. Hewitt Associates (c)	$568.0	3,807	$538.0	3,294	
19. Aon Consulting (l)	$472.9	4,370	$318.1	2,080	
20. Bain & Company	$450.0	1,350	$240.0	675	
21. American Management Systems	$440.0	2,960	$300.0	2,000	
22. Woodrow Milliman (m)	$350.0	1,150	$188.0	500	
23. Grant Thornton (n)	$306.0	886	$66.0	495	
24. Sedgwick Noble Lowndes	$261.9	3,142	$78.2	532	
25. The Hay Group	$259.0	1,035	$119.0	460	
26. Buck Consultants (o)	$228.0	2,557	$171.0	1,588	
27. A. Foster Higgins & Co.	$208.0	1,300	$164.0	950	
28. CSC Index (p)	$200.0	350	$150.0	275	
29. Monitor Company	$181.0	700	$117.0	400	
30. Proudfoot PLC	$135.0	430	$37.0	100	
31. Mitchell Madison Group	$100.0	305	$60.0	200	
32. Technology Solutions Co. (TSC) (q)	$97.6	995	$87.8	835	
33. George S. May International Co.	$91.1	460	$59.8	280	
34. The LEK Partnership	$90.0	300	$25.0	100	
35. The Segal Co.	$87.6	584	$85.9	572	
36. Kurt Salmon Associates (r)	$85.0	563	$65.0	401	
37. A T & T Solutions	$70.0	1,200	$46.0	950	
38. Thomas Group, Inc.	$65.0	171	$47.0	130	
39. Marakon Associates	$57.0	140	$29.0	85	
40. First Consulting Group	$51.3	325	$51.3	325	

*revenues, less reimbursed expenses, in millions of dollars for calendar 1996, unless otherwise noted. †Definitions of consultant varies. ††Average growth of 40 largest was 15%.
NOTE: All estimates are by *Consultants News*, primarily comparing firms with significant U.S. presence. (a) Andersen Consulting and Arthur Andersen are business units of Andersen Worldwide. (b) Fiscal year ended October 31, 1996. (c) Fiscal year ended May 31, 1996. (d) Figures in # of consultants columns reflect total consulting. (e) Fiscal year ended August 31, 1996. (f) Fiscal year ended May 31, 1996. (g) 76% of world revenues reflect William M. Mercer and 19% reflect Mercer Management Consulting. Figures in # of contributors columns reflect number of employees. (h) Provided audited revenue figures. (i) Fiscal year ended June 30, 1996. (j) Figure in # of consultants U.S. column reflects U.S. and Canada. (k) Revenue figure is projection for fiscal year ending March 31, 1997. (l) Revenue and # of consultants reflect acquisitions including Alexander & Alexander Services. (m) Millman & Robertson is U.S. member. (n) U.S. fiscal year ended July 31, 1996. Worldwide fiscal year end varies by country. (o) Revenue and # of consultants reflect acquisition of W F Corraon. (p) 1995 revenues for CSC Index were $170M. (q) Fiscal year ended May 31, 1996. (r) Growth is based on updated '95 revenue figures of $80.5M worldwide and $60.1M U.S.

SPECIAL REPRINT 1997
Copyright © 1997 Consultants News. Reprinted from Consultants News ® March 1997, published monthly since 1970 by Kennedy Information, LLC, Fitzwilliam, NH 03447.
Phone: 603 585301
Fax: 603 5856401
E-mail editor@kennedypub.com
Giles Goodhead, Publisher
Tom Rodenhauser, Managing Editor
www.kennedypub.com

In 1996, the universe of consulting firms was roughly divided across four dimensions: strategic consulting, information technology (IT) based consulting, specific situation consulting, and hybrid accounting/consulting firms.

Strategic consulting. These generalist strategy firms recommended and often implemented solutions to the complex business problems faced by the senior management of large corporations. The market leaders in the segment in 1996 were Bain & Company, Boston Consulting Group (BCG), and McKinsey & Company. The client base of these firms was typically quite diverse and ranged from financial service providers to high technology companies to large utilities. The scope of work performed was also broad, and included everything from general corporate strategy to mergers and acquisition and privatization advice.

Information technology consulting. These firms were built around a specialization in IT infrastructure planning, design, and procurement. In 1996, the leading firm, and largest company in the industry overall (with $2.5 billion in 1995 revenues), was Andersen Consulting. These firms typically worked with the same firms as the strategy consultants, but interacted at different levels of those organizations to provide more "nuts and bolts" operational advice and installation of computerized systems. Other firms in the segment included IBM Consulting Group and American Management Systems.

Specific situation consulting. This was the broadest and least quantifiable segment of the industry. Included here were companies specializing in particular industries (First Manhattan Group for banking or Watson Wyatt Worldwide for benefits) or certain types of problems (The Hay Group for human resources or ICF Kaiser for environmental issues). Also included in this strata were the "one-man-band" consultants and small partnerships that specialized in unique, smaller-scale situations and traded upon the personal relationships and network of their founders. Finally, there were firms that had grown quite large implementing specific management concepts. A prime example was CSC Index, which rode the coat tails of re-engineering to the Top 40 list of management consulting.

Hybrid accounting/consulting. This segment consisted of the consulting arms of the major accounting firms. These companies were among the largest in the industry and generated high revenues by defining their consulting services very broadly. These services included financial, tax, regulatory, and benefits advice, as well as substantial amounts of the traditional IT and re-engineering work. Some firms even had strong industry specific concentrations, such as Ernst & Young in health care. Other segment leaders included: KPMG Peat Marwick, Coopers & Lybrand, and Deloitte & Touche.

INDUSTRY TRENDS

The industry had undergone dramatic change in the early 1990's— change expected to continue as consulting moved into the 21st century. Three themes proliferated and continued to dominate the attention of firm partners: growth, integration, and globalization.

In 1995, the world market for management consulting grew 18%, to more than $40 billion. While this rate of overall growth was not expected to continue, it was predicted that growth would average a compound annual rate of 12% into the 21st century. This would create an industry with more than $65 billion in revenues by the year 2000.

The growth rates of individual firms had been even more dramatic. Of the top 40 firms in 1995, 16 had growth rates in excess of the 18% world wide rate. Several firms, including Coopers & Lybrand, IBM Consulting Group, and Booz-Allen & Hamilton, expanded at rates more than 30% per year. Differences in revenues between the top forty firms also increased. Tom Rodenhauser, *Consulting News* managing editor, said "We're seeing a greater disparity between the largest and smallest firms on our list—the drop-off in 1995 revenues was almost $2.45 billion from #1 to #40 on our list, a full $1 billion more than in 1990. That indicates a few mega-firms will battle for the title of largest management consultancy." Geographically, the United States was expected to keep pace with the overall industry growth rate and remain the premier market for consulting services. On a growth percentage basis however, the Asia/Pacific and Latin American regions were expected to explode due to their relatively small current base and their desire to become more competitive in the global marketplace.

The industry also saw an integration of services and expertise within firms through mergers, acquisitions, and alliances. The largest firms were not only growing faster but also broadening their offerings. According to *Management Consulting International*, "It is becoming increasingly difficult ... to define consulting ... Depending on the consultancy, services range from high-end strategy advice to operational consulting; from human resource strategy to employee benefits administration; and from customized business transformation to off-the-shelf software solutions."

EDS, for example, sought to consolidate client relationships by selling upstream consultancy services in addition to its core IT outsourcing and systems integration business. In 1995, EDS acquired A.T. Kearney, one of the oldest consulting firms, for $600 million. The fledgling Management Consulting Services unit of EDS was then merged with Kearney to create a top 15 company. EDS could then package consulting services with IT outsourcing, as it did with a billion dollar pact (including a $100 million of consulting) with Britain's Rolls Royce. Other firms also acquired or merged with small or medium size consultancies to fill specific location needs or expand services. For example, Ernst & Young merged with Kenneth Leventhal, a hybrid firm that specialized in advising on real-estate issues.

Andersen Consulting, in contrast, used alliances to fuel its growth. In 1995, Andersen partnered with GE Capital, Grupo Financiero Banamex-Accival, and PeopleSoft to achieve greater presence in the IT outsourcing, Mexican, and manufacturing markets, respectively. Ernst & Young by comparison formed a global alliance with Tata Consultancy Services of India to provide a broader array of software expertise and services.

Finally, as their clients became multinational, consulting firms had to follow suit and go global. Top-tier strategy consultants led the way. McKinsey started the overseas trend with the opening of an office in London in 1959. By 1989, McKinsey had 42 offices in 21 countries, and today the firm is represented in 36 countries by 70 offices. In fact, more than 60% of McKinsey's revenues were generated abroad. Bain & Company provided a similar story. The firm had 6 offices in 5 countries at the beginning of 1989; by 1996 it had 25 offices in 19 countries. In peak years, Bain added as many as 4 new offices each year.

Other consulting companies satisfied the need for an international presence through mergers and acquisitions. In 1995, Coopers & Lybrand merged with 12 overseas firms. Including its traditional accounting offices, Coopers & Lybrand was now represented in 140 countries. IBM Consulting acquired 6 companies and opened 4 new offices, adding representation in India, South Africa, Finland, Belgium, and Brazil.

The end result of this ongoing expansion, integration, and globalization was a continued widening of the definition of consulting and an overall democratization of the industry. Increasingly, firms offered more and more types of overlapping advice. The extraordinary growth of the IT firms, Big 6 hybrids, and top tier strategists meant that the consulting consumer had an ever-expanding menu of companies to choose from, and understanding the differences between firms was becoming more difficult.

MARKETING PRACTICES

From a marketing perspective these trends forced the industry to re-examine its aversion to self-promotion. The dramatic expansion experienced in the 90's forced firms to attempt to build a brand identity and differentiate themselves from their competitors in order to continue growing. Traditionally, the old-line strategy firms eschewed advertising and instead used a limited "narrowcasting" approach to sell themselves. This entailed identifying and communicating with a small set of qualified, sophisticated corporate consumers. The typical tools were targeted publications, executive conferences, books, and articles. This low-key approach maintained the mystique of these organizations and, when combined with their longevity and network of existing relationships, allowed them to grow quite easily.

However, as the field expanded and the number of new entrants increased, there was a move by many competitors toward a "broadcast" approach to marketing. They adopted mainstream marketing techniques, ranging from sports sponsorship to television and print advertising. A consultant at Mercer Management summed up the trend well, "Ten years ago, if I'd suggested we advertise, I'd have been shot; five years ago I'd have been whipped." In 1996, Mercer advertised in *Forbes* magazine. In 1996, industry giant Andersen Consulting spent upwards of $30 million on advertising and promotion. Many other firms, especially the Big 6 hybrids, have followed suit.

David Bechhofer surveyed the consulting landscape and noticed the substantial increase in marketing by all firms, as well as the fiercer competition generated by the many new entrants into the business. He also saw a growing need for increased local awareness as Bain opened offices in new markets. The greater size of the company required a more coordinated effort to "prime the pipeline" for new business. David knew that Bain wanted to continue growing and that these changing marketing dynamics had to be considered and evaluated. But, it was not clear what Bain's response should be. Marketing varied by type of consulting firm and understanding these differences was the first step to fully analyzing the problem.

BCG and McKinsey focused their marketing budgets on building "word-of-mouth" about their services and networking with prospective clients. Specifically, each firm focused on publishing articles and books and meeting high-level managers at industry and CEO-focused conferences. McKinsey published the "McKinsey Quarterly," which contained articles (written by partners) on current management topics, and resembled the *Harvard Business Review*. BCG published single topic thought pieces under the banner "Perspectives." White papers and various other special studies often were produced to supplement *Perspectives*. Both companies maintained extensive contact databases of business and academic leaders to whom these publications were mailed. In the case of the *McKinsey Quarterly*, circulation was estimated to be 45,000.

Each firm also encouraged partners to author books and articles for publications such as the *Harvard Business Review* and *Wall Street Journal*. McKinsey partners typically published 5 to 10 books annually and also spoke publicly on a wide variety of business topics. Both firms also held and attended select high-level, CEO-oriented, management conferences. Underwriting a conference, which could cost upward of $100,000, allowed a partner to address attendees and provided a tremendous networking opportunity through various break-out sessions and social events.

McKinsey even took the tactic of funding a Global Institute and a Change Institute. Both these institutions generated awareness and press for the firm, and helped position McKinsey as a "thought leader." McKinsey also used a public relations firm and image consultant to help promote and position the company. BCG did little in this regard, but did produce a brochure for general image building, something McKinsey declined to produce.

The IT, hybrid, and specific situation consultants took a more expansive approach to marketing. These firms used many of the same tactics as the strategy firms, including: brochures, captive publications (e.g., *McKinsey Quarterly*), thought pieces (white papers), PR firms, book publishing, and conferences. However, these methods tended to be focused more on specific products, like re-engineering, than on general business ideas and problems. These forms of marketing also tended to be targeted to a broader audience. In the case of conferences, these firms focused on all levels of an organization, not just top management. In the case of CSC Index, the pioneers in re-engineering, conferences were targeted to all functions and levels of an organization; so many were held that they grew into their own profit center. The specific skills these firms offered were needed and could be purchased at many different levels of the organization. Re-engineering, for example, could be applied to everything from mundane processes, such as credit approval, to the wholesale re-ordering of a company's production systems.

The IT, hybrid, and specific situation firms also took consulting into the marketing mainstream. In order to rapidly develop awareness and differentiate themselves, they turned to traditional media vehicles, such as print and television. CSC Index spent millions a year to promote re-engineering; in the process it turned to print advertisements in the general business press. Awareness of the firm increased dramatically. Gemini went so far as to trademark the term TRANSFORMATION to symbolize its line of products. This was followed with a multi-million dollar ad campaign in magazines such as *Fortune, Forbes* and *Business-Week* to promote the line.

Andersen Consulting pushed the boundaries even further by expanding into television. In a series of television and print advertisements the company used images of an elephant crossing a gorge on a downed tree trunk and a school of fish swimming in concert to highlight the firm's ability to help companies "marry size with nimbleness" and "reshape the entire enterprise," (Exhibit 1.13). Andersen even dared to enter the realm of sports sponsorship previously populated by consumer products companies such as Phillip-Morris and Coca-Cola. Examples of its foray into sports marketing include the:

- Andersen Consulting World Championship of Golf—a head-to-head match play competition featuring 32 of the world's best golfers and golf's largest purse.
- Andersen Consulting Stakes: Melbourne Cup—a Listed Race for two-year old horses that is seen by an estimated 350 million people worldwide.
- Corporate Sports Battle (CSB)—the world's largest corporate sports competition, which features American corporations competing in Olympic-style regional events and culminates in the ESPN-televised National Finals.

Andersen also sponsored individual athletes and teams including Jay

Exhibit 1.13 Advertisement for Andersen Consulting

What shape is your business in?

In response to unprecedented market pressures, many organizations are reconfiguring themselves They've recognized that isolated improvements no longer ensure survival. They're seeking cohesive solutions that dramatically strengthen their entire enterprise. Andersen Consulting helps organizations successfully transform by refining and re-aligning all vital components. Our work with hundreds of the world's leading companies has given us a unique balance of skills in strategy, tech-nology, process and people. So instead of just pointing you in a new direction, we can help make sure your whole organization moves forward aggressively. As one.

For more information, please visit our web site at http://www.ac.com.

ANDERSEN
CONSULTING

Siegel, a golfer on the PGA Senior Tour, and Rothmans Williams Renault, a Formula One racing team.

This extreme spectrum of marketing activities left David with a range of opportunities far broader than Bain or any of the other strategy firms had ever pursued.

CONSULTING AT BAIN & COMPANY

Bill Bain started his consulting career with BCG in 1967. By 1973, he had risen to group vice president. Disenchanted with the current state of consulting, he and 6 others left that same year to start Bain & Company. Bill Bain was unhappy with the existing industry paradigm:

> The product of consulting firms at the time was the report. In addition, the scope of what was being done by consulting firms was pretty narrow, or if it was broad, pretty shallow. I saw four major flaws in the traditional consulting practices: One, most projects were of short duration. Two, there was little use of data to support recommendations. Three, there was little or no attempt to follow through on recommendations. Finally, performance measurement emphasized a consulting firm's internal peer review rather than external measures of success.

Based on his analysis of the consulting industry, the new company was centered on the following principles:

Relationship consulting. Bill Bain decided that to have the greatest impact on its clients, the firm needed to be deeply involved and aligned with those companies. Only by building a high level of trust and buy-in could real change and the adoption of Bain's recommendations occur. He committed the firm to both client exclusivity and the development of long-lasting relationships with the highest levels of management, particularly the CEO. While Bain & Company today still occasionally offers exclusivity to clients, it is a small part of their total client mix.

Data driven analysis. Using an "outside-in," fact based approach to its clients' problems Bain delivered customized, creative, breakthrough strategies. Typically, a case team intensively studied a client's industry and how that client was viewed by its customers, competitors, and suppliers. This process surfaced all the given company's potential alternatives and possible solutions. Specific analytical tools then were used to evaluate these options and provide a series of final recommendations. This rigorous "data driven" approach, and emphasis on realistic options, ensured that solutions were both feasible and implementable.

Results. Bain's desire to produce meaningful change engendered a healthy disdain of written reports. The common firm feeling was that reports just sat on shelves. A weighty tome, instead of prompting action, often merely gathered dust. At Bain there were no reports. Graphical presentations told the "story" of a company's problem and offered a set of change recommendations—recommendations that had to pass the test of both being implementable by the client and capable of generating a sustainable competitive advantage. To Bain, an unimplementable strategy, no matter how intellectually elegant, was useless. Orit Gadiesh was fond of saying, "It's Monday morning, 8 a.m. What are you going to do?" As she explained, "At the end of the day, you have to be able to translate what you do into something that the client can, and wants to, implement. Next Monday, at 8 o'clock, when the client walks into his office, what is he going to have to do differently to make things happen?"

Performance measurement. Because the bottom line for Bain was results, the next question was how to measure them. The company's goal was to generate value that was an order of magnitude greater than the fees being charged. Bain's answer was to create and track a theoretical portfolio of their clients' stock and compare its performance with that of the S & P 500 index. Between 1980 and 1996, the return on this theoretical portfolio was approximately twice that of the S & P 500 index (Exhibit 1.14).

Culture. To augment its principles, Bain developed a unique and very strong cultural identity. This culture revolved around drive, teamwork, and creativity. Within the industry, employees were referred to as "Bainies" and were renowned for their iron discipline and gung-ho spirit. A "single-firm" culture and teamwork were core values promoted at all levels of the organization. As Tom Tierney, Worldwide Managing Director, describes it: "We promote a 'single-firm' culture and emphasize teamwork at all levels within Bain. Although we have offices around the globe, we operate seamlessly across them. We often staff teams with consultants from different offices, and people frequently transfer between cities to broaden their skills, all of which helps to build our 'one-firm' identity."

Extraordinary teams were another key aspect of the Bain culture. The case team was the essential functional unit at Bain and typically

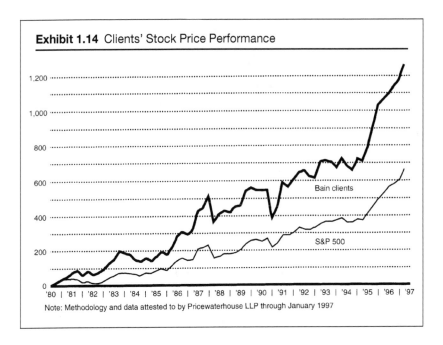

Exhibit 1.14 Clients' Stock Price Performance

Note: Methodology and data attested to by Pricewaterhouse LLP through January 1997

consisted of a partner, a manager, 2 to 4 consultants (recent MBA's), and 2 to 4 associate consultants (recent college graduates). This unit worked alone or in conjunction with other teams depending on the size and scope of a client's problem. The speed and intensity of the work required from a case team necessitated close cooperation and communication among all members. The ability to succeed and flourish in this environment was highly prized at Bain. One company veteran said, "We succeed because we are a team, we hunt as a pack. In my priority scheme, first, I would rather succeed together, but my second desired outcome would be to fail together, instead of succeeding alone."

Bain's culture attracted unique and creative people; this assertion was personified through the post-consulting career choices made by former Bain employees. Instead of joining the strategic planning or business development departments of large corporations, more than 60% of Bain alumni went into line general management, private equity, or small business/entrepreneurship positions. Less than a quarter took strategic planning positions after leaving the company.

The end result of these ideas was a firm with estimated 1996 revenues of $450 million. Annual revenue growth from 1973 to 1996 had averaged 34% and individual years had exceeded a 50% rate. Bain's strategy was so effective that year over year the firm retained as much as

85% (1996 over 1995) of its clients. From the initial 7 professionals based in Boston, in 1996 the firm numbered 1,800 employees in 24 offices spanning 5 continents and 19 countries (Exhibit 1.15).

In its capacity as a global strategy consultant, Bain handled a broad range of clients and problems. In 1996, the most prevalent client industries were technology, telecommunications, consumer products, and financial services (Exhibit 1.16). In terms of the specific services provided, corporate and business unit strategy dominated. Growth, turn-around, portfolio management, and competitor concerns, as well as mission/vision development and operational improvement, were the primary problems addressed. Bain also provided substantial organizational change, sales and marketing and mergers, and acquisition advice (Exhibit 1.17).

The "KGB" of Consulting

Historically, Bain was fortunate enough to be able to ignore marketing. Bill Bain's philosophy was that if everyone did excellent work, clients

Exhibit 1.15 Worldwide Office Location

Atlanta	Brussels	Beijing
Boston	Geneva	Hong Kong
Chicago	London	Seoul
Dallas	Madrid	Singapore
Los Angeles	Milan	Sydney
Mexico City	Moscow	Tokyo
San Francisco	Munich	
Toronto	Paris	
	Rome	
	Stockholm	

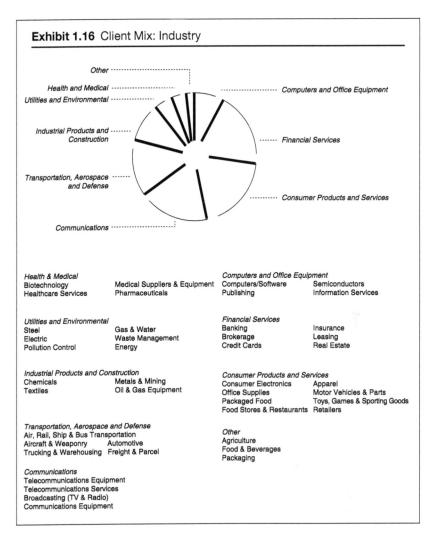

Exhibit 1.16 Client Mix: Industry

Health & Medical		Computers and Office Equipment	
Biotechnology	Medical Suppliers & Equipment	Computers/Software	Semiconductors
Healthcare Services	Pharmaceuticals	Publishing	Information Services

Utilities and Environmental		Financial Services	
Steel	Gas & Water	Banking	Insurance
Electric	Waste Management	Brokerage	Leasing
Pollution Control	Energy	Credit Cards	Real Estate

Industrial Products and Construction		Consumer Products and Services	
Chemicals	Metals & Mining	Consumer Electronics	Apparel
Textiles	Oil & Gas Equipment	Office Supplies	Motor Vehicles & Parts
		Packaged Food	Toys, Games & Sporting Goods
		Food Stores & Restaurants	Retailers

Transportation, Aerospace and Defense	
Air, Rail, Ship & Bus Transportation	
Aircraft & Weaponry	Automotive
Trucking & Warehousing	Freight & Parcel

Other
Agriculture
Food & Beverages
Packaging

Communications
Telecommunications Equipment
Telecommunications Services
Broadcasting (TV & Radio)
Communications Equipment

would beat a path to the company's doors. The partners understood that there was a high degree of inter-locking membership among corporate boards. CEOs consequently served on a variety of boards besides their own. Bain's relationship consulting and top level executive interaction thus lead to a very high level of referral business. This, plus the high level of repeat business, meant that firm capacity was often sold out many months in advance.

The outgrowth of this client exclusivity and aversion to marketing was secrecy and a dislike for publicity, which led Bain to be called the "KGB" of consulting. The company's initial refusal to use business

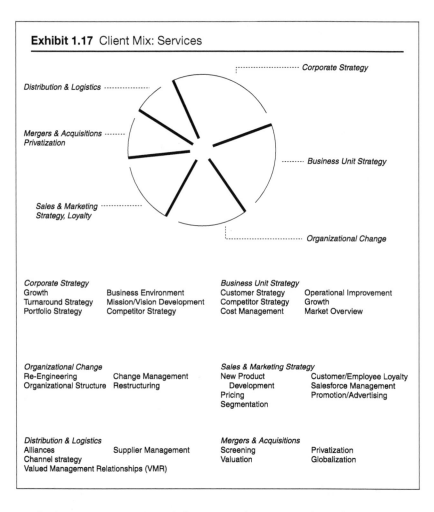

Exhibit 1.17 Client Mix: Services

Corporate Strategy
Growth
Turnaround Strategy
Portfolio Strategy
Business Environment
Mission/Vision Development
Competitor Strategy

Business Unit Strategy
Customer Strategy
Competitor Strategy
Cost Management
Operational Improvement
Growth
Market Overview

Organizational Change
Re-Engineering
Organizational Structure
Change Management
Restructuring

Sales & Marketing Strategy
New Product
  Development
Pricing
Segmentation
Customer/Employee Loyalty
Salesforce Management
Promotion/Advertising

Distribution & Logistics
Alliances
Channel strategy
Valued Management Relationships (VMR)
Supplier Management

Mergers & Acquisitions
Screening
Valuation
Privatization
Globalization

cards (a practice continued for more than 5 years) and strict policy forbidding interaction with the press enhanced this image. The "results not reports" tactic left Bain with no weighty documents to tout. The "one client per industry" policy, plus the customized and proprietary nature of each case, left no reason for Bain to publicize its work. Advertising as well as brochures were anathema.

However, as Bain moved into the 1990's, circumstances began to change. In 1990, control of the firm passed from Bill Bain and a small cadre of top executives to the partner group at-large. The rapid growth of the firm both domestically and overseas, and the desire to maintain a one-firm image, began to require greater internal and external communication and more extensive coordination among offices. As the company "grew-up" it was becoming harder to remain anonymous. In order to attract the best clients and employees, in the volumes needed to sustain such a large and rapidly growing organization (the company hired hundreds of new people a year), Bain needed to increase its awareness among a broader audience as a global leader in management consulting. The democratization of the industry, and the desire by an ever greater number of firms to try to upsell strategy work with an underlying specialty, only further confused clients about Bain's positioning.

A seminal event occurred when the CEO of one of Bain's largest multinational clients asked a simple question. As the CEO and a group of partners sat at dinner, the CEO, who prided himself on his company's global image, laid out the business cards of seven partners. Each card was designed differently and contained slightly different information. The CEO then asked, "What does this tell me about Bain's global one-firm image?"

DAVID'S DECISION

It was David's hypothesis that though there were a variety of segments in the industry, strategy consulting was a very distinct niche that had little crossover with the IT, Hybrid/Big 6, and situation specific sectors. To validate this hypothesis, David undertook a variety of surveys to understand how Bain sold itself and how the market viewed Bain. To understand how Bain sold itself, David conducted a survey of over 100 partners in the firm and followed this with in-depth, one-on-one interviews with 25 of them. This was complemented by a survey of the senior executives of 262 U.S. corporations with more than a billion dollars in revenue—the prime consumers of consulting.

The partner survey revealed that internally Bain's primary focus was consistent—produce results. Out in the world this was the key selling point used by partners and purchased by clients. A Chicago partner summed it up well:

Bain partners felt that they sold an understanding of change and the specific types of business situations that their clients faced. Understanding only one industry or an individual analytic concept (e.g., re-engineering) tended to prevent dynamic "out-of-the-box" thinking and only led to simple incremental change. Bain instead sold the breakthrough strategy that obsoleted a company's competitors.

The research survey confirmed David's belief that executives categorized consulting firms along a continuum from strategy firms to specialist expertise providers. The survey showed broad recognition amongst business leaders that there were three primary strategy consulting firms: Bain, BCG, and McKinsey. Competitors such as Andersen Consulting and CSC Index represented the IT and re-engineering segments respectively. Some firms, such as Booz-Allen, just evoked confusion as they mixed strategy with "expertise in a specific area."

Even within the strategy subset executives perceived the three companies differently. Bain was perceived as generating primarily financial results and secondarily breakthrough strategy. BCG was most cited for breakthrough strategy followed by a highly conceptual approach. McKinsey scored highest on advice to CEO's followed by quality people. David saw his industry segment positioning with Bain as the "Results Achiever," BCG the "Idea Generator," and McKinsey the "Advice Giver."

Bearing in mind his research, the current state of the industry and Bain's history, David continued his gaze out at Boston's South End and pondered the recommendations he would make at next week's meeting of the management committee.

Part 2

Major Practice Areas

Introduction

Case 2.1a

BAE Automated Systems (A): Denver International Airport
Baggage-Handling System
(Ramiro Montealegre, H. James Nelson, Carin Isabel Knoop, and
Lynda M. Applegate, University of Colorado)

Case 2.1b

BAE Automated Systems (B): Implementing the Denver
International Airport Baggage-Handling System
(Lynda M. Applegate)

Case 2.2

Mega Corporation (A, B, C, D)
(Larry Greiner and Arvind Bhambri, University of Southern California)

Case 2.3

Hunter Business Group: *TeamTBA*
(Elizabeth Caputo and Das Narayandas)

Case 2.4

Western Casualty
(David Upton and Sari Carp)

Case 2.5

Vandelay Industries, Inc.
(Andrew McAfee)

INTRODUCTION

Clients hire consultants for their leading edge knowledge and expertise in a variety of specialized disciplines. This section provides cases concerned with the five major practice areas in management consulting: (1) Information Technology, (2) Strategy and Organization, (3) Marketing, (4) Human Resources, and (5) Operations Management. Together, these five areas of specialization comprise approximately 80% of the total consulting market, with 45% in IT, and the remainder of the market roughly divided equally among the other four areas. Each of the five practice areas is represented by one case in this section, though we will see overlap among them.

All consultants need to be knowledgeable, if not experts, about all the major practice areas. Increasingly, client problems cut across the five specializations, making it imperative to know the limits of one's efforts as well as how to relate solutions to other disciplines. The five largest consulting firms have already established a broad-based profile dominated by IT, yet they also market a portfolio that includes most of the other practice areas. Other consulting firms, especially local and regional ones, typically prefer to specialize within one or two areas. In Greiner and Poulfelt's book[1], various experts discuss each of the four areas in more detail.

The first three cases in Part 2 of the casebook examine the three specializations of Information Technology, Strategy and Organization, and Marketing consulting. The IT area is considered in the *BAE Automated Systems (A)* case, which describes the difficult implementation of Denver's airport-wide computer-based baggage-handling system. It provides an opportunity for students to reflect on both the system design problems and the challenges of implementing IT-enabled change initiatives. The Strategy and Organization consulting practice area is represented by the *Mega Corporation (A), (B), (C) and (D)* cases. These cases focus on how a consultant works with a new CEO and his team to facilitate strategic and organizational changes. This series is unusual for its portrayal of the dynamic sequence of strategic decisions made in the top team. Finally, with regard to Marketing consulting, the *Hunter Business Group (HBG)* case raises a serious question facing many consulting firms today—how far should a firm go in directly involving itself in the management of part of a client's operations. Here we see *HBG* take over a sales unit and produce some initial success, but later when revenues begin to fall, several questions are raised about what to do next.

The fourth and fifth cases are devoted to human resources and to operations management consulting. The human resources case, *Western Casualty*, shows how consultants (MCG) improve productivity in their insurance client by introducing what are called "high involvement" methods that empower employee teams to come up with innovative solutions. This case also touches on a broader issue of consultant compensation, since the MCG consultants put their fees at risk, depending on results with the client. *Vandelay Industries, Inc.* is an Operations Management consulting case that involves the installation of a new IT system in a factory environment. It illustrates several problems facing the Deloitte & Touche consultants in understanding the work flow and deciding what kind of an IT system is most appropriate for the situation.

There are also many subspecializations within these broader practice areas. The diversity in service offerings has expanded greatly in recent years, not only leaving clients and consultants racing to keep up with the latest innovative practice area, but also raising questions about what legitimately can be called consulting and how it should be compensated.

NOTE

1.   Greiner, L. & Poulfelt, F. 2009. *Management Consulting Today and Tomorrow*, Taylor & Francis.

Case 2.1a

BAE AUTOMATED SYSTEMS (A): DENVER INTERNATIONAL AIRPORT BAGGAGE-HANDLING SYSTEM

(Ramiro Montealegre, H. James Nelson, Carin Isabel Knoop, and Lynda M. Applegate, Univesity of Colorado)

ABOUT THE AUTHORS

Assistant Professor Ramiro Montealegre and Research Associate H. James Nelson of the University of Colorado at Boulder, Research Associate Carin Isabel Knoop, and Professor Lynda M. Applegate prepared this case as the basis for class discussion rather than to illustrate either effective or ineffective handling of an administrative situation. Some names have been disguised.

No airport anywhere in the world is as technologically advanced as the Denver International Airport.[1]

It's dramatic. If your bag [got] on the track, your bag [was] in pieces.[2]

In November 1989, ground was broken to build the Denver International Airport (DIA). Located 25 miles from downtown Denver, Colorado, it was the first major airport to be built in the United States since the opening of the Dallas-Fort Worth Airport in 1974. In 1992, two years into construction, the project's top managers recommended inclusion of an airport-wide integrated baggage-handling system that could dramatically improve the efficiency of luggage delivery. Originally contracted by United Airlines to cover its operations, the system was to be expanded to serve the entire airport. It was expected that the integrated system would improve ground time efficiency, reduce close-out time for hub operations, and decrease time-consuming manual baggage sorting and handling. There were, however, a number of risks inherent in the endeavor: the scale of the large project size; the enormous complexity of the expanded system; the newness of the technology; the large number of resident entities to be served by the same system; the high degree of technical and project definition uncertainty; and the short time span for completion. Due to its significant experience implementing baggage-handling technology on a smaller scale, BAE Automated Systems Inc., an engineering consulting and manufacturing company based in Carollton, Texas, was awarded the contract.

Construction problems kept the new airport from opening on the originally scheduled opening date in October 1993. Subsequently, problems with the implementation of the baggage system forced delays in the opening of the airport another three times in seven months. In May 1994, under growing pressure from shareholders, the business community, Denver residents, Federal Aviation Administration (FAA) commissioners, and the tenant airlines and concessionaires, Denver mayor Wellington Webb announced that he was hiring the German firm Logplan to help assess the state of the automated baggage system. In July, Logplan issued an 11-page report to the City of Denver that characterized BAE's system as "highly advanced" and "theoretically" capable of living up to its promised "capacities, services and performances," but acknowledged mechanical and electrical problems that "make it most improbable to achieve a stable and reliable operation." Logplan suggested that it would take approximately five months to get the complete BAE system working reliably. It also suggested that a backup system of tugs, carts, and conveyor belts could be constructed in less than five months.

In August 1994, Mayor Webb approved the construction of a backup baggage system. At the same time, he notified BAE of a $12,000-a-day penalty for not finishing the baggage system by DIA's original October

29, 1993 completion date. Webb also demanded that BAE pay for the $50 million conventional tug-and-cart baggage system. Gene Di Fonso, President of BAE, knew that his company could demonstrate that flaws in the overall design of the airport and an unsystematic approach to project changes had affected implementation of the integrated baggage system. He wondered whether he should just cancel the contract and cut his losses, or attempt to negotiate with the city for the support required to finish the system as specified, despite the severe deterioration in communication and rising hostility. Could the problems with the automated system be overcome with the dedication of additional resources? Given that the system represented a significant departure from conventional technology, would reducing its size and complexity facilitate resolution of the problems that plagued it? And, if the city could be persuaded to accept a simplified system, would the tenant airlines, particularly those with hubbing operations that had been promised more advanced functionality and better performance, be likely to sue?

BUILDING THE MOST EFFICIENT AIRPORT IN THE WORLD

Until about 1970, Denver's Stapleton Airport had managed to accommodate an ever-growing number of airplanes and passengers. Its operational capacity was severely limited by runway layout; Stapleton had two parallel north-south runways and two additional parallel east-west runways that accommodated only commuter air carriers.

Denver's economy grew and expanded greatly in the early 1980s, consequent to booms in the oil, real estate, and tourism industries. An aging and saturated Stapleton Airport was increasingly seen as a liability that limited the attractiveness of the region to the many businesses that were flocking to it. Delays had become chronic. Neither the north-south nor east-west parallel runways had sufficient lateral separation to accommodate simultaneous parallel arrival streams during poor weather conditions when instrument flight rules were in effect. This lack of runway separation and the layout of Stapleton's taxiways tended to cause delays during high-traffic periods, even when weather conditions were good.

Denver's geographic location and the growing size of its population and commerce made it an attractive location for airline hubbing operations. At one point, Stapleton had housed four airline hubs, more than any other airport in the United States. In poor weather and during periods of high-traffic volume, however, its limitations disrupted connection schedules that were important to maintaining these operations. A local storm could easily congest air traffic across the entire United States.[3]

The City and County of Denver had determined in the mid-1970s that Stapleton International Airport was in need of expansion or replacement. In July 1979, a study to assess the airport's needs was commissioned by the City of Denver to the Denver Regional Council of Governments. Upon completion of the study in 1983, a report was issued saying that, due to its size and geographic location, and strong commitments by United and Continental Airlines, Denver would remain a significant hub for at least one major U.S. carrier. The study recommended expansion of Stapleton's capacity.

Political Situation[4]

The City of Denver's 1983 mayoral race precipitated initiatives to improve the airfield infrastructure. Three candidates were vying for mayor: Monte Pascoe, Dale Tooley, and Frederico Peña. Pascoe, a prominent Denver attorney and former State Democratic Party co-chair, seized upon the airport issue, forcing other candidates to adopt stronger positions on airport expansion than they might have otherwise.[5] Peña and Tooley, however, drew the highest numbers of votes in the general election, and were forced into a runoff. At the persistent urging of the Colorado Forum (a collection of 50 of the state's top business executives), Peña and Tooley signed a joint statement committing themselves to airport expansion. Peña won the runoff. Committed by a public promise that could have been enforced, if necessary, by the most highly motivated members of the region's business leadership, Peña immediately restated his intent to expand Stapleton.

The City of Denver and neighboring Adams County began to develop plans for long-term airport development in 1984. In 1985, a new site northeast of Denver was chosen. Consummation of the airport siting issue, however, was left to Adams County voters, which had to vote to permit the City of Denver to annex property therein. The city hired a consulting firm to help organize its resources and its efforts to work through the legal process. The data that was gathered through the master planning and environmental assessment later proved useful for public education.

An "Annexation Agreement" between Adams County and the City of Denver was reached on April 21, 1988. Adams County voters approved a plan to let Denver annex 43.3 square miles for the construction of an airport. In a special election on May 16, 1989, voters of Denver endorsed a "New Airport" by a margin of 62.7% to 37.3%. According to Edmond, "Those two referendums passed largely on the merits of the economic benefits: jobs and sales tax revenues."

Economic Considerations

A number of trends and events in the mid-1980s alarmed bank economists and others of the region's business leaders in the mid-1980s. The collapse of oil shale ventures between 1982 and 1986 saw mining employment fall from 42,000 to 26,000 jobs, while service support jobs fell from 25,300 jobs to 13,700.[6] Construction jobs fell from 50,700 to 36,600 jobs, and the value of private construction plummeted from $24 billion to $9.5 billion.[7]

A lackluster economy led many government officials in counties and municipalities, as well as in Denver, to embark upon an unprecedented policy of massive public construction to save the region from what was regarded in 1987 as an economic free-fall. A $180 million-plus municipal bond was issued for public improvements, including a new downtown library, neighborhood and major roadway improvements, and a host of overdue infrastructure investments. During the same period, the Peña administration moved decisively to confront an increasingly aggressive Chamber of Commerce leadership that was promoting airport relocation.

The determination of the "pro-New-Airport" clan was growing. The project was being marketed as a technologically advanced, state-of-the-art structure to draw businesses, import federal capital, and fund the creation of new jobs with bonded debts to overcome the short-term decline in the economy. The airport was to become a grandiose project to revive the Colorado economy and a master showcase for the Public Works Department. "The entire business community," recalled a member of the Mayor's administrative team:

> the Chamber of Commerce, members of the city council, the mayor, and state legislators, participated in informational discussions with other cities that had recently built airports. [This enabled] everybody to understand the magnitude of the project. So we studied the other two airports that had been built in the United States in the last 50 years and said, "Tell us everything that you went through and all the places you think there will be problems." We were not going into it blindly.

Forecasts of aviation activity at Stapleton by the Airport Consultant team, the FAA, and others, however, did not anticipate events such as a new phase of post-deregulation consolidation, the acquisition in 1986 of Frontier Airlines by Texas Air (the owner of Continental), significant increases in air fares for flights in and out of Stapleton, and the bankruptcy of Continental. Consequently, the level of aviation activity in Denver was overestimated. Instead of rising, Stapleton's share of total U.S. domestic passenger enplanements fell 4% per year from 1986 through 1989.[8]

THE MASTER PLAN

The City of Denver's approach to preparing a master plan for the airport was typical. "One hires the best consultants on airfield layout, noise impacts, terminal layout, on-site roadways, off-site roadways, cost estimating, financial analysis, and forecasting," observed DIA administrator Gail Edmond. "They brainstorm and generate as many alternate layouts as possible." Alternatives were discussed and eliminated at periodic joint working sessions, and a technical subcommittee was organized to gather input from the eventual airport users, airlines, pilots, and the FAA. "Everybody knows how to begin an airport master plan," Edmond added.

Following a bid, the consulting contract was awarded to the joint venture of Greiner, Inc. and Morrison-Knudsen Engineers for their combined expertise in the fields of transportation and construction. The consulting team, working under the direction of the DIA Director of Aviation, focused first on four elements: site selection; the master plan; the environmental assessment; and developing support by educating the public on economic benefit. The final master plan presented to the city by the team in the fall of 1987 called for the construction of the world's most efficient airport. It was to be created from the ground up with no predetermined limitations.

The plan was to allow the airport to grow and expand without compromising efficiency. Twice the size of Manhattan at 53 square miles, the nation's largest airport was to be designed for steady traffic flow in all weather conditions. It was to comprise a terminal with east and west buildings joined by an atrium structure, three concourses, an automated underground people mover, and five parallel 12,000-foot-long runways on which as many as 1,750 planes could take off and land daily. Its flow-through traffic patterns would allow planes to land, taxi to concourse gates, and take off again all in one direction. The ultimate buildout, projected for the year 2020, was to include up to 12 full service runways, more than 200 gates, and a capacity of 110 million passengers annually. Estimated cost (excluding land acquisition and pre-1990 planning costs) was $2 billion. By the end of 1991, the estimated cost had increased to $2.66 billion. Plans called for the project's completion by the fall of 1993.

In September 1989, Federal officials signed a $60 million grant agreement for the new airport, which was to be financed in multiple ways—by issuing revenue bonds and securing federal grants—supplemented by a sizable investment by the city [county of Denver 1991]. Estimated federal grants for the new airport originally totaled $501 million. Portions of these were forthcoming from the FAA, for federal fiscal year 1990 in the amount of $90 million and for federal fiscal year 1991 in the amount of $25 million. The remainder of the $501 million letter of intent was to be received on an annual basis through fiscal year 1997. The revenue bonds assumed the "Date of Beneficial Occupancy" (DBO) to be January 1, 1994, with bond repayments to begin on that date. At that time, the city determined that DIA would meet the DBO no later than October 31, 1993. A member of the Mayor's administrative team described the approach.

> What we did was plan the DBO date and then we planned an extra six months just in case there was a lag in the opening, which, in essence, allowed us to create stability in the market. The other thing we did was that we conservatively financed and filled every reserve account to the maximum. So we borrowed as much money as we could at the lower interest rate and were able to average the debt cost down, not up, as we thought it would be.

A Build-Design Project

By the time construction began at DIA in November 1989, a transfer of authority was taking place in the City of Denver. Wellington Webb was elected the new mayor. According to one of his assistants, the Peña administration had announced that the airport would be operational in October 1993. "This was a build-design project, which means that we were building the airport [while] we were designing it," he explained. "Because of the delays early on in the project, we had to accelerate construction immediately. There was a lot of pressure and too many players. This was an airport built by committee. We had regular meetings to straighten things out, but it didn't always work."

Although the Webb administration inherited the airport project without a commitment on the part of the major carriers, the support and input of concerned airlines were absolutely key, not only financially, but also in terms of input on overall airport layout, scope, and capacity, and supporting systems, such as fueling and baggage handling. Denver launched the DIA program without specific commitments from either of Stapleton airport's two major tenant airlines, United and Continental, which together accounted for more than 70% of existing passenger traffic. Continental committed to the new airport in February 1990, United in December 1991. Fundamental changes were made to the airport layout plan and facilities (some already under construction) to accommodate the operational needs of these carriers.

The Webb administration followed the predecessor administration's emphasis on assuring that the project's greatest beneficiaries would be local businesses. The desire was to involve as many individual firms as practicable and to use Denver area talent. It was reasoned that local talent was easily accessible to the program management team (PMT), knew Denver building codes and practices, and had available the necessary professional labor pool to accomplish the design in accordance with the demanding schedule. In addition, existing law stated that 30% minority-owned firms and 6% women-owned firms had to participate in a public works program. The result was a contracting philosophy that maximized opportunities for regional businesses and the local workforce to compete for the work. At least five of 60 contracts awarded for the design of DIA went to Denver-area firms. These 60 design contracts generated 110 construction contracts. Eighty-eight professional service contracts also had to be coordinated. Many local firms had to be hired and the program was chopped up into many small projects. Involvement totaled 200 to 300 firms and reached 400 during the construction phase. Five different firms designed the runways, four the terminal. The city's emphasis on encouraging everyone to compete and yet be part of the project increased the potential for interface and coordination problems.

Denver's flat economy led the administration to keep construction money within the city. Although this benefited the city, it introduced an additional burden on administration. As many as 40–50 concurrent contracts involved many interrelated milestones and contiguous or overlapping operational areas. The estimated daily on-site work force population exceeded 2,500 workers for a 15 to 18-month period beginning in mid-1991 and peaked at between 9,000 and 10,000 in mid-1992. Adding to the human resource coordination problems was a forecasted 4,000 deliveries daily. Construction volume for six months in mid-1992 exceeded $100 million per month.

The prolonged period of assessment and negotiation prior to final approval of the project, and the financial plan selected (which required that bond repayments begin on January 1, 1994), pressured the PMT to push the project ahead at all cost. Because the project had to assume the characteristics of a "fast-track" project early in the construction startup, the compressed design period precipitated a more dynamic construction effort than might be anticipated for a "competitively bid, fixed price" program. Reliance on a design/build method for the project was, according to one DIA official, "unusual because projects this complex normally happen during separate stages. For example, you need to finish up the site selection before you begin the master planning."

Moreover, communication channels between the city, project management team, and consultants were neither well defined or controlled. "If a contractor fell behind," a resident engineer who reported to one of the area managers said,

> the resident engineer would alert the contractor and document this. The resident engineer would document what would have to be done and what additional resources were necessary to get back on schedule and finish the contract on time. As a public agency it was enormous, the amount of documentation that we did. I don't know how many trees we cut down just for this project. The resident engineer had about five to eight 12-drawer filing cabinets of documentation and this was nothing compared to what the area manager had. It was just incredible. There were at least four to six copies of everything.

The scheduling manager described the evolution of the tracking system that was used.

> One of the biggest problems we had was keeping track of all the changes. So we developed a database system that was installed at each one of the resident engineer's trailers and each contract administrator was then charged with keeping that system up to date and feeding us disks, which we would then merge together periodically to produce an integrated report. But every party had developed their own tracking system before the start of the project. That worked well for each group, but there was no way to take each one of these divergent systems and combine it into one, comprehensive report. So when we introduced the change tracking system everybody said, "fine, that's wonderful, and I'll update it when I get to it and when I get time." It took three years to implement the tracking system.

Project Management

In a fast-moving, ever-changing environment such as the development of a new airport, the management structure must be able to rapidly produce engineering alternatives and the supporting cost and schedule data.[9] But because DIA was financed by many sources and was a public works program, project administrators had to balance administrative, political, and social imperatives.[10]

The City of Denver staff and consultant team shared leadership of the project and coordinated the initial facets of DIA design. "The initial thought," reflected one staff member, "was that the city staff would do their thing and the consulting staff do theirs and later we would coordinate. It became evident within a very short time that we were doing duplicate duties, which was inefficient. Finally, the city decided to coordinate resources."

The city selected a team of city employees and consultants and drafted a work scope document that clearly separated the city's from the consultants' responsibilities. The elements the city did not delegate to consultants included ultimate policy and facility decisions, approval of payments, negotiation and execution of contracts, facilitation of FAA approvals, affirmative action, settlement of contractor claims and disputes, selection of consultants, and utility agreements. The city delegated some elements, such as value engineering, construction market analysis, claim management, on-site staff and organization, and state-of-the-art project control (computerized management of budget and schedule). Exhibit 2.1 depicts the DIA management structure.

The program management team became the organization dedicated to overseeing planning and development for the new airport. Headed by the associate director of aviation, the team was partially staffed by city career service employees. To add experience and capability, the city augmented the PMT with personnel from the joint venture of Greiner Engineering and Morrison-Knudsen Engineers, the consulting team. Observed one program management team member, "This working partnership of the City of Denver and consulting joint venture team developed into a fully integrated single organization, capitalizing on the best to be offered by all participants, and optimizing the use of personnel resources."

DIA's operational project structure comprised five different areas subdivided into smaller units. The working areas were: site development (earthmoving, grading, and drainage); roadways and on-grade parking (service roads, on-airport roads, and off-airport roads connecting

Exhibit 2.1 Organization Chart

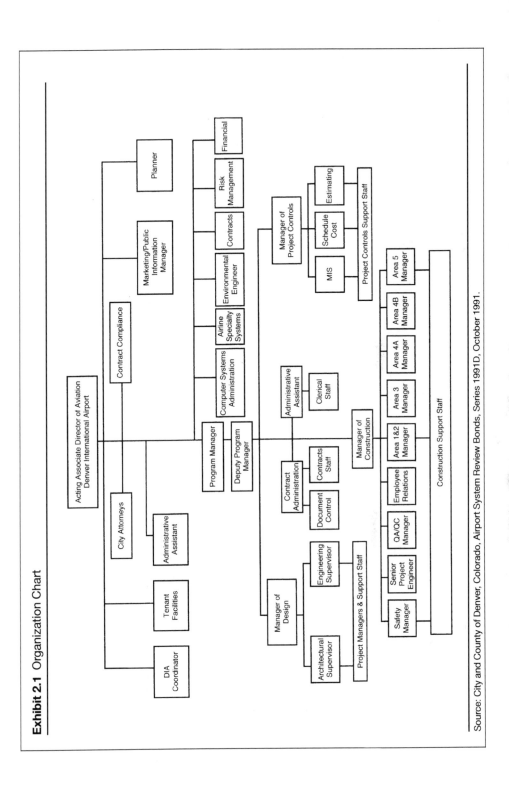

Source: City and County of Denver, Colorado, Airport System Review Bonds, Series 1991D, October 1991.

to highways); airfield paving; building design (people-mover/baggage-handler, tunnel, concourses, passenger bridge, terminal, and parking); and utility/special systems and other facilities (electrical transmission, oil, and gas line removal and relocation). An area manager controlled construction within each area. Area managers were responsible for the administration of all assigned contracts and, in coordination with other area managers, for management of the portion of the overall site in which their work took place.

UNITED AIRLINES' BAGGAGE SYSTEM

From the public's perspective, the "friendliness" of any airport is measured by time. No matter how architecturally stimulating a new airport structure, the perception of business or leisure travelers is often registered in terms of efficiency in checking luggage at the departure area or waiting to claim a bag in the arrival area. The larger the airport, the more critical the efficient handling of baggage. Remote concourses connected by underground tunnels present special problems for airport planners and operators because of the great distances passengers and baggage must travel. The purpose of an airport being to move passengers as efficiently as possible, moving bags as quickly is part and parcel of that responsibility. Rapid transport of frequent flyers accomplishes very little if bags are left behind.

DIA's Concourse A, which was to house Continental Airlines, was situated some 400 meters, and United Airlines' Concourse B nearly 1,000 meters, north of the main terminal. Concourse C, home to other carriers including American, Delta, Northwest, America West, and TWA, sat parallel to the other two concourses more than 1,600 meters north of the main terminal. The initial project design did not incorporate an airport-wide baggage system; the airport expected the individual airlines to build their own systems as in most other American airports.[11] United Airlines, which in June 1991 signed on to use DIA as its second-largest hub airport, proceeded to do just that.

Needing an automated baggage handling system if it was to turn aircraft around in less than 30 minutes, United, in December 1991, commissioned BAE Automatic Systems, Inc., a world leader in the design and implementation of material handling systems, to develop an automated baggage handling system for its B Concourse at DIA. The contract, which included engineering and early parts procurement only, was valued at $20 million; and the task was estimated to be completed in two and one-half years. "We began working at DIA under a contract directly with United Airlines," recalled Di Fonso. "Obviously, United Airlines has experience with airports. They concluded that the schedule had gotten totally out of control from the standpoint of baggage and they acted to serve their own needs, basically to protect themselves. We contracted with United and were already designing their portion of the system before the city went out for competitive bidding."

BAE was founded as a division of Docutel Corporation in 1968. Docutel, which had developed the Telecar (a track-mounted automated baggage system), constructed an automated baggage system for United Airlines at San Francisco Airport in 1978. When Docutel ran into financial difficulties during this installation, United asked Boeing, a major supplier of its aircraft, to take over the company. Boeing agreed and the new company, a wholly-owned subsidiary dubbed Boeing Airport Equipment, completed the San Francisco installation. In 1982, Boeing sold the company to its senior management, which renamed it BAE Automated Systems. In August 1985, BAE became an operating unit of Clarkson Industries, a wholly-owned subsidiary of London-based BTR plc. BTR plc (formerly British Tire and Rubber), was a $10 billion conglomerate with global interests in building, paper and printing products, and agricultural and aircraft equipment.

In 1994, BAE's 365 employees worked on projects across the United States and in Europe and Australia. In-house engineering, manufacturing, and field support capabilities enabled BAE to develop, design, manufacture, install, and support every project it undertook from start to finish. BAE also provided consulting, engineering, and management services for airport projects and a variety of material handling applications.

With sales of $100 million in 1994, up from approximately $40 million in 1991, BAE accounted for 90% of U.S. baggage sorting equipment sales. Between 1972 and 1994, the company had successfully designed, manufactured, and installed nearly 70 automated baggage handling systems (worth almost $500 million dollars) at major airports in the United States, in New York, Dallas-Fort Worth, Chicago, San Francisco, Atlanta, Miami, Newark, and Pittsburgh. It had also installed systems in Vancouver and London and was selected, in 1992, as a consultant to the $550 million main terminal for the New Seoul Metropolitan Airport in South Korea.

BAE was a very self-contained, integrated company structured along two business lines: manufacturing and engineering. Its approximately

200,000 square foot manufacturing facility was capable of producing nearly all of the components required by BAE systems save motors, gearboxes, and bearings. The engineering department was structured according to major projects. Each project was assigned a project manager who reported directly to the company president.

IMPLEMENTING AN INTEGRATED BAGGAGE-HANDLING SYSTEM

BAE had already commenced work on United's baggage system when the PMT recognized the potential benefits of an airport-wide integrated baggage system. Moreover, as one DIA senior manager explained, "airlines other than United simply were not coming forward with plans to develop their own baggage systems." Airport planners and consultants began to draw up specifications and the city sent out a request for bids. Of 16 companies contacted, both in the United States and abroad, only three responded. A consulting firm recommended against the submitted designs, on the grounds that the configurations would not meet the airport's needs.

BAE was among the companies that had decided not to bid for the job. BAE had installed the Telecar system at a number of other airports and the basic technologies of the Telecar, laser barcode readers, and conveyor belt systems were not new. What was new was the size and complexity of the system. "A grand airport like DIA needs a complex baggage system," explained Di Fonso,

> Therefore the type of technology to be used for such a system is the kind of decision that must be made very early in a project. If there is a surprise like no bidders there is still time to react. At DIA, this never happened. Working with United Airlines, we had concluded that destination-coded vehicles moving at high speed was the technology needed. But quite honestly, although we had that technology developed, its implementation in a complex project like this would have required significantly greater time than the city had left available.

A United project manager concurred: "BAE told them from the beginning that they were going to need at least one more year to get the system up and running, but no one wanted to hear that." The City of Denver was getting the same story from the technical advisers to the Franz Josef Strauss Airport in Munich. The Munich Airport had an automated baggage system, but one far less complex than DIA's.

Nevertheless, Munich's technical advisors had spent two years testing the system and the system had been running 24 hours a day for six months before the airport opened.

Formulating Intentions

As BAE was already working on United's automated baggage handling system and enjoyed a world-wide reputation as a superior baggage system builder, Denver approached the company. BAE was asked to study how the United concept could be expanded into an integrated airport system that could serve the other carriers in the various concourses. BAE presented the City of Denver with a proposal to develop the "most complex automated baggage system ever built," according to Di Fonso. It was to be effective in delivering bags to and from passengers, and efficient in terms of operating reliability, maintainability, and future flexibility. The system was to be capable of directing bags (including suitcases of all sizes, skis, and golf clubs) from the main terminal through a tunnel into a remote concourse and directly to a gate. Such efficient delivery would save precious ground time, reduce close-out time for hub operations, and cut time-consuming manual baggage sorting and handling.

Although an automated system was more expensive initially than simple tugs and baggage carts, it was expected that it would reduce the man-power which was required to distribute bags to the correct locations. Bags unloaded from an aircraft arriving at a particular concourse would barely be touched by human hands. Moved through the airport at speeds up to 20 mph, they would be waiting when passengers arrived at the terminal. To prove the capability of its mechanical aspects, and demonstrate the proposed system to the airlines and politicians, BAE built a prototype automated baggage handling system in a 50,000 square foot warehouse near its manufacturing plant in Carrollton, Texas. The prototype system convinced Chief Airport Engineer Walter Slinger that the automated system would work. "[The City of Denver] approached us based on one core concept," recalled Di Fonso. "They wanted to have a fully integrated, airport-wide baggage system. The city had two major concerns. First, they had no acceptable proposal. Second, United was probably going to go ahead and build what it needed and the rest of the airport would have been equipped with something else." Di Fonso continued,

> When we arrived on the scene, we were faced with fully defined project specs, which obviously in the long run proved to be a

major planning error. The city had fallen into a trap, which historically architects and engineers tend to fall into as they severely underplay the importance and significance of some of the requirements of a baggage system, that is, arranging things for the space into which it must fit, accommodating the weight it may impose on the building structure, the power it requires to run, and the ventilation and air conditioning that may be necessary to dissipate the heat it generates.

In April 1992, BAE was awarded the $175.6 million contract to build the entire airport system. According to Di Fonso, company executives and city officials hammered out a deal in three intense working sessions. "We placed a number of conditions on accepting the job," he observed.

> The design was not to be changed beyond a given date and there would be a number of freeze dates for mechanical design, software design, permanent power requirements and the like. The contract made it obvious that both signatory parties were very concerned about the ability to complete. The provisions dealt mostly with all-around access, timely completion of certain areas, provision of permanent power, provision of computer rooms. All these elements were delineated as milestones.

Denver officials accepted these requirements and, in addition, committed to unrestricted access for BAE equipment. Because of the tight deadlines, BAE would have priority in any area where it needed to install the system. Di Fonso elaborated,

> When we entered into the contract, Continental Airlines was still under bankruptcy law protection. The city was very concerned that they would be unable to pay for their concourse. They only contracted for about 40% of the equipment that is now in concourse A, which was the concourse that Continental had leased. Beyond that, concourse C had no signatory airlines as leaseholders at the time. The city, therefore, wanted the simplest, most elementary baggage system possible for concourse C. The outputs and inputs were very, very crude, intentionally crude to keep the costs down because the city had no assurance of revenue stream at that point in time. The city did not get the airlines together or ask them what they wanted or needed to operate. The approach was more along the lines of "we will build the apartment building and then you come in and rent a set of rooms."

Project Organization and Management

No major organizational changes to accommodate the new baggage system were deemed necessary, although some managerial adjustments were made on the DIA project. Design of the United baggage system was frozen on May 15, 1992, when the PMT assumed managerial responsibility for the integrated baggage system. The direct relationship with BAE was delegated to Working Area 4, which also had responsibility for building design efforts, such as the people-mover, airside concourse building, passenger bridge, main landside building complex and parking garage, and various other smaller structures. The area manager, although he had no experience in airport construction, baggage system technologies, or the introduction of new technologies, possessed vast experience in construction project control management.

BAE had to change its working structure to conform to DIA's project management structure. Di Fonso explained,

> There was a senior manager for each of the concourses and a manager for the main terminal. The bag system, however, traversed all of them. If I had to argue a case for right of way I would have to go to all the managers because I was traversing all four empires. In addition, because changes were happening fast at each of these sites, there was no time to have an information system to see what is concourse A deciding and what is concourse B deciding. We had to be personally involved to understand what was going on. There was no one to tie it all together and overlap all these effects because the basic organization was to manage it as discrete areas. It was pandemonium. We would keep saying that over and over again. Who is in charge?

For the first two years of the project, Di Fonso was the project manager. The project was divided into three general areas of expertise: mechanical engineering, industrial control, and software design. Mechanical engineering was responsible for all mechanical components and their installation, industrial control for industrial control design, logic controller programming, and motor control panels, and software design for writing real-time process control software to manage the system.

At the time the contract with BAE was signed, construction had already begun on the terminal and concourses. Substantial changes had to be made to the overall design of the terminal and some construction already completed had to be taken out and reinstalled to accommodate the expanded system. Installation of the expanded system was initially estimated to require more than $100 million in construction work.

Walls had to be removed and a new floor installed in the terminal building to support the new system. Moreover, major changes in project governance were taking place during the baggage system negotiations. In May 1992, shortly after the baggage system negotiations commenced, the head of the DIA project resigned.

The death in October 1992 of Chief Airport Engineer Slinger, who had been a strong proponent of the baggage system and closely involved in negotiations with BAE, also exerted a significant impact on the project. His cooperation had been essential because of the amount of heavy machinery and track that had to be moved and installed and the amount of construction work required to accommodate the system. His replacement, Gail Edmond, was selected because she had worked closely with him and knew all the players. Her managerial style, however, was quite different from Slinger's. A Public Works manager recalled his first reaction to the change: "[The airport] is not going to be open on time." A United Airlines project manager summarized Edmond's challenge thus:

> Slinger was a real problem solver. He was controversial because of his attitude, but he was never afraid to address problems. He had a lot of autonomy and could get things done. Gail was in a completely different position. Basically, she had a good understanding of how the project was organized and who the key players were, but didn't know much about the actual construction. Also, the city council didn't give her anywhere near the autonomy and the authority that Slinger had and she had to get approval from the council on just about all decisions. They really tied her hands and everyone knew it.

Di Fonso echoed the project manager's assessment:

> Walter [Slinger] understood that one of the things we had to have was unrestricted access. I think he clearly understood the problem the city was facing and he understood the short timeframe under which we were operating. He was the one that accepted all of the contractual conditions, all the milestones of the original contract. He really had no opportunity to influence the outcome of this project, however, because he died within months after the contract was signed. I think Gail did an excellent job [but] she was overwhelmed.[12] She just had too much. The layers below focused inward, worrying about their own little corners of the world.

"Not only did we not get the unrestricted access that was agreed upon," Di Fonso emphasized, "we didn't even have reasonable access." Ten days after Slinger's death, a BAE millwright found a truck from Hensel Phelps, the contractor building Concourse C, blocking her work site. She asked someone to move the truck or leave the keys so it could be moved. According to a BAE superintendent, "she was told that 'This is not a BAE job and we can park anywhere we please: is that clear?' " Elsewhere, BAE electricians had to leave work areas where concrete grinders were creating clouds of dust. Fumes from chemical sealants forced other BAE workers to flee. Di Fonso pleaded with the city for help. "We ask that the city take prompt action to assure BAE the ability to continue its work in an uninterrupted manner," he wrote. "Without the city's help, the delays to BAE's work will quickly become unrecoverable."[13]

To further complicate matters, the airlines began requesting changes to the system's design even though the mechanical and software designs were supposed to be frozen. "Six months prior to opening the airport," Di Fonso recalled, "we were still moving equipment around, changing controls, changing software design."

In August 1992, for example, United altered plans for a transfer system for bags changing planes, requesting that BAE eliminate an entire loop of track from Concourse B. Rather than two complete loops of track, United would have only one. This change saved approximately $20 million, but required a system redesign. Additional ski-claim devices and odd-size baggage elevators added in four of the six sections of the terminal added $1.61 million to the cost of the system. One month later, Continental requested that automated baggage sorting systems be added to its west basement at an additional cost of $4.67 million. The ski claim area length was first changed from 94 feet to 127 feet, then in January 1993, shortened to 112 feet. The first change added $295,800, the second subtracted $125,000, from the cost. The same month, maintenance tracks were added to permit the Telecars to be serviced without having to lift them off the main tracks at an additional cost of $912,000. One year later, United requested alterations to its odd-size baggage inputs—cost of the change: $432,000.

Another problem was the city's inability to supply "clean" electricity to the baggage system. The motors and circuitry used in the system were extremely sensitive to power surges and fluctuations. When electrical feedback tripped circuit breakers on hundreds of motors, an engineer was called in to design filters to correct the problem. Although ordered at that time, the filters still had not arrived several months later. A city worker had canceled a contract without realizing that the filters were part of it. The filters finally arrived in March 1994.

A third, albeit disputed, complication related to Denver's requirement, and city law, that a certain percentage of jobs be contracted to
minority-owned companies. The City of Denver had denied BAE's
original contract because it did not comply with hiring requirements,
where upon BAE engaged some outside contractors in lieu of BAE
employees. Di Fonso estimated that this increased costs by approximately $6 million, a claim rejected by the Mayor's Office of Contract
Compliance. Then, in September 1993, BAE's contract negotiations
with the City of Denver over maintenance of the system resulted in a
two-day strike of 300 millwrights that was joined by some 200 electricians. BAE negotiated with Denver for maintenance workers to earn
$12 per hour on certain jobs that the union contended should be worth
$20 per hour. As a result, BAE lost the maintenance contract.

Project Relations

Much of the effort for implementing the baggage system was directed
within one of the four working areas. "The relationship with the
management team was very poor," recalled Di Fonso.

> The management team had no prior baggage handling competence
> or experience. This was treated as a major public works project.
> The management team treated the baggage system as similar to
> pouring concrete or putting in air-conditioning ducts. When we
> would make our complaints about delays and access and so forth,
> other contractors would argue their position. The standard
> answer was, "Go work it out among yourselves." . . . With con-
> tractors basically on their own, this led almost to anarchy. Everyone
> was doing his or her own thing.

Another perspective was offered by a project manager from Stone &
Webster, a consultant to the PMT, reflecting on the work done by BAE:
"This contractor simply did not respond to the obvious incredible
workload they were faced with. Their inexperienced project management vastly underestimated their task. Their work ethic was deplor-
able."[14] PMT management insisted that access and mechanical issues
weren't the problem. "They were running cars in Concourse B all summer (1993)," Edmund observed. "The problem was that the programming was not done and BAE had full control of the programming."[15]

LAWSUITS AND A BACKUP BAGGAGE SYSTEM

In February 1993, Mayor Webb delayed the scheduled October 1993 airport opening to December 19, 1993. Later, this December date was changed to March 9, 1994. "Everybody got into the panic mode of trying to get to this magical date that nobody was ready for," a senior vice-president for BAE recalled. In September 1993, the opening was again postponed—this time until May 15, 1994. In late April 1994, the City of Denver invited reporters to observe the first test of the baggage system, without notifying BAE. Seven thousand bags were to be moved to Continental's Concourse A and United's Concourse B. So many problems were discovered that testing had to be halted. Reporters saw piles of disgorged clothes and other personal items lying beneath the Telecar's tracks.

Most of the problems related to errors in the system's computer software, but mechanical problems also played a part. The software that controlled the delivery of empty cars to the terminal building, for example, often sent the cars back to the waiting pool. Another problem was "jam logic" software, which was designed to shut down a section of track behind a jammed car, but instead shut down an entire loop of track. Optical sensors designed to detect and monitor cars were dirty causing the system to believe that a section of track was empty when, in fact, it had held a stopped car. Collisions between cars dumped baggage on tracks and on the floor; jammed cars jumped the track and bent the rails; faulty switches caused the Telecars to dump luggage onto the tracks or against the walls of the tunnels.

After the test, Mayor Webb delayed the airport's opening yet again, this time indefinitely. "Clearly, the automated baggage system now underway at DIA is not yet at a level that meets the requirements of the city, the airlines, or the traveling public," the mayor stated. The city set the costs of the delay at $330,000 per month. Recognizing that his reputation was staked on his ability to have a baggage system performing to a point at which the new airport could be opened, Mayor Webb engaged, in May 1994, the German firm Logplan to assess the state of the automated baggage system. In July, Logplan isolated a loop of track that contained every feature of the automated baggage system and intended to run it for an extended period to test the reliability of the Telecars. Jams on the conveyor belts and collisions between cars caused the test to be halted. The system did not run long enough to determine if there was a basic design flaw or to analyze where the problems were. Logplan recommended construction of a backup baggage system, and suggested using Rapistan Demag, a firm it had worked with in the past. Construction of a backup system was announced in August 1994. The system itself cost $10.5 million, but electrical upgrades and major building modifications raised the projected cost to $50 million.

In the meantime, the City of Denver, as well as many major airlines, hired legal firms to assist with negotiations and future litigation. "We will have enough legal action for the rest of this century," a city administrator mused. The City of Denver had to communicate with such parties as the United States Federal grand jury, Securities Exchange Commission, and the General Accounting Office. The federal grand jury was conducting a general investigation concerning DIA. The SEC was investigating the sale of $3.2 billion in bonds to finance DIA's construction, and GAO the use of Congressional funds.

Di Fonso, reviewing Mayor Webb's letter and requests that BAE pay a $12,000-a-day penalty for missing DIA's original October 29, 1993 completion date, as well as assuming the costs of building the $50 million conventional tug-and-cart baggage system, summed up the situation thus: "We have gotten to the point with the city that literally we are not talking to each other. Consultants recommended a backup baggage system, and the minute that the decision was made, the city had to defend it. We are left out in limbo."

NOTES TO CASE

1. Fred Isaac, Federal Aviation Administration regional administrator, quoted in "Denver Still Working Out Kinks as Its First Birthday Arrives," *USA Today*, February 28, 1996, p. 4b.
2. Fred Renville, United Airlines employee quoted in "Denver Still Working Out Kinks as Its First Birthday Arrives," *USA Today*, February 28, 1996, p. 4b.
3. According to James Barnes [1993], "By 1994, Stapleton was one of the top five most constrained airports in the U.S. There were over 50,000 hours of delay in 1988 and by 1997 the FAA had projected that Stapleton would experience over 100,000 hours of delay per year."
4. Extracted from: Moore, S.T.: "Between Growth Machine and Garbage Can: Determining Whether to Expand the Denver Airport, 1982–1988," Annual Meeting of the Southern Political Science Association, Atlanta, Georgia, November 4, 1994.
5. Ibid.
6. *Colorado Business Outlook Forum*, University of Colorado School of Business, 1990.

7. *Small Area Employment Estimates; Construction Review,* U.S. Department of Commerce, 1990.

8. Furthermore, when selling the project to voters, planners at one point forecast up to 36 weekly flights to Europe by 1993. The number recorded in 1993, however, was four. The number of passengers departing from Denver was to rise from 16 million in 1985 to some 26 million by 1995. The 1994 figure, however, was about the same as the number of passengers in 1985, or half of Stapleton's capacity.

9. The DIA project used the so-called "fast-tracking" method, which made it possible to compress some activities along the critical path and manage the construction project as a series of overlapping tasks.

10. These included considerations, such as affirmative action, local participation, neighborhood concerns, civic pride, input from the disabled community, art, secondary employment benefits of contract packaging, concern for the environment, and political interest.

11. Rifkin, G.: "What Really Happened at Denver's Airport," *Forbes,* SAP Supplement, August 29, 1994.

12. In addition to her role as Chief Airport Engineer, Edmond kept her previous responsibilities as Chief of Construction and Acting Director of Aviation.

13. *Rocky Mountain News,* January 29, 1995.

14. *Forbes,* SAP Supplement, August 29, 1994.

15. *Forbes,* SAP Supplement, August 29, 1994.

Case 2.1b

BAE AUTOMATED SYSTEMS (B): IMPLEMENTING THE DENVER INTERNATIONAL AIRPORT BAGGAGE-HANDLING SYSTEM

(Lynda M. Applegate)

ABOUT THE AUTHORS

Assistant Professor Ramiro Montealegre and Research Associate H. James Nelson of the University of Colorado at Boulder, Research Associate Carin Isabel Knoop and Professor Lynda M. Applegate prepared this case. HBS cases are developed solely as the basis for class discussion. Cases are not intended to serve as endorsements, sources of primary data, or illustrations of effective or ineffective management. Some names have been disguised.

Copyright © 1996 President and Fellows of Harvard College. To order copies or request permission to reproduce materials, call 1-800-545-7685, write Harvard Business School Publishing, Boston, MA 02163, or go to http://www.hbsp.harvard.edu. No part of this publication may be reproduced, stored in a retrieval system, used in a spreadsheet, or transmitted in any form or by any means—electronic, mechanical, photocopying, recording, or otherwise—without the permission of Harvard Business School.

BAE, blaming delays on lack of site access and permit delays for which it held the City of Denver responsible, went public on September 7 with a $40 million claim against the city. The essence of BAE's counterclaim was that the entire airport was behind schedule and constant design changes had prevented BAE from installing its system. A major issue had been the city's alleged inability to meet agreed-upon deadlines to build the space that would house different elements of the baggage-handling system. The claim also accused the city of breaking contractual promises to make the BAE system the top priority by allowing other contractors' jobs to take precedence.

When the airport finally opened in late February 1995, it was 16 months behind schedule and close to $2 billion over budget. The first flight to land at the airport, nearly three years after BAE was retained to build the automated integrated baggage system, encountered not one state-of-the-art integrated baggage handling system, but three.

BACK TO SQUARE ONE

On August 31, 1994, the *Rocky Mountain News* reported that in an effort to avoid legal action the City of Denver had proposed a "stand still" agreement whereby major parties (the city, United Airlines, and BAE) would waive certain previous agreements and rights until the new airport was opened and operational. "Of course," the reporter emphasized, "the legal departments of these parties are going to be busy until the end of this century with this case."

The moratorium nevertheless broke the deadlock. Problems had arisen between the City of Denver and United Airlines around the design of the backup baggage system. United Airlines objected to the manual system, saying it would not accommodate the airline's heavy schedule. United offered a plan to modify the automated system to deliver bags to the planes and rely on tugs and carts to deliver most of the baggage for arriving passengers. United and the City of Denver, unable to agree who should pay for the modifications, approached BAE executives, who indicated they would not continue without a signed contract from the City of Denver.

Both United and Continental Airlines had geared up for protracted negotiations and possible litigation. The law firm retained by United pointed out that it was hired to negotiate the proposed back-up baggage system at DIA—not to initiate litigation procedures. Continental, which had engaged a law firm for "assistance with both DIA and Stapleton issues," maintained that the last minute baggage system was a breach of contract for which it could sue the city or choose to cancel its lease of DIA gates. United urged the city to bring in mediators "because of the deteriorating relationship with BAE."

As a result of the negotiations, the original contract was broken into two pieces: the United contract; and the remaining piece of the city contract. Under the new contract, United used BAE's system to serve its Concourse B. It also took over and used at reduced speed two loops of track that served Concourse C. It isolated its operation from the BAE system that served Concourse A. The number of cars was reduced from 3,100 to 2,300 and the spacing between cars extended. The rest of the baggage system was designed around conveyor belts and propane-powered tugs and carts. Warning lights were installed in the baggage tunnels to guide the tugs.

The negotiations also brought about a change in the organization structure. United immediately hired a construction manager with full decision-making authority and contracted with a consulting company for further assistance. BAE hired its own consultant to develop and write test plans and prepare commissioning documents.

"When we changed from working directly for the city to working for United," Di Fonso recalled:

> It was like the sun came up. We were now working for people who fully understood the technology and its needs. We signed the contract with United in September 1994. Five months later we opened this airport. The contract with United required us to make $35 million worth of changes. That's an example of what can be done when people are working together as opposed to against one another.
>
> We formed a team; everybody had the same goal; we developed a schedule. Anytime we hit a problem—a building interference, a code—they would clear it up almost immediately. We never had to wait more than 24 hours for a problem to be resolved, as compared to sometimes waiting two or three months for a problem to be resolved by the City. That's how dramatic the change was.

Integrated testing continued through the fall and winter of 1994. In January 1995, a full-scale, three-hour, 10,000 bag practice run of the substitute baggage system was completed without any problems.

OPEN FOR BUSINESS

On the sleety, snowy, icy morning on February 28, 1995, the DIA opened with ceremony, the thunder of jet engines, and a sense of relief. The first scheduled passenger arrival, United Flight 1474 from Colorado Springs, was to land at 6:05 a.m. Former mayor and then Secretary of Transportation, Federico Peña, and current mayor, Wellington Webb, the two politicians responsible for the new airport, were on hand to greet the first passengers in the presence of a large crowd that included 1,725 journalists. The waiting was finally over. The airport opened with five runways and 88 gates (20 fewer than Stapleton), at a cost of $5.2 billion and an $18.80 average per-passenger airline fee—the nation's second highest. The airport's opening also offered the possibility of political relief for Mayor Webb, who was running for re-election that spring.

As the first flight approached the terminal, a switch controlling the movement of the enclosed passenger walkways reportedly malfunctioned at the gate where dignitaries waited for the airplane. The historic load of passengers had to wait an extra ten minutes while the plane was backed out and moved to another gate. Their luggage, however, arrived as they finished the hike from the gate to the luggage claim. Despite minor problems, including one of six lines breaking down for short periods, BAE's automated baggage system worked well. Nor did airlines served by the backup system report any major difficulties.

The baggage system was almost back to the original plans, with United, the airline that carried the most passengers at DIA, using an automated baggage delivery system and others using a conventional system. United's $300 million system, which comprised 22 miles of rollercoaster-like track, 3,500 cars, and 55 computers that could handle up to 30,000 pieces of luggage per day, controlled more of the airport rights of way than originally planned.[1] A simplified automated system served United's Concourse B. Continental used a tug-and-cart system on its Concourse A but was expected to shift to the automated system in the future. Other airlines were operating a very conventional, highly labor-intensive system. Airlines on Concourse C would have an automated system only if BAE installed new track, and United granted rights for access. Given that the backup system was designed to be "100% independent" of BAE's system, United's baggage consultant explained, "There's no longer an integrated baggage system. What we have is three baggage systems."

NOTE TO CASE

1. Robert Davis, "Denver Still Working Out Kinks as Its First Birthday Arrives," *USA Today*, February 28, 1996, p. 4b.

Case 2.2a

MEGA CORPORATION (A)

(Larry Greiner and Arvind Bhambri, University of Southern California)

ABOUT THE AUTHORS

This case was prepared by Professors Larry Greiner and Arvind Bhambri of the Marshall School of Business, University of Southern California, as a basis for class discussion, rather than to illustrate either effective or ineffective handling of administrative situations. Certain names and figures have been disguised to preserve confidentiality.

Six months after Tom Rice became CEO of Mega, he invited one of his former MBA professors, Mark Drake, to visit the company as a consultant. Drake and Rice had remained close friends and colleagues since Rice's graduation ten years before. Over the years, Drake had advised Rice on his career, which had been largely in management consulting, and on several occasions Rice had asked Drake to work with him on consulting assignments.

On Mark Drake's initial visit to Mega, Tom Rice asked Drake to interview his senior executives for issues that "they believe need to be addressed in the development of a long-term strategic plan," as well as "to get a reading on how I'm being perceived." They agreed that the interviewing effort should take place over about two days, and that Drake should give both an oral and written report to Rice upon completion. The consultant's fees were to be billed on a per diem basis. Drake was assisted by Jim Dunn, an academic colleague of Drake's, who served as a researcher/consultant on the Mega assignment.

The Mega Corporation, with revenues exceeding $900 million, was the fifth largest marketer of liquefied petroleum (commonly called propane) in the U.S. Headquartered in Denver, Mega employed 2,500 people and served over 300,000 domestic, industrial, agricultural, and motor fuel customers nationwide through a network of wholesale and retail outlets. These outlets were fed by a distribution system that utilized pipelines, rail tank cars, and a fleet of trucks located strategically at rail and truck terminals.

Mega was a major subsidiary of Alpha Industries, a $3.5 billion diversified corporation recently taken private through a leveraged buy out (LBO). According to Bob May, Chairman and CEO of Alpha, the corporation's previous stock price on the NYSE was under-valued at nearly half its book value, and he became worried about a hostile takeover. In commenting on the implications of the LBO for both Alpha and Mega, Bob May made the following observation:

> "The LBO flipped Alpha from having $300 million in equity and $100 million in debt to just the reverse. It made us private and more in control, but the cost of the increased debt was $45 million each year in interest. I was unhappy with the performance of Mega and its ability to contribute to paying off the debt so I brought in Tom Rice to be CEO of Mega."

The decision by Bob May to bring in Tom Rice as CEO of Mega was a difficult one that he hoped would produce a turnaround in earnings at Mega. Bob May had hired Rice as a management consultant immediately after the LBO to assist him in developing a cost reduction program at three of Alpha's subsidiaries, one of which was Mega. At the same time, and unrelated to Rice's project, Bob May terminated the CEO of Mega and assigned one of his corporate vice-presidents to serve as the interim president until a permanent CEO could be selected. With regard to May's selection of Tom Rice, Bob May told the case writer:

> "I think everybody was shocked by my bringing in a consultant and putting him in a line role, but I think it's something that Tom wanted to do, and my feeling was that he had a lot of ability, so why not turn him loose at it."

Rice was an ex-Air Force pilot with a BA in English and an MBA from the University of Southern California. His initial job was in real estate finance for a large bank but he soon left that job to join a management consulting firm in Chicago. Over the next few years, he moved to two other management consulting firms where he quickly became a partner and senior officer, eventually heading the Chicago office of the second firm. In deciding to accept the job at Mega, Rice said:

> "Even though I had some qualms about moving to Denver, I took it because I wanted a shot at managing a major company. Also, I respected Bob May, and I felt like I had some respect from him coming in the door. I didn't see the Mega job as an end in itself. Once it was up and running, I could move on to something bigger. Bob gave me lots of incentive with an ownership interest."

ARRIVAL OF TOM RICE

Tom Rice became CEO of Mega on his 38th birthday. He was introduced to the senior management group by the outgoing and interim CEO at a hastily called meeting. Rice was surprised to learn that the departing CEO had provided no advance notice of Rice's arrival and appointment as CEO.

> "We were about to go into the meeting together when I asked the former CEO if he had told them about my appointment, and he said, 'no'. So I suggested that maybe he ought to go in and have a few minutes alone with them so they could adjust to the news. He went in and, in essence, said, 'I'm going off to work at Alpha headquarters, and Tom Rice is going to be your new President, so I'll bring him in." And I went in. They were all sitting there looking stunned and demotivated as hell. Nobody had told them that any inside candidates were being considered."

During the meeting, Rice made a few brief comments about how he looked forward to working with the group. "It was very uncomfortable . . . they just stared at me." Shortly after the meeting, Mega's former CEO called Tom Rice to tell him that he had planned to fire one of Mega's senior executives (the person in charge of Marketing) because he didn't want "to leave Rice with a cancer in the organization." Rice thanked him for his call.

Tom Rice was so angry at the way the ex-CEO had treated Mega's senior executives that he decided not to heed the advice of the former CEO to fire one of them.

> "I didn't trust the judgment of the ex-CEO. I decided to keep all

of the people, give them incentives, go through the annual planning process, and if it didn't work, then clean house."

Tom Rice entered a functional organizational structure (see Exhibit 2.2) where he found the senior group, as he put it, "in a low state of executive morale." Rice was Mega's third CEO in two years and, according to one senior executive, "teamwork had all but disappeared, with everyone defending their own turf." During his first few days on the job, Tom Rice observed that Mega's senior executives tended to remain in their offices, and no one was speaking to him or to each other. "I felt like they all had their eyes on me, waiting for me, and even daring me to do something."

INITIAL ACTIONS

Tom Rice quickly discovered that Mega was 25% behind its annual profit plan, with only five months remaining in the fiscal year. As a result, he decided to begin a series of meetings with his executive committee to plan how they could achieve the annual profit goal. Rice's decision to hold these planning meetings was in contrast to the previous CEO's approach, which was to deal with people on a one-on-one basis. Rice described the subsequent meetings in these terms

"It was an excellent forum that enabled me to ask questions, and that's why I enjoyed it. Very quickly, I learned a lot about the company. We came up with a laundry list of key issues, and airing them was a major improvement even though we couldn't solve all

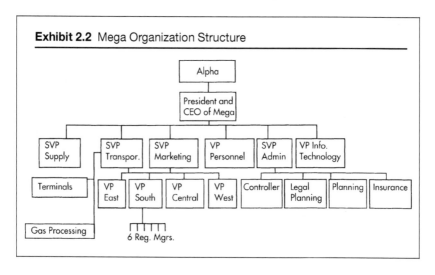

Exhibit 2.2 Mega Organization Structure

of them. What came out of all this was a commitment to achieve our profit goal for the year—and to hell with whether it was the right level, we would still try to achieve it."

Over the next few weeks, the planning meetings resulted in two major decisions and action steps taken by Tom Rice. One step was to arrange with Bob May for a revised incentive bonus for his key executives if they made the annual profit plan. A second decision was to raise prices immediately in order to increase revenues. The executive committee resisted Rice's pricing decision, but he stuck to it, saying "trust me."

At the end of five months, Mega exceeded its original profit plan by 10%, with half of its profits coming from the price increase and the remainder from increased unit sales. Rice then called his executive committee together, congratulated them, and told them that they would all receive a substantial bonus. He also gave a gold clock to each member to remind them of "what they could do under time pressure." Rice was highly pleased with their accomplishments, and he felt that he could work with them in building upon their backgrounds and prior experience (see Exhibit 2.3):

"From the start I liked what I saw. They were young, educated, and hadn't been in the company long enough to tell war stories. And then they really pitched in to pull it out."

The consultant, Mark Drake, following his interviews with Mega's executives, prepared a brief written report (see Appendix A), which listed several major issues, including whether Mega should diversify out of propane, the adequacy of its present organization structure,

---

Exhibit 2.3 Background of Mega's Senior Executives

Name	Title	Age	Education	Seniority
Tom Rice	Pres. & CEO	38	M.B.A.	New
Pat Cook	SVP of Supply	37	B.S.	5 yrs.
John Larch	SVP of Transp.	43	M.B.A.	7 yrs.
Andy Davis	SVP of Mktg.	40	M.B.A.	5 yrs.
Bill Hope	SVP of Admin.	39	M.S.	10 yrs.
Sam Smith	VP of Personnel	44	B.A.	20 yrs.
Ron Mix	VP of Info. Tech.	41	B.S.	3 yrs.
Jerry James	Legal Counsel	38	L.L.B.	10 yrs.

and coordination problems arising from "turf protecting" behavior among certain senior managers. Mark Drake told Rice that, while the executives differed among themselves over proposed solutions to the strategic issues, they were "uniformly much happier under Rice's leadership." The consultant recommended that a retreat be held soon, and designed so that the top group could discuss strategic issues and come up with proposed solutions. Rice agreed because, "We seemed to be making real progress as a team."

DISCUSSION QUESTIONS

1. What is your assessment of the "business issues" facing Mega in its marketplace and its relationship with Alpha?
2. Give your evaluation of how Tom Rice proceeded during his first six months. What critical actions did he take? What were the results and how did these affect Rice's position as CEO and his ability to proceed? Would you have acted in the same way as CEO?
3. Assess the relationship between the consultant and Tom Rice. What are its strengths and weaknesses? If you had been Tom Rice, would you have sought out Mark Drake or another kind of consultant with different qualifications?
4. Evaluate the way in which the consultant proceeded and comment on his written report to Rice. Is the report what you expected? Do you think a "retreat" makes sense for proceeding, or would you recommend another course of action? How would you organize the retreat? What should be the roles of Rice and Drake in the retreat?

APPENDIX A

Consultant's Report

Dear Tom:

The purpose of this letter is to expand on what I outlined at dinner after my interviews. Your executives were very open and constructive in their comments. As we agreed before my arrival, the purpose of the visit was to get a feel for the company through confidential interviews, and to report the major areas that need further attention from top management. Listed below are the main issues that I detected running across all the interviews.

I. The Top Group

How do we structure the group better? Do we need two groups, one composed of Rice and the SVPS to drive strategy and a larger group to review and set policy? How often should various groups meet, and what should be their character? How can we improve the way we work together informally? How do we improve the level of trust, and reduce turf protecting? Can we discipline ourselves more in meetings? How can we divide up various corporate tasks and hold people accountable?

II. Producer Flow/Distribution Process

Should we develop an in-depth study to determine the real costs of moving propane through the system, and the best ways to manage the flow? Can we articulate better how customer problems and inquiries get handled so that our response is better? Should we go to a transfer pricing system from Supply to Marketing? How can the SVPS of Marketing, Supply, and Transportation work more closely together to improve the efficiency of the process?

III. Corporate Strategy

What short-term (1 to 2 years) strategies should we set for ourselves? How do we improve inaccuracies in market forecasting? Should we keep the wholesale business? How do we go about capturing greater market share against sleepy competitors? What should be done about the southeastern region? Should we concentrate our focus on certain market segments? What do we do about terminals and gas processing? What long-term (3 to 5 years) strategies should we adopt? What kind of diversification strategy, if any, should we have? Should we develop a supply business for other LPG firms? What R&D should we undertake? What do we do about Alpha and the LBO?

IV. Organization Structure

Do we have the right balance in our structure? Is Marketing too large as a single organization (80% of our employees)? Should we divide Marketing into two departments, east and west? Should Transportation be folded into Supply? Do we have too many levels in Marketing? Should IT and Personnel report to the CEO? Should Training and Safety continue to report to Legal? What should be our overall position on centralization versus decentralization?

V. Corporate Staff

Do we have too many people in some staff groups, especially Accounting and IT? How do we improve the response of IT to our information needs? What do we do about the general staff attitude, which seems to be slow and still attuned to the regulation days? Do we have enough high-powered talent below the top level? Do we need a few sharp analysts working directly for Rice and the top group? Do we have enough people in Legal to handle lobbying? Are we short on Safety people?

VI. Reactions to Tom Rice

You seem to be well received. Their comments reflected these observations: He wants us to achieve together. He needs to reflect a positive image to the employees and to the industry. He can be more direct in sharing his beliefs and opinions with us. We are not sure if he really wants to solve problems in a team. We need to do more cross-training and job rotation. How do we learn to solve conflicts better without making them a threat or a personal issue?

RECOMMENDATIONS

The above areas cover the main questions evoked during the interviews. There is a lot of agreement on most of these issues, although there are a lot of differences in proposed solutions. Everyone expressed a strong desire to work together with you.

My suggestion is that we design a retreat: for all of us to meet together to discuss these topics, flesh them out some more, and develop whatever action plans that are needed. If you decide to hold a retreat, we will need to design a format to approach the various issues in the most constructive manner. It may be that some issues deserve more focused discussion, while others can be tabled for another meeting.

You may want to pass a copy of this letter on to the others so that they know what I reported to you. It could also serve as a basis for planning a future meeting.

I look forward to seeing you again in the near future. Please give my thanks to the others for their warm reception.

Sincerely,

Mark Drake

Case 2.2b

MEGA CORPORATION (B)

(Larry Greiner and Arvind Bhambri, University of Southern California)

ABOUT THE AUTHORS

This case was prepared by Professors Larry Greiner and Arvind Bhambri of the Marshall School of Business, University of Southern California, as a basis for class discussion, rather than to illustrate either effective or ineffective handling of administrative situations. Certain names and figures have been disguised to preserve confidentiality.

Mark Drake and Tom Rice planned the agenda for the first retreat (see Exhibit 2.4). They organized it around three broad topics: strategy for the company, organization structure, and the top management team. The retreat was held at a "no frills" hotel (requested by Rice), lasting from Friday noon to Sunday noon. Rice and his seven senior executives, all of whom were members of Mega's executive committee, attended the retreat along with Mark Drake and his assistant, Jim Dunn. Rice requested that Drake serve as moderator so that Rice could participate with the others.

> "The group is looking to me too much, and I don't have all the answers. They have to become more active and vocal with their points of view."

In opening the retreat, Rice told the group, "I have no hidden agenda. I just want us to dive in and see where it takes us." The consultant began with a short lecture based on Michael Potter's (1980) strategy

Exhibit 2.4 Tentative Agenda for First Retreat

Friday, February 8

12:00–1:00	Lunch
1:00–4:00	Strategic Issues and Opportunities— We will try to identify the short-term and long-term strategic issues and opportunities facing Mega. In particular, we will try to gain a clearer focus and specify the alternatives, along with their pros and cons.
4:00–5:30	Overall Corporate Organization Structure— We will analyze the present structure and its strengths and weaknesses. How well does the current structure fit the current strategy? Then, before adjourning, we will begin a discussion on what types of organization structure best fit the strategic alternatives identified in the prior session.
6:00–7:30	Dinner
7:30–9:30	Team Building Session— We will use some self-evaluation techniques to take a closer look at the functioning of the group, and talk about plans for building an even more effective team.

Saturday, February 9

8:00–10:00	Overall Corporate Structure— We will continue from yesterday by examining the relationship between different structures and the strategies already identified.
10:00–12:00	Distribution Flow— We will discuss the present situation and how it can be made more effective, ranging from how to price it, how to measure it, and how to make it more responsive to the customer.
12:00–1:30	Lunch
2:00–5:00	Corporate Staff Organization— This discussion will focus on the structure of the staff in Denver and the climate in the office. We will look at how we can become more effective, running from who reports to whom to norms for performance.
5:30–	Dinner

Sunday, February 10

| 9:00–10:30 | Committee Organization at the Top— Discussion of what is the best way for the top executives to organize themselves. What kinds of committees do we need, who should be on them, and what should be their charter? |
| 10:30–12:00 | Action-Planning— We will review and summarize the specific plans that we made during the meeting. Who will do what to follow up? |

framework, and then he used the framework in leading a discussion of Mega's competitive situation. Several flipcharts were filled when a heated interchange took place between Tom Rice and two members of the group:

Rice: "Why do you guys see so many threats and so few opportunities?"

March: (VP of Transportation) "Because the market for propane is so mature and customers for propane are limited."

Cook: (VP of supply) "Besides, even if we could sell more propane, we don't have enough money for investments because all our cash goes to Alpha to pay off the LBO debt."

Rice: "I feel that we can take control of our own destiny, no matter what the others say. Let's don't blame others for why we can't take control."

The consultant then intervened to suggest that the group divide into two sub-groups for the purpose of, "Identifying two to four alternative strategic directions for Mega, along with the pros and cons for each alternative." Two hours later, they reported back, initiating a debate over two particular strategic alternatives: (1) diversification, or (2) exclusive focus on propane. Although Mega had already diversified into a limited number of non-propane businesses before Rice was appointed CEO, several members of the group were not as pleased with this direction, and the IT member said, "There are still lots of opportunities in propane if we make acquisitions and are more selective in our geographic markets." But another member, Andy, who was in charge of Marketing, argued strongly for diversification out of propane. Tom Rice remained quiet throughout this discussion, despite having participated actively in one of the sub-groups.

The second day of the retreat again involved the use of sub-groups to examine the issue of determining the best organization structure for Mega. The groups met after the consultant gave a short lecture on various structural alternatives, along with describing the various conditions under which they might apply. In their sub-group reports, one group proposed a decentralized product structure divided between industrial and retail divisions, while the other group advocated staying with the current functional organization structure.

The ensuing discussion became argumentative and wandering, with one member finally observing, "We can't solve this problem until we decide on our overall business strategy." Everyone seemed to agree, at which point Rice suggested that the group return to the strategy discussion. The second consultant then gave a brief lecture on designing a strategy/mission statement. He told the group that the statement should, "sum up the company's desired identity, be brief and clear, put into writing, and be made understandable to all employees." Two new sub-groups were then assigned to draft suggested statements of strategic direction for Mega.

At the end of the second day, each sub-group presented surprisingly similar strategy statements. Both groups seemed to agree that Mega should, as they said, "concentrate exclusively on the propane industry," "become more marketing oriented," "make acquisitions," and "set high financial goals." Their sub-group discussions had determined that Mega, despite being in a mature industry, could still "clean up," as they put it, because its major competitors were "badly managed" and there were many small "mom and pop" operations that might sell out.

The remaining discussion centered on how high their financial goals should be; a central concern was how could Mega still generate cash for Alpha while also making investments in acquisitions and additional marketing programs? A way out of this dilemma was found when one member proposed selling the non-propane assets, closing down low profit propane outlets and cutting operating costs. When another member suggested that the company should try to "double profits in five years," Tom Rice said, "I could get very excited by that goal, and I know I can sell it to Alpha."

The retreat ended on Sunday with Tom Rice complimenting the group and leading them in a discussion about follow-up steps. It was agreed that each person should draft a separate strategy statement and give it to another member, Bill Hope, for final drafting of a single statement. Rice asked that the final draft be, "subjected to some hard market and financial analysis," and that, "it should be tried out in some group meetings with middle managers for their reactions." Rice then announced that the group should meet again in six weeks for a second retreat to, "ratify a new strategy statement and resume discussion on organization structure."

SECOND RETREAT

The second retreat began with a presentation by Bill Hope of the final draft strategy statement (see Exhibit 2.5 for agenda). Everyone quickly indicated approval, with one member thumping his agreement on the table. For the rest of the morning, two sub-groups met to evaluate the statement against a number of criteria provided by the consultants, including these questions: "Is it realistic in its assumptions about the marketplace and what we might be able to achieve?" "Is it sufficiently clear and easy to communicate?" "Do we find the statement exciting and challenging?" "Is it enduring but also selective enough to aid in screening major decisions?"

When the two groups returned, they reported that the draft statement met most of the criteria, but they also wanted it shortened and to include a more explicit focus on increased propane marketing. Jim Dunn then drafted an abbreviated statement over lunch. When Dunn read the following redrafted statement to the group in its afternoon session, spontaneous applause broke out:

> "Mega is a leading marketing and distributor of propane and related services. We set aggressive financial goals and achieve growth through market development and acquisitions. Our people establish a competitive advantage in selected market segments through a unified effort that demands:
>
> • A strong marketing orientation
> • High standards of safety
> • Outstanding service "before our customers need us"

The remainder of the retreat proved far more difficult as the group turned to discuss the company's organization structure. The consultant presented two alternatives that had received the most attention at the first retreat: (1) a new product structure divided between wholesale and retail markets, and (2) the existing functional structure. Again, the two sub-groups were sent off separately to review the alternatives in terms of their pros and cons. This time, however, each sub-group was asked by the consultant to determine which structure, or refinement thereof, would best implement the new strategy statement.

Exhibit 2.5 Agenda for Second Retreat

Saturday

9:00–12:00	Fine-Tuning the Strategy Statement— Key Questions: 1. What is effective about Bill Hope's statement? 2. What is missing in his statement? 3. Will it give us direction? 4. Will it box us in or liberate us? 5. How can it be communicated effectively?
12:00–1:00	Lunch
1:00–3:00	Developing a Management Philosophy Statement— Key issues: 1. Values about what level decisions should be made. 2. Values about involvement of employees in decision making, planning, and goal setting. 3. Values about performance appraisal. 4. Values about employee development. 5. Values about staff orientation.
3:15–5:30	Reevaluating Basic Organization Structure— Last time we had two structures proposed to us. Can we examine them to determine how consistent they are with the strategy statement we have prepared? Which is more consistent? How might we make a transition toward one of these structures? What actions are most feasible now, one year from now, two years from now?
5:30–7:00	Drinks and Dinner
7:00–9:30	Fine-Tuning Present Organization— Last time we had several suggestions about improvements that could be made with our present organization. What should we do about: 1. Supply-Transportation interface—should they be combined? How can they work together more effectively? 2. Marketing organization—Does it need new functions (e.g., director of domestic sales, director of industrial and national accounts)? Should some functions be divested to other groups (e.g., acquisitions, truck fleet, wholesale sales, etc.)? Should regions be consolidated and better balanced? 3. Do we have some functions in the wrong place? For example, there are likely some unrelated units under marketing, and also there is safety now under legal,

	and training is scattered around, and what about wholesale pricing in IT?
Sunday	
8:00–11:30	Improving the Corporate Staff Organization
	Last time we had some alternative models suggested, as well as a philosophy of how staff should relate to the line organization.
	Key questions:
	1. Should all staff be consolidated under one SVP of administration?
	2. If not, what is the logic for a second set of staff responsibilities, such as one for administration and one for corporate development?
	3. What is the position with regard to decentralization? How can that be implemented more effectively?

Upon returning from their sub-group meetings, both groups indicated a strong preference for the current functional structure, contending that the wholesale market did not show enough profit potential to warrant a separate product group. But here the agreement ended. One member argued for an entirely new marketing department that would develop new products and sales programs, and transform the current marketing department into an operations group responsible for sales and distribution. But Andy Davis, the current head of marketing, retorted, "I can take care of all that in my department." When one member proposed the consolidation of all staff functions under a single SVP of Administration, the directors of legal, human resources and data processing all argued that they should continue to report directly to Tom Rice. Time was running out when one member said, "Well at least we know that we don't want a product structure, but will we ever agree on what we do want?"

The retreat ended with Tom Rice expressing his personal commitment to the new strategy statement, and then he added, "We need to do some more thinking about our organization structure, so let's keep talking about it until our next retreat in one month."

DISCUSSION QUESTIONS

1. Assess the first retreat. How did the design of the retreat help to facilitate resolution of issues, and where did it inhibit resolution? Why was the group not able to cover all of the agenda?

What was the role of the consultant and his impact? What was the role of Tom Rice and his input? Would you have acted differently in either role? What were the key contributions by other members of the group?

2. Assess the second retreat. In addition to considering the same questions mentioned in #1 above, why is the subject of organization structure proving so difficult to resolve?

3. How would you design the upcoming third retreat? Should the consultant or Tom Rice change their behavior so as to develop a resolution of the organization structure? Should the same group attend the retreat? Would you attempt to address any additional issues beyond organization structure?

Case 2.2c

MEGA CORPORATION (C)

(Larry Greiner and Arvind Bhambri, University of Southern California)

ABOUT THE AUTHORS

This case was prepared by Professors Larry Greiner and Arvind Bhambri at the Marshall School of Business, University of Southern California, as a basis for class discussion, rather than to illustrate either effective or ineffective handling of an administrative situation. Certain names and figures have been disguised to preserve confidentiality.

Tom Rice decided to become more directly involved in planning the agenda for the third retreat (see Exhibit 2.6 for agenda). He told the consultants:

> "We need to move these meetings off the discussion level and into action. I'm ready to move and the group seems ready too. They seem to be waiting for me to make a decision, so I will do it. All our financial and marketing checks on the strategy statement make sense and the middle managers like it. They say it isn't us now, so the question centers on implementation—especially, organization structure and who fills what jobs."

During a four-hour planning meeting prior to the third retreat, Tom Rice and the consultants drew up a proposed organization structure (see Exhibit 2.7). Rice wanted to lead off the retreat with a presentation of the proposed structure, including a statement of key charters for each major function. He also wanted to hold an open discussion about

---

Exhibit 2.6 Agenda for Third Retreat

Objectives —
1. Reach consensus on a shared vision of what Mega should be in the future.
2. Design organization structure, key roles, and personnel assignments.
3. Make commitment to a specific plan of action to implement vision and organization.

Friday, June 28

1:00   Vision and Organization Discussion
        1. Presentation by Tom Rice
        2. Group Discussion
           a. Does the vision make good sense to us?
           b. Does the vision fit our first and second retreats' statements of strategy and values?
           c. Does the organization fit the vision?
5:00   Adjourn
7:00   Casual Dinner

Saturday, June 29

8:00   Continental Breakfast
8:30   Personnel discussion
        1. What are the skill requirements for the key jobs?
        2. Who should fill these jobs? What are the individual preferences?
        3. Who will do what and when?
5:00   Adjourn
7:00   Dinner

Sunday, June 30

8:00   Continental Breakfast
8:30   Continuation of Plan of Action Discussion
12:00   Adjourn — Sunday Brunch in the Main Dining Room.

---

who should fill what positions. The consultants agreed to design a format for handling this delicate discussion. Rice further decided to invite only the four SVPs of the major functions to the retreat because, "These guys are most crucial to making this happen, and I have to focus on their anxieties."

The third retreat began with Tom Rice making a presentation of his recommended organization structure, shown to them on a flip-chart. It contained several changes from the current organization: a new marketing department for developing new programs; renamed

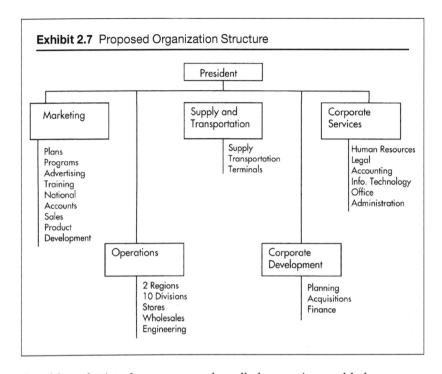

Exhibit 2.7 Proposed Organization Structure

President

Marketing
- Plans
- Programs
- Advertising
- Training
- National Accounts
- Sales
- Product Development

Supply and Transportation
- Supply
- Transportation
- Terminals

Corporate Services
- Human Resources
- Legal
- Accounting
- Info. Technology
- Office Administration

Operations
- 2 Regions
- 10 Divisions
- Stores
- Wholesales
- Engineering

Corporate Development
- Planning
- Acquisitions
- Finance

the old marketing department to be called operations; added a corporate development group for acquisitions; combined the supply and transportation departments into a single functional group; and placed human resources, data processing and legal all under a single SVP of corporate services. In addition, Rice explained to the group that he wanted to reduce the number of zone managers from four to two and regional managers from 24 to 10 in operations (the old marketing department), so as to, "tighten up management and put our best field managers against the marketplace." When Tom Rice had finished his presentation to the four SVPs, he invited them to, "criticize my proposal for how well it implements our new strategy . . . feel free to shoot holes in it," he said.

The group's discussion started slowly with mainly questions of clarification. The most silent member, Andy Davis, the head of marketing in the current organization, suddenly spoke up with a dissenting opinion, "I'm worried about the new marketing group being separated from my operations group." Rice responded sharply, "Andy, I want us to talk about these functions without putting ourselves in certain jobs." Rice went on to explain that he felt marketing issues would not receive sufficient attention if left in operations, and that he was trying to be consistent with the group's expressed desire to emphasize marketing in the new strategy statement. Other members seemed to agree with Rice's reasoning. Then one member suggested that national sales should be placed under the new marketing department, and Rice agreed. Another SVP felt that ten division managers were too few, so four more were added. After two hours of discussion and modifications, no one seemed to be raising further objections to the new structure, including Andy, who had confined his concerns to the new marketing department. Late in the day, one of the group said, "It looks good to me, let's go ahead with it." The rest of the group vocally concurred, with Andy quietly nodding his head.

The next morning began with an active discussion to define key responsibilities for each top position in the new structure. When the group had finished drawing up these responsibilities, Tom Rice said, "Now, I would like to talk about who should fill each job, and I'd like to get your opinions and preferences." The consultant then asked the group to engage in an exercise where the participants were asked to put down on paper which jobs were their first and second choice, and who besides themselves, from inside or outside the group, would best fit each job?" Much nervous laughter accompanied completion of the written assignment. When the final results were posted on a blackboard, the group was astonished to see exact agreement between their personal job preference and the nominations by their colleagues, but with one notable exception. The group preferred that Andy take the new marketing job, but he wanted to stay in his old job, which was now to be called operations. The marketing job was Andy's second choice.

Much of the subsequent discussion involved members of the group trying to persuade Andy to take the marketing job, but he strongly resisted. Finally, Tom Rice stepped in to say:

> "Look, I feel very good about the way we have handled this. We seem to know where our basic talents match up. It's been a long day, so why don't we go off and relax a bit, and then we can return to our discussion after dinner."

Just as Rice was leaving the room, he quietly told the consultants, "to order champagne and dinner for 7:00 . . . we are going to celebrate." Then he ran out the door after Andy, and they headed off into the woods together. Three hours later the group returned for dinner where Andy announced that he wanted to take the new marketing job. The group applauded, and Tom Rice raised his glass to say:

"I'm ready to go with all of you in new positions, so let's toast our goal of doubling over the next five years and all of us having a lot of fun doing it."

When the consultant later asked Tom Rice what had happened in the woods with Andy, he explained:

"I told Andy that I really needed him in the marketing job because he was the best marketing person in the company. He still resisted. So I asked him what it would take to get him in the job, and to my surprise he said that he wanted responsibility for recruiting a bunch of young high potential managers to the company. And I said that was fine with me, at which point he jumped up and shook my hand. I was amazed, because I was ready to let him go."

DISCUSSION QUESTIONS

1. Assess the change in the role taken by Tom Rice in preparing for and leading off the third retreat. Was he being too directive in proposing a single plan? Did he go too far in deciding not to invite three members from the prior retreats? How did these decisions affect the dynamics and the outcomes of the retreat?

2. Assess the role of the consultant, Mark Drake. Did he defer too much to Tom Rice? What contribution did he make, if any, to the third retreat?

3. Assess the "substantive' " changes that were made. How does the new structure differ from the old structure? Is the new structure more consistent with the new strategy than the old structure? Were the personnel changes more in line with getting the most competent people in the "right" jobs to implement the new organization?

4. How should the implementation of the new strategy and structure take place? What specific steps would you, as a consultant, recommend? What would you do as Tom Rice? How rapidly should the plan be put in place? What should be done in handling the three key executives who did not attend the third retreat?

Case 2.2d

MEGA CORPORATION (D)

(Larry Greiner and Arvind Bhambri, University of Southern California)

ABOUT THE AUTHORS

This case was prepared by Professors Larry Greiner and Arvind Bhambri at the Marshall School of Business, University of Southern California, as a basis for class discussion, rather than to illustrate either effective or ineffective handling of an administrative situation. Certain names and figures have been disguised to preserve confidentiality.

The week following the third retreat was a busy one for Mega's senior executives. The CEO, Tom Rice, met separately with each of the three executives who were not invited to the retreat. One of them, the head of Legal, had been nominated at the retreat and approved by Rice to be the new SVP of Corporate Services, which would include Information Technology, Human Resources, Accounting and Legal. The Legal executive was elated to hear about his promotion, but the other two executives were disappointed yet supportive of the overall structural changes. Rice asked the new SVP of Corporate Services to meet immediately with the other two managers to discuss, "How can we work together effectively as a team in the new organization."

Mega's CEO also asked the new Executive Committee, now consisting of five SVPs instead of the earlier four SVPs and three VPs, to meet in an all day session. Rice asked each person to prepare in advance a new organization chart for each of your departments, and to bring a list of nominations for persons in each job in their revised organizations.

This meeting, attended by the consultant, saw the group review, modify, and approve various structural changes within each department. During the discussion about personnel appointments, two members argued over wanting to recruit the same manager, and Tom Rice intervened to say, "Why don't you both talk to her and see which position she really wants to take?"

Two weeks later a large celebration was held in the company's central warehouse with all field managers and corporate employees in attendance. A gigantic banner, "Double in Five Years," was displayed prominently, and a Dixieland band played. Tom Rice gave a speech about the new strategy and the organization changes. Other senior executives stood nearby and spoke briefly with enthusiasm and support for the many changes. Employees in the audience seemed excited, and one manager asked Tom Rice, "Will we have an opportunity to buy stock in the company?" Rice responded that it would be legally impossible in the LBO arrangements, but that, "We will try to share the benefits with you."

During the following year, numerous changes occurred in Mega, and its performance increased significantly. The first month saw thirty-nine executives change positions within the company, including all of the top executive team except for Tom Rice. Dramatic improvements in morale were cited by many employees. Several people reported numerous examples of senior and middle-level managers involving their subordinates more frequently in team decision making, and many employees were recognized for coming forward with new ideas and suggestions for additional changes. The new head of Marketing, Andy Davis, recruited six new young managers, including the captain of the Cal Berkeley football team. The SVP of supply and transportation dominated the futures market on propane, and became a supplier to other major propane users at a substantial profit. The asset base of the company changed dramatically as various non-propane assets were sold off and six acquisitions were made of smaller propane companies.

Midway through the first year, Tom Rice called a fourth retreat for the executive team to "extend the change effort down to the lowest levels of the company." The consultant, Mark Drake, moderated the meeting, although Rice and his team designed its format beforehand. During the meeting, the two remaining zone manager jobs in operations were eliminated and their job occupants transferred or retired, removing one entire level from the field hierarchy. Additional initiatives were launched leading to several programs with different senior executives taking responsibility for each new program. For example, a training program was created for sales managers, and a sales incentive program was introduced. A new profit sharing plan was also created for all employees. Finally, all store managers were invited to bring their best salesperson with them to a two-day conference in Denver where Tom Rice discussed the company's strategic goals, followed by small group discussions and group reports on how to improve performance at the store level.

The groups proposed several steps, and implementation followed, to repaint all the delivery trucks, require all drivers to appear in new uniforms, and for them to receive training in how to treat customers in a friendly, service oriented manner.

A manager two levels removed from the senior group commented later on the effects of the many changes in the company on him personally:

> "I was just about ready to leave when the lights came on. I got a new boss who finally listened to me. He was giving me more work than I had ever done."

Still another manager at the store level said:

> "Before Tom Rice, the guys at the head office rarely ever visited my store, and then it was to find something wrong. Now I feel like they are actually trying to help me. My sales have gone up a lot, and my paycheck is a lot fatter too."

At the end of one year, the company had greatly exceeded its profit plan, and its return on assets was up 40%. A sizeable reward distribution was made to many employees from the profit sharing plan. Special recognition was given to the SVP of Corporate Services who came in $500,000 under budget. After two years, Tom Rice reported to Bob May that Mega would double its profits in less than three years.

DISCUSSION QUESTIONS

1. Identify the key decisions and events that took place in implementing the new strategy and organization. How did these affect motivation and productivity among the middle management and the workforce? Are there additional steps that you would have taken or might recommend for the future?

2. How did the CEO's role and the consultant's role differ

during this period from the earlier retreats? Who was giving leadership to the changes during this period?

3. Looking back over all four cases, how would you conceptualize the total change process? Did it proceed through certain identifiable phases? The process was largely driven from the topdown—were there other alternative approaches? Would the approach used at Mega work in other situations, or did it depend on certain conditions that were unique only to Mega? How important were the roles of Tom Rice? ... the consultant? ... the top group? ... in facilitating the change process?

Case 2.3

HUNTER BUSINESS GROUP: *TEAMTBA*

(Elizabeth Caputo and Das Narayandas)

ABOUT THE AUTHOR

Research Associate Elizabeth Caputo (MBA '99) prepared this case under the supervision of Professor Das Narayandas. This case was developed from published sources. HBS cases are developed solely as the basis for class discussion. Cases are not intended to serve as endorsements, sources of primary data, or illustrations of effective or ineffective management.

Sometimes you have a secondary product line that is moving in a direction different from that of the firm . . . You think that everything is OK, that it is just an incremental business, but in fact, it becomes more like an anchor . . .

Vic Hunter, Chairman and CEO, Hunter Business Group

Such was the dilemma that Star Oil faced during the summer of 1992. Its tire, battery, and accessory (TBA) business, the "ugly stepchild" of its gasoline station services division was now unprofitable and consuming valuable field resources. Its downward trend in profitability had led to a growing sentiment within the firm toward abandoning Star's branded TBA business. Yet, a recent survey of the firm's service stations produced a surprise finding. Customers who had their cars serviced at the 2,200 U.S. gasoline service stations[1] selling Star-branded TBA products bought four times more gasoline than those who bought only gasoline there. This suggested that Star's branded TBA products played a strategic role in boosting Star's gasoline sales. The decision to exit the TBA business, therefore, no longer appeared easy. In the face of increasing competition, Star could not afford an erosion of customer loyalty that might damage its well-known brand. However, the unprofitable nature of the business was unacceptable to the firm's top management. Star executives sought a way to retain the branded TBA business and restore profitability. At this point Star turned to the Hunter Business Group (HBG) for assistance.

HUNTER BUSINESS GROUP

The Hunter Business Group (HBG) specialized in reorganizing the sales and marketing efforts of large and small firms, in industries ranging from computers and biomedical supplies to office supplies and auto parts. Vic Hunter (an alumnus of the Harvard Business School), the company's President and CEO, had founded HBG in 1981 after amassing a wealth of direct marketing and sales management experience. Hunter believed that strategic use of direct marketing technologies could revolutionize the face of business-to-business (B2B) marketing. Seeing direct marketing as more than just a technique, Hunter expressed his vision:

> Our goal is to facilitate the *transformation of change* within our clients' businesses. We believe that direct marketing is a *highly personal* form of marketing that respects and recognizes the unique needs of each customer. A properly designed and maintained database allows communications to be derived from specific information attached to a given customer account. When a seller's communications provide genuine value to a customer, direct marketing programs result in solid relationships, high retention rates and increased profitability.

HBG achieved these objectives by stepping beyond traditional approaches to sales and marketing to find new ways to increase brand penetration and customer satisfaction, while cutting sales and marketing expense. Consequently, HBG had become widely recognized as a "Statue of

Liberty," both for fatigued and impoverished divisions of large companies and for healthy firms looking to revolutionize their sales and marketing efforts. Over the years, HBG had built a highly diversified client base, including IBM, Du Pont, Hallmark Cards, 3M, Monsanto, and BellSouth.

When presented with the details of Star's dilemma, Hunter found it an ideal match for HBG's unique expertise. In fact, based on his experience, he was confident that HBG could turn around the TBA division and make it profitable within a year. Of course, this required fundamentally altering the way Star's gas station operators approached their business. It also meant that Star's sales reps would need to redefine the way they managed dealer relationships, using HBG's integrated direct marketing model to maximize their sales and marketing effectiveness.

DIRECT MARKETING AND HBG'S CUSTOMER CONTACT MATRIX

Direct marketing had long held a mixed reputation. In the consumer arena, for example, manufacturers and service providers saw it as the lowest-cost approach for promoting to attractive customer segments by using databases and linked, automated telephone and mailing systems. For many consumers this meant endless dinnertime phone calls offering low-rate credit cards, long-distance rate deals, and other kinds of "come-ons."

In the arena of business marketing, however, direct marketing techniques had not been fully explored until the 1980s. In this domain, telemarketing methods were often put to more careful use, supplementing rather than replacing expensive face-to-face sales calls. Hunter defined direct marketing as "an interactive marketing system that employs *integrated*, organized contacts to effect a measurable customer response." The effectiveness of integrating mail, telephone, and field contacts, he believed, would always be greater than that resulting from using each medium independently (Exhibit 2.8).

Central to the HBG approach was the use of an economic model—a customer contact matrix—developed by Hunter. The foundation for the model (Exhibit 2.11) rested upon the research of the service management group at the Harvard Business School.[2] This group developed groundbreaking methods to measure customer loyalty and adjust customer contact frequency based on current and future revenues. Therefore, even in a dying industry like typewriters where sales had

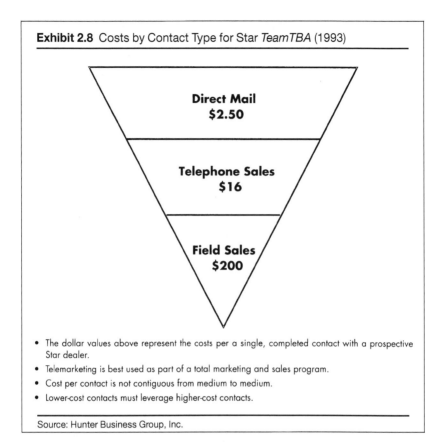

Exhibit 2.8 Costs by Contact Type for Star *TeamTBA* (1993)

Direct Mail
$2.50

Telephone Sales
$16

Field Sales
$200

- The dollar values above represent the costs per a single, completed contact with a prospective Star dealer.
- Telemarketing is best used as part of a total marketing and sales program.
- Cost per contact is not contiguous from medium to medium.
- Lower-cost contacts must leverage higher-cost contacts.

Source: Hunter Business Group, Inc.

gone down 20% in one year, there would be stability and sustainability as long as selling expenses declined more rapidly than revenues.

THE EVOLUTION OF GASOLINE SERVICE STATIONS AND THE BRANDED TBA MARKET

The concept of the modern-day gasoline service station evolved during the 1950s with the advent of the U.S. Interstate system. In order to differentiate themselves in a highly competitive gasoline market, service stations began providing "under the hood" checks during fill-ups and replaced worn-out tires, batteries, and other accessories with their own branded products.[3] Station operators discovered that offering these "expert/advisory" services gave them an opportunity to strengthen their bonds with customers. Many also discovered that their customers often were willing to pay a premium for branded TBA products. By the 1970s, it was common for major gasoline retailers, including Amoco,

Shell, and Star (all of which had very strong brand images) to offer their own branded TBA products and services. These stations used their branded components to maintain a competitive edge in retail gasoline sales. In addition to providing a point of differentiation and margins of more than 20%, branded TBA products could often represent half or more of a service station's overall contribution while accounting for only a small portion of its revenues.

Although gasoline retailers like Star dominated the TBA market during the 1960s and 1970s, the market's high margins soon attracted the attention of specialty competitors that included high-volume/low-price service models (Kmart, Wal-Mart), specialty service chains, (NTB, Jiffy Lube), and independent dealers. These firms aggressively entered the TBA market in the 1980s and gained significant share at the expense of traditional players like Star, who encountered market share declines as high as 70% versus 1960s levels. This trend continued in the 1980s with the closing of nearly 72,000 service stations throughout the decade—an additional 35% decline. By 1990, 80% of repairs on the nation's 190 million automobiles were made, almost equally, by car dealerships, private garages, specialty repair shops, and gasoline service station dealers. The "do-it-yourself" market made up the remaining 20%.

THE STAR OIL ACCOUNT

The branded TBA business was not new to HBG. The firm had recently ended an eight-year relationship with Amoco, a global gasoline retailer like Star. Amoco had partnered with HBG to increase lagging TBA sales at its nearly 6,000 service stations (hereafter referred to as *dealers*). Despite the implementation of a highly successful, integrated, direct marketing program at Amoco, the HBG partnership was discontinued in 1991 when Amoco decided to outsource its entire branded TBA business to the National Automotive Parts Association Supply Company (NAPA).

When Star approached HBG soon thereafter, Vic Hunter was delighted. Star recognized the importance of the TBA business in supporting its ubiquitous, industry-dominant logo. To Hunter, the importance that Star's management ascribed to preserving this brand image suggested its long-term commitment to the TBA business— something he had found lacking in the Amoco relationship.

Nonetheless, with revenues having fallen over 20% in the past twelve months, Star managers were finding it difficult to justify maintaining the TBA division despite its importance in supporting the brand. Hunter described the situation:

> In 1991–92, Star was losing money. They were unsure how much but knew the amount was substantial. On a variable cost basis, the small part that they could track, the loss was about $8 million. Further, the TBA division had become unattractive not only from the financial standpoint, but also from that of human resources. TBA was not an exciting place to be. Yet, a significant amount of Star's brand equity rested in its TBA product lines. Strong customer relationships had been built around these products throughout the marketplace.

I was convinced that the integrated approach we had used at Amoco would also work well at Star. Consequently, we told them we would turn their business around within a year. We also promised that we would design a sales and marketing program to maintain their brand image and increase dealer satisfaction while simultaneously reducing sales and marketing expenses. Their reaction was 'yes, but what about the dealer/employee relationships? We have seasoned people who were hired to work for Star forever and you're telling us that you can do things better and with a significantly lower budget?' Star's managers were clearly skeptical about our ability to deliver on our promises, but their only alternative was to give us a chance.

TEAMTBA

HBG began by establishing an entirely new company to address the Star business. It was named *TeamTBA*. The company operated out of HBG's Milwaukee headquarters under the leadership of Julie Kowalski, a member of HBG's management team. The initial agreement between the firms stated that HBG would license the Star brand, and independently manage a direct marketing operation that would include marketing, sales, manufacturing, and product design. Star would receive no compensation on sales below $20 million per year, but was entitled to 2% of *TeamTBA* revenues exceeding that. Additionally, Star would retain control over the product—HBG would need to obtain Star's approval before making changes to current TBA products. This included dropping existing products, changing vendors, and introducing new products and services. Star also wanted *TeamTBA* to live up to its word and reduce operating costs by fifty percent in the first year. Star retained the right to terminate the agreement if this condition was not met.

TeamTBA began operations by creating an extensive branded TBA dealer database. Prior to 1992, Star had maintained dealer profile databases by product line. However, like other firms in this industry, it maintained this information entirely on paper. Rebecca Nguyen, HBG's Information Systems Manager at the time, recalled:

> When we began work with Star, all service station (hereafter referred to as dealer) information was stored on paper and much of it was incomplete. We used that information to create a master that would then be updated as our salespeople called on the various dealers and collected current information. It took us more than six months to gather all the pertinent information. By September 1992, our dealer master database had grown to include all 2,200 dealers.

TeamTBA organized its sales and marketing effort around sales teams, each consisting of a field sales representative (FSR), an internal telesales representative (TSR), and a customer service representative (CSR). In contrast to Star's field sales force of 84 reps, *TeamTBA* began with just 18 sales people (16 HBG employees or new hires and two former Star field sales representatives). Hunter explained:

> It is not that we did not want to hire Star's reps. In fact, we gave them an option to join us. However, most stayed on at Star to focus on gasoline sales, or left because they lacked confidence in our approach. Some felt the transition would be too difficult to handle.

TeamTBA's FSRs were assigned sales territories and teamed with a headquarters-based TSR. This partnership formed the field customer interface (Exhibit 2.9). FSRs were to advise dealers on how to better manage and grow their service bay operations, thereby stimulating demand for TBA products. Also, internal TSRs would proactively initiate contacts with station owners, in close collaboration with FSRs, to solicit orders, conduct and coordinate predefined sales strategies, and maintain/update customer profiles in the dealer master database. Inbound CSRs, also located at headquarters, would augment the process by providing order status, order processing support, and immediate customer problem resolution. Weekly conference calls (between the FSR and the TSR) would be conducted to share information about recent dealer contacts and to develop future contact strategies. These calls would also be taped so that management could ensure that the sales teams were working effectively to develop value-added, integrated, contact plans. Further, contact and coordination with the existing Star

Exhibit 2.9 *TeamTBA* Process Chart

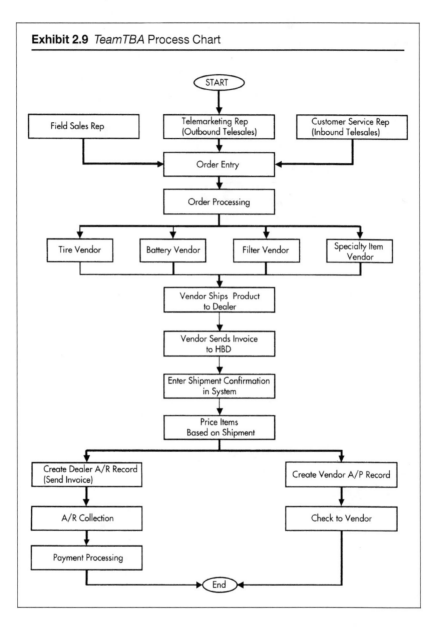

gasoline sales force would be part of the overall contact plan and the responsibility of the FSRs.

Marketing and promotional resources were to be provided through a marketing coordinator located centrally. This coordinator was responsible for overseeing production and distribution of key marketing elements by working with Star (as required) and with outside vendors. An initial 1993 promotion calendar had already been created to guide these efforts.

Accounting resources had been established to handle order entry, vendor invoice processing, accounts receivable, financial analysis and reporting, pricing analysis, sales analysis, and auditing of intra-company transactions.

Information Systems was charged with maintaining and enhancing software and hardware resources, developing new systems to support the business process, training and communicating with all system users, managing a "help desk" function, and managing the EDI process with vendors.

Vendor negotiations and relationship management were the responsibilities of the general manager. Hunter explained:

> We took a radically different approach with vendors. To begin with, in each category we short-listed those vendors we thought capable of meeting our quality standards. Based on their experience, most of these vendors came to the negotiating table expecting to talk price and play "hardball." They were surprised when we refused to talk about price. Not that price was unimportant, we were more interested in hearing what these vendors had to offer in terms of added value that would help us differentiate *TeamTBA* products in the eyes of our dealers and the end consumers. We were looking for partners, not suppliers. We offered long-term, single-source contracts to these vendors in return for their commitment to customize existing products and to develop new ones for us. Interestingly, several vendors walked away from the table because they were unprepared to do business this way. Those that remained were committed to making *TeamTBA* a success.

By December 1992, *TeamTBA* had selected Kelly Springfield as its main tire vendor, Delco-Remy for batteries, and Champion for filters—each a well-known manufacturer in its industry. A vendor decision on chemicals was to be made before the end of December. All TBA products, regardless of vendor, would be labeled and marketed under the Star brand name.

In order to ensure a smooth transition, *TeamTBA* had assumed some of Star's telemarketing, order processing, and customer service responsibilities in August 1992. By the end of December of that year,

TeamTBA's field sales representatives were in place, and the new sales plan was launched at the beginning of January 1993.

USING THE STAR CUSTOMER CONTACT MATRIX

Understanding and applying Hunter's customer contact matrix was the backbone of *TeamTBA*'s customer (gasoline service station) management strategy. The process began by projecting revenues for 1993 (Exhibit 2.10). Hunter forecasted revenues at $20 million—a significant reduction from the 1991 and 1992 levels. *TeamTBA* made this downward projection based on their belief that the earlier Star TBA revenues had been overreported. Further, a large portion of the TBA volume had resulted from Star reps "pushing" TBA products. Finally, the negative impact of the Persian Gulf War was expected to hit the industry that year. Assuming reduced product costs (now budgeted at 80% of revenues) as a result of stronger relationship management and the consolidation of suppliers, *TeamTBA* projected a gross margin of $4 million for 1993. With this in mind, *TeamTBA* began to think about a reasonable estimate for direct marketing expense.

Star wanted *TeamTBA* to honor Hunter's verbal commitment that his team could implement their program successfully while reducing operating costs by 50% of the expected 1993 revenues. This meant that HBG's projected operating costs had to be reduced from 35.5% to 17.75% as a percentage of revenues, or to $3.55 million. "**Operating costs**," as noted in Exhibit 2.10 comprised two expenses: the **direct marketing and sales expense** (which included mail, phone, and field operations, salaries) and **fixed operating expense** (which included rent, salaries for internal office support, database management, and miscellaneous costs associated with *TeamTBA*'s Milwaukee headquarters). HBG's experience suggested that fixed expenses would run between 40–45% of operating costs, or about $1.5 million. Consequently, the team established a baseline of $2 million for direct marketing and sales expense.

Exhibit 2.11 illustrates the cost and corresponding frequency of contacts by medium—mail ($2.50 per contact), phone ($16 per contact), and face-to-face meetings ($200 per contact)—and shows the number of active dealers by sales volume grade. *TeamTBA* knew from experience that as the amount of sales visits fell, the frequency of phone and mail contacts would need to go up. The question for *TeamTBA*, however, was whether or not this could be done more effectively given their $2 million budget. The next step was to determine the optimal

Exhibit 2.10 Star Financial Information, 1991–1992 (actual); 1993–1994 (projected); in millions

	1991	As % of 1991 Revenues	1992	As % of 1992 Revenues	1993 (Team TBA projection)	As % of 1993 Revenues	1994 (Team TBA projection)	As % of 1994 Revenues
Revenue	$36.7		$39.4		$20.0		$16.0	
Product Costs	32.3	88.0	33.6	85.3	16.0	80.0	12.8	80.0
Gross Margin	4.4	12.0	5.8	14.7	4.0	20.0	3.2	20.0
Operating Costs	11.3	30.8	14.0	35.5	3.55	17.75	2.84	17.75
Operating Income	(6.9)	(18.8)	(8.2)	(20.8)	.45	2.25	.36	2.25

Source: Hunter Business Group, Inc.

Exhibit 2.11 Customer Contact Matrix

Customer Grade	Dollar Sales Range	Actual Avg Sales Revenue per Account	# of Accounts	Sales Revenue	Avg Mail Contacts per Account	Total Mail Contacts	Mail Cost *Avg Cost per Contact $2.50*	Avg Phone Calls per Account	Total Phone Calls	Phone Cost *Avg Cost per Contact $16.00*	Avg Field Calls per Account	Total Field Sales Calls	Field Sales Cost *Avg Cost per Contact $200*	Total Cost	Expense to Revenue Ratio
Target Customers															
AA (5%)	>$30,000	$50,000	88	$4,400,000	72	6,336	$15,840	48	4,224	$67,584	24	2,112	$422,400	$505,824	11.50%
A (15%)	$20,000–$30,000	$25,000	264	$6,600,000	72	19,008	$47,520	24	6,336	$101,376	12	3,168	$633,600	$782,496	11.86%
B (25%)	$10,000–$20,000	$12,000	440	$5,280,000	48	21,120	$52,800	18	7,920	$126,720	4	1,760	$352,000	$531,520	10.07%
C (25%)	$5,000–$10,000	$6,500	440	$2,860,000	24	10,560	$26,400	12	5,280	$84,480	0	0	$0	$110,880	3.88%
D (30%)	<$5,000	$1,650	528	$871,200	12	6,336	$15,840	6	3,168	$50,688	0	0	$0	$66,528	7.64%
Total			1,760	$20,011,200		63,360	$158,400		26,928	$430,848		7,040	$1,408,000	$1,997,248	9.98%

Source: Hunter Business Group, Inc.

combination of mail, phone, and field contacts within the budget, yet still meet the new sales target.

Dealers graded by purchase volume: Dealers were sorted into buckets based on their TBA purchase volumes. The buckets were labeled "AA" (more than $30,000), "A" ($20,000–$30,000), "B" ($10,000–$20,000), "C" ($5,000–$10,000) and "D" (less than $5,000). Using past purchase data, *TeamTBA* established the average dollar sales for each grade, as shown in the table.

Number of dealers: It was HBG's standard industry practice to sort customer accounts (dealers in this case) according to a 5/15/25/25/30 rule, designating the "top 20%" accounts as AA and A respectively. Thus, regardless of industry, the percentage of accounts allocated to each grade always remained constant.

Sales revenue: HBG's customer contact matrix usually extended the "20/80" rule across industries–the AA and A accounts typically generated 80% of the overall sales revenues. However, this was not the case with TBA, where the AA and A dealers only accounted for about one-half of all sales revenue.

Average field calls per dealer account: Field calls were the most expensive yet most effective component of the program, and therefore were the starting point for decisions on the allocation of marketing efforts. As Julie Kowalski, head of *TeamTBA*, described:

> Profit for *TeamTBA* needed to be considered for each grade. For a dealer account in the D grade, bringing in around $1,650 of revenue and $330 of margin, a single field contact costing $200 would be ineffective and unprofitable, hence the zero demarcation in the model. In contrast, AA accounts might justify as many as 24 visits a year, or $4,800 in field expense.

Average mail contacts per dealer account: The number of times a dealer would be contacted by mail was determined by HBG's experience. Virtually all direct mail solicitation was performed at least monthly; thus, even for C and D accounts, 12 contacts per year were reasonable. For higher-level accounts more frequent mailings (including targeted offerings and marketing calendars) were added (72, 48, 24, and 12).

Average phone calls per dealer account: Telephone contact frequency was also based on HBG's experience. *TeamTBA* believed that every dealer should be contacted at least every two months. As with mail contacts for higher volume dealers, more frequent phone contacts were planned.

TeamTBA planned to adjust the number of mail, phone, and field contacts to reflect changes in incoming revenue throughout the program.

"GOLD" ACCOUNTS

In order for the *TeamTBA* approach to be successful, sales teams had to provide incentives to dealers: not only so dealers would purchase larger volumes of Star products, but more importantly, so they would purchase a *wider assortment* of these products. To do this, *TeamTBA* established the "Gold Account" program. A Gold Account was defined as a dealer who purchased $17,000 or more from *TeamTBA* during a given year. This $17,000 had to include at least 25 batteries ($1,250), 50 tires ($2,500), $250 in filters, and $250 in chemicals every 90 days. This translated to sales of $4,250 per quarter, or $17,000 annually. Kowalski explained:

> The heart of our methodology is to identify dealers who take a proactive approach to TBA products. Based on experience, we found that the easiest way to identify such accounts is to look at their purchase patterns. A dealer who routinely orders a certain amount of product in each category is presumably committed to selling those product categories. We are therefore interested not just in volume, but also the breadth of products purchased.

Based on this definition, an AA account that purchased $50,000 of "product" consisting only of tires would not receive Gold Account recognition. But, a B account purchasing an $18,000 combination of filters, batteries, tires, and chemicals would achieve Gold Account status due to the combination of products purchased. Consequently, Gold Accounts were not limited to AA accounts and included some in each of the AA, A, and B accounts.

Using Star information from the end of 1992, *TeamTBA* discovered that of 2,200 stations, only 14 qualified for Gold status. Vic Hunter remarked: "What looked like a very strong brand because 80% of dealers purchased Star-branded products, proved to be poor brand foundation with weak market penetration. We were very disappointed."

TeamTBA encouraged its sales teams to increase the number of Gold Accounts by offering them $100 bonuses for each net addition to the number of Gold Accounts in their territory. Exhibit 2.12 shows the dramatic increase in the number of Gold accounts during 1993, the first year of the program. Hunter credited the surge to active manage-

Exhibit 2.12 Number of Gold Accounts—Year One (1993)

Month	Gold Accounts
January	–
February	14
March	46
April	55
May	87
June	116
July	105
August	122
September	136
October	145
November	154

Source: Hunter Business Group, Inc.

ment of customer needs. Unlike the past, when TBA representatives "pushed" products onto dealers, *TeamTBA* representatives now showed dealers how to sell TBA products more efficiently. Hunter explained:

We helped dealers learn to market. Under the new model, our representative would notice, for instance, when a station had not purchased filters for a given time period. The *TeamTBA* rep would then demonstrate how offering a discounted oil change with every 50 gallons of gas purchased would increase the dealer's revenues.

TEAMTBA RESULTS

A few months after *TeamTBA* started operations, it conducted a satisfaction survey of the 2,200 dealers (Exhibit 2.13). The survey results were encouraging and surprising. First, in all but one category dealer satisfaction had risen after *TeamTBA* had taken over the business. Second, and perhaps more striking, was the seemingly counterintuitive increase in territory sales manager (TSM) contact frequency, despite *TeamTBA* decreasing its number of field representatives from 83 (Star) to 18 (*TeamTBA*), and decreasing its frequency of direct personal contact by 70%. Hunter clarified this point:

Classic marketing suggests that if I [the Star rep] call dealers less frequently, I get less business . . . we went from 83 to 18 field reps—this should have spelled disaster. The survey showed that dealers' perceptions of the frequency of face-to-face contacts had

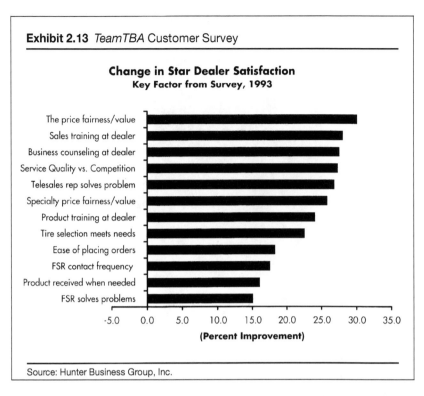

Exhibit 2.13 *TeamTBA* Customer Survey

Change in Star Dealer Satisfaction
Key Factor from Survey, 1993

Source: Hunter Business Group, Inc.

actually risen. This is not as counterintuitive as it seems at first. People don't differentiate between contact media. They differentiate based on the frequency of "valued communications." If you generate valued communications by phone and through the mail that are seamlessly integrated with field activities, the overall perception is that face-to-face contact frequency has increased. Previously, a Star representative, for instance, would ordinarily visit a retailer or owner in San Antonio, 50 times a year. Now, (with the *TeamTBA* model) field visits were reduced to 12 times a year, but when a dealer was asked the question "How many times does a TBA rep visit you?" they responded that the frequency had increased 17% (59 visits), much higher than it actually was (12 visits).

The survey results demonstrated the effectiveness of Hunter's integrated marketing approach. In fact, by contacting dealers through a variety of media, *TeamTBA* had actually increased the number of contacts by 600%. Hunter concluded:

Star's main problem had been a lack of understanding about what dealers really needed—it was not face-to-face contact from field representatives. Before *TeamTBA*, Star reps had focused on the politics of the relationship between Star and its dealers, rather than focusing on tires, batteries, and accessories. Dealers saw their relationship as confrontational at best, involving prolonged meetings that accomplished little. Meetings typically had concluded with dealers buying Star's products based on a sense of obligation, or to gain access to co-op marketing funds.

Within the new business approach, the starting point was a dealer specific plan based on information recorded in the dealer master database. Next, a phone conversation between the *TeamTBA* telesales rep and the dealer would ensue to confirm the dealer's needs. More research would then be done before the first field visit. Following the visit, another four or five phone/mail contacts would be made before the next field trip. As Hunter described:

> When a Team member makes an initial phone contact, they say something like "I would like to talk to you about the battery program. What are some of the problems that you encounter that are not currently being addressed . . .? And, by the way, Vic Hunter will be in your area next week. Would you like him to come in and show you our line?" If the dealer expressed an interest, the field rep would call on the dealer personally, discussing any unmet needs or other issues. Dealers then feel better about buying our products because their needs are addressed and value is being exchanged.

Other Survey Results

Several other dealer responses piqued HBG's interest. For instance, the survey confirmed the impression that a majority of the dealers carried branded TBA products. However, tires and batteries—which generated a significant portion of *TeamTBA* revenues—were being sold by only a small percentage of accounts. Secondly, it appeared that dealers' perceived value of the Star brand varied with the type of products they purchased. For example, across all dealers in the survey, 65% considered the Star brand to be of equal or greater importance than price. Yet, among those who also sold tires, this number rose to 80%. Finally, dealers reflected in their responses their reluctance "to throw out the TBA baby with the bath water." Eighty percent of respondents reported that service bay repairs were highly important to their overall business, with an additional 16% describing such services as having average or above average importance.

EARLY SUCCESSES

Within six months of the *TeamTBA* launch, the program looked like a great success. The number of active Star accounts (those accounts having purchased within the previous 30 days) had increased 24%. Even more impressive was the significant increase in the number of Gold Accounts, which had exceeded 100 by June. Jim Jaskoske, chairman of Star's National Dealer Council, wrote a letter to council members reporting on a *TeamTBA* sales training meeting that he had attended in mid-1993:

> I can assure you that *TeamTBA*'s only objective is to help us earn a profit. Their only business is selling Star branded TBA products. We can look forward to competitive pricing, point-of-sale materials, award programs, quantity discounts, and the fastest possible delivery service.

Hunter was delighted that the results of the dealer satisfaction survey seemed to prove the merits of his firm's customer contact matrix. Even though face-to-face contact had decreased by 70% or more in many cases, dealers were more satisfied with the sales interactions they had under the *TeamTBA* program than they ever had been. Over 85% of respondents in the survey considered *TeamTBA* to offer equal or better service than that of Star, and nearly 30% found that service to be "much better" than previous service offerings. Nearly 40% of dealers reported that the Star brand added a 15% premium to the prices they were able to charge.

Through 1993, the good news continued for *TeamTBA*, as cumulative first year sales passed the target of $20 million. While this represented about half of the revenue generated a year earlier, the cost of sales had plummeted, thereby meeting the initial goal of attaining profitability for the *TeamTBA* program.

However, one concern was beginning to grow. By the beginning of 1994, it looked as though the number of active accounts and total sales volume had begun to level off. Further, Star had launched a program to convert franchised service stations at major intersections (usually *TeamTBA*'s best customers) into convenience stores with no service facilities. The number of service stations with service bays was also expected to fall from 2,200 to 1,700 in the next year or two.

PLANNING FOR THE JOURNEY AHEAD

As she reviewed the situation for the coming year, Julie Kowalski made an assumption that there would be 1,500 active accounts. Based on the data and projections she had before her, she also expected the average sales volume within each account grade to decline, and that *TeamTBA*'s sales revenues would drop to around $16 million in 1994. Along with Vic Hunter and the rest of the management team, she set out to develop a plan that would allow product costs and margins as a percentage of revenues to remain constant for the next year, leaving *TeamTBA* with an expected operating income of $360,000 for 1994. Based on this, Kowalski began evaluating her options, knowing that *TeamTBA*'s strategy could take any of several approaches.

As one approach, Kowalski could assume that *TeamTBA*'s fixed costs would remain constant at $1.5 million. This meant that they would not shut down any facilities, abandon any territories, or scale back operational expenses associated with running the TBA program. By freezing these fixed costs, *TeamTBA* would have only $1.34 million to spend on direct marketing and sales efforts. They would thus have to reduce sales and marketing expenditures by $660,000 from 1993 in order to meet their $360,000 profitability target.

This scenario raised several obstacles. First, there was the sales force question. At present, the cost of salaries for the *TeamTBA* sales force exceeded $1.6 million (Exhibit 2.14). It appeared impossible, then, to meet the new profitability target without drastically cutting back the sales and marketing force—whether in mail, telesales, or field sales. Indeed, Kowalski even wondered if there was any merit to eliminating the field sales force entirely and establishing *TeamTBA* as a premier

---

Exhibit 2.14 *TeamTBA* Direct Marketing Sales Force Salary Information (1993)

Employee Category	Number of Employees	Fully Burdened Salary	Total Salary Cost to HBG	Total Contact Cost for HBG	% of Total Contact Cost Attributed to Employee Salary
Field Sales	18	$70,000	$1,260,000	$1,408,000	89%
Telesales	6	$56,000	$336,000	$430,848	76%
Mail	1.5	$36,000	$54,000	$158,400	34%
Total	25		$1,650,000	$1,997,248	

telesales operation. Just looking at the original matrix, she recognized that such a move could eliminate $1.4 million in costs.

Kowalski knew that making such a move could create a serious morale problem within the team, so she weighed the expected cost recovery against the likely adverse reactions among the remaining *TeamTBA* sales force and the Star dealers who were their valued customers. She also knew that the fruits of such cost recovery would be partially consumed in the investments required to expand telemarketing capacity.

A second strategy would be to maintain the fixed component of *TeamTBA*'s operating expenses at a constant *percentage of revenue*, or 40–45%. This would equal $1.28 million, given Kowalski's projection of $2.84 million for total 1994 operating costs. Such a move, however, would leave only $1.56 million for sales and marketing costs—a figure that included salary expense. Consequently, a certain number of jobs would still have to be cut.

A third alternative strategy would be a hybrid approach. This scenario involved reducing fixed costs as well as sales and marketing costs by 20%, consistent with the 20% decline in revenues from 1993. *TeamTBA* could do this in a variety of ways. They could make wholesale changes in the frequency of contacts by mail, phone, or field; they could try to increase the number of Gold Accounts and make an effort to boost sales volume among the highest performers, while decreasing or terminating contacts among C and D accounts; or they could experiment with a combination of the two: adjusting contact frequency and encouraging more dealers to "step up" to the Gold Account level.

There were several questions that needed to be addressed with this hybrid approach. Would reducing the number of contacts hasten the decline in revenues? Was it possible for *TeamTBA* to improve its effectiveness over 1993 levels by developing Gold accounts? Was the team capable of getting these dealers to buy more TBA products? After all, TBA products were not their primary source of revenues. Was this asking for too much from the dealers?

Amidst all this, Hunter, Kowalski, and the management team were debating whether this was the time to change their sales compensation structure from trying to maximize revenue to maximizing contribution margin. Hunter explained: "By educating the sales force on the costs of TBA products and the types of purchasing arrangements that would be most conducive to *maximizing contribution margin*, we could get them to make more autonomous decisions on how to manage individual dealer accounts. This would align their efforts with our goal of managing the sales-to-expense ratio." Would this move be counter-productive as well?

In the face of all the questions associated with each of the options, Hunter and Kowalski needed to come up with a plan to counter the forthcoming decline in revenues.

NOTES TO CASE

1. Gasoline service stations typically had one or more service bays in addition to multiple self-serve and full service gasoline pumps. Based on the availability of labor, these establishments offered a range of services from simple maintenance jobs (replacement of tires/batteries/wiper blades/engine oil/transmission oil/windshield washer liquid) to more complex repairs (repairing brake-pads/mufflers/struts, tuning engines, etc.)

2. James L. Heskett, Earl W. Sasser Jr., and Leonard A. Schlesinger, *The Service Profit Chain: How Leading Companies Link Profit And Growth To Loyalty, Satisfaction And Value.* (New York: Free Press, 1997).

3. Gasoline retailers like Star had traditionally sold branded TBA products through their gasoline service station dealers.

Case 2.4

WESTERN CASUALTY

(David Upton and Sari Carp)

In mid-1995, Linda Hurlburt, Vice President of Operations and Information Services at Western Casualty, had launched a restructuring effort aimed at revitalizing the company's underperforming Other Party Liability (OPL) department. A year later, Hurlburt's restructuring initiative had succeeded spectacularly. OPL was arguably the most competent organization of its kind in the Western United States. Success spawned further quandaries, though, and Hurlburt now faced a new dilemma.

OPL, Casualty's subrogation arm, recovered costs incurred by Casualty policyholders but resulting from the actions of a third party. OPL's newfound efficiency rendered its services attractive to competing insurers. One major insurer had already offered to contract with the department to manage its recovery needs. This proposal represented a superb opportunity for OPL. For Casualty as a whole, however, it signaled potential termination of a lucrative competitive advantage: exclusive access to the best subrogation team. Hurlburt was unsure if OPL's potential gain would outweigh its parent's implied loss.

THE INDUSTRY: PROPERTY/CASUALTY INSURANCE

History

There is little reason to suppose that ancient peoples were any less rational or risk-averse than we. Therefore, it is not surprising that insurance is anything but a modern phenomenon. The first known form of insurance was marine insurance, developed in ancient Babylonia. Classical Greeks and Romans enjoyed life and health insurance, while trade between far-flung imperial cities soon engendered a demand for property insurance.

Assisted by regulatory favoritism, English insurers like Lloyd's of London dominated the American colonial market. However, several local mutual insurance companies did develop and corporate insurers mushroomed after 1776. The first U.S. casualty policy was underwritten in 1832; the first burglary premium paid in 1885. In step with technology, the Travelers insurance group introduced an automobile bodily injury policy in 1898.

Many early property/casualty companies suffered from incompetent management and excessively speculative investment policies. Most insurers failed to provide adequately for potential catastrophes, so the industry experienced severe attrition following the Great Chicago Fire of 1871 and the San Francisco earthquake of 1906. Federal and state governments made few attempts to regulate insurers and false advertising and frequent default on distributions to policyholders undermined consumer confidence in the industry. It was also impossible for insurers or customers to identify efficient premium levels in the absence of extensive data on accident frequency, etc. As information and regulation improved, however, the property/casualty industry grew steadily. By the end of the 1980s, the United States was home to 3800 property/casualty insurers. Many of these transacted considerable business abroad: U.S. insurers underwrote 37% of all premiums worldwide.

The 1990s

The national insurance market embraced three major sectors: life, health and property/casualty. Multi-line insurance companies underwrote policies in all three areas, but most insurers specialized in one. The property/casualty sector was probably the most diverse, encompassing auto (roughly 40% of the market), homeowners (9%), workers compensation and other types of insurance. The property/casualty industry had swelled significantly during the mid-1980s, enjoying year-on-year premium growth of up to 22%. Growth slowed considerably, though, during the late 1980s and early 1990s. In 1994, property/casualty insurers underwrote $250.7 billion in premiums, a mere 3.6% increase over 1993. Commercial premiums (e.g., commercial auto or worker's compensation) rose three times as much as personal premiums.

1994 was a disastrous year for most property/casualty insurers. Record natural and man-made disasters, in conjunction with high interest rates, devastated the industry. The year began with the North-ridge, California earthquake and ended with the bankruptcy of Orange County. In a disturbing parallel to their nineteenth century counter-parts, property/casualty insurers had simply failed to put aside enough cash to deal with such emergencies. This was especially true of com-panies underwriting municipal bond insurance: the Orange County failure represented a massive shock to an industry in which defaults rarely occur. Orange County also contributed to a significant bond market decline, which hurt insurers' investments. As industry profit margins narrowed over the preceding decade, most insurance firms had become dependent on investment income. The unpredictable nature of potential payouts mandated highly liquid, conservative investments like bonds. As the Federal Reserve raised rates and bond prices fell, insurers lost a lot of money.

Western Casualty

The panic-inducing events of 1994 encouraged many national insurance carriers like State Farm and Allstate to withdraw entirely from the California market. Such departures, in addition to 1994's many insurance company failures, left California's insurance industry in chaos.

Not all insurers enjoyed the ability to jettison their California busi-nesses. Western Casualty was the largest regional property/casualty insurer in the West. California represented its largest market by a con-siderable margin. If it ceased to operate in that state, Casualty would probably be unable to survive. Management also believed that the industry's recent shakeout suggested new opportunities for the more efficient of the remaining insurance providers to increase profits.

Established in 1956, Western Casualty became the Golden State's most powerful property/casualty insurer by 1972. A decade later, it dominated the Western region. By the early 1990s, however, Casualty's market share had declined from over 65% to less than 20% in California, while national property/casualty insurers threatened to take control. Observers ascribed Casualty's collapse in market share largely to a cumbersome cost structure and to complacency in marketing.

Now, however, Casualty could not afford to be complacent. Management introduced a new organization plan and promised to streamline costs. Before 1994, the company had been divided along functional lines: sales, retention (the care of existing customers), and service and claims processing. Each department performed its tasks and handed the file to the next department; no department had a complete understanding of any customer's needs. The new plan mandated that Casualty's 3000 employees be grouped by insurance sector. One group dealt with homeowner policies, another with auto, a third with worker's compensation, etc. Core support functions such as the legal and OPL departments, however, remained distinct from these groups.

Casualty's reorganization effort was hampered by the backward state of the company's information technology. The company lagged far behind its competitors, who had long ago shifted their claims processing from a paper to a digital system. During 1995, Casualty invested $9 million in new technology. Most of this was spent on data processing and communications systems. Casualty initiated a corporate-wide "information warehouse" (a large database), installed computer networks within and between departments and promoted scannable enrollment forms.

Casualty's reorganization did seem to pay off. By late 1996, the free fall of the company's market share had been arrested, and management even projected a rise of 2–4% in 1997, though some of this rise was undoubtedly due to the exit of competitors from the market.

The Department: Other-Party Liability

By June 1995, Western Casualty had completed its reorganization. Hurlburt was appointed to the newly-created position of Vice President of Operations & Information Services. Hurlburt, a CPA and MBA, had joined Casualty in 1993. Prior to the reorganization, she had served as the company's Director of Operations Processing, supervising the entry of claims and eligibility data into Casualty's systems. Hurlburt characterized the difference between her new job and her previous position: "Before, I wasn't involved in how the machinery ran, just in getting information into the machinery. Now I look at both."

Hurlburt's new responsibilities encompassed several support departments, including Other Party Liability (OPL). Before the corporate reorganization, OPL had been split into two departments: Bodily Injury and Property Damage. Both departments had been engaged in recovering costs incurred by policyholders but caused by a third party. For example, if Casualty had paid a policyholder's claim for treatment of an auto accident-related injury, Bodily Injury would attempt to recover Casualty's expense from the party responsible for the accident (assuming, of course, that this was not its own policyholder). Similarly, if the company reimbursed a policyholder for fire damage caused by a contractor working on the policyholder's property, Property Damage would pursue recovery from the contractor or his insurer. Now the functions of Bodily Injury and Property Damage were united in one 40-person department, OPL.

About 65% of OPL's business was related to bodily injury: although these cases were fewer, they tended to be of much longer duration and to entail significantly higher sums. Ideally, employees would be cross-trained to work on both bodily injury and property damage cases. Department members dealt directly with Casualty's policyholders and with the attorneys and insurers of the third parties. They also liased with outside sources of information, such as local Departments of Motor Vehicles. While OPL employees were not required to possess formal legal training, those most involved in negotiating with third parties' lawyers usually developed relevant expertise in the course of their responsibilities.

The Outsourcing Dilemma

At the time it began reporting to Hurlburt, OPL had 20,000 unresolved recovery cases with values averaging $7500 each. It typically handled 8,500 cases per annum: in 1994, its efforts yielded $55 million for Casualty. Total recovery activity in the market in which Casualty operated was $550–600 million. Since Casualty's market share was about 20%, management reasoned, it should enjoy an equivalent portion of total recoveries. OPL's performance fell far short of this benchmark.

OPL had always been a "marginal performer." In March 1995, a proposal was made to outsource the department's functions. Since the beginning of 1993, the information technology for all of Western Casualty had been outsourced to ABD Information Services Inc., a global supplier of information systems and services. ABD had a loose alliance with the PAX Group, a subrogation firm. PAX now proposed to take over Casualty's subrogation activities from the OPL department. General uncertainty and flux during the company's reorganization process prevented Casualty from arriving at a firm decision about outsourcing OPL before Hurlburt inherited the department in June 1995.

Hurlburt compared PAX's proposal to the costs of keeping OPL in-house. She concluded that outsourcing would cost Casualty 20% more than retaining the department in its current form. There were also strategic reasons in favor of an internal subrogation division. The greater the knowledge about the case, the argument went, the more efficient the recovery. An in-house department would have easier and more extensive access to information on specific cases than would an external provider. Also, the marketing value of an internal watchdog was significant. Although the functions performed by an in-house OPL department and those of an outside provider would be almost identical, clients seemed to prefer Casualty to provide a "complete package" including subrogation services.

Despite these arguments, senior management favored outsourcing OPL. Casualty was on the margin of fulfilling its reserve requirements and managers were anxious to "get more cash through the door" as soon as possible. This would have been facilitated by outsourcing OPL, as more recoveries could be performed in the immediate future. Hurlburt, however, remained certain that the best choice for Casualty was to retain its OPL department. She decided to go out on a limb to save the department: she promised senior management that, if permitted to keep OPL in-house, she would increase recoveries by one-third during the following year. Senior managers agreed to let her try.

The Consultants

Hurlburt's professional reputation and OPL's future were both at stake. Hurlburt had to stimulate productivity very rapidly. She felt that outside consultants would be able to catalyze the process. Hurlburt was especially eager to work with Carl Doenitz and Robert Drury, consultants with the McClellan Consulting Group (MCG). Unlike many larger firms, MCG focused primarily on one industry: property and casualty insurance. Doenitz had only joined MCG three years previously, but he benefited from twelve years of experience as a Casualty manager. Drury, in contrast, brought thirty years training as a consultant, but no exposure to property/casualty insurance.

Hurlburt's proposal to work with MCG met with considerable resistance at Casualty. The company had recently had several disillusioning and expensive experiences with consultants hired to work on corporate-wide initiatives. These consultants rarely remained on-site long enough to obtain more than a cursory understanding of the company or to implement their recommendations. They also made little attempt to involve Casualty employees in developing strategies for change. A million-dollar reengineering study performed by a high-profile consulting firm was generally perceived to have been "useless," as was a $2 million project by another major firm two years previously. These negative impressions of outside consultants were exacerbated by the assumption, shared by employees at many firms, that the arrival of consultants heralded the involuntary departure of employees.

In the hope of rendering the consultants' presence more palatable to Casualty management and to members of the OPL department, Hurlburt adopted a novel approach. She made the consultants "at risk," defining their total compensation (after assessment and project design, which were on a flat-fee basis) as 5% of OPL's year-on-year increase in recoveries (net of additional costs) during the following 18 months. This was an unprecedented arrangement both for Casualty and for the consultants. The consultants welcomed the potentially enormous rewards of such a scheme, believing, in Drury's words, that Casualty represented "fertile ground in which to be successful." Nonetheless, they recognized the risks. If OPL's productivity failed to increase for reasons beyond their control, Doenitz and Drury would suffer directly. This was not entirely improbable. The consultants were convinced that significant productivity rises at OPL could not be effected without major technological change, but they were unsure of Casualty management's willingness to enable such change.

Despite the limited downside potential to which the "at risk" plan exposed Casualty, the company's legal department was still concerned. The lawyers feared that Hurlburt's compensation scheme would identify the consultants as Casualty employees for tax purposes. The finance department was also nervous about unusual accounting problems the scheme might create. It took Hurlburt two months to secure these departments' consent to her arrangement with MCG.

OPL employees proved somewhat easier to win over than the Casualty lawyers. Hurlburt offered a copy of the consultants' contract to any department employee who wished to see it. Most employees accepted this opportunity and read the contract, observing immediately that the "at risk" compensation arrangement identified MCG's interests with those of OPL. Hurlburt and the department manager, Scott Rosenthal, also emphasized that Doenitz and Drury were present, not to help OPL downsize, but to make it more productive.

The consultants themselves wanted to take a different approach from that exhibited by their predecessors at Casualty. Unlike previous efforts, MCG's initiative was focused on one department only, rather than diffused across the corporate spectrum. This offered Doenitz and Drury, who planned to remain on site for 18 months, the chance to develop a meaningful partnership with their client. Arriving in late 1995, the consultants knew little about the day-to-day operations of an OPL department. They were convinced that employees' input would be essential to providing them with the necessary knowledge to assess the department's needs and determined that the change process they facilitated would be participatory, not directive.

Brainstorming

From the commencement of the OPL restructuring initiative, Hurlburt, Doenitz and Drury emphasized the participation of department employees in identifying and implementing change strategies. This conviction was shared by Rosenthal, the OPL department manager. Rosenthal had joined Casualty in 1986 and managed Bodily Injury since 1992. For two years (mid-1993 to mid-1995) following Casualty's acquisition of Golden Gate Property Network, Property Damage had been managed by Joe McIntosh, who had originally administered Golden Gate's subrogation division. Following the 1995 reorganization, though, Hurlburt chose Rosenthal to head the new OPL unit.

Other senior department members often participated in the brainstorming sessions held by Hurlburt, Rosenthal and the consultants. They, too, were concerned that if associates worried about the restructuring and felt excluded from the process, they would become impediments. Paramount among employees' fears, according to their supervisors, was the suspicion that change must eventually mean downsizing. Associates, however, claimed that, while many of them were moderately concerned about the broad effects of change, few worried about downsizing. This lack of anxiety arose partly because associates believed managerial assurances that downsizing would not occur, but largely because it was obvious that the workload at OPL already far exceeded the capacity of the current workforce.

A primary objective of the restructuring team was to persuade OPL employees of the need for change. Before Hurlburt took over, OPL had no tradition of benchmarking its performance against its competitors. Most department members, therefore, were unaware of the extent to which the company's market share exceeded its share of recoveries. The results of benchmarking, which demonstrated that OPL's recoveries amounted to barely half of the sum suggested by Casualty's market share, represented a crisis. Hurlburt and Rosenthal took advantage of this crisis to illustrate the urgency of the drive to improve OPL's productivity.

All OPL associates were randomly assigned to 9 to 10 person discussion teams. The teams met weekly for at least one hour to exchange ideas and generate suggestions for change. Each team elected a captain to chair the meetings and report back to Rosenthal and the consultants. Many employees offered little input to team discussions, but others were highly vocal. Bernadette Voelker, a team captain, and other associates estimated that about half of the department's employees participated actively. Voelker described the situation: "We were given the opportunity to focus on our own process improvement. Some people were overwhelmed by that opportunity; others seized it."

Rosenthal and other managers considered that the feedback they received throughout the change process, both through the team discussion system and through informal conversations with individual associates, was instrumental in defining change goals and strategies. By talking with associates, Rosenthal said, he learned that his employees "felt they had to do everything, but didn't have the time to do anything well." Bill LePage, Lynda Brown and Shelly Wissner, all managerial-level department members, spoke with enthusiasm about their own roles in problem identification and idea development. They felt that they had worked closely with the consultants and had a significant influence on the changes in the OPL department. LePage affirmed that "any change that's been made has been a product of our own recommendations." He noted that the brainstorming sessions represented opportunities for discussion of both sweeping goal-related issues and "little problems, like [supervisors] yelling across the floor to one another and distracting the associates." Associates actively participating in the team discussions were also pleased to see their suggestions, such as file reorganization and hardware upgrades, implemented. However, when their recommendations were not taken, an explanation was seldom provided. The majority of associates interviewed also said that they would not feel comfortable approaching Doenitz or Drury with individual ideas or questions.

A New Structure

Hurlburt, Rosenthal and the consultants reorganized the OPL department into four task-based teams: Negotiation, Telephone, Written Correspondence and Recovery. By the end of 1995, the Negotiation and Telephone Units each employed 9 associates; the Written Unit, 12; and Recovery, 6. Four staff members reported directly to Rosenthal. These numbers included 7 temporary workers, concentrated principally in the Telephone and Written Units.

The Negotiation Unit handled all negotiations with third parties' attorneys. The Telephone and Written Units respectively took all calls and letters concerning OPL cases. The Recovery Unit's main function was the adjustment of Casualty's claims database to reflect recoveries made by OPL. For example, if a Casualty policyholder suffered property damage, Casualty would be obliged to pay that policyholder's claims. The payment would be entered in the insurer's mainframe system. If OPL later recovered some portion of Casualty's outlay from a third party, the Recovery Unit would go into the database and subtract the recovered amount from Casualty's payment to the policyholder.

Each unit had a supervisor, called a "team leader." The team leaders, all current department members, were selected principally by Rosenthal. Some, possessing outstanding experience or leadership skills, he recognized as "obvious choices"; others, he identified through an interview process. Chosen early in the restructuring initiative, team leaders then participated in the design and implementation of change strategies.

Associates were also assigned to their units by Rosenthal, with some input from the team leaders. Rosenthal intended the composition of the various units to reflect associates' individual skills. Choosing the Negotiation team was fairly straightforward, as certain associates already spent the majority of their time negotiating and had developed expertise in that area. Assignments to the Telephone and Written Units seemed more random. Rosenthal and the supervisors tried to place associates who were somewhat more competent in one type of communication in the corresponding unit, but the skills required for each task were very similar. Employees' own preferences were not consulted and they were never made aware of any particular criteria.

Before the official drive to increase productivity commenced, OPL had no budget for hiring temporary workers or paying overtime. Shortly after the arrival of the consultants, however, it was given such a budget. The number of temps at OPL during 1995–96 fluctuated between 7 and 15. Many of the temps stayed with the department for considerable periods. LePage attributed much of OPL's success to increased staffing and flexibility.

Wissner characterized OPL's new structure as "finally, a permanent solution, not just a 'work-around'." The other team leaders were equally enthusiastic. Brown, who had been promoted from negotiator to Negotiation team leader, was clearly pleased by the opportunity to exercise managerial skills. Her team experienced the least change, since most negotiators' jobs had already been quite specialized. Nonetheless, Brown believed that the reorganization had clarified their roles still further and streamlined the unit's operations. Wissner, Recovery Team leader, had been in a managerial role before the restructuring. She now supervised only half the number of employees that she had previously, a change which she felt offered her greater control and clearer communication. Wissner also considered that the new structure had freed her team from "extraneous tasks" like typing and basic administration and allowed team members to focus on their primary function. She herself felt less harried since the reorganization; before it, she had been one of only two department managers constantly being asked questions outside their sphere of competence. Now, she could concentrate on developing the specialized knowledge she already had, rather than attempting to become an expert in fields in which she had no background. LePage, the other pre-reorganization supervisor, agreed that it was a relief to no longer be managing dozens of individuals with multiple functions. He now worked shorter hours and "felt like things on [his] list were actually getting done." LePage could also devote time to corporate-wide issues and bring the expertise gained in those pursuits to his work in OPL. For example, he had been deeply involved in OPL's systems development and in integrating its technology with that evolving in the rest of the company.

The associates were not as uniformly overjoyed by OPL's restructuring as were their supervisors. Bernadette Voelker, a Negotiation Team policyholder with 10 years tenure in the OPL department, was one of the most positive. She explained that before the changes, OPL had always been understaffed, "operating on the finger in the hole in the dike principle." Everyone's job had been "whatever needed doing at the time." Voelker was now involved only in negotiation, while she had previously been required to process correspondence as well. With newly increased accountability and flexibility in settling negotiations, she now took "more personal pride" in achieving the most advantageous resolution of a case. Members of the Telephone and Written units were less enthusiastic, however. Joely McGathy, a Telephone team policyholder, said she missed following one case and seeing what happened to it rather than dealing merely with isolated phone calls relating to various cases. McGathy felt that her unit tended "to get more problems" than the other units and that few Telephone associates were pleased with the new structure. Kregg Baur, of the Written unit, had also enjoyed "doing a bit of everything" before the restructuring. Now, he was "not very unhappy, but definitely less happier than before." McGathy and Baur conceded that increased access to their supervisors was a benefit of the new structure. However, they considered that their performance could no longer be measured by supervisors, since they did not receive credit for resolving cases. All the associates interviewed agreed that, post-reorganization, an "it's not my job" attitude was decidedly more prevalent in the OPL department.

Teamwork

The restructuring team was concerned by what it perceived as a lack of departmental unity. As well as encouraging them to become involved in the change process, the MCG consultants hoped to shift the employees' focus away from their individual functions to the department's ultimate objectives. OPL's mission statement ("To become the premier recovery organization in the Northwest through technology and teamwork") was posted around the work environment. In an effort to clarify expectations, Rosenthal established standards of how much each employee should accomplish each day. Emphasizing the need to increase productivity, he also made dollar recovery a universal incentive. This represented only 2% of total compensation, however, and most associates did not consider it a significant motivator. Associates did, though, seem to feel that individual effort could make a true impact on OPL's progress toward its goals. They also appeared more confident that the department was capable of superior performance: Voelker said, "we now know that we can do a better job [with recoveries] than anyone outside the corporation."

Departmental unity was fostered by projects including an OPL newsletter and by social events such as cookouts and "crazy hat day." Brown stated that she had "never before been in a company where [she had] seen the kind of appreciation of people doing a good job" exhibited in the OPL department. Supervisors tried to recognize extra effort by associates. On several extremely stormy days, OPL took pride in boasting the highest proportion of employees showing up for work of any organization in its building. Managers rewarded these eager employees by ordering pizza for lunch and printing certificates of appreciation.

The consultants underscored the value of strong leadership skills and met often with team leaders during the change process. Team leaders were positive about these meetings, feeling that Drury and Doenitz used constructive criticism well and helped them focus on what they could do to ameliorate the functioning of their respective teams. LePage recalled the consultants requesting him to list the improvements he felt needed to be made in the department. When he handed them his list, Drury and Doenitz returned it to him, telling him to "actualize" the changes he had listed. The consultants also wanted the team leaders to be more creative in searching for solutions, to "think outside the box." Most of the leaders did seem to internalize this rhetoric: at any rate, they employed the consultants' phrases with relish and frequency. Team leaders were also encouraged to hold frequent team discussions. Wissner described her team meetings as "vocal" and believed that the associates she supervised now felt more comfortable expressing their opinions. Wissner asserted that significant changes had come about as a result of suggestions made in team meetings. Most of these changes were "workflow-oriented," concerning processes within the team. Questions like systems development, which required corporate cooperation, could not be resolved by the team alone.

Technology

At the time that Hurlburt inherited OPL, it was dependent on its IT supplier, ABD, to provide all the technology it needed. The department felt strongly that ABD fell short of supplying an effective case management system: OPL had no computer database recording its more than 20,000 outstanding cases. Its claims processing was done through TPS, a mainframe system which afforded little flexibility or access to detail. The OPL team knew that obtaining approval from Casualty management to change suppliers or develop its own software from scratch would be, at best, time-consuming, and at worst, impossible. So, the team determined to work around what the department already had.

Microsoft Access, a database creation application, had been provided on all OPL employees' PCs. In early 1996, Rosenthal commissioned a temporary programmer to construct an Access database that managed the outstanding cases and made that information available to all computers on the OPL network. The computerized database would allow OPL employees to manipulate case data more efficiently and rapidly. Its automatic follow-up system would facilitate customer relationships. Managers could monitor employees' productivity by observing case activity on the database. Essentially, the database would eliminate the confusion, information lags and information losses which tend to accompany a paper filing system. Possession of its own, internally-designed and operated case management system promised OPL a degree of independence from its IT supplier. This could be achieved while circumventing company bureaucracy: the OPL technology initiative did not entail a supplier change or a significant increase in expenditure, so Hurlburt and her team were not required to obtain management's approval for it. Hurlburt remarked later, "If we had had to get management's approval, we'd probably still be waiting."

By mid-1996, the OPL technology initiative was about one-third complete. Further programming of the database was scheduled to be finished by autumn. Document imaging, an essential component of OPL's metamorphosis to a "paperless environment," would be complete by the end of the year. The major task remaining was entering OPL's 20,000 outstanding cases into the new database. This was targeted for completion by mid-1997. Entering the cases was obviously necessary in order to apply the database, but it occupied a considerable portion[1] of OPL employees' time. This time might otherwise have been spent dealing with customers' needs.

Rosenthal and the restructuring team were confident that the immense effort required to establish the database was easily justified, as the new technology would enable OPL to become much more proactive about case management. Because most of its work was with the corporate-wide system, Wissner's department, the Recovery Unit, remained "stuck with" the original mainframe arrangement. However, Wissner believed that OPL's new technology, coupled with the department's increasingly aggressive attitude toward problem-solving, rendered the "huge undertaking" of modernizing her unit[2] "more doable than it ever was [before the change initiative]." Brown, the Negotiation team leader, claimed the new database was helping her to manage much more effectively, as it facilitated keeping track of settlements and monitoring individual negotiators' performance.

Employees lower on the totem pole also recognized the database's enormous potential and described its advent as a major change in their department's method of operation. Baur said, "we're all eagerly anticipating imaging," while Voelker looked forward to a time when "the most stressful aspect of my job, actually retrieving the files from the file room" would no longer be necessary. However, employees often did not exploit features of the new database. For example, many employees complained that, because their jobs no longer required them to follow a case to resolution, they never found out what happened in specific situations. However, few employees had used the database to follow up on cases which interested them. Employees were also critical of the lack of time which had been allotted to organize and enter all the case files into the database. Voelker considered this the most significant defect of the restructuring effort.

Results

The restructuring team's initial target had been to expand recoveries by one-third before the MCG consultants were scheduled to depart in May 1997. By the end of 1996, it was apparent that OPL would end up increasing recoveries considerably more than this target. Recoveries in 1994 had been valued at $55 million; in 1995, this number rose to $70 million. Rosenthal estimated that recovery activity in 1996 would be around $105 million, nearly twice 1994's figure. According to him, OPL's rate of improvement was constantly increasing. Casualty management was so impressed that it gave Hurlburt even more departments to supervise.

Most department members were content with OPL's reorganization. When asked if anything could have been done better, the only item supervisors mentioned was more effective communication with associates to avert fears of redundancies. Associates, while often somewhat dissatisfied with the effects of the changes on their own jobs, tended to feel that the change process itself had been fair and efficient. They also recognized the necessity of changes to improve productivity. The team units were working cohesively and seemed to be developing a sense of group identity. When two team leaders left Casualty in mid-1996, team members took the initiative of interviewing potential replacements and identifying candidates who harmonized with their own styles of work.

The consultants were also pleased by the results of their work. Doenitz attributed much of OPL's success to a "paradigm shift": employees viewed their own and their department's roles from a new perspective. They now felt "empowered to go ahead and do whatever needed to be done" without waiting for orders from their superiors. Drury observed the team leaders becoming more effective and adventurous managers, taking the initiative in changes within their areas. The consultants expected that by the time they left, continuous improvement would be a fact of life in the OPL department.

A New Dilemma

OPL had now become so efficient that it had the potential to market its services as a recovery organization. Casualty's competitors wanted to take advantage of OPL's flexibility and cost structure. Pegasus, a large Oregon-based insurance company, had offered to contract with Casualty to use OPL's database for its own subrogation. This represented a wonderful opportunity for OPL to expand its revenues, in which its parent shared. Since it would not have to program an entirely new database in order to process another company's claims, the Casualty department could also benefit from economies of scale. The more cases it processed, the lower its cost per case would be.

However, if OPL subrogated Pegasus' claims, it might well be in competition with the needs of its parent, Casualty. By providing subrogation services to other insurers, OPL would cost Casualty the competitive (and marketing) advantage of exclusive access to the "West's premier recovery unit." Rosenthal believed that this concern did not represent a major obstacle. He pointed out that OPL could focus on offering its external services to non-Casualty insurers, such as health insurers. Thus, it would not be aiding firms in direct competition with Casualty. Hurlburt also believed that if OPL priced its services correctly, it could easily compensate by additional revenue for any loss of competitive advantage.

There was another issue, too: the OPL negotiators had developed close relationships with the ouside lawyers with whom they worked. On one occasion, Hurlburt was mystified to receive a memo from the sales department thanking her for OPL's help in landing a large account. In the process of negotiating an excellent settlement, an OPL negotiator had also managed to convince the law firm he was bargaining with to adopt Casualty as its malpractice insurer! This kind of cozy relationship would be jeopardized if OPL negotiators represented companies other than Casualty.

Nonetheless, department members were eager to expand the use of their winning formula. By 1997, most expected OPL's future to include work for insurers beyond its parent and Hurlburt and Casualty's Board of Directors was considering spinning the department off as a wholly-owned subsidiary. Should they give OPL the opportunity to pursue glory as an independent processing organization or would the costs to its corporate parent be too high?

NOTES TO CASE

1. Approximately 1½ hours per employee per day.
2. For example, by creating an interface between the TPL and corporate systems, which might allow the Recovery unit to perform its work within the TPL database.

Case 2.5

VANDELAY INDUSTRIES, INC.

(Andrew McAfee)

On a Monday morning in January, 1996, Elaine Kramer was in her Philadelphia office catching up on e-mail. She had been in Minneapolis the previous week for a series of meetings between her firm, Deloitte & Touche Consulting Group/ICS, and the executives and plant managers of Vandelay Industries Inc., a major producer of industrial process equipment. The week had ended with the two companies signing a contract to work together on a large information systems implementation project.

Her phone rang.

"This is Elaine Kramer."

"Hi, Elaine, this is George Hall. I manage Vandelay's Dunbarton plant; we met at the project kick-off meetings last week."

"Oh, yes—how are you, George? I really enjoyed the presentation on your pull-based manufacturing project. You guys have generated some really impressive results. What can I do for you?"

"I was just wondering if I could start getting my people signed up for training on the R/3 system. I know it's early, but we're really eager to dig in here. Your presentation got a lot of people excited about getting rid of our plant's old mainframe. We want to get an R/3 team together so we're ready to work on the system as soon as it's installed at Dunbarton."

"Well, we haven't started putting training schedules together yet . . ."

"Well, keep us in mind when you do. Like I said in the presentation, we're a bunch of tinkerers, and that's what has helped us improve so much over the past few years. We think R/3 can really help us past some of our current roadblocks, so we're eager to start experimenting with it."

"OK, let me get back to you once we're further along with training plans."

After Kramer hung up the phone she mentally replayed the conversation; it raised an issue that had been in the back of her mind since the meetings. How much should the plants in the network be encouraged to modify their local set-up of the new computer system once it had been installed?

Project Background

Vandelay had decided in 1995 to implement a single Enterprise Resource Planning (ERP) information system throughout the corporation. The firm had chosen the R/3 system from SAP AG, a German company that was the market lead in ERP products. Vandelay hoped that the R/3 implementation would end the existing fragmentation of its systems, allow process standardization across the corporation, and give it a competitive advantage over its rivals.

Vandelay managers realized that putting R/3 in place would be an enormous effort, of which installation of hardware and software was only a small part. For help with all aspects of the project, from the technical details of an ERP system to widespread business practice changes, Vandelay had engaged the Deloitte & Touche Consulting Group/ICS. ICS assisted clients in managing fundamental changes of the kind entailed by an ERP system, and had significant expertise with SAP's R/3 product.

Kramer, who had been with the firm for over 5 years, had been chosen to lead the project. At the meetings in Minneapolis she had been impressed with Vandelay's enthusiasm for the project. The plant managers seemed especially excited; many of them had said that they considered their existing information systems an impediment, rather than an aid, to efficient production.

George Hall certainly seemed pleased at the thought of R/3 in his plant, but Kramer was not entirely calmed by their conversation. Hall had evidently assumed that Dunbarton would be free to modify the system at will; Kramer knew that this would not be the case. She wondered how to respond to his request for training, and how to let him and the other plant managers know that all decisions about R/3 were not under their control.

VANDELAY INDUSTRIES

Company Background

Vandelay Industries, Inc. was an $8B corporation that manufactured and distributed industrial process equipment used in the production of rubber and latex. The company was founded in Minnesota during World War II; its initial products proved important on the Home Front, enabling the much greater productivity required by the war effort. From the beginning, Vandelay's offerings were known for their design quality and innovative engineering; company lore held that this was because wartime rubber shortages necessitated precise, wasteless production.

Markets for Vandelay products were extremely healthy throughout the following decades, and the firm steadily expanded, partly by building new sites and partly by acquiring smaller firms[1]. The company also steadily expanded its product lines, eventually supplying a range of process industries. Vandelay plants were treated as revenue centers and typically were allowed a high degree of independence, provided that they maintained acceptable profit margins. At its peak, the company employed 30,000 people and manufactured on four continents. Employees tended to remain with Vandelay for a long time, taking advantage of generous pay and benefits and a stimulating work environment.

The company began to experience difficult times beginning in the mid-1980s as a result of market shifts and severe competitive pressures. Three strong foreign competitors emerged, offering less expensive alternatives in many of Vandelay's product lines. These machines typically did not include all of the features of the comparable Vandelay product, but were substantially (20–30%) cheaper. As a result, the American company's traditional emphasis on features and customizability became a liability. Its manufacturing operations were never intended to be low cost, but its products could no longer command a large price premium once suitable substitutes were available. The firm's traditionally long lead times also became a problem; the new entrants could fill customer orders much more quickly.

Vandelay fought hard over the next ten years to learn new technologies and new ways of doing business. It adopted lean production methods, rationalized its product lines, and introduced new, simpler and cheaper machines. It also closed three plants, leaving eight in operation[2] and had the first layoffs in its history, reducing its total headcount to 20,000 people. Many of these efforts paid off, and the company returned to profitability in the mid-1990s.

During this decade of realignment, Vandelay's executives realized that they would have to accord much higher priority to manufacturing and order fulfillment in order to further drive down costs. They also needed to become quicker; the company's new machines were popular, but still had longer lead times than competitors. Internal investigations had shown that actual manufacturing and material movement times accounted for less than 5% of total lead times experienced. Large parts of the remaining time, Vandelay found, were devoted to information processing and information transfer steps. This was partly because the computer systems in use across the firm to guide order fulfillment and production activities were poorly integrated, and in some cases, completely incompatible.

Information Systems

Each plant had selected its own system for manufacturing resource planning (MRP), the software that translated customer demands into purchasing and production requirements. In addition, many sites had also installed specialized software to help with forecasting, capacity planning, or scheduling. Information systems for human resources management had also been selected individually. There was a single corporate financial information system, to which each site had built an interface for automatic electronic updates, but this was the only example of corporation-wide systems integration.

As Vandelay reviewed its operations, it uncovered several examples of how this patchwork of information systems added time and expense to the production cycle. Examples included:

- *Scheduling:* The plants' dissimilar manufacturing software often made integration across sites difficult. For example, one of Vandelay's American plants made a variety of machined and stamped metal parts which were used by the other North American assembly sites. This plant used an outdated MRP system which required all data to be entered manually. Requirements from all downstream users were keyed in at the beginning of each week, a task that required almost a full day. No other inputs were allowed during the week, and the plant was deluged with complaints about its responsiveness.
- *Forecasting:* Vandelay's European planning group used a forecasting program which grouped all demand for an item into one monthly "bucket." Plants were then free to decide when to build the product within that month. Customer orders, however, usually requested delivery within a specific week. If these requests did not line up with the month's production plan by chance, late shipments resulted.
- *Order management:* Customer orders were taken manually by an inside sales organization in each region (North America, Europe, and Asia), then routed via fax to the appropriate plant where they were keyed in to that site's order entry system. Faxes, and therefore, orders, were sometimes lost.
- *Human resources:* When a Vandelay employee transferred from one location to another, her complete employee record had to be copied. Because of incompatible human resources software, this data often had to be manually re-entered. In addition to being redundant and time-consuming, this meant that the confidentiality of the information was difficult to guarantee.
- *Financials and accounting:* The manufacturing software used within most Vandelay plants was not integrated with the site's financial package, so information such as labor hours charged to a job,

materials purchased, and orders shipped had to be entered into both systems. This introduced potential for error, and necessitated periodic reconciliations.

Business Practices

Vandelay sites' operations practices were as varied as their information systems. There was no uniformly recognized "best" way to invoice customers, close the accounts at month end, reserve warehouse inventory for a customer's order, or carry out any of the hundreds of other activities in the production process that required computer usage or input. At the kick-off meetings, Kramer had heard "horror stories" about flawed processes uncovered by plant managers. Some of them were quite vivid:

> "I walked down to my receiving dock a few days ago and just watched what happened each time a supplier's truck unloaded. First, our receiving guys would verify the quantities. Then they'd leave the boxes on the dock and take the packing lists over to a terminal for our quality system. If it said that the part needed incoming inspection, they'd move the boxes over to quality control. If there was no inspection, they'd take the list over to another terminal and enter the received quantities into the purchasing system, then they'd move the boxes and the list over to stores. Meanwhile, the stores guy is working through a backlog of these boxes, entering the stockroom bin numbers of all the items he's shelved. And if there's a discrepancy in the packing list or a high-priority item hits the dock, things get *real* complicated."
>
> Teri Buhl, Fort Wayne (IN) plant manager

> "When I started at the plant last year, I couldn't believe how work got scheduled on the floor. They'd started a system of putting a green tag on high priority workorders to flag that they should be at the head of the queue. That worked for a while, but then someone decided that *really* high priority jobs should get a red tag. You can guess how it went from there. By the time I got there, no job had a prayer unless it had some kind of tag on it and there were at least a half-dozen color combinations in play. Our starting queues looked like Christmas trees."
>
> Alain Barsoux, Marseilles plant manager

To alleviate these problems with systems and practices, Vandelay decided to purchase and install a single ERP system, which would incorporate the functions of all the previously fragmented software.

The company would also use this effort as an opportunity to standardize practices across sites.

Vandelay saw one other major benefit from an ERP system: gaining visibility, in a common format, over data from anywhere in the company. The company anticipated that once the software was in place, authorized users would be able to instantly see relevant information, no matter where it originated. This would provide the ability to coordinate and manage Vandelay sites more tightly than ever before; plants could see what their internal customers and suppliers were doing, and network-level managers could directly compare performance across locations.

After a review of leading ERP vendors and implementation support consultants, Vandelay decided to purchase SAP's R/3 software and put it in place with the help of Deloitte & Touche Consulting Group/ICS.

THE SOFTWARE VENDOR: SAP

Company Background

SAP AG was founded in 1972 in Walldorf, Germany, with the goal of producing integrated application software for corporations. These applications were to include all of the activities of a corporation, from purchasing and manufacturing to order fulfillment and accounting. SAP's first major product was the R/2 system, which ran on mainframe computers. R/2 and its competitors came to be called Enterprise Information Systems (EISs). Within manufacturing firms they were also known as Enterprise Resource Planning (ERP) systems to reflect that they incorporated and expanded on the functions of previous MRP systems.

SAP was one of the first ERP vendors to realize that powerful and flexible client-server computing technologies developed in the 1980s were likely to replace the established mainframe architectures of many large firms. The company began work on a client-server product in 1987 and released the R/3 system in 1992. R/3 capitalized on many of the advantages of client-server computing, including:

- *Ease of use.* Client-server applications often used personal computer-like graphical user interfaces. They also ran on the familiar desktop machines used for spreadsheets and word processing.
- *Ease of integration.* The flexible client-server hardware and operating systems could be more easily linked internally (to process control

equipment, for example) and externally, to Wide-area networks and the Internet.

- *Scalability*, or the ability to add computing power incrementally. Companies could easily expand client-server networks by adding relatively small and cheap machines. With mainframes, computing capacity had to be purchased in large 'chunks.'
- *More open standards.* The operating systems most used for client-server computing were non-proprietary, so hardware from different manufacturers could be combined. In contrast, most mainframe technologies were proprietary, so a mainframe purchase from IBM or Digital locked in the customer to that vendor.

As Figure 2.1 shows, R/3 was extremely successful and fueled rapid growth at SAP. By 1995, the firm was the 3rd largest software company in the world (see Exhibit 2.15). Expansion was especially rapid in North America, where SAP went from a very small presence in 1992 to $710M in sales in 1995. This success was due to several factors, including:

- *Client-server technology.* As large firms moved from mainframe to client-server architectures in the early 1990s, the R/3 system was available to them. Meanwhile, many suppliers of existing "legacy systems" did not have client-server applications ready for market.
- *Modularity, functionality, and integration.* R/3 functionality included financials, order management, manufacturing, logistics, and human resources, as detailed in Exhibit 2.16. Prior to the arrival of ERP, these functions would be scattered among several systems. R/3

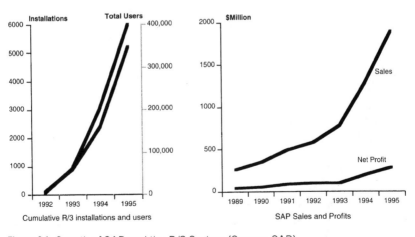

Figure 2.1 Growth of SAP and the R/3 System (Source: SAP)

Exhibit 2.15 World's largest software companies

Vertical and Cross-Industry Applications Worldwide Software Revenue, Top 10 Vendors Worldwide, 1993–1995 ($M)

Company	1993	1994	1995	1995 % Share	1994 % Share	Growth 1994–95 (%)
Microsoft	1,246	1,688	2,484	6.2	4.8	47.1
IBM	1,647	1,607	1,711	4.3	4.6	6.5
SAP AG	414	843	1,322	3.3	2.4	56.9
IBM/Lotus	281	401	540	1.4	1.1	34.6
Computer Associates*	431	425	478	1.2	1.2	12.5
Autodesk	351	392	455	1.1	1.1	16.1
Novell	603	477	443	1.1	1.4	−7.1
Adobe Systems	324	387	438	1.1	1.1	13.3
Cadence Design	336	391	435	1.1	1.1	11.2
Siemens Nixdorf	350	365	361	0.9	1.0	−1.1
All other vendors	24,238	27,895	31,240	78.1	79.9	12.0
Worldwide solutions revenue	30,273	34,930	39,989			14.5

* Includes revenues of Legent Corp. for entire year

Source: International Data Corporation, 1996

integrated all of these tasks by allowing its modules to share and transfer information freely, and by centralizing all information in a single database which all modules accessed.

• *Marketing strategy.* SAP partnered with most large consulting firms. Together, they sold R/3 to executives as part of a broader business strategy, rather than selling it to Information Systems managers as a piece of software.

R/3 Usage: Transaction Screens and Processes

On a user's machine, R/3 looked and felt like any other modern personal computer application; it had a graphical user interface and used a mouse for pointing and clicking. Users navigated through R/3 by moving from screen to screen; each screen carried out a different transaction. Transactions included everything from checking the in-stock

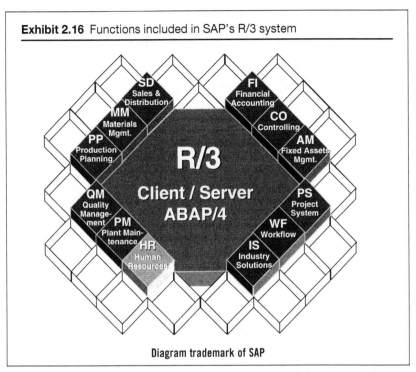

Exhibit 2.16 Functions included in SAP's R/3 system

Diagram trademark of SAP

status of a component to changing an assembly's estimated cost; Exhibit 2.17 gives an example of a transaction screen.

A full SAP implementation, including all standard functions, incorporated hundreds of possible transactions. Most common business processes included multiple transactions and cut across more than one functional area or software module. Figure 2.2 outlines the process of taking a customer order, and shows the SAP modules involved at each step. It shows that without ERP this process could involve three separate information systems—Sales and Distribution, MRP, and Accounting and Financials. With R/3, each step would require a different transaction screen, but they would all be part of the same system. They would thus be sharing and updating the same information. This elimination of redundant entry and "hand-offs" between applications was one of the chief advantages of ERP systems.

R/3 Usage: System Configuration

Configuration Tables
Although R/3 was intended as a "standard" application that did not require significant modification for each customer, it was still necessary

Exhibit 2.17 Sample SAP screen

Create Standard order: Overview - Single-Line Entry	_ 8 X

Sales document   Edit   Overview   Header   Item   Environment   System   Help

Business data-item	Business data-header	Schedule lines	Pricing	Partners

Sold-to party	customer1		
Purch. order no.	test order	Purch. ord. date	05/27/1996
Req. deliv. date	T 05/27/1996	Pricing date	05/27/1996
Sales order		Net value	0.00

All items

Item	Material	Order quantity	UoM	Description
	testpart	100		

SDB [1] i:mko.dec   OVR 06:09PM

© 1996 SAP America, Inc.

to configure the system to meet a company's specific requirements. Configuration was accomplished by changing settings in R/3 configuration tables.

R/3's approximately 8000 tables defined every aspect of how the system functioned and how users interacted with it; in other words, they defined how all transaction screens would look and work. To configure their system, installers typically built models of how a process should work, then turned these into "scripts," and finally translated scripts into table settings. For example, after writing a script that defined how a new customer order would be entered, Vandelay would know whether the order taker should have the ability to override the product's "price" field on the order entry screen.

During an implementation, this configuration activity had to be replicated for all relevant processes and required a great deal of time and expertise. People who were adept at this work, and who understood the impact of each table change, were a feature of every R/3 implementation. Kramer would be relying on several of them at ICS to work closely with the Vandelay project team.

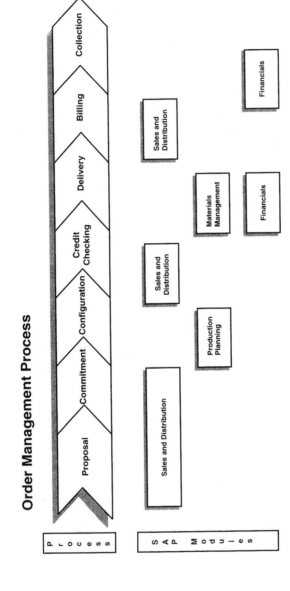

Figure 2.2 SAP modules involved in a single business process (Copyright ICS, 1995)

Added Functionality

Although the R/3 system was generally recognized to contain more functionality than its competition, it typically could only satisfy 80–95% of a large company's specific business requirements through standard configuration table setting work[3]. The remaining functionality could be obtained in four ways:

• Interfacing R/3 to existing legacy systems
• Interfacing R/3 to other packaged software serving as "point solutions" for specific tasks
• Developing custom software that extended R/3's functionality, and was accessed through standard application program interfaces
• Modifying the R/3 source code directly. (This approach was strongly discouraged by SAP and could lead to a loss of support for the software.)

THE CONSULTANTS: DELOITTE & TOUCHE CONSULTING GROUP/ICS

Company Background

Deloitte & Touche Consulting Group (the Consulting Group) was the consulting division of Deloitte & Touche, one of the 'Big 6' audit and tax firms and the product of the 1989 merger of Deloitte, Haskins & Sells and Touche Ross. Consulting had been an important activity for the predecessor firms since the 1950s, and accounted for over 15% of total Deloitte & Touche revenues by the mid-1990s[4]. In 1995, the Consulting Group generated slightly over $1 billion in revenues and employed 8,000 professionals in more than 100 countries.

Deloitte & Touche Consulting Group/ICS was the subsidiary of the Consulting Group which specialized in SAP implementations, offering complementary software products, education and training, and consulting in business process reengineering and change management. ICS was one of the largest worldwide providers of SAP implementation services and one of the most rapidly growing sections of the Consulting Group, employing over 1300 professionals on four continents in 1995.

ICS had developed a considerable knowledge base in SAP systems; over 50% of its consultants had more than two years experience with the products. ICS had won SAP's Award of Excellence, which was based on customer satisfaction surveys administered by the software maker, every year since its inception. SAP had also named ICS as an 'R/3 Global Logo Partner.' According to SAP[5],

> "The aim of these partnerships is to establish, extend and enhance R/3 expertise. In order to keep these logo partners up to date with the latest developments, SAP maintains very close contact with them, providing an intensive flow of information and offering the following services:
>
> • an R/3 System for internal training;
> • regular R/3 logo partner forums, workshops and training sessions;
> • access to SAP InfoLine, SAP's internal information system;
> • second level support from SAP Consulting, including the consultant hotline."

ICS professionals ranged from general management consultants to SAP specialists. The specialists focused on a functional or technical area of SAP and worked as, for example, experts on the Materials Management functions or programmers in the systems' native ABAP/4 language. Management consultants, meanwhile, had experience with process re-design, systems implementation, change management, or project management. More senior personnel often combined both types of skills.

Technology-Enabled Change

ICS consultants had adopted a common set of principles for leading large-scale change in a firm. According to Kramer:

> "Change occurs at several levels in an organization: strategy, process, people, and technology. Depending on the particular client situation, there are two approaches which can be taken. The first is 'clean sheet,' where all four dimensions of organizational change are explored without constraints. The second is 'technology-enabled change.' In this situation, the primary technology is selected early in the process and more strongly influences the other three dimensions of strategy, people, and processes, but still enables significant overall business change. The introduction of powerful, flexible, enterprise-wide solutions such as SAP is driving this approach as clients are looking to concurrently replace mainframe legacy systems and achieve significant operating improvement.
>
> The 'right' approach to change is determined based on the

client's situation. In Vandelay's case, the latter approach is more appropriate since they have already made the decision to go with SAP. To guide a client through all phases of implementation, ICS uses a structured approach tailored to the client's situation. This methodology captures the collective learning of the practitioners and creates a roadmap for the SAP implementation."

Figure 2.3 illustrates how ICS viewed the difference between the "technology-enabled" and "clean sheet" approaches to process redesign.

THE VANDELAY PROJECT

Vandelay management projected that the implementation would take 18 months and require the full-time efforts of 50 people, including consultants (both process redesigners and SAP specialists) and employees, as well as part-time involvement from many employees at each site. The total budget for the project was $20 million, including hardware, software, consulting fees, and the salaries and expenses of involved employees. Based on her prior experiences, Kramer felt that the time-line and budget were very aggressive for the scope of the implementation; she wondered whether all of the elements were in place to achieve the desired change.

R/3 software was to be implemented at Vandelay's eight manufacturing sites and four order entry locations[6], and at the corporate headquarters in Minnesota. The plant installations would take the longest; each one would require a lengthy preparation period to align its operations with the new business practices. Kramer estimated that two-thirds of all Vandelay employees would need training on how to use the new system, with the amount of training required ranging from one day for casual users to two weeks for those who would use R/3 heavily in their jobs.

Initially, the project team would focus about 80% of its effort on designing the "to be" process model of the organization, and 20% on issues relating to the system implementation. This reflected the fact that the project would begin by establishing the need for business change and setting performance targets, rather than installing software. In the later phases of the implementation the required mix of consulting skills would shift to deeper SAP expertise. During the activities of system configuration, testing, and delivery, the emphasis would be reversed; 80% concentration on SAP implementation, 20% on process design.

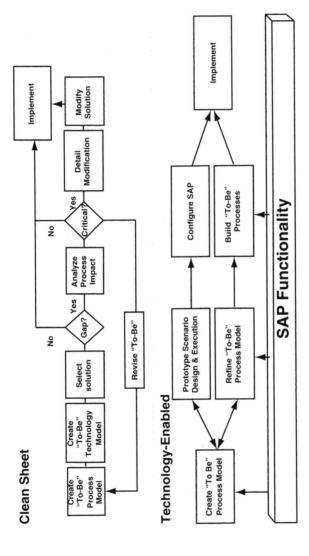

Figure 2.3 ICS's view of two models for business process re-design (Copyright 1995, ICS)

Team Structure

As Kramer put it:

> "A project like this one requires a variety of skills. I think the most important are project management ability, SAP expertise, business and industry understanding, systems implementation experience, and change leadership talent. We'll need to field a joint client/consultant team with the right mix of skills at the right time."

Vandelay and ICS had decided to use two teams for managing the project. While senior management on the steering committee would decide strategic issues relating to the implementation, Table 2.1 shows that the project team would be responsible for the bulk of the decisions made, and for the ones which determined how the system would actually work. For this reason, Kramer was eager to structure this team correctly.

Kramer's experience had shown her that there were two basic ways to select participants for the project team. She could simply present a list of the required skills and characteristics for team members to senior-

Table 2.1 Vandelay Project Team Structure

Team name	Team composition and time commitment	Issues addressed by team	% of total issues addressed by team
Steering Committee	Division VPs 8 people, meeting monthly	*Business Strategy*, e.g., sequence of site installations, planned changes in mfg. strategy.	5%
Project team	Operations employees, e.g., planner/buyers, financial accountants: 20 people, full-time*.	*Implementation specifics:* e.g., rules for reserving inventory for a customer order, horizons for planning and scheduling.	95%

* Includes only client business operations team members; does not include consultants, IT resources, or other staff for project activities such as testing, training, and documentation.

level management and ask them to nominate and approach the people who they felt would be best for the job. Alternatively, she could mandate that the team contain at least one representative from each of Vandelay's implementation sites around the world. While this approach might sacrifice some quality and depth on the team, it could also help to ensure that each site would have a project champion from the outset.

Managing Change

Selecting the best development team was only one of Kramer's considerations as she prepared to dig in on the Vandelay engagement. She had led ERP implementations before and was aware of the challenges involved in assisting a large organization as it attempted to change and standardize its practices. She placed these challenges into a few categories:

Centralization vs. Autonomy

There was no way to involve all users in the decisions that would affect them and their jobs. This could create a strong temptation for people to second guess these choices, and to alter the system that was delivered to them. This was especially true at Vandelay, which had a strong tradition of encouraging innovation and autonomy among its employees, as George Hall had demonstrated. Should this tinkering be encouraged, or should systems and processes be "locked-down" as much as possible? Could Kramer and her teams be confident that their decisions were the right ones throughout Vandelay? If so, should processes be tightly centralized and controlled, and tinkering (and therefore possible innovation) strongly discouraged? If not, what was the point of the long and thorough development and implementation cycle? Kramer had a strong bias toward "input by many, design by few," but how could she put this rule into practice?

She knew that this issue was particularly important for global companies like Vandelay. Just as cultures and currencies varied across countries, so did standard business practices, outlooks, and relationships between customers and suppliers. The implementation team would have to be sure that any universal processes did not run afoul of local ones.

A closely related question concerned standardization on externally defined "best practices." Much of the consultants' expertise came from their previous engagements; they knew what had worked and what hadn't for other clients. In addition, SAP's standard capabilities were the result of the firm's accumulated knowledge about the requirements for ERP software. There was thus a set of outside practices involving systems, operations, and processes that could be used at Vandelay. Kramer wondered how they should be incorporated into the project—were they a starting point or the final word?

Kramer could already see one area where plants would have to give up some of their autonomy. R/3 required that each item have a single, unique part number, and Vandelay executives wanted common part numbers across all sites so they could see accurate consolidated information about production, orders, and sales. Each plant, however, had developed its own internal part numbering system over time. Replacing these schemes would be a major effort, involving everything from stock-room storage bins to engineering drawings to part stamping equipment. In addition, plant personnel would have to forget the previous numbers, which they often knew by heart. Kramer saw that part number standardization would be part of the Vandelay R/3 implementation, that the plants would probably resist it, and that they would have no choice in the matter.

Change Agents and Organizational Inertia

Kramer also knew from experience that large implementations went best when a critical mass of early leaders—people who were enthusiastic about the work of change and who were respected within the firm—had been built. She also knew, however, that even with committed change agents in place, most people did not completely accept a new system until they really believed that it was inevitable. She found this paradoxical; companies committed substantial resources up front and stated clearly that the new system was a given, but most employees remained skeptical for a long time. Why was this, and what could she and her early movers do about it?

Software

Although R/3 had broad capability, there would be situations where it would not exactly fit the desired Vandelay process design. Kramer had observed three primary alternatives to addressing this situation:

1. Change the business process to match the capabilities of the software
2. Interface R/3 to another package or custom solution
3. Extend the R/3 system to precisely match the business requirements

What guidelines should she follow in selecting among these options?

Kramer knew that she would have to get back to George Hall soon about training for his site, but she was unsure what to tell him. If his people weren't allowed to experiment with the system as much as they wanted, would his enthusiasm for the project turn into hostility?

NOTES TO CASE

1. Half of all new Vandelay sites from 1945 to 1985 were bought rather than built.
2. Four in North America, 2 in Europe, and 2 in Asia.
3. According to an SAP estimate.
4. "Professional Service Trends: Deloitte & Touche" Dataquest® report, February 25, 1994.
5. From SAP Web site. http://www.sap.com. Download 3/1/96.
6. Order entry locations: 2 in North America, 1 in Europe, and 1 in Asia.

Part 3

Data Gathering, Analysis, and Engagement Management

Introduction

Case 3.1

Bob Baker: MBA Student and Internal Consultant
(Larry Greiner, University of Southern California)

Case 3.2

Integron Incorporated
(David Upton, Michelle Jarrard, and Laurie Thomas)

Case 3.3

Deloitte & Touche Consulting Group
(David Upton and Christine Steinman)

INTRODUCTION

Consulting services are often delivered by firms using their own unique concepts, models, and methodologies. These different approaches have been developed by consulting firms not only to analyze and solve substantive problems but also to achieve competitive advantage through branding their particular approaches. Many firms within the consulting industry have been successful in developing conceptual models that have later turned into well-established brands such as the Boston Consulting Group Portfolio Matrix.

The five major practice areas also differ significantly in their commonly employed data gathering methods and analytical frameworks.

As Greiner and Poulfelt's book[1] indicates, the strategy and organization specialization typically relies heavily on interviews and economic data, while marketing consulting makes heavy use of surveys, focus groups, and statistics. The practice areas also vary in their different analytical models for framing problems and proposing solutions. For instance, strategy and organization consultants might use a systemic model, such as the McKinsey "7S" approach, for understanding the degree of fit between strategy and organization, or operations management consulting might use a work-flow model for an analysis of the value chain, and then turn to "just-in-time" solutions.

The first of three cases in Part 3, *Bob Baker: MBA and Internal Consultant*, reveals the value of interviewing as a method for gathering data, as well as the use of a simple model devised by the consultant to re-frame the problems at hand and thereby gain added insight for the client. This case is interesting because it is not only an operations management case but also involves an internal consultant working from within the organization, thus prompting questions about the differences between internal and external consulting. The second case, *Integron Incorporated*, involves the consultants' use of benchmarking as a method for gathering data and framing the issues in a plant setting. It raises several questions about the adequacy of benchmarking in this situation, and what other methods might have been employed.

Cutting across all five practice areas are many similarities in the ways that projects are managed. Consultants in all specializations typically work in teams, managed by a more experienced member. Team composition reflects the unique disciplines and special skills needed for a given project. These teams proceed through a fairly predictable set of phases, beginning with negotiating the proposal, data gathering, analysis, action planning, and sometimes direct involvement in implementation. Teams require a great deal of interaction within themselves so as to combine individual findings and agree on conclusions.

In the *Deloitte & Touche Consulting Group* case, the problems of managing engagements are explored. Here we find the manager of the consulting project team deeply concerned about the client's expectations for immediate positive results from an ongoing project. The case asks the student to think about effective and ineffective ways of managing consulting engagements, especially in terms of how consultants interact with each other on the project team, as well as with the client to create an appropriate and acceptable course of action.

NOTE

1.   Greiner, L. & Poulfelt, F., 2009. *Management Consulting Today and Tomor-row*, Taylor & Francis.

Case 3.1

BOB BAKER: MBA STUDENT AND INTERNAL CONSULTANT

(Larry Greiner, University of Southern California)

ABOUT THE AUTHOR

This case was prepared by Professor Larry Greiner of USC's Marshall School of Business as the basis for class discussion rather than to illustrate either effective or ineffective handling of an administrative situation. All names are disguised.

Prior to starting his second year of MBA training, Bob Baker dropped by the office of one of his first-year professors to talk with him about his summer job experience. After listening to Baker for about five minutes, the professor asked if he could record the discussion on a tape recorder. Baker agreed, and the conversation took place without notes or preparation. The interview is transcribed below.

Before entering the MBA program, Baker had worked for four and one-half years as a general foreman, production foreman and plant engineering supervisor in two plants of a chemical company in California. He also served for three and one-half years in the Navy as an engineering officer on two destroyers. Baker majored in philosophy at Amherst. At the time of the interview, he was 30 years old and married with two children. According to Baker, his decision to attend an MBA program was part of an "overall plan which hopefully would lead to my rapid rise in general management."

The first five minutes of the interview (not included here) were devoted to a brief description of how Baker obtained his summer job at a plant of Steelco, a $2 billion manufacturer of heavy duty presses and aerospace equipment. He was hired, along with five other MBA candidates, to work at the Long Beach, California plant of Steelco. Upon arriving at the plant, he was assigned to work for the Pneumonic Drive Division and its Controller, Charlie Terrell. During his first meeting with Terrell, Baker was offered four potential projects, among which Baker indicated that his primary interest was in a "computer project designed to speed up the processing of sales orders," because it sounded like an area to become "better informed about," and which "sounded important to the company's future."

Baker explained to his professor that the Pneumonic Drive Division had been in existence for only one year, but that it had already experienced a rapid growth in sales. It specialized in servo-mechanism devices, such as gear reducers, which were in heavy demand by the aerospace industry. In Baker's opinion, the division was a "marketing oriented" organization that lacked only in manufacturing facilities. All production operations were performed at Steelco's main plant, which was located a short distance from the division's offices. Baker described the main plant as a "huge job shop" designed primarily to produce large presses for forming aerospace parts. The plant also manufactured products for other Steelco Divisions, such as Pneumonic Drive, as a way of making up for a slackening demand for press machines.

Professor: Could you tell me something about your first few days there, and what struck you, and what made an impression on you, and so on?

Baker: Well, I walked into the office and everybody was very nice, and they were all interested in telling me that they had a lot of problems. And I thought that this was kind of unusual that they should want to open up . . . letting me know what all their problems were at the beginning. But it turned out that the problems that they were opening up about weren't their problems; they were problems of the factory. The factory is separate from the Pneumonic Drive division, which is principally a marketing division as it sits right now. It receives orders, and it places them with the factory, and then it deals with the customer and then the factory ships out the order. Now, it also has pricing problems, and it has a few inventory problems. It doesn't carry its own inventory and it doesn't determine how much inventory to carry. Then, in a second area, in the area of government contracts and special products, they have a great deal to do with the Engineering department that tries to design these products. And then once the factory has built the parts or the components that are required, they assemble the products. This is only in special areas. In the standard product line the factory does all this . . . the engineering, the inventory of parts, the assembly; everything is . . . ordering of raw materials . . . everything is done by the factory.

Professor: You said you were surprised that people were telling you about their troubles. You just walked in and . . . did they ask you to go around and see people?

Baker: Yes, what I did was I started out by getting involved in the sales order system and I went around trying to follow an order through the system. And I got to see a lot of people and to get a pretty good knowledge of how the company worked in a mechanical sense of the term.

Professor: Did you decide to do this yourself, to follow something around?

Baker: Well, yes, I had a choice among four projects. I looked at this one and thought it would be a good place to start because it would get me out and get me to know a lot of people. As I started around asking embarrassing questions, I was surprised at the answers. Most of the answers were in terms of, "Well, the factory can't do this for us, and we don't get any of that from the factory and we never know when the factory is going to ship the product." And what looked to be problems from their side . . . then I went over to the factory and got almost the opposite view. They were all saying, "The problem is the people over in Pneumonic Drive who never tell us anything. We never know what to do and we're always three weeks late before we get started with an order." Well, I was able somehow to keep an open mind through this a little bit.

Professor: You don't think the factory people saw you as a spy?

Baker: No, and I think this was one of the important things that I . . . I'm not quite sure how I did this but I managed to make everybody think that I was a little bit on their side. I wasn't deceitful about it; I didn't go around with two faces. But I was very careful not to criticize either side too much and to try and understand the problems of people with whom I was talking. If I was talking to the manufacturing people, I would try to see their view and try to understand what troubles they were having . . . rather than try to say, "Well, the marketing people can't live with this." I wasn't criticizing either side; I was trying to take a positive view of, "What's your problem and how can it be fixed." And in a lot of cases I think . . . just in the beginning . . . they began to see from the questions that I was asking that they had problems that didn't . . . that they hadn't thought about because they were blaming them . . . it was very easy to pass the buck to the other side.

Professor: What kinds of questions were you asking them?

Baker: Well, I was asking sort of . . . I was just trying to get deeper and deeper into the system as it worked. I tried to find out about the particulars that they were discussing . . . an order that was placed too soon . . . I was trying to find out how they thought an order got placed and what they did with it after they got the order and then just try and, I suppose, follow it through as logically as I could to what would happen. And I tried to avoid drawing conclusions but tried to let them draw their own conclusions.

Professor: What did these people know about you . . . you know, in terms of what they had heard ahead of time . . . was there any announcement or was it word of mouth?

Baker: There was a letter sent around to the department heads in the Pneumonic Drive Division explaining the four projects on which I would work, and that I was a summer project student from USC. That was all, none of the people under them knew. And most of the people I was dealing with were under them, at least in the beginning. They were under the department head level, and none of them knew who I was until I arrived on the scene and I was introduced as a summer student who was working on the sales order system. Over in the factory they knew even less. The department heads hadn't been told . . . no one had been told about my existence. So I arrived on the scene with the same spiel about being a summer student and working on projects. Also, I tried to put across the fact that I wasn't there to tell them how to run their organization, which would have been silly. But I wanted to try and find out what the organization did, and then see if there was anything I could see from an outsider's point of view that might be different.

Professor: Did they know you had access to anyone who might be able to do something about their problems?

Baker: There were perhaps only two ways . . . first, they knew I worked for Charlie Terrell. He's the controller of the company, and he's a pretty influential guy in the division. The second thing was that the first day that I arrived, and every Monday thereafter, except well it wasn't always Monday but it was supposed to be Monday, there was a department heads meeting and I went to most of these meetings. I'm sure that people noticed this and that may have been some indication, but these were the only things that I can think of that would have indicated where I stood in the organization. It didn't show, except, well, I had an office and not everybody had an office. I suppose there was a little status there. But the people in the factory didn't know even that much.

Professor: So one of the impressions that you got from going around was this blaming between the factory and Pneumonic Drive?

Baker: There was a lot of buck-passing going on.

Professor: What were some of your other initial impressions of the place?

Baker: Well, the company was behind the times in terms of . . . well, they used a full cost system that sort of hid a lot of what I thought were the relevant costs of projects. They didn't do very much planning or advanced thinking. Production control was very loose but inventory control was very good. And then, the very fact that they had these two organizations caused quite a bit of repetition. In Pneumonic Drive there was production coordination, and in the factory the same function was called production control. These people were doing the same job twice and any planning that was done was done twice because nobody in the factory got any benefit from the planning that was done in the Pneumonic Drive Division and vice versa. So I had the feeling that they were pretty far behind in terms of an organization that's ready to move out on a new product. This was a new product; it was only about 18 months old and really it only had about a year of sales on it. A few samples were out for the first six months, but it was barely beginning to build a sales volume.

Professor: Did you get the impression that people were concerned about the same things you were, or did people seem pretty self-satisfied?

Baker: No, I got the impression that the one thing that really made the organization tick was that they had come to work to catch up and to get moving. And they were all very anxious to do it. They didn't all have the same idea about what had to be done, and because they didn't get together, they were going in different directions. I think some of my bigger value to them for the summer was the fact that I served as a link between a lot of different groups, between the group at the factory and the group in Pneumonic Drive. I think that's the biggest and most obvious one. But I also served as a link between marketing and engineering, production coordination and marketing. Just by being or appearing to be a neutral, people would come to me and say, "Gee, you know, I wish we could get those guys over there to understand this." And these weren't solicitations. I hadn't said, "Well, come to me with your problems," because I didn't really feel that was my job.

Professor: How did you feel about being in this kind of neutral role, or trying to be in it? Is this something you had been in before and were accustomed to doing?

Baker: No, it was certainly not something I had been in before. I had always been, I think just by my nature I tend to be very partisan. I tend to side or associate myself with a group that I'm involved with, and any challenge that comes to the group I take personally. This was certainly not the situation in my previous job at Smith Manufacturing. Probably some of these same problems existed, but I'm sure my blinders were on there, just as much as the blinders were on some of these fellows at Steelco. In my previous job, I wasn't about to take criticism about plant operations as opposed to the engineering area or some other area. On the other hand, I think I was a little more open about my thoughts in the operations area. In other words, I wouldn't hesitate to criticize myself or someone else within operations. But if the challenge came from outside the group, then I was the first one to toot the horn. The idea of being a sort of a neutral with no home was unusual for me, that's for sure.

Professor: Did it bother you, or did you enjoy it?

Baker: It bothered me at first but I think I got to enjoy it more and more as I found that it worked. When a guy came to me with a problem and I'd listen . . . one thing that is in my nature is that I try to listen, perhaps too much. When someone comes to me with a problem, I get interested in it, and sometimes this means that I just don't have time to do what I was doing before they came to see me. But getting interested in it and doing something about it in terms of just passing this information on to somebody else and seeing that, by golly, you know, this other guy listened as well. And I knew that he was listening when he wouldn't have listened to the guy who was first bringing it up because there were lots of closed minds in the organization. If somebody from Marketing came in to tell the Production Coordination group what to do, or the Production Control group, or even the Engineering group, it was automatically wrong because Marketing thought of it. I don't mean to single out Marketing because this kind of conflict was true of a lot of the groups. So my position of being a neutral was very important, I think, in getting the information across the lines. I'd like to think that later on in the summer, as a result of some of the things that I had passed back and forth, these guys understood a little bit more about what the other half was doing. And they were a little more willing to talk about it. But at the beginning, it was very surprising to have a guy come up to me who had been working in this business for a while . . . in fact, most of the guys that were involved had been in the business for fifteen years or so at least. And they would come to me without any real reason . . . they just sort of appeared at my door and would want to talk, and they'd sit down and talk. I'm afraid that this idea sort of snowballed because I guess they saw me as a kind of tool that they could use because it seemed to get results sometimes. So more and more there would be people appearing at my door. I was surprised . . . you know, as I was just sitting there working on the sales order systems. It was very interesting but it was unusual to me.

Professor: What happened as you began to get this information? Did you put together a report?

Baker: Yes, I started working on the sales order system and probably being very analytical in trying to create a flow chart. And I was reading a book on the side about computers and there was a guy in the factory that had some computer experience and I'd done some talking with him. So, as I was really looking at this as a computer problem (very analytical, very dry), it probably seemed—at least to me—that it was getting very boring. But it did provide me with a lot of information to start. And I guess I had one other thing that really helped, and that was a set of financial reports that came out every month. And I spent a few hours in the first week trying to play with this information as if it were a case and see what kind of things I could make out of it in terms of finance, in terms of marketing. I was just playing around because I really didn't know where to go or what problems were really important and what problems weren't. After playing around with this information for awhile, I began to get a good picture of what was going on. I found later, although I didn't really know at the time . . . what was really going on in the company. I guess it was the second department head meeting that I attended where it struck me that the manufacturing manager and the marketing manager were talking about two different things. The manufacturing manager was saying that, "Gee, I'm just getting out all the product that I can get out, and it is too bad we weren't making money." And the marketing guy was saying, "Gee, we are selling all we can; it's too bad the factory isn't producing enough so we can make money." I sort of sat quietly in the meeting and thought about this. And then when I got out of the meeting, I talked to my boss about it, and I tried to point out a couple of things that I had seen in the numbers. He got very interested in my comments, and asked me to follow it up a bit. The result was that we made several different tries at trying to explain this problem in terms of numbers because . . .

Professor: What was the problem?

Baker: The problem was that the factory was unable to produce the products that marketing required. The reason behind this was probably that marketing hadn't asked for them long enough in advance so that the factory could plan and get the equipment ready, get the capacity ready. Even today I don't think the company has the capacity to meet its sales requirements because its sales are growing very fast. Back then, it was getting worse and worse, and it was hard to show this to a general manager who had been looking at sales figures going down every month. They were going down because the backlog of orders was building up behind them. And they were trying . . . they were shuffling around . . . instead of producing 100 units of all one size, they'd build five units of that size and then shift to another size because another customer needed it badly, and they were just locked into a situation where sales were bound to level off or even in fact go down. And I was trying to pinpoint this, but nobody in the organization had made the distinction to themselves between a product shipped out the door and a product sold in terms of the customer calling up and placing an order. So I started talking about shipments and orders as if they were different things, and it didn't make much sense to them but it gradually began to sink in.

Professor: You got the interest of your boss?

Baker: Yes, I got that right away. There were several times during the first few weeks when I was worried because I wasn't involved at all in the projects that we said I was going to be working on. But three different times during that period I went back to him and said, "Now look, we're not doing what we said we were going to be doing, but I think what we're doing is important . . . I just want to be sure that you understand that I'm really not working on the sales order system, or any of these projects . . . this is something different." Every week I tried to make some report . . . I don't know whether it was for me to collect my thoughts or to pass on to him, or what. It just seemed like a good idea. And in all my reports, I tried to make it obvious that I had shifted my emphasis, and I was working on something that was entirely different from what we started out doing.

Professor: How did he respond to this?

Baker: Well he responded . . . he was worried that I wouldn't have something concrete to hang my hat on at the end of the summer. He wanted me to be able to say, "Well, I went to work for Steelco and I did this, and here it is." But he was, I guess, willing to take a chance for awhile in order to get something that he thought was worthwhile. And it became obvious that there was something that you could hang your hat on very easily; in fact, to me it seemed a great deal more important than the sales order system or any of the other projects.

Professor: Now the "this" that you could hang your hat on, is it this difference between orders and shipments?

Baker: Yes, well, the first problem was to make this distinction so that people could understand that there was a difference. And the second problem seemed to be, from both sides, to determine how much we could ship in a month, or whatever period. And the third problem was to try to determine how much we were selling. Then we could say, "All right, we're not getting what we need." From there, we went on to produce a forecast which would show what we, what the people in the organization thought could be sold in the future, and from that, once again to follow it up, we tried to make a schedule of what equipment was needed, what size of a factory we needed, and did we have enough plant? We didn't know the answer when we started. So we tried to determine all the implications that we could think of along the way. And this kind of helped me a little bit in my neutral plan too, because I became an oracle of information from both sides. Lots of times, people found that they didn't have the information . . . I wasn't just a middle man, I had the answer. Perhaps these were better answers than had been around before, but none of the stuff I came up with was original. I didn't go out and do marketing research, and I didn't go out in the plant and make a time study of how much time it took to do certain operations. I took information that was already there in some form and changed it into another form that looked usable, and then tried to point out to people how it could be used, and this was the result. One of the final results was that we came to the conclusion that we didn't really have enough capacity to meet our forecasts for this year. And for next year it was going to be worse and for the year after that it was going to be even worse. We actually set up a plan to move to a new plant eventually. We worked with the facilities, the equipment and the people that we'd need. We took a big view toward what we would do, all toward setting up a new completely autonomous division.

Professor: Now, who is the "*we*" here?

Baker: Well as I told you before, I rapidly associated with the people I worked with. The "*we*", I guess, is the Pneumonic Drive Division, but it's not the Pneumonic Drive Division that exists now. It includes the manufacturing manager who works for the factory, it includes the production scheduling clerk who works in the factory, and it includes the foreman, the manufacturing engineer, as well as my boss, and the marketing department.

Professor: Were you meeting with these people as a group or were you going around to each individually and sort of gradually bringing them to some consensus about what needed to be done?

Baker: Well, mostly, we took it step by step. In other words, I started out with the marketing problems of trying to forecast what sales would be in the future and as I went through it, the word got out that this kind of information was available and the people came looking for it. That's when I got involved with the manufacturing manager who was newly appointed to the job and very anxious to find out what my information was going to say and what he should be doing about it, and the second half of the summer was almost exclusively spent in the area of facilities planning . . . how to determine what kind of facilities and what kind of organization we'd like to have in the future.

Professor: This planning . . . was it all going on sort of informally . . . and were you doing the major bulk of it and then presenting your ideas to these people?

Baker: I was asking questions and then taking their answers and trying to work it into something that looked feasible.

Professor: Did you write a report on what looked feasible?

Baker: I didn't write a formal report but I produced a ten year sales forecast, and I broke it down into different areas. Then I produced a chart trying to show how many hours of work would be required on each machine in the different years involved. Also, I estimated how much floor space was needed, and how many people were required. Then we developed charts for all of these issues and used them later in a presentation to top management about implementing the plan. But the planning itself . . . we didn't have a meeting and say, "O.K., we're going to have a planning meeting today." It came from moving from one step to another, and I guess I was the one who produced the format in terms of what steps should we go to next. I would go and talk to somebody and try to find out some answers. He might not particularly know where I was going or why I was going there, although I tried to let them know as much as I could about the background involved. But sometimes I didn't know myself until I got back and looked over what I had and knew where I was going. It involved a lot of duplication . . . if I sat down and thought very carefully just exactly where I wanted to go, I might have been able to go to one guy and ask a series of questions and come up with a series of answers, and then go to the next guy and the next guy and never go back. But the way I did it produced two results, or maybe three. First of all, I wasn't tied to a procedure that, perhaps, could have locked me into an answer that I didn't like, or not that I didn't like but an answer that wasn't the best one as I saw it at the end. The second thing was it got them interested in what I was doing . . . it got them some knowledge about what I was doing so that the answers they gave me weren't just pat answers . . . they were really interested in giving me answers that were worthwhile. Several times they'd come back and say, "You know, I've been thinking about that . . . I think there's a better answer, or there's a better way to answer it, and we should look at it this way or that way." And the other thing, of course, was that I got almost all my ideas from them, by talking with them, and trying to find out how they thought the situation worked. Then I'd go back and think about it, and then I might come back to ask another question or check to make sure, "Is this really what you mean . . . now, does this, you know, this seems to imply that we don't have enough product? Is this really what you mean? Did you really mean that we could do it this way?" I can't think of a specific example right now . . . well, I guess in the government sales forecasting area, the government marketing manager had given me a forecast for two years and then for five years and ten years. And he had given me a forecast one way for one and two and another way for five and ten. And when I was trying to develop the different categories involved, I found that I had categories for one year here and then I didn't have anything in that category for 5 and 10 years, but I had other categories for 5 and 10. So I thought about them and tried to relate the two categories, and had to go back and say, "Is this really what . . . if you meant this in this category, it seems as if you must have meant it this way in another category." And I tried to get him to agree . . . all the way along the line I tried to do this, especially in the Marketing area, to get them to agree that these are the numbers that they like the best. In fact, it got so that they were coming to me for these numbers because they had given them to me in one form and I'd spread them out into several forms, and they knew this . . . they knew what the form was so they'd come back and say, "Hey, you've got that number . . . I've been looking for a number and I think you've got it somewhere in there." So the information we had was really getting used because people knew where it was, and they knew what it was.

Professor: I was just going to say, could you tell me how all this finally worked out? You mentioned a report to top management, a new plant, and I'm getting interested in what was its final form and impact?

Baker: Sure, what we developed, and a lot of people were pushing for this . . . the factory was pushing it and the Pneumonic Drive Division was pushing it . . . and when I say "we" now, I think I mean myself and the manufacturing manager at this point, because we were talking about building a new facility. And we would each talk with the people, and they'd ask questions, and we'd answer, "Yeah, that's a good question . . . we should have thought of that before and we'll work that out." And finally, we came up with a plan that both the factory and the Pneumonic Drive Division were behind, and the general manager of the Pneumonic Drive Division and the plant manager of the factory went to the president of Steelco and made a presentation to him, using our charts and our numbers, and they agreed to obtain the money to make the plan work.

Case 3.2

INTEGRON INCORPORATED

(David Upton, Michelle Jarrard and Laurie Thomas)

> **ABOUT THE AUTHORS**
>
> This case was prepared by Professor David Upton, and MBA candidates Michelle Jarrard and Laurie Thomas as the basis for class discussion rather than to illustrate either effective or ineffective handling of an administrative situation. Names and data have been disguised.
>
> Copyright © 1995 by the President and Fellows of Harvard College. To order copies or request permission to reproduce materials, call 1-800-545-7685 or write Harvard Business School Publishing, Boston, MA 02163. No part of this publication may be reproduced, stored in a retrieval system, used in a spreadsheet, or transmitted in any form or by any means—electronic, mechanical, photocopying, recording, or otherwise—without the permission of Harvard Business School.

THE INTEGRATED COMPONENTS DIVISION (ICD)

Gary Lloyd, vice president of the Integrated Components Division (ICD) of Integron Inc., pondered over his computer as he put together his slides summarizing the benchmarking study recently completed for his newly unleashed Multichip Module (MCM) manufacturing organization. In January 1994—two months previously—his division had assumed full profit and loss responsibility for the first time, and became able to compete for business outside the Integron group.

Lloyd had commissioned the study for two reasons. First, ICD had launched several improvement programs in an effort to boost competitiveness; and Lloyd wanted the benchmarking study to guide further initiatives and to determine which improvement steps should continue to be pursued. Second, he planned to use the results as a basis for setting a new strategic direction. Lloyd knew that his team of managers was technically skilled and excited about tackling the new challenges, but he was concerned about their lack of experience in external markets. This study would be an important step in building what had once been a manufacturing cost center into an organization that could exploit its capabilities to generate new commercial opportunities.

The results of the study, however, were worrisome. They implied that the MCM organization needed to make some radical changes in order to meet prevailing market needs. Although Lloyd agreed that the MCM group had to make some fundamental changes, he had several nagging doubts and questions regarding the consultants' findings:

1. How well did benchmarking the current competition really help determine the path for developing new operations capabilities in the future? The MCM market was in its infancy, and the slate of competitors had by no means stabilized. Industry experts seemed unable to agree on an outlook; credible predictions ranged from explosive growth to complete dissolution. Lloyd worried that focusing on a goal based on current standards might leave them behind in this fast-paced, capricious industry.
2. How should ICD focus its marketing strategy? The MCM market comprised several diverse segments, and focusing on the development of one set of capabilities might preclude ICD from serving other segments as well as they could in the future.
3. Should ICD's manufacturing improvement plans focus on one element of performance, such as quality, to the exclusion of the others, such as quick-response and cost? ICD had embarked on a number of quality-improvement schemes over the years and last year had placed highest emphasis on customer-service improvement. This year ICD was implementing widespread cost-cutting initiatives.

Evolution of the Current Organization

Integron Inc. was the third largest telecommunications equipment supplier in the United States. The ICD division had its beginnings in the early 1960s when Integron developed technology for building hybrid integrated circuits. Internal demand for these circuits boomed and by the mid-1970s, five or six manufacturing plants had been built to provide much-needed capacity. At the same time, telecommunications became much more software intensive and demand for dedicated hardware slowed. Manufacturing of hybrid integrated circuits, (a technology combining digital and analog technologies) was consolidated into the single plant in Kincher Falls, Oregon. In 1990, with the formal integration of R&D and manufacturing organizations, the unit shifted from its functional reporting structure to a business unit structure as a self-contained cost center.

Because ICD had been a captive supplier to other groups within Integron, its organization was designed around the support of internal customers. Products were passed from unit to unit at cost, and the business was driven by research and the resulting technological needs in Integron as a whole. The $30 million business unit was organized on a product and customer basis, and even though R&D engineers had been integrated into the organization, there were lingering barriers between the functional areas. Demand for any given product usually evolved through informal channels of communication between the design engineers at Kincher Falls and design engineers at the "customers" (other Integron) units. Such a customer would either approach ICD's design engineers with a technical problem or ICD's design engineers would call the down-stream customers to discuss some new technological development or opportunity. If there was a match, design engineers from both units would team up to develop a product. While each new product was a result of a customized design, its technical characteristics did not change after entering production. A new product might be produced for years without significant modification. So, paradoxically, while the development group felt pressure to be agile and responsive, *manufacturing* at the Kincher Falls facility was organized for high-volumes with dedicated lines and a heavily specialized workforce.

STANDING ALONE

By the late 1980s, business units within Integron knew they would have to become independent and start to find external sources of business. In 1987, Henry Dornberg, Integron's CEO, let it be known that the 50-year-old company could no longer be managed as a hierarchical behemoth. His goal was to decentralize decision making so that operating units felt solely responsible for setting strategic direction, implementing competitive initiatives, and meeting financial hurdle rates. Although Dornberg did not specify required hurdle rates publicly, unit managers knew they would be held responsible for attaining aggressive financial results very quickly.

With the chill winds of change blowing through the company, ICD initiated several improvement programs in an effort to become more competitive in the external market. Continuous quality improvement had long been a central theme at ICD. Indeed, the business unit was part of a group winning the prestigious Skinner Award[1] for Quality in 1993. Most employees in the plant were members of at least one quality team.

In January 1994, ICD was formally converted from a cost center to a profit center. At the time of the benchmarking study, the fledgling marketing department was six weeks old, and the unit still lacked a dedicated sales force. New marketing personnel were wrestling with novel and unfamiliar issues such as billing policy, pricing, segmentation analysis, and sales strategies for external customers, most of whom were original equipment manufacturers (OEMs).

This new responsibility came to ICD at a very difficult time. First, the hybrid integrated circuits product line, the majority of ICD's revenues, was reaching maturity. These products were used by telecommunications customers—primarily a captive market. The overall market was projected to grow at just 4% per year, and Lloyd knew his Integron customers were starting to seek out external suppliers in search of a better price for given levels of performance. Additionally, the most promising growth area, the emerging multichip module market, was so new that it was astonishingly difficult to predict how large it would grow, which market segments would grow the most, and which specific substrate technology would be in highest demand.

MULTICHIP MODULES

A multichip module (MCM) consisted of several microelectronic components bonded onto a common substrate. A module began life as a substrate onto which conductive material was patterned to form circuit interconnections. Different combinations of integrated circuits or "chips," placed on the substrate formed a hybrid circuit that was capable of performing more complex functions than would be practicable on a single chip. The MCM itself consisted of several layers of hybrid integrated circuits separated by a thin-film polymer. The module incorporated passive components, such as resistors and capacitors, which provided it with functionality beyond that of existing integrated circuits.

MCMs provided cost-effective, custom solutions for technically advanced applications requiring high speeds in space-constrained systems. However, as speed requirements increased, the density of electrical components on the MCMs had also increased, causing routing problems that manifested themselves as signal delays and interference on the circuit.

There were three basic substrate types, which distinguished the various MCM families: MCM-C (Ceramic), MCM-L (Laminate) and MCM-D (Dielectric). Each family of MCM varied in terms of the solutions it offered. MCM-Cs were based on a thick-film technology substrate. The MCM-L technology was similar to surface mount technology (SMT), in that it achieved high densities and was the cheapest to produce. Finally, the MCM-D technology was the most technically advanced of the three product types. Based on a thin-film technology substrate, it was excellent for routing and density problems. MCM-Ds were also capable of working at very high frequencies, currently those above 100 MHz, as compared to printed circuit boards, which were limited to applications below 50 MHz. ICD offered products in the MCM-D class and was also working on an advanced technology product in the MCM-D category that would enable it to offer a much lower-cost dielectric solution.

THE DESIGN AND MANUFACTURING PROCESS

Product Realization

The creation of multichip modules at ICD was a process characterized by heavy early interaction between the customer and ICD applications engineers and designers. Prior to the actual bid, a team comprising customer engineers and ICD personnel determined whether there was a technical match and whether ICD had the operational capabilities to meet necessary lead times and produce the required volumes.

Next, the customers and ICD designers decided upon the technical specifications and layout of the module. Agreement regarding the specifications was acknowledged by a formal acceptance letter. This step ensured that all team members had clearly laid out their designs and product criteria. The team then embarked on a prototyping process to build and test the models and prototype batches. Throughout this process, (known to all as the product realization process, PRP), arduous functional testing was done to simulate the lot in full production with the highest possible fidelity. The customers checked the design of the sample product for their application after this first group of models had been built and tested within ICD. This step was documented with a customer model acceptance letter. The period from the original design acceptance letter until the model acceptance letter was typically four weeks.

During the final 10 week phase before volume production, the design team built an engineering pilot batch, usually a group of 10 to 20 modules that the customer would use in his or her design process (rather than simply check for functionality). This process was similar to the model process. Design changes were incorporated and the manufacturing process was fully documented to facilitate volume production. After completion of the lot, the customer again signed off with a product acceptance letter, indicating that she or he was ready to begin volume production (see Exhibit 3.1).

Volume Production

The volume production process at ICD began with either a forecasted order, generated in anticipation of a "win," or with a hard order. After the order was entered into the system, the material for the substrate was ordered. The lead time to receive the silicon was 16 weeks—a bottleneck for the entire process. The master scheduling system checked for bill of material availability and calculated available capacity in the factory. If material and capacity were available, the system automatically scheduled the build without the intervention of a planner.

Once scheduled, a route card and shop order were created and dispatched to the first step of the manufacturing process. A strong union ingrained custom-and-practice dictated very specific roles for each operator, necessitating a stable of material handlers, dispatchers, and "regular" operators. Each operator carefully documented, on the route card, his or her contribution to the process and moved the lot through the line. At the end of the process, the parts were entered via a bar code reader into the on-line tracking system, and in-process yield losses were calculated. The product was packed and shipped in a small room just next to the manufacturing area.

In the early 1990's, as part of ICD's commitment to improving its manufacturing abilities, the manufacturing area began transforming itself from a functional layout to three focused factories, each focusing on a different type of electronic packaging. Under the new system, all orders for a given product type would be produced on the same line. ICD's managers were sure this layout would help reduce manufacturing leadtimes and increase flexibility to volume demands and design

Exhibit 3.1 Product Realization Process

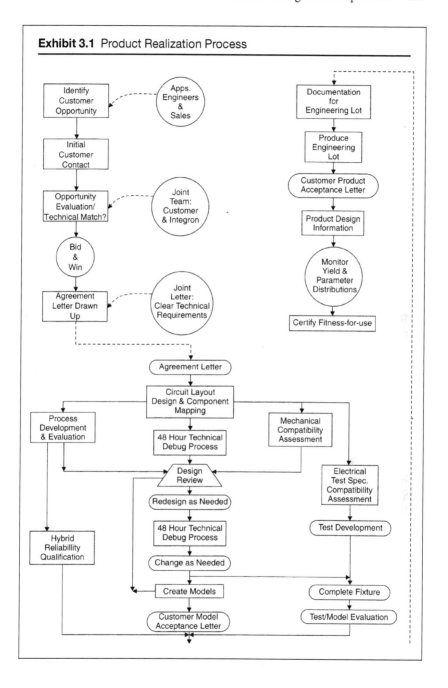

changes. The first line, for specialty products, was scheduled for completion in June 1994 (see Exhibit 3.2).

THE MARKET FOR MULTICHIP MODULES

Market forecasts for multichip modules were frustratingly varied and uncertain. One industry research organization, Dataquest, estimated the current market at $300 million and expected it to grow to $18 billion by the year 2000. However, these market size estimates had been decreasing substantially every year. Dataquest also estimated that 30% of all chips would be sold as part of a multichip module by that time. The federal government was supporting the growth of the market by deeming it a critical technology, and in late 1993, it appropriated $70 million in funding from the Defense Advanced Research Projects Agency (DARPA). There remained, however, other industry observers with less optimistic views. They believed that multichip modules would be confined to small niches, because current single-chip packaging techniques coupled with further shrinking of traditional microprocessors would offer the most cost-effective technical solution.

Not only was the overall growth of the multichip module market uncertain, but the *relative* growth of each of the highly diverse segments was also difficult to predict. There were three primary market segments: personal computers, wireless, and automated test equipment.

Personal Computers & Workstations

ICD projected this segment would grow from about $70 million in 1993 to about $1.1 billion in 1995. Although it was the largest single segment, it would most likely have the most stringent competitive requirements. Product life cycles were very short, customers demanded fast prototyping abilities, and cost pressures were tremendous. Also, most current multichip module competitors were focused on this segment. ICD had focused on the high-end workstation portion of this segment in order to leverage its leading-edge technology capabilities, but managers were certain of the need to develop a new, cheaper technology to remain a contender in this segment.

Wireless

Internal projections estimated this segment would grow from about $40 million in 1993 to $280 million by 1995. This segment currently had longer product life cycles than the PC market, and the required production runs were also longer. However, the wireless market was facing tough cost pressures and was moving to the use of "platform"

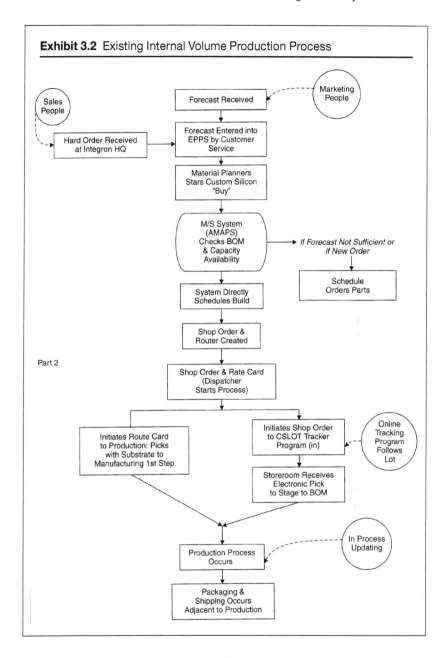

Exhibit 3.2 Existing Internal Volume Production Process

products—base products that could be modified or upgraded over time without a full-scale redesign. To compete in this segment, ICD might have to reorient its whole "custom-design" process to shift from 100% custom to a much more incremental approach.

Automated Test Equipment and Instrumentation (ATE)

The targeted areas of the ATE market included vision systems, high-speed instruments, integrated circuit testers, and circuit board testers. This market was expected to grow from $28 million in 1993 to $72 million by 1995. The high technical requirements in this segment fitted well with ICD's MCM-D technology. ICD had already acquired a prestigious external customer in this segment, and several others were in the pipeline.

THE COMPETITION

Because the multichip module market was so new, and might offer huge growth possibilities, a range of different types of competitor had been attracted, each trying to capture a piece of the market.

Vertically Integrated Systems Companies

Integron was a member of this category along with companies such as IBM, AT&T, Fujitsu, and DEC. These companies originally developed multichip module expertise to solve internal technical challenges and were now looking for external commercial opportunities to leverage their technical abilities. Each of these firms had substantial internal demand that could sustain them through early, uncertain external market developments. However, their specific market approach tactics were beginning to diverge. IBM, AT&T and Integron had kept MCM capabilities in-house, but recently, DEC had divested its capabilities into an independent company, Micro Module Systems (MMS).

Technological Competitors

Potential competitors in this group included Cypress Semiconductor, Motorola, Harris Semiconductor, Pacific Microelectronics, and Texas Instruments. These players competed primarily through their abilities with monolithic silicon, but some were entering the MCM market. The market was attractive to these companies not only as a source of growth but also as an opportunity to offset the commoditization of their core products. Many of them hoped MCMs would provide price premiums and opportunities to differentiate on the basis of performance and service. While these competitors did have expertise in packaging multiple chips in one unit, most did not yet have the capabilities to integrate passive components (individual components that enabled increased functionality of MCMs, such as capacitors and diodes) into products without the assistance of OEMs. These competitors had strong relationships with potential MCM customers through their other product offerings. Several of them were beginning to work with OEMs to build requisite skills.

Contract Assembly Houses

Companies in this segment included nChip, Flextronix, and Promex. Historically, these competitors had lacked the high-performance multi-chip module design capabilities and were thus relegated to providing manufacturing outsourcing for chip makers and systems houses (e.g., Sun Microsystems). Additionally, the MCM industry lacked specific standards, making it difficult for assembly houses to replicate modules for appropriate specifications—many of the standards that did exist had done so only tacitly, among larger companies' engineers. However, with the development of third-party software-suites of standard design tools, contract assemblers were expected to acquire design capabilities quickly. In addition, the Micro-electronics and Computer Consortium was developing industry-wide standards. If these competitors overcame their current obstacles, they would be in an excellent competitive position, because end users wanted the flexibility to use different companies' chips in any given design.

Within these competitive segments, the specific players were not solidly established and changed from week to week. At the time of the benchmarking study, several companies had exited the multichip module market while a number of others were just entering. Industry experts believed that the winning competitors would be those who had the most financial staying power and who bet upon the right technological option: either high-end, technically complex products or cheaper, standardized products. It seemed to Lloyd that everyone was simply gambling on their best hunch.

THE PROBLEM

Gambling, according to Lloyd, was not good enough for his manufacturing organization, and so he was determined to develop abilities across a broad front to cover all of the possibilities.

Lloyd knew ICD had to become externally competitive in order to grow, and the organization had developed a *to do* list to help boost its abilities (see Exhibit 3.3). He noted:

> I would love to think that there is some perfect, focused strategy out there that would ensure our success. But the fact of the matter is that we have to perform well in all aspects of our business.

Exhibit 3.3 Current List of Operations Development Programs

ME INITIATIVES	ME OBJECTIVES	OPERATIONAL PROGRAMS
IMPROVE CUSTOMER SATISFACTION	CUSTOMER SATISFACTION	1. ISO9001 Certification 2. Customer Satisfaction Planning Organization 3. DQI Program 4. Customer Service and Quality Improvement Forums 5. Customer Removal Rate 6. Customer Change Notification & Acceptance Program 7. T2 Rating
	ORDER REALIZATION	1. Manufacturing and Order Management Systems 2. Service to Customer Want Improvements
	NEW PRODUCT INTRODUCTION	1. New Product Realization Improvements 2. MCM Product Realization Process 3. FCP Migration Program 4. FCP Product Realization Process
	SKINNER DISCIPLINE	1. Skinner Assessment
INCREASE PEOPLE INVOLVEMENT	PEOPLE INVOLVEMENT	1. Quality Improvement/Task Teams 2. Support Team 3. Employee Suggestion Program 4. Customer Focus
	LEADERSHIP	1. Leadership Training 2. Management Team Initiatives 3. Performance Appraisal 4. Skills Enhancement Program
COMPLETE TURNAROUND PLAN	PROFITABLE GROWTH	1. Microelectronics Transition 2. Domestic Sales Growth 3. International Sales Growth
	FINANCIAL COMMITMENT	1. ABC Implementation 2. MCM Focus Factories 3. FCP Focus Factories 4. Expense Reduction Initiatives

TECHNOLOGY	1. MCM-L Introduction 2. Low-cost Metallization Introduction 3. New Polymer Introduction 4. MIT Introduction 5. FCP Development (12 programs)
ENVIRONMENTAL	1. CFC/CHC Eliminations 2. SARA 313 (Air) 3. Paper Recycling and Reduction

Specific strategic initiatives are typically the result of some personal vision. My old boss, Mike McManus, started to focus on quality. My current boss, Jenny Dudley, thinks we need to strengthen the voice of the customer; therefore, we have launched several customer service initiatives including a satisfaction survey.

Lloyd brought in two consultants from Hantwood Associates, to conduct a benchmarking study of the manufacturing operation for two reasons. First, he wanted to assess the progress that had been made in the various, periodic improvement initiatives in the past. Second, he wanted a method by which the manufacturing group could set operational goals for itself. The consultants, Debra Spooner and Charlene Crandall, both recent graduates of a well-known Eastern business school, initially embarked on the generic steps of a benchmarking study but quickly ran into problems as they thought about the design of this particular study.

What Attributes Should Be Benchmarked?

The consultants wanted to benchmark a specific operational attribute as it applied to a single market segment. However, Lloyd had expressed strong feelings that his organization had to build a set of general capabilities that could serve all segments. He hoped that the study would help unearth this set of required skills; thus, he did not want the consultants to narrow the study in any way.

How Should Data Be Collected?

Because there were no clear industry leaders, the consultants did not want to focus solely upon competitors' skills. They also suspected that if competitive plant tours were granted, they would be too general to be helpful. Talking to customers was a potential alternate source of information; however, ICD had very few OEM customers at the time of the study. Additionally, the consultants suspected that these OEMs had very little contact with other MCM producers. Thus, Spooner and Crandall were faced with the task of benchmarking a broad set of performance criteria across four market segments with little access to competitors.

They also recognized some risks associated with benchmarking in the multichip module industry:

- Should benchmarking be used *at all* to set long-term objectives in this fast-paced, new industry? If ICD set specific objectives based on the past performance of competitors, it ran the risk of focusing on achieving performance levels that those competitors might already have surpassed.
- Would the benchmarking process cause the firm to overreact in developing its strategy? For example, if technical capabilities were the current basis of competition and ICD focused on boosting those skills, would they be able to react if cost began to gain influence over the buying decision?

Initial Approach

Because of the problems and risks, the consultants settled on an approach that deviated slightly from a traditional benchmarking study but would help set directional targets. They developed a questionnaire (Exhibit 3.4) designed to answer three broad questions:

- Which manufacturing performance criteria most influenced a customer's buying decision?
- How well did ICD perform against these criteria?
- How well were competitors performing?

The questionnaire was given to OEMs in each customer segment as well as ICD's applications engineers. Applications engineers served as the primary interface with OEM customers, solving their applications needs and generating sales for ICD. Indeed, as ICD had no sales force, they were the only day-to-day contacts for customers. Spooner and Crandall felt that the application engineers' contribution would help compensate for the small number of customers. The consultants also wanted to compare the internal perspective of ICD people with customer evaluations. In this way, the study might reveal two types of gap: First, the difference between ICD's self-assessment and customer

---

Exhibit 3.4 Benchmarking Questionnaire

Integron Benchmarking Questionnaire

Intent of Questionnaire

Our goal in analyzing this questionnaire is to gain an understanding of customer's needs, perceptions of Integron, and perceptions of the competition in the high-end multichip module market. The results will be compiled and used to help determine Integron's strengths and weaknesses. Please take a few minutes to look over the questions. We will call to discuss your responses.

A. Overall Perception of Integron
1. Has been, or are they now, a supplier to you? — if so, what do they supply?
2. What is your general impression of their:

Criterion	Good	Average	Poor
Quality	/		
Delivery	/		
Technical Competency	/		
Price		/	
Other			

3. What is Integron's strongest capability?
   Engineering design talent and financial strength

B. Who makes the purchase decision regarding this type of technology?
1. Is it the engineer/purchasing or a coalition? *Coalition*
2. How long do you spend talking with the Integron Sales rep prior to the buy decision? *About 1 month*
3. What is the critical factor needed to finalize a purchase from Integron? *Ability to meet our design requirements*

C. What criteria are important to you when considering the purchase of MCMs? Please rank these on a scale of 1–7 (1 = not important, 3–4 of average importance, 7 critical). At the end, please rank your top five criteria by writing their rank next to them.

Rank	Criterion	1	2	3	4	5	6	7
5	Cost to you vs. other MCMs					×		
4	Cost to you vs. substitute technologies					×		
	Quality (adherence to spec.)					×		
1	Meet current technical requirements							×
	Degree of customization available				×			
	Difficulty and costs of changing from current tooling/designs: i.e., switching costs			×				
2	Length of time to get prototypes						×	
3	Length of time to get volume production						×	
	Adequate documentation of process specs.		×					
	Ability for supplier to be primary supplier			×				
	Continuing ability to offer leading-edge technical solutions			×				
	Reputation/longevity of supplier				×			
	Ability to order any lot size	×						
	Ability to produce at high volume		×					
	Other:							

(Continued)

Exhibit 3.4 Continued

D. Please rank how well you feel Integron performs on the same criteria below. (1 = poorly, 3–4 average, 7 excellently). Also, please rank Integron's five strongest characteristics.

Rank	Criterion	1	2	3	4	5	6	7
	Cost to you vs. other MCMs				×			
	Cost to you vs. substitute technologies			×				
	Quality (adherence to spec.)				×			
5	Meet current technical requirements					×		
3	Degree of customization available						×	
	Difficulty and costs of changing from current tooling/designs: i.e., switching costs					×		
	Length of time to get prototypes			×				
	Length of time to get volume production			×				
	Adequate documentation of process specs.				×			
3	Ability for supplier to be primary supplier						×	
2	Continuing ability to offer leading-edge technical solutions						×	
1	Reputation/longevity of supplier							×
4	Ability to order any lot size						×	
	Other:							
	Other:							

E. Please define what "flexibility" means to you.
   1. If you had to choose, would you prefer more customization ability or shorter lead times to receive your prototype lots?

   Shorter lead times – also engineer who returns calls promptly.

   2. If you had to choose, would you prefer lower cost & limited Engineering Change Orders (ECOs) or higher cost and ECOs?

   Lower cost & limited ECOs

F. What MCM alternatives to Integron do you know of? This can include substitute technologies as well as direct MCM competitors.

Competitor	Strengths	Weaknesses
MMS	Performance, cost	Financial stability
nChip	Marketing dept, density, thermal performance	Financial stability
Fujitsu		Cost, flexibility
IBM	Process/staff	Cost, responsiveness
AT&T	Engineering, performance	
TI		
Kyocera	Quality	Cost

G. Is your physical proximity to a supplier important?

   No.

Exhibit 3.4 Continued

H. For each criterion below, please determine Integron's strongest competitor and rank its performance on a scale of 1–7 (1 = poor, 3–4 average, 7 excellent)

Company	Criterion	1	2	3	4	5	6	7
MMS	Cost to you vs. other MCMs					/		
Kyocera	Cost to you vs. substitute technologies					/		
Kyocera	Quality (adherence to spec.)						/	
MMS	Meet current technical requirements					/		
MMS, nChip	Degree of customization available					/		
	Difficulty and costs of changing from current tooling/designs: i.e., switching costs				/			
	Length of time to get prototypes					/		
	Length of time to get volume production					/		
	Adequate documentation of process specs.?							
IBM, AT&T, Kyocera	Ability of supplier to be Primary supplier						/	
IBM, AT&T	Continuing ability to offer leading-edge technical solutions					/		
Kyocera	Reputation/longevity of supplier						/	
MMS	Ability to order any lot size			/				
	Ability to produce at high volume						/	
	Other:							

I. What are the three most important things Integron could change to improve their relationship with you?

1. Give me a single point of contact who can act as a liaison with all functional groups.

2. Lower your prices!

J. Please add any other information that would help us assess Integron's relative competitiveness.

Thanks for your help!

evaluations; second, the difference between competitors' performance and ICD's performance, as reported by customers.

RESULTS OF THE STUDY

Exhibit 3.5 shows a typical response from the telephone survey conducted by the consultants. To assess the fit between ICD's manufacturing strengths and customers' buying criteria, they asked customers to rate ICD's performance on each of their criteria. Next, the consultants analyzed the differences between ICD's performance ratings and its competitors' ratings to determine the magnitude of any competitive

Exhibit 3.5 Survey Response Summary Data

BUYING CRITERIA	IMPORTANCE TO BUYING DECISION (Customer Avg.)	ICD PERFORMANCE		COMPETITOR PERFORMANCE	
		Customer Average	App. Eng. Average	Customer Average	App. Eng. Average
Cost to you vs. other MCM	5.25	4.60	2.50	5.75	7.00
Cost to you vs. substitute technologies	6.00	3.70	1.50	5.00	6.00
Quality (adherence to specifications)	6.40	6.00	5.00	5.75	5.00
Meet current technical requirements	6.80	6.00	5.00	5.50	5.00
Degree of customization available	5.10	6.25	4.50	5.00	4.50
Difficulty and costs of changing from current tooling/designs	4.50	5.00	3.50	7.00	4.50
Length of time to get prototypes	5.50	3.70	4.00	5.50	4.00
Length of time to get volume production	5.60	3.50	4.50	5.50	4.00
Adequate documentation of process and specs.	4.20	4.75	4.00	6.75	5.50
Ability for supplier to be primary supplier	3.20	6.00	6.50	6.00	4.50
Continuing ability to offer leading-edge technical solutions	5.20	6.75	5.00	7.00	5.50
Reputation/longevity of supplier	5.80	6.70	7.00	7.00	4.50
Ability to order any lot size	5.00	5.50	4.00	5.50	4.00

gaps. Although ICD fared well in these comparisons, the analyses also highlighted a number of weaknesses (see Exhibit 3.5).

The consultants also made several observations based on comments that arose during the survey.

- Each market segment cited similar buying criteria but assigned different priorities to each (see Exhibit 3.6).
- While applications engineers also generated a similar list of criteria, they assigned relative importance quite differently from the customers (see Exhibit 3.7).
- The most serious disparity in perception concerned the importance of cost. Customers cited cost as only one of many barriers dissuading

---

Exhibit 3.6 Comparison of Buying Criteria by Segment

Workstation	ATE	Wireless
1. Meet current technical reqs.	1. Service	1. Quality
2. Quality	2. Meet current technical reqs.	2. Meet current technical reqs.
3. Cost & ability to produce high volumes	3. Quality	3. Ability to test
4. Longevity / reputation	4. Cost	4. Cost
5. Length of time to get volume production	5. Continuing ability to offer technical solutions	5. Ability to produce at high volume

---

Exhibit 3.7 Internal and External Rankings of Buying Criteria

Integron Applications Engineers	Workstation Customers
1. Cost	1. Meeting current technical requirements
2. Meeting current technical requirements	2. Quality
3. Longevity/reputations	3. Cost & ability to produce at high volume
4. Quality	4. Longevity/ reputations
5. Continuing ability to offer technical solutions	5. Length of time to get volume production

them from adopting MCMs—while applications engineers consistently saw it as the most critical element in the buying decision.

- The manufacturing organization, in choosing a general approach to all segments, might have been failing to meet the needs of any one segment (see Exhibit 3.8). For example, one customer who was willing to pay a high price required product characteristics that were too difficult to manufacture. Another customer felt that the costs required to produce a very simple product were too high.
- Applications engineers felt that ICD's approach was unfocused and that it inadequately met the specific needs of each segment. They also felt they were being asked to fill two different roles, one as a salesperson and one as a technical consultant (see Exhibit 3.9)

After hearing the consultants' findings, Lloyd realized there were some critical decisions to be made before charting ICD's future path. He left

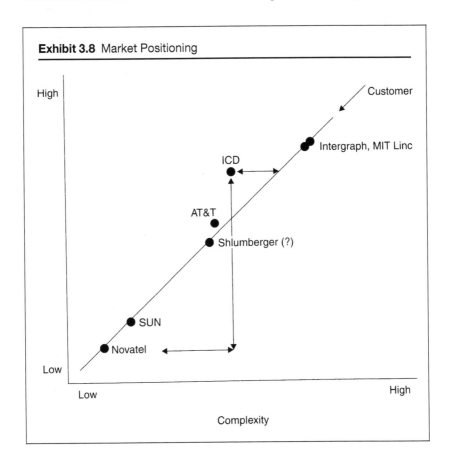

Exhibit 3.8 Market Positioning

Exhibit 3.9 Selected Applications Engineer Comments

"ICD either needs to find new niche markets for high-priced products or low-cost fabrication of MCMs."

"I'm not sure if one organization can adequately address all four markets: I know our products can't."

"Am I supposed to help customers solve problems or close deals? I feel like I'm asked to do two jobs."

---

the presentation, went back to his office, and started to put together his recommendations.

LLOYD'S DILEMMA

The following Tuesday, Gary Lloyd looked down at the recommendations he had developed. They implied major changes for his organization, and he had several lingering doubts about the study.

First, the survey results were based on a very small number of respondents. Lloyd's feeling was that the results were generally accurate, but he had to admit they were by no means statistically significant. Second, ICD had plenty to do without the upheaval of the radical change implied by the findings of the survey, not the least of which was to continue serving internal customers. Other Integron units needed his organization to remain at the forefront of technological developments, and he did not want to do anything to put that capability at risk.

Lloyd was frustrated. He could not predict how the market would change, but the study had shown that each of the emergent lily pads was moving in a different direction, at unknown speed. Each needed different capabilities from its supplier. At the same time, his manufacturing people desperately needed to know if their improvement plans were headed in the right direction.

Lloyd could act now or wait and repeat the study when there were more customers available to participate, and the market had become more stable. Postponing action was very tempting. The MCM market was changing quickly, and he did not want to gamble on a strategy that could quickly become outdated.

Lloyd's direct reports were waiting to hear his recommendations and action plan in the conference room next door. "Okay," he thought as he got up from his desk, "let's see what I have to say . . ."

NOTE TO CASE

1. The Skinner Award was an internationally recognized award for quality.

Case 3.3

DELOITTE & TOUCHE CONSULTING GROUP

(David Upton and Christine Steinman)

ABOUT THE AUTHORS

Professor David Upton and Research Associate Christine Steinman prepared this case as the basis for class discussion rather than to illustrate
either effective or ineffective handling of an administrative situation.

June 14, 1995, was unseasonably warm and humid. Maria Chen, a
senior consultant at Deloitte & Touche Consulting Group, was halfway
through a twelve-week engagement with SKS Manufacturing, a Pontiac,
Michigan based auto supplier. SKS had engaged the Consulting Group
to reduce inventory levels in its main plant. After six weeks, however,
work-in-process inventory had actually increased by 13%.

Early that afternoon, Chen had retreated from the shop floor to the
relative calm of the second-floor conference room to pick up her messages and to briefly escape the stifling heat and throbbing noise from
the floor below. She fell into the first available chair, leaned back,
breathed in the coolness and tried to relax, but her concerns about the

engagement interfered. To make things worse, she had been stopped on her way up by Jack Skidmore, the SKS president. He had tersely requested an explanation for the plant's lackluster inventory improvements. She had no solid answer. She took a deep breath, picked up the phone, punched in her password, and felt her stomach tighten as she listened to not one but two urgent voice messages from David Hendry, the partner leading the project. She dialed the number he had left, and listened to him say:

> Maria, I talked to some folks at SKS this morning and they are not at all pleased with the way this thing is going. Listen, I know you're doing your best there, but next Monday at the steering committee meeting—we have to make them understand we're moving in the right direction. I'll be out there tomorrow. Let's get together with Annette and Ben to decide what you might do.

As she dropped the phone into its cradle, she realized she wasn't certain about what to do, but thought there were probably two options. She could either build a presentation for the steering committee based on all the positive changes that occurred over the past six weeks (however, most of the evidence would be qualitative) or she could focus the next couple of days on trying to produce a noticeable reduction in inventory, which would be a long shot at best.

DELOITTE & TOUCHE CONSULTING GROUP

In 1995, Deloitte & Touche Consulting Group was officially designated a wholly owned subsidiary of Deloitte & Touche LLP. Deloitte & Touche LLP, known as one of the "big six" accounting firms, was formed in December 1989, by a merger between Deloitte, Haskins & Sells and Touche Ross.[1] Traditionally, Deloitte & Touche had been thought of as an audit and tax service firm, but at year end 1993, the Consulting Group, which had a client base significantly different than the audit and tax practices, comprised 28% of the firm's total revenue. In the United States, the Consulting Group was comprised of 2,700 professionals (including 250 partners) and 5,600 consulting professionals worldwide.

The Consulting Group focused on delivering services in four main areas: operations, information technology, financial management and strategy development in a broad set of industries, including manufacturing, healthcare and financial services. In addition to the core, the Consulting Group teamed with its wholly-owned subsidiaries to deliver services. Those organizations included Braxton Associates, a Boston-based strategy consulting firm; DRT International and CMD Systems, application and systems development firms. In 1995, the Consulting Group merged with ICS, a firm specializing in the implementation of large scale SAP projects.

The Consulting Group's primary competitors included Andersen Consulting, Price Waterhouse, Ernst & Young, as well as McKinsey, BCG, Booz Allen and CSC Index. Industry-wide, the range of management consulting services could be described as a spectrum with strategy consulting on one end and systems implementation on the other. The Consulting Group viewed its strength and position in the market as an "implementation" consulting firm. The firm's ability to offer a fully integrated solution of strategy, operations, and information technology was key to its success.

The Consulting Industry

Since the early 1990s, considerable transformation had occurred within the consulting services industry. Due to a number of factors, clients had become much more informed and demanding, which had resulted in the following:

- **Integrated teams.** As late as the early 1990s, consultants often worked alone. Now, work teams almost always included key client employees as well as consultants. This arrangement usually allowed both parties to learn from the other more effectively, as well as help the client to participate more fully in defining and implementing business solutions. At the same time, the breadth of personalities involved, their disparate backgrounds and a lack of common understanding of approaches could often add additional complexity to the situation.
- **Knowledge transfer.** In the past, the norm had been to perform the agreed upon services and then to move on, once the consulting assignment was complete. However, clients began to realize that the benefits from their consulting investment were very short lived unless its employees could carry on effectively where consultants had left off. Clients expected critical knowledge to be transferred from the consultants to key employees. *Teaching* had became an integral part of successful consulting.
- **Third party ratings.** The proliferation of consulting firms had fueled increased scrutiny and the birth of independent organizations which compiled evaluative reports and cross-industry ratings.

The Gartner Group, for example, evaluated a range of factors, from success of implementations to "completeness of vision."

- **Integration of approaches.** Clients were beginning to require consultants to have the ability and resources to develop and implement solutions that linked strategy to operations and technology more closely than they had in the past. Additionally, clients increasingly expected consultants to have industry-specific knowledge and an ability to provide solutions world-wide.

Career Progression

A new professional at the Consulting Group could expect his or her career to progress through the following levels, with a partner being the most senior position:

- **Consultant/Analyst.** While consultants performed many of the same tasks as the senior consultants, they generally lacked the experience level of their senior colleagues. Consultants were typically hired as undergraduates fresh from college. Although some consultants made their way through the ranks, many in this position chose to return to graduate school. Analysts were also hired straight from undergraduate programs, and were expected to provide the analytical support needed to make informed decisions during the engagement process. In addition, the Consulting Group hired Summer Associates, usually MBAs between the first and second year of their coursework. Summer associates' responsibilities were similar to the senior consultants.
- **Senior Consultant.** Senior consultants were usually hired from MBA programs, often with two or three years of industry experience. Major tasks included collecting and analyzing data, focusing and taking responsibility for particular sub-projects and presentations, facilitating and managing client teams and helping to prepare proposals to clients. They were often supported by an analyst.
- **Senior Manager/Manager.** Senior managers dealt with the upper levels of client management, particularly with issues and problems that arose during the course of an engagement, and sometimes worked with multiple clients at one time. They also handled proposal presentations to prospective clients. Managers supervised several senior consultants on a single client engagement.
- **Partner.** Just under 10% of the firm's consulting professionals earned this title, which generally took six to eleven years to achieve. As senior managers became partners, their focus shifted from the

work involved in engagements to managing the client relationship. Partners typically handled two or three clients at one time, and focused on applying their experience to finding solutions and making sure the client remained satisfied with the Consulting Group. Partners were also responsible for selling consulting group services, and usually developed specialization in a particular industry or service line.

No fixed rules existed regarding progression up the ladder, but a framework of "expectations" outlined what professionals were expected to master in order to proceed. Professionals received appraisals at the end of each engagement. In general, new hires with undergraduate degrees entered at the analyst or consultant level, and could expect to be promoted to senior consultant within approximately three years. New hires with graduate degrees or a minimum of five years of work experience were given the senior consultant title. Training for the new consultant was a combination of new hire/new position retreats and on-the-job training. The Consulting Group put a great deal of emphasis on learning from doing.

Roughly two-thirds of new hires came from industry, with the remainder coming from universities like Harvard, Wharton, Chicago and Kellogg. About 75% of the latter category had advanced degrees (primarily MBAs) and therefore also had some prior work experience. Turnover at the Consulting Group was between 15 and 20% annually. The consultants that decided to leave the firm often cited a desire for a change in lifestyle or decided to join a client in management and executive positions. Additionally, some consultants left to apply their "implementation" skills in start-up businesses.

SKS MANUFACTURING—THE CLIENT

The Company

SKS Manufacturing, a metal stamping manufacturer, was founded in 1959 by two General Motors trained engineers, Allen Kramer and John Stefanski. SKS supplied a variety of exhaust system components to Tier I and Tier II suppliers, as well as after-market distributors (See Exhibit 3.10). Since its founding, SKS had been, for better and for worse, completely tied to the automobile industry.

In the beginning, Kramer and Stefanski made the most of their "big three" connections and translated them into a solid and steadily growing

Exhibit 3.10 Selected SKS Products[a]

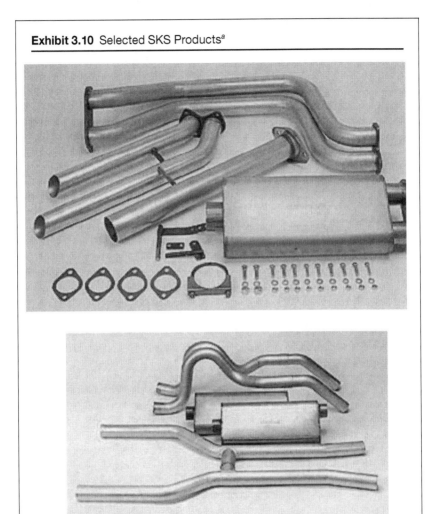

[a] http://www.edelbrock.com/catback.html

business. In the early 1960s, a third partner, Robert Skidmore, came aboard. Skidmore, a renowned charmer, was able to win new contracts quickly and ultimately set the company on its current trajectory. Still privately held, Kramer's eldest son, Jack, was named president in 1989. Ownership was split between the Kramer and Skidmore families, Stefanski was bought out in 1977. Since those early days, SKS had grown into a formidable competitor and a leader within its industry; 1995 year end sales were projected to be just under $570 million, and SKS now employed over 5,700 people (See Exhibit 3.11).

Exhibit 3.11 Selected Operating Results and Balance Sheet (SKS)

	1995	1994	1993	1992	1991
Operating Results					
Sales	567	536	482	464	397
Gross Profit	88	90	86	83	71
Sales and administrative expense	56	60	58	60	52
Depreciation	5	4	3	7	5
Earnings before interest and taxes	11	19	23	17	14
Net Income/(Loss)	(4)	14	16	9	4
Assets					
Cash	0.4	4	9	0.7	2
Receivables	112	79	61	94	73
Inventory	126	117	82	67	78
Net Properly, Plant and Equipment	115	107	97	101	86
Other	20	7	59	27	33
Total Assets	373	314	308	290	272
Liabilities & Net Worth					
Accounts Payable	73	51	33	37	30
Long term debt	123	108	112	98	86
Other	80	56	57	58	54
Net Worth	97	99	106	97	102
Total Liabilities and Net Worth	373	314	308	290	272

The elder Skidmore had brought a vision to the company of industry leadership and sales figures that were far beyond his partners' original conservative projections and careful cash flow analysis. He firmly believed sales focus was the vehicle with which long term success would be attained, and instituted a sales structure that had remained intact. SKS salespeople focused on direct sales and kept existing customers happy within Region I (Michigan—especially Metro Detroit, Ohio, and western Indiana). Manufacturing representatives were used to cover the rest of the United States and to a small, but growing, degree Mexico and Canada. Sales were heavily concentrated with three major customers, which comprised 65% of the total. SKS had only begun exporting in the last five years, and consequently only 3% of sales were outside of the U.S. The current generation of managers realized this would have to be changed to insure ongoing viability.

SKS's main plant was located in Pontiac, Michigan, an industrial suburb north of Detroit. The facility was 450,000 square feet, which gave the company ample capacity for current volume plus a little room to grow. Most of the manufacturing processes were performed at this location. Some items required special coatings, and were shipped out to one or two nearby suppliers. One warehouse was also located on the premises, but a second was inconveniently located six miles to the south of this facility.

The SKS shop-floor was a dingy, noisy place—smelling of the lubricating oil used to coat the metal to help it flow in the presses. In the press section, brake-presses, making between 20 and 60 blows per minute, stamped out metal parts from raw sheet metal, then spat the newly trimmed components into a chute, which emptied into a wire-cage bin on a pallet. The presses were drawn from a variety of vintages—from new, automatic presses with computer control to a few battered old WWII-vintage presses, with automatic guards incongruously retrofitted. Testament to the bad old days of press-work were the occasional old-timers who would shake one's hand absent a full complement of digits. In general, press work involved some vigilance for safety's sake, but was primarily a machine-tending job. Over the previous few years, SKS had seen more pressure to change between components more quickly as their product range grew and customer demands for responsiveness became stronger. As a result of this, runs had become shorter and die-changes more frequent. Operators had become involved in this activity, but press-*setting* was still, primarily, a job for a skilled setter. Most people on the floor agreed that it was now a much better place to work than it had been, but that it was still a little chaotic on occasion, with many components sitting between presses and "split-batches" making the job of keeping the production shop orderly very difficult.

SKS's new products were conceptualized and, for the most part, designed in-house. SKS had a full-time engineer pool of nine, with an average experience level of twelve years. The in-house design engineers used manual drawings and CAD applications. On occasion, for specialized applications, SKS would seek the help of an outside engineering and design firm.

Key Personnel

The majority of the SKS management had been with the company for most of their respective careers, and had fairly homogeneous backgrounds. SKS management stated that employees were treated

"like family." From the Consulting Group's perspective, it was important to work well with the following people.

Jack Skidmore had been the SKS president since 1989. The eldest
son of Robert Skidmore, he was, they said, "molded in his father's
image." So, quite naturally, he began a career in sales after he graduated
from Central Michigan University in 1972 with a BA in history. He
successfully worked for a few firms outside the family business (including starting his own insurance agency), and then moved into the business thirteen years ago. Within SKS, he proved himself as a sales
manager, tightening long term relationships that had begun to unravel
with escalating industry competitiveness. Skidmore was known to
"promise the world" and then somehow find a way to deliver. This
behavior solidified several teetering customer relationships, but made
his sales trips dreaded among the core group of workers that could be
counted on to, in Jack's own words, "make things shake." Often out of
the plant on customer visits, Skidmore relied heavily on David Fletcher
to run the day-to-day operations.

David Fletcher had been the SKS plant manager for the last eight
years. Fletcher, with an engineering background and twenty-two years
experience in the automotive industry, had joined SKS about fourteen
years previously. Since then he had held a variety of positions, including material manager, production control manager, chief engineer and
assistant plant manager. Fletcher was known as a hard working and fair
person, and although his temper could flare unexpectedly, he had won
the respect of many SKS employees. He knew the plant inside and out,
and tolerated little less from his core management staff.

Stan Janovich was the first shift supervisor, and had been for nearly
nineteen years. Janovich was just a few years from retirement, and,
although he was looking forward to spending time at his northern
Michigan cabin, he wondered aloud how things would continue to
work without him around. He took a great deal of pride in his contributions to SKS, and felt things were "pretty much in place." Janovich
had been with SKS almost since its beginning, and had seen the ebbs
and flows of the auto industry, so, as he explained at the last staff
meeting, things will "work themselves out."

The Engagement

SKS had sought out the help of a third party several months earlier. The
company was experiencing a critical cash flow shortage and had delayed

payment to several suppliers in order to service its payroll obligations. Additionally, SKS was unable to maintain acceptable customer service levels, shipping only 77% of customer orders in time to make required delivery dates. By April 1995, SKS management realized it no longer had the luxury of time, or the internal capability and focus to turn around the situation; they interviewed several consulting firms before ultimately engaging the services of the Deloitte & Touche Consulting Group.

The Consulting Group initially considered a longer term "reengineering" approach that would focus on redesigning cross-functional business processes. This approach would be a radical change from the "functional silos" from which SKS currently performed business tasks. However, to begin with, the Consulting Group proposed a shorter, and more focused, twelve week engagement that would stabilize the current cash position. The consultants advised that a radical "reengineering" approach, with the company in a cash crunch, might introduce a level of risk that the firm might not recover from. The Consulting Group viewed the twelve week engagement as a necessary foundation to start the longer term project, and SKS, with little previous experience with consultants, thought this would be a good time to "test drive" the firm.

The SKS project fell onto David Hendry's line of responsibility, and Annette Wattley-Davis, a senior manager, would be second in command. Together, they selected a team of three consultants and two business analysts for the first 12 week project to stabilize operations. Additionally, they obtained commitment from Jack Skidmore, David Fletcher, and Stan Janovich that they would spend at least 25% of their time working with the team.

The engagement began in early May 1995.

The Engagement Team

A typical Consulting Group engagement of this scope involved four to five professionals: a partner, a manager or senior manager, two to three senior consultants, as well as a couple of analysts. The team for the SKS engagement included the following people:

David Hendry was a partner based in the Detroit office. Hendry had spent the last eighteen years heavily involved in the automotive industry. He had worked with the three major automotive manufacturers and many of the major automotive part suppliers around the world. An MIT-trained engineer, Hendry began his career as a design engineer at

Ford Motor Company, and after several years and an MBA from the University of Chicago, moved into the consulting world. He had been a partner for seven years, and his concentration in this industry made him one of the Consulting Group's automotive "gurus." Hendry had recently taken on even greater responsibility for bringing in new business, and was successfully shouldering his new load. Over the years he had acquired a reputation for results in the industry, which was a source of personal pride and continued motivation.

Annette Wattley-Davis joined the Consulting Group as a senior consultant eight years ago, fresh from an MBA at Wharton. Based in Cleveland, she has focused, for most of her Consulting Group tenure, on business process reengineering for manufacturing firms. As a manager, she was nominated by her local office to participate in a six-month national effort to develop Consulting Group's next generation Reengineering for Results™ methodology. Since Wattley-Davis became a senior manager last year, she has focused almost exclusively on the automotive industry.

In addition to the SKS engagement, she was finishing up another project in Dallas that required between 2–3 days of her time over the first six weeks of this engagement.

Maria Chen worked for three years after finishing her BA in economics (Amherst '89) for General Electric as an associate in their management training program. In this program she was exposed to many different areas of operations including finance, internal audit, manufacturing, and engineering. At the Harvard Business School (MBA '94), Chen performed well academically, and had a knack for quantitative analysis. After her arrival at the Consulting Group in August 1994, Chen reflected, "I came to this firm to get some diversified "hands-on" operations experience." Since that time, she had been undergoing training and assisting with various projects. SKS, although her second direct manufacturing experience, would be the first project where she had direct responsibility for significant pieces of the work.

Ben Rohan and Ramesh Patel were the other two consultants on the engagement team. Rohan was an experienced senior consultant based in the Detroit office. He had a BS in computer science from the University of Illinois and an MBA from Dartmouth, and a number of years of procurement and manufacturing experience. Since he joined the Consulting Group last year, he had been on three different engagements, one in health care, one in financial services, and the last one in manufacturing. Patel joined the Consulting Group as a summer associate. A Cornell-trained engineer, his objectives were to gain some practical client experiences and to evaluate the Consulting Group as a future employer. The firm looked for Patel to be an active team member and to provide analytical support. The Consulting Group also wanted to recruit him for the following year.

The Planning Meeting

Wattley-Davis recognized that a multiple pronged approach would be required to address the SKS short term business and manufacturing problems. A quick analysis of the company's cost structure and inventory levels indicated that an effort to both reduce cash investment in raw material and to synchronize production and procurement would alleviate the immediate problems.

About a week before the start date, she brought the team together to discuss the preliminary issues and to make sure everyone knew what they were expected to accomplish and were comfortable in their roles. One team would be led by the industry-hire Ben Rohan. His job was to attack the material procurement processes and raw material levels. The second team was led by Maria Chen. She would address the production scheduling processes and synchronize production operations with purchasing. They were expected to work together on this "quick hit" opportunity to reduce inventory.

Chen walked away from the meeting excited and was eager to begin the project. When she returned to her office, she reviewed her notes to make sure she knew exactly what she needed to accomplish over the next twelve weeks. As she saw it, her main goals were:

- To develop production scheduling rules and processes that would smooth production, relieve the most severe bottlenecks and reduce the number of crises the plant was experiencing, which would decrease the need for "buffer" inventory;
- To design and implement a pilot of a pull-based synchronous manufacturing cell in twelve weeks, as well as a new factory layout design and roll-out plan;
- To work with Ben Rohan to reduce overall inventory levels by $10M within twelve weeks.

Additionally, the Consulting Group wanted to position itself for the larger reengineering opportunity, and identify any further add-on work.

Time Zero

Chen was very anxious to make a good first impression with the client. She had spent the weekend before reading up on synchronous manufacturing techniques, and had placed a few calls to a few Consulting Group colleagues that she had heard worked on similar engagements. She flew into Detroit Metropolitan airport the night before and was the first to arrive at the plant.

Upon arriving, Chen notified the receptionist that she was with the Deloitte & Touche Consulting Group reengineering team, and, although early, asked to see the plant manager, David Fletcher. In a few minutes, Fletcher came into the lobby, and approached Chen. She expected a warm welcome, but realized immediately that either Fletcher was not pleased she was there or hadn't had his requisite caffeine intake that morning. After a perfunctory handshake, Fletcher wanted to know "What exactly did she think she was doing there?" Chen was shocked with the cold reception and Fletcher's lack of information, and did not understand why Jack Skidmore had not informed Fletcher about the start of the engagement, the use of consultants, and the scope of the project. Fletcher suggested Chen leave the plant site until he had time to sort the whole thing out.

Soon the rest of the consulting team arrived in the lobby, and Chen relayed her story to Hendry and Wattley-Davis. Hendry phoned Skidmore, catching him on his way to the airport, and found Fletcher had just that day returned from a ten-day vacation. Skidmore agreed to smooth everything over, and the Consulting Group team entered the plant an hour and a half later. The engagement had begun, but Chen could not imagine a rockier beginning.

Ramp Up

Annette Wattley-Davis recognized that Chen, as a fairly new consultant, was taking on a lot of responsibility and was being thrown into a difficult and vague situation with this engagement. She spent some extra time with Chen talking her through some of the issues she would likely run into in the next few weeks. Wattley-Davis relayed lessons she had learned the hard way, for example, the importance of gaining consensus around new ideas and the difficulty of making changes on the factory floor. She also worked with Chen to develop a detailed work plan for her part of the project, and suggested ways to integrate the work into the team's overall work plan.

The first week was hard but after the second week, Chen had started to settle into the SKS culture. The team had made a spartan, but comfortable, conference room on the second floor their headquarters. They spent the first few weeks there collecting data, creating a spreadsheet model of material flow, and eating late night pizzas. The team had begun to work well together, and although Jack Skidmore and David Fletcher only spent parts of their work day with the consultants, they had begun to spend more time with them after hours. Chen was working at full speed on a complex spreadsheet model that she believed would "knock the socks off" both Wattley-Davis and their client. Because the spreadsheet turned out to be a bit more complex than she had first designed, she ended up having to sacrifice some of the other items on her list of things to do.

At the end of the third week, the team members, including client team members, prepared summaries of their analysis and previewed them with selected members of the plant staff. In a group of eighteen, the team members individually presented their overheads. Chen's presentation on her material flow simulation did not go nearly as well as she had anticipated. Stan Janovich, whom she had wanted to talk with earlier in the week (but had run out of time), pointed out many issues that had not been accounted for in the model. She grudgingly realized Janovich was completely on target with his criticisms, and jotted some notes for the simulation revisions.

After the meeting, Wattley-Davis took Chen aside and quizzed her about how much of the modeling effort had been reviewed with Janovich and other key people on the floor prior to the meeting. She also asked how much time she had actually spent on the factory floor and with the other team led by Rohan over the last few weeks. Wattley-Davis's displeasure was obvious as she suggested Chen move her work space from the conference room to the factory floor. Chen dejectedly agreed and as she turned away, the senior manager continued, "And, pull the plug on that spreadsheet for a while."

Phase Two

By the end of the fourth week, Chen began to realize the value of her manager's mandate to move down to the shop floor. After staining and nearly ruining her new Donna Karan suit, she wore jeans and an equally replaceable shirt. Her first encounters with Janovich left her with the distinct impression that he was gruff, unapproachable, and not at all interested in Consulting Group's work, but as she came to know him, she realized that was not completely true. She began to have casual conversations with him about his twin grandchildren (Nicole and

Nicholas), the history of the plant, and eventually how scheduling work was really done outside of the computerized program which she had been briefed on.

She gradually learned that there were two sets of procedures being followed on a daily basis—a formal documented process and the way work was really done. Alterations from the formal process were sometimes for the sake of a short cut and other times to avoid the computerized system which many folks on the floor felt was basically useless. Chen also found that Janovich's opinion carried a lot of weight in the SKS world even though he only held the title of day shift supervisor.

As she spent more and more time with Janovich, she realized he consistently "bad mouthed" the sales group for dumping orders at the end of the quarter and changing priorities of jobs once they had been launched. He also explained his computer mistrust; the bills of material and parts lists developed by engineering were always out-of-date. He pointed to a dented gray (and "rust") filing cabinet that contained marked-up parts lists and prints that were the plant's "true" records. Janovich also admitted that inventory accuracy had always been a problem. Chen also discovered that in addition to poor data in the system, most of the applications were not integrated. Much of the basic data for an order had to be reentered when moving from order entry to the manufacturing system. Betty Ranowski, a long time SKS clerk, was responsible for re-keying the orders into the manufacturing system every Monday.

Chen mentioned this new information to some of her team-mates. They suggested she meet with the sales, engineering, and information technology managers to contrast their points-of-view with Janovich's. This made sense to Chen, but she decided to stick closely to the directives given by Wattley-Davis—stay on the floor until you fully understand the production system. The memories of the first day and her sinking spreadsheet model seemed very fresh, and she was intent on redeeming herself as quickly as possible. She did, however, talk to the clerk, Betty Ranowski, about the time and effort required to re-enter all of the manufacturing orders.

During the fifth week, Wattley-Davis evaluated Chen's progress (versus her original work plan), and asked again that she spend more time working with Rohan and key information technology people at SKS. By the end of the week, Chen began to feel like things were back on track. She had started to make some changes in the floor layout with Janovich's input. One of the major bottlenecks in material flow started to ease, and jobs seemed to be moving much faster. She began collecting data and posting the performance trends by stamping line in a location where they couldn't be missed. The trend lines looked unchanged, and Skidmore had the charts showing poor on-time deliveries taken down just before a major customer was scheduled to tour the facility.

After the customer meeting and tour, Skidmore found Chen and asked for a quick update on the progress that was being made. He also expressed his concern that Chen was giving his employees the impression that the Consulting Group work at SKS meant some people were going to be fired. Chen was shocked to hear this, fumbled with her response, and ultimately promised to look into it. Skidmore, not seeming overly pleased, dismissed her and walked away. Chen was stunned, and had no idea how something she had done could have resulted in such a conclusion. She later learned that her chat with Ranowski had been interpreted, by Ranowski, as "the beginning of the end."

"White Knuckle" Time

Chen sat tensely at the conference table, and considered her options. She knew progress was being made, but not at the accelerated pace that she had initially envisioned. She also knew the steering committee meeting would be a showdown if she had no substantive improvements to show. She wanted desperately to show a major improvement in inventory reduction for her first six weeks of effort.

The performance metrics she had just graphed showed that although on-time delivery had improved slightly from 77% to 79%, total work-in-process inventory had actually increased by 13%. She heard the warning words of Janovich ringing in her head. Maybe he was right. Maybe this business was unique, and inventory levels needed to be at a higher level, especially at the end of a quarter, to buffer the poor forecasts generated by sales.

Chen also reflected on Hendry's counsel two weeks earlier to start a formal change management and communications process, even during this first phase of the project. She had that on her work plan, but she wondered if that would have really helped calm Ranowski's fears. How could she have jumped to the conclusion that she was going to get fired?

Deep down, Chen knew that she had made progress, even if the numbers didn't reflect the results. For the first time in the company history the individual managers were starting to act as a team, and were taking a cross functional view of their business. She had raised their level of awareness above the finger pointing between functions for problems, and complaints of the "stupid mainframe system" to really focusing on the underlying problems. Fletcher, who had nearly thrown her out of the plant the first day, was now spending more time with her testing different plant floor layouts and trying to reduce work-in-process inventory.

Chen feared that if she didn't have the hard numbers, the project would be shut down before it could be successful. She also worried that the early termination of a strategically important engagement would virtually eliminate her firm's ability to sell the larger reengineering engagement to this client. And finally, she believed that she had been placed in a very difficult position, and that her evaluation would not accurately reflect the degree of difficulty of this situation, and what she had accomplished.

NOTE TO CASE

1.   *Professional Service Trends: Deloitte & Touche*, Dataquest ® report, Dun & Bradstreet Corporation, February 25, 1994, was referenced for this section.

Part 4

Consulting to Implement Change in Different Contexts

Introduction

Case 4.1

Case of the Retiring CEO
(Larry Greiner, University of Southern California)

Case 4.2

Bain & Company: International Expansion
(Peter J. Williamson and Michael Y. Yoshino)

Case 4.3

The Bridgespan Group
(John Kalafatas and Allen Grossman)

Case 4.4

Datavision (A, B, C)
(Gregory C. Rogers and Michael Beer)

Case 4.5

Mercer Management Consulting (A, B)
(Thomas J. DeLong and Michael W. Echenberg)

INTRODUCTION

Clients want solutions that work and add value to their organizations' performance. Otherwise, it is hard to justify the expense and resources consumed in a consulting assignment. At the same time, it is difficult to measure the real benefits of a project because so many variables are outside the control of consultants. This is further complicated by the normal time delay between a client's taking action and achieving improved signs of financial performance. The more immediate test is represented in this question: Has the consulting project prompted the client to take action that is consistent with initiatives set within the scope of the project? Presumably, these actions will lead to better performance, but those outcomes may not be known for some time.

The issue of implementation has been on the consulting agenda for years. Conducting studies, undertaking analyses, and coming up with recommendations are all part of the consulting repertoire. But the real value of consulting is not achieved until action is taken by the client. Therefore, the role of a consultant as a change-maker must receive high priority in consulting, and this begins with the training of consultants in the planning of projects and continues through to their skills at implementing change. Part 4 in Greiner and Poulfelt's book[1] discusses in some depth how consultants can intervene more effectively to promote change in client organizations.

Consultants must also be highly sensitive to the surrounding context for their projects, from the type of industry to the size of clients, and to global versus local conditions. All of these factors greatly (and usually do) affect what choices consultants make among alternative intervention methods to fit the context. For example, introducing change in the government arena is likely to encounter barriers not present in private firms. Or working at the CEO level will raise issues about change not found in solving problems at the plant level. Further, the processes of implementing change in Chinese firms will obviously be different from working with clients in the United States. Many of these situational issues are addressed in Part 3 of Greiner and Poulfelt's book, Consulting in Different Contexts.

Five cases are included in this part to address the problems of implementing change in different contexts. The *Case of the Retiring CEO* examines the issue of politics within a client's top team as it affects the outcomes of a major strategy project. It suggests that clients behave according to other agendas than the rational business issues being addressed by the consultants. The *Bain & Company International Expansion* case turns the focus back on changes within Bain as it takes a comprehensive look at the changing consulting industry and the question of where in the new global marketplace it should open new international offices. *The Bridgespan Group* case takes the reader into the nonprofit world where a Bain offshoot consulting group, *Bridgespan*, digests its initial success and decides what changes to make in handling increased client demand. The cases in *Datavision (A)* and *(B)* reveal a sequence of facilitation interventions made by a consultant in trying to help a small computer company. It allows students to follow the interventions through the two cases—to discuss what to do next and then to observe what actually happens. The *Mercer Management Consulting (A)* case examines the effects of a leading consulting firm's acquisition strategy on its internal culture, raising numerous issues about how to absorb and assimilate new units.

We learn from these cases that consulting is rarely a linear and rational process because it must deal with uncertainty and anxiety among employees in a client organization. Too often, consultants view implementation as merely the last phase after entry, diagnosis, and action planning. However, implementation should be on the consultant's planning agenda from the very beginning, considering issues such as: To what extent should the client and other stakeholders become involved with the consulting team and participate in the diagnosis, and solution process? Where in the organization are the likely pockets of resistance? What political issues exist in the senior management group? What are the cultural taboos in the organization? How much change can a client absorb, and in what sequence should the phases of change be introduced? What types of interventions are called for by the situation, and who on the consultant team is most qualified to perform these interventions? Many questions are raised in the above cases, and the resultant learning should be useful to preparing consultants as change-makers.

NOTE

1. Greiner, L. & Poulfelt, F. 2009. *Management Consulting Today and Tomorrow*, Taylor & Francis.

Case 4.1

CASE OF THE RETIRING CEO

(Larry Greiner, University of Southern California)

ABOUT THE AUTHOR

This case was prepared by Professor Larry Greiner of USC's Marshall School of Business as the basis for class discussion rather than to illustrate either effective or ineffective handling of an administrative situation. All names are disguised.

Gamma Industries is a Fortune 100 company with a diverse product line and extensive international operations. In early 2001, the company was facing a third year of declining profits and the possibility of red ink for the first time in its history. This downward trend had continued despite a recent large infusion of $800 million from a European investor, which had taken a majority position in Gamma.

Prior to 2001 and the period of declining profits, Gamma had been led for ten years by a dynamic and dominating CEO and Chairman, John Amato, who had greatly increased profits, sales and market share during his tenure. When Amato retired in 1998, his second-in-command, Ralph Hines, succeeded him at age sixty-one. Hines had been a loyal but undistinguished subordinate to Amato. In contrast to the charismatic Amato, Hines was seen as a "quiet gentleman" who had emerged from years of obscurity while working in Gamma's finance department.

Shortly after becoming Chairman and CEO, Hines divided the company into two major industry groups, with one group representing an industry for old-line products, and the other group focused on new products in a different but more rapidly growing industry. Hines chose Bill Sheldon, age fifty-one, to be President of Gamma, and gave him responsibility for the old-line group. In addition, Hines selected Harry Katz, age forty-two, to be Vice-Chairman in charge of the group for more recent products. Bill Sheldon had arrived at Gamma three years before and was widely seen as the "cool intellectual" in the top management group, while Katz, recruited from a competitor in 1998, was known for his "aggressive but warm personality." Hines assigned responsibility for daily operations to Sheldon and Katz, while devoting his attention to the Board, the financial community, and the European investor.

In late 2000, Ralph Hines, at the urging of Harry Katz, decided to replace the retiring Vice-President of Human Resources with an outsider, Chris Miller, age fifty, who had been a personnel director at a Fortune 100 company. Miller was given the title of Executive Vice-President and member of the Executive Committee, which included Hines, Sheldon, Katz, and James Samuels, who resided in Brussels as Vice-Chairman in charge of Gamma's International operations.

Chris Miller spent his first three months interviewing executives and workers throughout Gamma. In his report of findings to the Executive Committee, Miller stated that "significant morale problems exist at all levels," and that "many people perceive a lack of strategic direction for the company." He also noted but did not report to the Committee that there seemed to be a "growing feeling that Gamma was being run like two separate companies." The Executive Committee directed Miller to look into the morale problem and to begin a program to deal with it. He then began a search for an outside consultant to provide assistance. Gamma had a long history of using management consultants in its functional areas and in strategic planning.

Through various contacts and referrals, Chris Miller phoned Professor Rob Frank at a local university, and asked Frank if he could stop by for a visit. Miller and Professor Frank met to discuss the situation for about one hour, at which point Frank referred Miller to a faculty colleague, Professor Barry Johnson, who was well known in the "motivation and job design" field. Frank did not feel sufficiently qualified himself to deal with the problems of low morale at Gamma.

Chris Miller, after meeting with Professor Johnson, was sufficiently impressed to invite Johnson to make a presentation to Gamma's Management Council. The Council consisted of fifteen members, including the Executive Committee members and their immediate subordinates. Miller asked Johnson to describe how a "quality-of-working-life" (QWL) program might be introduced in a selected part of Gamma's operations as an experiment to improve morale and performance.

Professor Johnson, upon returning from making his presentation to the Council, told Rob Frank that he had never attended a meeting where, as he put it, "so much one-upmanship was going on among the participants." He said that the Chairman, Ralph Hines, had remained quiet throughout the meeting and that Harry Katz acted "less than enthusiastic," leaving before the meeting was over. Chris Miller later left a phone message for Professor Johnson saying that Gamma had decided not to adopt a QWL program.

Two months later, Chris Miller phoned Professor Frank again to arrange a second visit for the purpose of locating another consultant. On this occasion, Miller reported that "political differences" made it difficult for Gamma's senior management to agree to do a QWL project. As a result, Miller asked Frank if he could recommend another consultant who might work with Gamma in "charting a new strategic direction." Miller also told Frank that an academic consultant probably would not be effective because of "top management's skepticism toward professors."

As they talked further, Miller went on to describe the political situation at Gamma as involving an underlying conflict between Chairman Hines, President Sheldon, and Vice-Chairman Katz. He said that Sheldon and Katz did not respect Hines, and that there was a lot of tension between the three. According to Miller, Hines believed that, "competition between key managers is healthy for the profit center concept." Miller then confided to Professor Frank that he had not told Hines about the fact that "Sheldon and Katz were not taking major decisions to Hines." Instead, as Miller explained to Professor Frank, "Sheldon and Katz had formed a Thursday-morning group"—composed of themselves, a couple of key subordinates, and Miller—to discuss important operating issues. According to Miller, "Sheldon and Katz each saw themselves as a logical successor to Hines." However, Miller pointed out to Frank that Sheldon and Katz were "not fighting publicly or privately with each other."

A few days later, Rob Frank called Chris Miller to recommend Strategic Management Associates (SMA), a major management-consulting firm that had established a strong reputation in strategic planning projects, as well as an ability to bring consensus to a top management group. Miller indicated an interest, so Frank arranged for Miller to meet with two of SMA's "most experienced consultants," Bob Hagen and Rich Jones. Miller had warned Frank previously that any consultant who worked on the project would have to be acceptable to Sheldon and Katz.

Chris Miller, in an initial meeting with the two SMA consultants, described his perceptions of Gamma's competitive problems, saying, "the company is drifting in the marketplace." He also spent consider-able time discussing the personalities of Sheldon and Katz. The two senior consultants listened intently and asked occasional questions, after which they described SMA's background and clientele, including how they would likely approach a study of Gamma's problems. Miller liked what he heard and decided to arrange for the consultants to meet with Sheldon and Katz.

The time of this second meeting was changed four times by either Sheldon or Katz, but finally after one month, a one-hour meeting was arranged. During this meeting, the SMA consultants did most of the talking in response to an initial question from Katz, who asked about their personal backgrounds and previous clientele. Both Sheldon and Katz reacted in a friendly manner, while both placed blame for Gamma's problems on "changes in the industry." At the end of the meeting, as they stood shaking hands, Katz invited SMA to submit a written proposal for a first stage of field research to "ascertain the nature of Gamma's strategic problem." Chris Miller was delighted with the outcome.

A proposal was written and submitted by SMA, stating, "The pur-pose of the project is to determine the nature of the strategic problem facing Gamma through interviews with the top seventy officers and an examination of financial and marketing data." The proposed fee was $900,000, and the proposal concluded by stating, "if this first stage goes well, a second stage focused on implementation planning will be proposed."

Two months passed before EVP Chris Miller called Bob Hagen to say that approval had been given for the project. He told Hagen, "I had an easy time getting agreement from the Chairman but it was difficult getting Sheldon and Katz together at the same time to sign off."

The first stage of the project was to be completed over a two-month period, yet it took almost four months to finish because of scheduling difficulties. During the project, the consultants had intended to meet informally with the Thursday-morning group every two weeks to report on their progress, but these meetings were postponed three times at the last minute. When these meetings did occur, Sheldon and Katz were rarely present together. In making their reports, the SMA consultants gave a brief summary, usually confined to data-gathering steps that had taken place. Any substantive comments made by the consultants were limited to general observations, such as, "We're finding a lot of different points of view about what the strategy of Gamma is and should be." The Thursday-morning group always listened with interest and encouraged the consultants to continue.

About halfway through the project, one of the senior consultants, Bob Hagen, happened to meet the Chairman, Ralph Hines, at the local airport. Hines invited Hagen to ride into the city with him. During the trip, Hines asked Hagen about the project, and Hagen gave him an informal report, highlighting one finding that "a large shortfall seemed to exist between budgeted cost savings and the amount that several key executives believed can actually be saved." Hines expressed surprise but did not inquire further.

Shortly after the airport incident, Chris Miller called SMA to request that Bob Hagen be removed from the project because Sheldon and Katz had complained separately to him about Hagen's comments about the budget shortfall on the airport ride with Hines. Apparently the Chairman had returned to his office from the airport ride and called in Sheldon and Katz separately, asking each to explain the budget discrepancy. Both Sheldon and Katz denied that a shortfall existed. Miller told SMA that Sheldon and Katz still wanted to complete the consulting project because of its potential value, but that Hagen had to be removed from the project. A different interpretation of these events was later given by the remaining senior consultant, who said, "We had learned too much about Gamma . . . lower-level executives were too favorable toward the project for us to be fired . . . so we replaced Bob Hagen, who had a lot of other work to do anyway."

The project continued as before, including sporadic meetings with the Thursday-morning group. Sheldon usually attended but Katz was seldom present. When the final report was ready, a presentation was made with slides to the Thursday-morning group, which reacted favorably. The report called attention to a "lack of agreement on corporate strategy among Gamma's senior executives, as well as to a number of formal systems that seemed to be in conflict with each other, such as budgets with compensation." The same report was also given to

Gamma's Management Council, including Ralph Hines in attendance. Again, the report was well received.

Shortly thereafter, Chris Miller asked SMA to prepare a second proposal on "implementation planning." The proposal was immediately written and submitted, with estimated fees of $700,000, which were to cover a further investigation of the strategy and preparation of an action plan. Within two weeks, Chris Miller called SMA to say that the proposal had been approved.

During the second stage of implementation planning, the same scheduling problems continued with the Thursday-morning group; only two meetings were held, but neither Katz nor Sheldon were in attendance at the same time. Nevertheless, both Sheldon and Katz separately indicated in contacts with Miller that they were pleased with the project to date.

As the final report neared completion, a surprising and unexpected event occurred. The European majority shareholder suddenly decided to take charge of Gamma, and sent its Vice-Chairman, Henry Francis, to reside at Gamma's headquarters. It had acted, with agreement of Gamma's Board and Ralph Hines, because of their shared concern for Gamma's deteriorating profit position. Francis was appointed as Vice-Chairman of Gamma, reporting directly to Hines. Francis planned to reside at Gamma headquarters until he completed a full assessment of Gamma's situation, after which he would submit recommendations to Gamma's Board and its European shareholder.

Gamma's senior management was stunned by the move, as were SMA's consultants. Chris Miller informed SMA about the move, and asked SMA to postpone its final report on implementation for a few weeks until he could become better acquainted with the new Vice-Chairman. Four weeks later, Chris Miller asked SMA to make its report on implementation to Henry Francis (the new Vice-Chairman). SMA gave its final report orally with slides to Francis, Ralph Hines, Chris Miller, as well as Harry Katz who requested at the last minute to be allowed to sit in. The Vice-Chairman listened thoughtfully, asked several questions, and took a few notes. The other parties remained silent. At the conclusion, Henry Francis warmly thanked the consultants, saying that he would like to meet privately with them in a few weeks.

SMA heard nothing from Gamma until four weeks later, when an SMA consultant learned from an executive at Gamma that Harry Katz was "rumored to be on his way out." One week later, the newspapers reported that both Katz and Sheldon had resigned. Three days later, the newspapers reported that a new President had been appointed from outside the company to replace Sheldon, but Katz's position was not filled. The new President was placed in charge of the entire company, reporting directly to Chairman Ralph Hines. The Vice-Chairman from the European shareholder, Henry Francis, announced that he was returning to his Brussels base.

Two months later, the SMA consultants, not having heard from Gamma, called Chris Miller, who said, "It is too early for SMA to make their report to the new President," and that "I will get back in touch with you as soon as it seems appropriate." Two months passed without a call from Miller. The consultants were puzzled; they had made over $1,600,000 in fees, yet there had been no call.

Case 4.2

BAIN & COMPANY: INTERNATIONAL EXPANSION

(Peter J. Williamson and Michael Y. Yoshino)

"Bain is back, engines on full thrust." This was the way one observer described the resurgence of Bain & Company by mid-1994. The firm had survived a difficult transition in control from its founder group to a worldwide partnership in 1991. Three years later, performance had dramatically exceeded the original plan: revenue had grown at more than 25% per year, more than 500 new employees had been recruited (most of whom had offers to join Bain's primary competitors), staff turnover was at an all-time low, and client requests for proposals had almost tripled.

BAIN 2000

Bain's managing director, Tom Tierney, knew it was time to take another serious look forward. With his fellow partners, particularly those on the Policy Committee, he needed to reassess what had worked and what hadn't, to prepare the business to meet the demands of a changing market for consulting services, and to decide on how and where to grow towards 2000.

The firm's bedrock would remain its core values which stressed delivering financial results for clients through strategic insight, effective implementation, and teamwork. Bain's existing mission statement (see Exhibit 4.1) which had guided the firm since its founding was re-affirmed. Consistent with this mission, Bain's overriding objectives for the year 2000 were twofold: double the value received by clients for each dollar they invested in Bain, and make Bain, by far, the most attractive strategy consulting firm to join and pursue a career with.

Deciding how and where to grow was a very real current issue for the firm. The partner group generated opportunities to grow in Bain's

---

Exhibit 4.1 Bain & Company, Inc., Mission Statement

Bain & Company's mission is to help our clients create such high levels of economic value that together we set new standards of excellence in our respective industries.

This mission demands:

- The Bain vision of the most productive client relationship and single-minded dedication to achieving it with each client.
- The Bain community of extraordinary teams.
- The Bain approach to creating value, based on a sharp competitive and customer focus, the most effective analytic techniques, and our process for collaboration with the client.

We believe that accomplishing our mission will redefine the management consulting business and will provide new levels of rewards for our clients and for our organization.

Firm Operating Principles
- One firm
- Teamwork
- Commitment to client success, individual success, and firm success
- Excellence/meritocracy
- Fun
- Trust

current geographic markets in greater numbers than could be pursued with the existing human resources. This constant stream of opportunities was forcing trade-offs to be made regarding client assignments. In addition, the company was faced with a series of major investment proposals: an unexpected opportunity to acquire a 600-person consulting firm in Europe, competitive pressure to open an office in Mexico, and opportunities to get in on the ground floor of a number of rapidly emerging Asian markets—markets where the future battle among global consulting firms might be won or lost. There were also questions about the shape of tomorrow's Bain & Company. Recent growth had been driven, in part, by aggressive international expansion. Over the past three years, Bain had opened offices in Hong Kong, Beijing, Seoul, Singapore, Costa Rica, Stockholm, Madrid, Warsaw, and Rome. It had also undertaken major expansions in Sydney and Moscow. Was further greenfield geographic expansion the best use of scarce resources? What strains would further growth put on Bain's cherished "one firm" culture? How should Tom Tierney and Bain's core management team go about managing a service business that was becoming increasingly diversified around the globe? What approaches were necessary to ensure consistent quality and to avoid duplication? How should Bain go about further integrating its business worldwide?

AN INDUSTRY IN FLUX

Primary demand for consulting was growing at between 5% and 15% per year in real terms. While emerging markets like Mexico and Asia were expanding at spectacular rates from a low base, there was still significant growth in the United States—the world's largest consulting market. There was also growth in Europe. While the industry was already well established in some European markets like the United Kingdom and Germany, in other countries, such as Spain, there was a large potential market among clients who had made little or no prior use of consultants.

Drivers of Industry Growth

Growth was being driven by a variety of factors. One important driver was the need to access specialized skills. In order to remain competitive, corporations needed to access increasingly specialized capabilities in everything from strategy and marketing to plant design and IT systems. Where demand for these skills varied as businesses developed (a large strategy team might be needed at one time and a specialist IT team at another), many firms could not justify keeping the necessary capacity in-house. At the same time, many companies had eliminated central services and staff functions in the drive towards a "lean" corporate center. These trends were generating increased demand for consulting services as a way to access external capabilities and help accelerate organizational change.

Another important factor was what some consultants argued was a decline in "shelf-life" of strategies. In the 1960s, a strategy might have been revisited only once in five years or more. By the 1990s, the accelerated pace of change meant that, while the basic strategic direction may be sustained for years, specific initiatives would have to be continually reevaluated and adapted to volatile market and competitor moves. This created demand for both general strategy and specialist consultants. Finally, more and more industries were facing "discontinuities" in their operating environment caused by factors such as deregulation, new technologies, major shifts in government spending (cutbacks in defense spending, for example), falling trade barriers, and "maverick" competitors who challenged industry norms. These changes demanded that an increasing number of companies, even those who had been comfortable industry leaders for decades, had to "reinvent" themselves. To meet this challenge, they needed to borrow experience from other industries and markets—a process where experienced consultants could play an important role.

In other cases, companies were being forced to look at entering unfamiliar, emerging markets, like China or eastern Europe, as a source of growth. These potential clients needed consultants who could help them build a bridge between their existing operations and skills and the demands of frontier markets emerging from fundamentally different economic systems and with different business cultures.

Segmentation

This diverse set of factors driving growth in demand for consulting meant that the business was further segmenting as it expanded. Lumping this multibillion-dollar industry under the single heading of "consulting" was something of a misnomer. Beneath this broad umbrella, consultants included the large, strategy generalists like McKinsey, Bain & Company, and The Boston Consulting Group (BCG); companies that specialized in a particular industry or type of problem (such as First Manhattan Group in banking, The Thomas Group in cycle-time reduction, Proudfoot in manufacturing efficiency); companies that built on enormous strength in a functional specialty like IT, such as Andersen Consulting—originally a spinoff from the accounting firm Arthur Andersen; "national champions" with a very strong base in their home market, such as Roland Berger in Germany (now a subsidiary of the giant Deutsche Bank); firms like CSC Index that had their roots in the dramatic growth of a single product like "re-engineering"; and "one-man-band" consultants or small partnerships that built upon the personal relationships of their founders.

Depending on the particular issue the client perceived, the strategy generalists might come into competition at the margin with any of these other groups. This was partly because a number of the more specialized firms had sought to build strategy practices as a way of "pulling through" the sale of their mainstream services like IT or plant efficiency studies on the back of a strategy review. In the more mature markets, however, major clients were becoming increasingly sophisticated buyers. If they were clear what the problem was or where they needed outside skills to augment in-house capability, they would approach the firms with proven expertise in that area. If, on the other hand, they needed a fundamental strategy review that would encompass an entire business and where the requirement was to frame the problem and to develop creative, bold-stroke solutions, they would be more likely to approach one or more of the leading global strategy generalists (or "top tier" firms as members of this group preferred to call themselves). As a result, when a company like Bain found itself in a "bake off" where the potential client requested proposals from a number of consultants, the competitors were most likely to include McKinsey and BCG (see Exhibit 4.2).

Buying Behavior

Increasingly sophisticated buyers were also demanding higher value-added from consultants. Many had war stories where past consulting experiences fell well short of expectations. Today, the potential clients often spoke in terms of success-related (contingency) fees and measurable results, and "house accounts" were opening up their business to competition. Some observers believed these trends would play to the strengths of specialists: it was often easier to demonstrate immediate cost savings or revenue enhancement when the problem was limited and well-defined than to measure the impact of a major strategic repositioning where a consultant's contribution was difficult to isolate and where the benefit might be spread over many years. At the same time, some specialist firms were suffering from client disenchantment with tools that had delivered far less than the consultants had promised.

Exhibit 4.2 Bain's Competitors in Bake-Offs

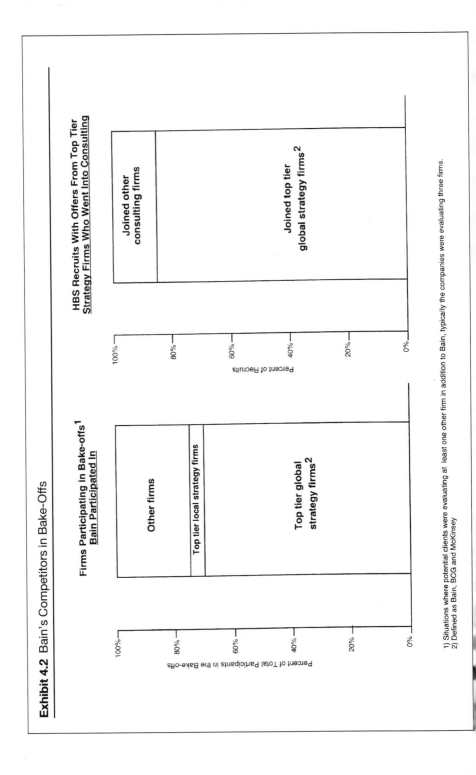

Firms Participating in Bake-offs[1] Bain Participated In

Percent of Total Participants in the Bake-offs

- Other firms
- Top tier local strategy firms
- Top tier global strategy firms[2]

HBS Recruits With Offers From Top Tier Strategy Firms Who Went Into Consulting

Percent of Recruits

- Joined other consulting firms
- Joined top tier global strategy firms[2]

1) Situations where potential clients were evaluating at least one other firm in addition to Bain, typically the companies were evaluating three firms.
2) Defined as Bain, BCG and McKinsey

Using one of the leading generalist consultants for a major strategy study also meant the client needed a substantial budget. As a result, the core market for leading strategy houses comprised those companies around the world with more than $1 billion in sales. It was estimated that there were around 500 of these billion-dollar companies in Asia, 1,100 in Europe, and 1,100 in North America (see Exhibit 4.3). In addition, there was growing demand for consulting among companies with revenues of between $200 million and $1 billion, especially those in growing markets.

Even among those with both the cash and the ambition for a fundamental reassessment of their strategy, clients were wary of paying generalist consultants to learn about their industry from scratch: the ability to demonstrate a basic knowledge of technology, cost structure, distribution, etc., was becoming a requirement just to enter the race.

Multinationals were a key segment within the target market of billion-dollar corporations. Traditionally, many of these companies had bought consulting from their headquarters. But the buying patterns of multinationals were changing as they moved closer to "transnational" structures. Regional management was becoming more important in the buying decision, especially in Europe, and country managers were emerging as increasingly autonomous buyers for some types of requirements. These changes were making it untenable to run an international consulting firm staffed out of one or two massive offices in which entire teams simply parachuted into another country only when a client project demanded. Equally important, as multinationals began to operate global networks, sharing products, manufacturing capacity, marketing and sales resources, and decision making, they expected their consultants to operate with a mirror image of this global network. These demands were straining the traditional management structures of those international consulting firms that were based on strong national offices run by a local partner group (which, in some cases, had begun to act like geographic fiefdoms).

Emerging Markets

The increased importance of emerging markets like China, India, and Latin America, was also presenting challenges as well as opportunities for the consulting industry. The market among multinational corporations operating in these regions was attractive: multinationals were sophisticated buyers for whom the fee levels would come as no shock. But they often wanted to be sure that the consultant already had some

Exhibit 4.3 Strategy Consultant Market

Country	Estimated Number of Companies with Revenues > $1 Billion	Estimated 1994 Strategy Consulting Market[a]
United States	1,035	
Germany/Austria	260	
United Kingdom	290	
Japan	360	
Italy	60	
France	200	
Canada	100	
G7 Subtotal	2,305	$3,500–$4,200MM
Scandinavia	160	
South Korea	15	
Australia/New Zealand	40	
Spain/Portugal	45	
Switzerland	50	
Benelux	100	
Hong Kong	20	
Subtotal	430	$400–$500MM
Mexico	20	
Brazil	25	
India	*	
Singapore	*	
Taiwan	*	
Malaysia	*	
Thailand	*	
South Africa	40	
Argentina	*	
Chile	*	
Venezuela	*	
Israel	*	
Subtotal	85	$100–$200MM
GRAND TOTAL	2,820	$4,000–$4,900MM

a Industry estimates, various sources
* Indicates less than five (5) companies

local experience so that they didn't end up financing the consultant's learning curve in a new environment; and because many of these large companies already had some local presence and regional organizations, they were looking for in-depth studies which put a greater premium on local knowledge, and not just "entry-level" products. Consulting firms wishing to enter emerging markets on the back of multinationals could therefore face a "chicken and egg" dilemma: an inability to sell cases without local experience, but no chance to build their experience without a case. The alternative was to gain experience by serving local clients. Here the problem was that potential clients often had little experience of using consultants, other than for highly specialized activities such as technology or plant design. While there were possible advantages to being a first mover in emerging markets, creating generic demand could be expensive, and willingness to pay was lower because consultants' fees could be relatively high compared with local wages. It was also unclear just how sustainable first-mover advantages would be.

The types of people needed to serve the two main customer groups might also be different. Local companies often preferred expatriates who knew what was going on among the world-class companies and could help them to catch up; multinationals often wanted access to the best local people with good connections and a detailed knowledge of how business in the country actually worked on the ground.

Competing for the Best People

Finally, firms in the consulting industry had to compete for the "right" people. Firms had to be able to attract and retain high-caliber individuals whose capabilities and experience were consistent with the ability to deliver differentiated services to their target customers. As with potential customers, there was little overlap between the recruits who were interested in and being pursued by the leading strategy firms and the other consulting firms. As a result, when Bain found itself competing with other consulting firms for a recruit, it was most likely to be facing McKinsey and/or BCG (see Exhibit 4.2). Some firms accorded particular emphasis to hiring individuals who possessed what they termed "a good cultural fit." Dave Johnson, a partner who also headed Bain's worldwide recruiting, described what Bain was looking for in the way of good fit.

> Superior analytical skills and creativity are the first hurdles that a recruit must clear in the evaluation process. We make decisions on whom within that group will receive offers based on our assessment of how well they would fit at Bain, which for us means asking ourselves the following questions: "Will they thrive in a highly team-oriented culture?" "Will they get excited about working hand in hand with the clients at all levels to drive to results?"

"Are they leaders who can successfully guide their clients and colleagues through difficult challenges?" "Do they share our values and our mission to create business success stories?"

New consultants were becoming increasingly demanding of consulting firms: they were looking for learning potential, diversity, career advancement, and lifestyle, not just financial reward. To deliver these rewards, a consulting firm would have to grow so as to generate opportunities for career advancement and a stream of new challenges. Working with the same clients in an established office for years or even repeatedly working on the same sort of problem in a long series of new environments may demotivate consultants. As one strategy consultant put it, "People don't line up to volunteer for another cost study if they've already done four." The alternative to growth was to pursue the "up or out" principle with consequent high turnover and continual reinvestment in training. The competition to recruit and retain people also limited a firm's ability to bully people into moving to less attractive cities or countries to build a new office or to force them to spend too much of their time on the road.

Depending on the type of consulting service they were selling, some firms hired people with industry experience. Others hired experienced local business people to lead their expansion into new markets. Hiring people away from directly competing consulting firms was another potential source of experienced people. Although a common practice in other professional service businesses like law or investment banking, hiring within the industry had been relatively rare in the consulting business. More recently, however, some of the IT firms entering the management consulting business had begun to hire aggressively on the open market, so much so that Arthur D. Little had recently taken out a court order to stop Electronic Data Systems from hiring any more of its staff. Another potential source of capacity was the constant stream of smaller consulting firms (and sometimes medium-sized local or regional firms) available for acquisition. Having built a business to a certain level, the founders of these firms usually wanted to "cash out." Selling the business to a larger firm provided an attractive exit route, offering a mix of cash for the owners and a degree of continuity for their staffs.

THE MAJOR PLAYERS

Bain's major competitors were the other leading strategy generalists. McKinsey and BCG, Bain's most direct competitors, are profiled below, along with a number of other consulting firms which, despite a different heritage and focus, occasionally appeared on the radar screen for particular types of projects. These included: Andersen Consulting, Booz Allen & Hamilton, Gemini Consulting, and Arthur D. Little.

McKinsey & Company, Inc.

Founded in 1926 by J. O. McKinsey, by 1993, McKinsey & Company had revenues estimated at $1.2 billion and 3,100 consultants in 60 offices around the world. Its approach to consulting and its culture were heavily influenced by its long-time leader, Marvin Bower. Bower told *Fortune* magazine in 1993: "My vision was to provide advice on managing to top executives and to do it with the professional standing of a leading law firm." His proud explanation of how he turned down Howard Hughes as a client ("it is our duty not to start an engagement with clients that aren't ready to be served") perhaps sums up something of the culture of the company that likes to describe itself simply as "The Firm."[1]

McKinsey began expanding internationally in 1959 when it opened a London office. By 1971 it already had 17 offices on four continents. It continued to spread its geographic reach aggressively during the 1970s, and then by 1980 it started systematically building up what is today a huge database of information on a range of industries worldwide which its consultants could tap into. It established think tanks in Brussels and Washington to facilitate "knowledge building" across its global network.

Few doubted the strength of Mckinsey's global brand, their wealth of accumulated experience, and their ability to hire and retain excellent people. They had deep pockets and could afford to invest substantial resources in developing new markets. But, as by far the largest firm in strategy consulting, they not surprisingly attracted critics. Former McKinsey partner and co-author of *In Search of Excellence* Tom Peters felt McKinsey was too much of "a left-brained (analytic) institution" and that he didn't "see enough creativity in the firm today."[2] Others pointed out that, despite a formidable growth record, it would inevitably take a long time for new consultants to attain senior positions in McKinsey's mammoth organization, and that there were bound to be fewer opportunities for champions to build something new than in smaller firms. Concerns had also been raised that McKinsey's partnership structure might be struggling to cope with its growth and global spread and that their size may present future problems for "The Firm." These potential disadvantages of size included challenges presented by trying to grow at the rate of the market without sacrificing selectivity with respect to new client assignments and recruits.

The Boston Consulting Group

Founded in 1963 by Bruce Henderson, a former Arthur D. Little consultant, The Boston Consulting Group (BCG) was the first large management consulting firm to specialize in strategy consulting. It took a highly analytical approach aimed at understanding the drivers of its client's competitive positioning and became recognized for its intellectual leadership. This included the thinking behind a string of well-known tools ranging from the "experience curve" and the "growth-share" matrix through to today's more sophisticated offerings like "time-based competition" and "competing on capabilities" which have spawned articles in the *Harvard Business Review*.

BCG began to expand internationally relatively early in its life cycle so that by 1970 it had offices in London, Munich, Paris, and Tokyo, as well as Boston and San Francisco. By 1994 it had some 1,100 consultants in 28 offices (including 8 in the Asia-Pacific region and 1 in Latin America) generating revenues of $340 million (1993 industry estimate).

BCG put little emphasis on formal structure, preferring to rely on a compensation system that rewards the individual for teamwork and cooperation. Respect for the individual was a deep-seated belief, as Barry Jones, head of BCG's London office put it: "They're relatively their own people with their own ideas." The support systems were coordinated on a regional basis and each region is represented on the global executive committee, although regional administration was described as "light." Some insight into this culture is perhaps best explained by BCG's approach to writing a statement of values in 1990 with the aim of solidifying a common ethos in the face of rapid growth. The company reportedly set up teams in each of the main regions to codify what they thought the Group's core values should be. When these statements were brought together, the partners were surprised and pleased to discover how similar they were. The "partnership" of around 140 partners meets together somewhere in the world every six months. BCG also urged its consultants to spend a period of their careers in a region away from their home base.

One of BCG's favorite phrases was "helping the client look outside the box"; another was "the voyage of discovery." While BCG had more recently stressed implementation, critics claimed it had not thrown off an excessively academic, "textbookish" approach. While the market was clearly demanding more of an implementation focus, BCG's heritage and culture had been an impediment to shifting with the market. It was unclear how BCG's consultants would respond to significantly shifting the mix of their time from strategy development to driving the client change management process. BCG was also finding that maintaining its intellectual leadership positioning in the marketplace was becoming increasingly difficult, given the rate at which the other firms "copied" their innovations. Finally, while some saw BCG's loose structure and individualistic culture as a strength, others believed it would impair their ability to achieve the level of coordination across offices required to best meet customer needs.

Andersen Consulting

The roots of Andersen Consulting went back to 1918 when Arthur Andersen's accounting practice had begun advising clients. By the 1970s, it had built a large information systems consultancy and, in the 1980s, began moving into strategy and organizational change consulting. In 1980, the consulting arm broke away from the accounting side to form Andersen Consulting. With a mix of business school recruiting and hiring from competitors, it had built a group of 600 strategy consultants and a change management practice with 1,200 professionals by 1993.

The difficulty for Andersen lay in integrating these strategy and change management people into an IT systems organization of more than 22,000 professionals with 71 offices in North America, 60 offices across Europe, the Middle East, Africa, and India, and a further 19 offices in the Asia-Pacific region, generating revenues of $2.8 billion (1993). The company's structure had been built for large-scale delivery of systems design and implementation. A ratio of junior staff to partners of 16 to one was common on a traditional systems project. Graduates were trained in The Andersen Way at the company university (critics called them Android clones) in a clear methodology that ensured delivery of consistent quality. While Andersen set the benchmark for service and knowhow in IT, it continued to grapple with managing an increasingly diverse group of professionals with varying skills, experience, and styles.

Booz, Allen & Hamilton

Arguably, the core of the Booz Allen business is one of its oldest and largest clients: the U.S. government, for whom the company had worked in defense, aerospace, artificial intelligence, and other programs since

World War I. This relationship had formed the foundation for a business that by 1994 employed 3,200 consultants in 44 offices with revenues of $800 million (1993).

Booz was one of the first of the large consulting firms to begin to build a global organization with both a worldwide technology practice and "Worldwide Commercial"—the firm's general strategy consulting arm. By 1994, 50% of revenues were earned outside the United States. The company was looking to grow at least as fast as the market in Asia and South America to maintain its share, and to grow market share in Europe, where it had historically been relatively weak. It was considered to be a potentially strong competitor to the strategy generalists in its core industries like defense and aerospace, where technology played a major role.

Worldwide Commercial was structured as a matrix of global industry practices and global functional practices. As part of the Booz "Vision 2000," consultants had been regrouped into cross-functional global teams based around the industry practices with substantial management authority delegated down to team level. The compensation system had been changed from individual bonuses to uniform percentage bonuses for each member of a team. As part of this new structure, Booz Allen had begun to set up what it termed "geographic footprints": concentrations of consultants specializing in a particular field large enough to provide critical mass in one location that would serve its "footprint" or hinterland. Booz had also recently appointed a "Chief Knowledge Officer" with a large budget to fund investment in support of technology and research and development.

Gemini Consulting

Gemini was the product of a series of major acquisitions by the French firm Sogeti, owners of the systems house Cap Gemini. Through the early 1990s, Sogeti purchased the strategy consultants MAC Group, United Research, and the German firm, Gruber Titze and Partners, to build Gemini Consulting. Despite its 1,700 consultants, 17 offices in the United States, Europe, Southeast Asia, and Africa, and revenues of $432 million (1993), Gemini remained the smallest unit within the Sogeti group.

Gemini and its parent had expressed determination to become a truly global consulting organization. It has targeted major global clients with whom it sought to build long-term relationships. A global matrix, which the firm introduced on January 1, 1994, has replaced the former regional organization. It aimed to take global industry specialists (with strength in strategy consulting to the financial services and telecoms industries) from the former MAC Group and merge these with the much larger United Research (with experience in operations consulting, especially in oil, gas, and chemicals). The aim was to form teams with consultants who have expertise in a series of functional disciplines including strategy, operations, marketing, and IT. This combined to form the favorite Gemini product, "The Four Rs": reframing (achieving a paradigm shift), restructuring (portfolio shifts and re-engineering); revitalizing (growing existing businesses and inventing new ones), and renewing (including growing people).

Critics pointed out that the merging of different consulting cultures had been unsettling and that the initial high staff turnover could remain a problem. Others suggested that the "one-stop-shop" concept is fundamentally flawed; no consulting firm can be excellent across the board, and objectivity is potentially sacrificed. "Gemini faces real challenges," stated one former Gemini partner. "Their amalgamation of organizations makes it difficult for them to deliver consistently high-quality results with clients. In addition, they will continue to struggle to integrate the diverse cultures of the business strategists and the technical consultants."

Arthur D. Little (ADL)

ADL grew out of a research laboratory founded in 1886 by a 23-year-old chemist, Arthur Dehol Little. By 1994, the company comprised three distinct businesses: management consulting accounted for around two-thirds of revenues; the remainder was equally divided between technology and product development, and environmental, health, and safety consulting. ADL employed 1,579 consultants in 34 offices around the world and generated revenues of $385 million (1993).

ADL's global business was structured into a series of regional practices: North America, Latin America, Europe, and Asia Pacific, plus an oil and gas unit. Each of these regions was a profit center with senior managers reporting to a board of directors which combined officers elected internally for a three-year term with a group of high-profile outside directors. ADL's strength was regarded as its consultants' expertise in specific industries and technologies. Critics claimed its aspirations to grow its strategy consulting business were unrealistic and it would be better off sticking to "nuts and bolts" consulting where its strength lay.

BAIN & COMPANY: GROWTH, CRISIS, AND RENEWAL

Bain & Company was founded in 1973 by Bill Bain, a former Boston Consulting Group vice-president. Bain's focus was on results-oriented, relationship-driven consulting, with heavy emphasis on implementation. Bain recognized that sustainable improvements in results were unlikely to be achieved as a result of a three-month study and that to really transform a company's strategy required a long-term relationship based on mutual benefit and trust. Therefore, Bain aspired to and often achieved a type of relationship with clients that was the exact opposite of the industry norm: Bain would commit to refuse to work with the client's competitors in return for an intensive, long-term working relationship (and the client's commitment not to hire one of Bain's competitors). Bain was convinced that this unique approach to working with clients was the best way to add significant value to a client's business.

Bain's basic formula worked well. Bain & Company grew rapidly, sometimes by as much as 50% in a single year, with revenues of $750,000 in 1973, rising to over $100 million by the mid-1980s. By 1994, Bain had more than 1,250 employees in 23 offices (see Exhibit 4.4). (Industry experts estimated Bain's 1993 revenues at $220MM.)

CRISIS AND RECOVERY

During this growth phase in the late 1980s, Bill Bain and seven other "founding" partners decided to sell 30% of the company into an ESOP (Employee Stock Ownership Plan). The company borrowed around $200 million to pay these eight partners for part of their equity. As a result, the firm took on the burden of $25 million per year in interest payments to be paid out of future revenues. As the growth of

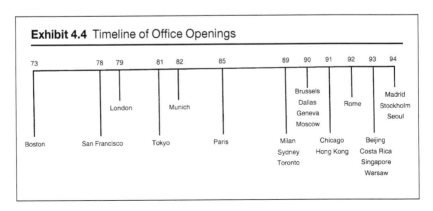

Exhibit 4.4 Timeline of Office Openings

the firm slowed during the late 1980s, the financial obligations created by the ESOP became onerous, creating both cash flow difficulties and tremendous tension between the vice-presidents and the founders. A difficult three-year period, 1988–1990 (during which the firm was forced to lay off a number of its employees), culminated with a fundamental restructuring of the ownership, organizational structure, and balance sheet of the company.

As part of the restructuring, the "founding" partners agreed to return approximately $100 million to the firm in cash and forgiven debt and to surrender the remaining 70% of equity they held. Bill Bain stepped down as chairman and CEO. Following the restructuring, Bain employees held 40% of the stock (through the ESOP), while 75 new partners owned the remaining 60%. This provided an incentive for Bain's key people to stay on and rebuild the firm. Rebuild the firm is exactly what this team did. As described above, the results of the first three years after the restructuring dramatically exceeded all expectations.

One of the first steps taken by the new owners of the firm was to adopt a new governance structure, partner compensation system, and organization chart (see Exhibit 4.5). Embodying what Tom Tierney described as "a partnership of equals,"[3] much more emphasis was placed on building consensus and getting widespread buy-in to major decisions. The crisis had dramatically strengthened the organization and reinforced its core values.

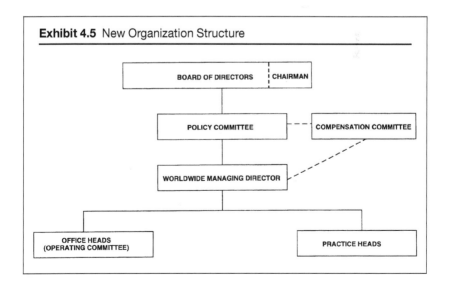

Exhibit 4.5 New Organization Structure

BAIN'S SOURCES OF DIFFERENTIATION

"Compare the marketing brochures from different consulting companies today," said Bain director Peter Tornquist,

> and one sees very similar words from a handful of top consulting firms—like soap powders one, two, and three. Our clients and our people know we are different, but the challenge is to communicate that to potential clients and recruits who have not worked with us yet.

Every firm in the consulting business had to have a pool of expertise to sell. The differences really came down to two things: the precise kind of expertise a consulting firm had accumulated, and how it chose to organize and deliver that expertise through its people.

THE PRODUCT

The Bain partners believed that the principal elements of their value proposition—a clear emphasis on achieving results through strategy implementation, an integrated approach to problem solving that employed tools specific to a client's needs, and innovative solutions that would draw on a wide experience base—afforded an important source of competitive advantage. This strong emphasis on helping clients achieve results was underscored by the firm's systematic tracking of both its clients' stock performance versus the market performance (Bain's clients had out-performed the market by two and one-half times since 1980) and the returns on investment in Bain fees that clients realized on individual assignments.

Many of Bain's competitors chose to build up and market expertise along industry or geographic lines. Industry practice areas or geographic profit centers would then dominate the structure of their global organizations. For example, McKinsey had tens of "practice areas," loosely affiliated groups charged with sharing, codifying and developing knowledge in particular sectors like electronics, banking, telecommunications, or retailing. These practice areas were headed by partners with worldwide responsibilities for that area.

In recent years, BCG had developed 10 practice areas (some industry-based like financial services or health care, others based on a concept like time-based competition).

In terms of the investment in industry and concept-based practice areas, Bain fell in between McKinsey and BCG. However, increasingly, the dominant axis of Bain's business was neither industry nor geography, but "problem type." This meant organizing its expertise around sets of customer needs, like large company transformation and industry redefinition. This approach meant the lessons learned in tackling a similar problem in other industries or geographic environments could more readily be tapped when addressing a client's particular circumstances. Bain believed this helped ensure its consultants were not trapped by the conventional wisdom of an industry. At the same time, it meant that Bain would not be overly dependent on particular tools like re-engineering, thereby avoiding the danger of a "solution in search of a problem" that had often led particular tools to fall out of favor through misapplication.

People and Culture as Differentiators

Bain & Company believed that its culture was another key differentiator through its influence on both the Bain product and the way it was delivered. Tierney described the Bain culture as "maniacal about results." Orit Gadiesh, Bain's chairman of the board, and widely recognized as "Bain's spiritual leader," offered her view of what is unique about the firm's culture in a companywide address regarding Bain's core values. The following is an excerpt from this speech entitled "True North Culture."

> When you listen to clients, employees, and alumni of Bain & Company talk about what is unique about our firm, what emerges is our TRUE NORTH! There isn't one single phrase or sentence that is used, but the individual anecdotes collectively build the theme. What comes through is a commitment to find out the *truth*, look it *square in the eye* with our clients and *stick* to it even when it is hard. What also comes through is our commitment to work with our clients to turn the truth into the best *results* possible for them. And what finally comes through is that our *kind of commitment* and the *extent* of it, are rare.

Framed copies of the excerpts from this speech, delivered on the firm's twentieth anniversary, appeared on the walls of Bain offices around the world (see Exhibit 4.6). Senior management felt very strongly that the firm's future success would depend on maintaining this culture.

With the aim of delivering results through the development and implementation of a highly customized product, Bain was looking for bright, well-rounded people with a line orientation who share the firm's values and sense of mission. Dave Johnson added:

Exhibit 4.6 Strategy Consultant Market

Excerpts from a speech by Orit Gadiesh, Chairman of the Board, Bain & Company, Inc.:

"We've all used a compass to navigate. Most of us, out on a simple camping adventure, use an ordinary compass to find north. But an ordinary compass points to magnetic north, and the direction of magnetic north changes, depending on both the time and your location. If you really need to find where true North is, you need a gyro compass that works based on its own *internal* system, rather than the external system of the very fickle magnetic field. Magnetic north is fine for an afternoon's walk. But if you're on a stormy ocean and the winds are shifting and you're running out of food and water—you had better know where true north is, or you may not survive."

"Companies and organizations that want to survive need to find their own TRUE NORTH. TRUE NORTH is what ultimately defines an organization and its core values. It's what should eventually be predictable about an organization, even if it is hard to stick to at times. It is actions, not words. It is not a mission statement about what the organization should be, but rather it is what really actuates an organization. And its dissemination, implicit or explicit, within the organization is what forms the basis for trust."

"TRUE NORTH is *not* about not changing with the time. On the contrary, it is about adjusting and growing, but without letting go of what defines you at the core. In fact, you only *really* know you have a TRUE NORTH when tradeoffs have had to be made, when your organization has been tested and it has emerged from the test still holding on to the same values."

"When you listen to clients, employees ad alumni of Bain & Company talk about what is unique about our firm, what emerges is our TRUE NORTH! There isn't one single phrase or sentence that is used, but the individual anecdotes collectively build the theme. What comes through is a commitment to find out the *truth*, look it *square in the eye* with our clients and *stick* to it even when it is hard. What also comes through is our commitment to work with our clients to turn the truth into the best *results* possible for the client. And what finally comes through is that our *kind of commitment* and the *extent* of it are rare."

"This approach and the way we apply it has always been one of our most important core values, and I believe that in our 20 years it has never diminished. If anything, it has strengthened and continued to define us over time. I'm not sure that 20 years ago we could truly articulate it. When a firm is founded, many things are said about how it is going to be different and better and braver than its competitors. But when a firm is founded it hasn't been tested yet. It is when the years pass and actions are taken and decisions are made that are consistent with the same themes, that a culture develops, and a TRUE NORTH is or is not established and maintained. Only then is it transferable to successive generations."

"This approach has caused us to take actions or make decisions that on the margin would have been easier—and at times more profitable—to make differently. Indeed, this is how all organizations get tested and by and large, as we have been tested, we have come out on the right side of things."

"I know that during our 20 years as a firm there were times when decisions were made that were not consistent with this TRUE NORTH theme. Those are the ones people actually remember best and, ironically, perhaps that's healthy. We remember them because they were inconsistent with what we feel in our gut is right."

"At the end of the day, though, it's the *cumulative set of actions* that our organization has taken in the past and will take in the future that defines its TRUE NORTH. That set of actions reflects back to us our values, and they can only thrive if we have the same vision and set of convictions, and are guided by the same principles."

"Every one of us is a *custodian* of TRUE NORTH. This is the one thing that *no one* can mandate. Every day, in everything that we do, our TRUE NORTH is either reflected in our reality or it is not. Its power comes from the fact that the overwhelming majority of us believes in it."

"Each person lives with these principles and strengthens our values every time he or she makes a choice. In making these choices we all become role models for each other and for all the people who will come behind us."

Continued

Exhibit 4.6 Continued

"I believe that if we can *continue* to be defined by what has carried us so far, and if we can *continue* to use and project the power that comes with our TRUE NORTH convictions, then no matter what we face, we will continue to be an organization that is both unique and remarkable."

More so than any other strategy consulting firm, we attract people who want to learn what it would take to be a successful general manager and whose alternative to going into consulting is getting on the general manager track at a company. The fact that well over half of the consultants who leave Bain go into line management positions, startups, or the venture capital business is indicative of the difference between our people and our competitors.

A key element of the Bain approach was also consistency around the globe. This depended on Bain maintaining the "one-firm" culture that had characterized the company from its inception. In the early years, the policy of centralizing the business in a small number of offices automatically encouraged consistency on a single culture. International expansion and the shifts in the way multinationals bought consulting, however, had challenged this philosophy because another plank of Bain's differentiation, what London's managing partner, Robin Buchanan, termed "OPERA," required a structure that mirrored the client's worldwide organization. "OPERA" stood for Overdelivering on quality, Personal relationship with the client, Extra delivery beyond the contracted brief, Reliability, and Availability. Buchanan said simply, "You can't deliver OPERA from thousands of miles away." This was a major challenge that had shaped the way Bain had set about building the global network. In particular, it was one reason that Bain favored organic growth and individual hiring over growth by acquisition.

Target Customer Profile

The Bain approach was particularly attractive to certain types of customers: general managers dissatisfied with the status quo who wanted to achieve breakthrough, not incremental improvements in strategic position and in profits. Experience had shown that when Bain successfully identified these situations, Bain had a high probability of initiating a relationship. Bain's historical overall win rate in competitive situations or "bakeoffs" was greater than 60%, and had remained at that level despite an almost tripling in number of "bakeoffs" participated in. Some examples of the kinds of projects Bain won and lost serve to illustrate:

A large, diversified multinational computer company finds its financial performance deteriorating. It does not have the luxury of a lengthy consulting project which will yield valuable facts and generate interesting debate. It needs to drive through real change quickly. Historically, they have used a variety of consulting firms and one particular competitor has done a number of technical expertise-based projects over the past five years. Given the enormous upside (and downside) they are not interested in using multiple suppliers—they want a single consulting relationship. They are attracted to Bain based on its experience of developing and implementing aggressive profit improvement programs that require major strategic shifts and buy-in from the organization.

* * *

A medium-sized electrical products manufacturer, competing in a low-growth industry, wants a strategy to achieve rapid growth in sales and profits over a five-year period. The management team, who together owned 70% of the company, have had no experience working with strategy consultants and are openly skeptical about the ability of consultants to deliver results. After several meetings with each of the leading strategy firms, the team chooses Bain because of its track record for successfully developing and implementing growth strategies (in particular for medium-sized companies) and Bain's interest in forging a long-term partnership focused on helping them to become a clear leader in their industry.

* * *

A defense contractor wants to implement a breakthrough strategy to address the discontinuous changes in its industry. Management are heavily incented to increase market capitalization. Bain is chosen over competitors who have worked for the company for many years, despite Bain's limited industry experience.

* * *

Bain is asked to tender for a case in Europe that must be regarded as a long-shot because it's up against competitors with well-developed practice groups in the client's industry. It decides to distinguish its proposal by leveraging its experience in distribution strategies in other industries by framing the problem from the standpoint of the final and intermediate customers rather than from the supplier's perspective. This approach is in part the result of the objectivity that comes from "industry blindness."

The kind of cases Bain lost or avoided were more likely to be clients who wanted to buy specific "information" or "expertise" as an input to their strategic planning process. They tended to be project buyers— although they may purchase multiple projects over a period of time —rather than forming a close partnership with a single consulting company. Examples included:

> The CEO of a billion-dollar retail and manufacturing company found the retailing division underperforming. Unsatisfied with the division's business plan, he requested proposals from three consulting firms to "evaluate the underlying dynamics of our industry and provide a basis for our future strategy." Bain proposed a strategic diagnostic aimed at uncovering the opportunities to fundamentally alter the company's performance trajectory ("retail dynamics" was a minor part of the effort). Bain lost, despite a strong introduction from a board member. The winning consulting firm proposed a more modest effort precisely fitting the CEO's original specification and relying heavily on industry expertise.

*   *   *

> A blue-chip consumer product company requests a proposal from Bain to undertake a project addressing frozen food pricing through a specific distribution channel. The company employs at least five different consulting firms on an ad hoc basis each year. The corporate planner had been chartered with completing this study as an input to future pricing strategy. The number of frozen food pricing studies that the firm had done was an important criterion for choosing a consultant. (Bain had done none.) Bain lost.

*   *   *

The type of clients that stood to profit most from Bain's services, Tierney believed, were those contemplating fundamental changes in the way they did business. Bain tried to steer clear of clients that simply wanted to buy products as a way to capture "hot" concepts or conventional industry expertise. The observation of another senior partner echoed Tierney's sentiment: "We want to work for those clients where we can really help achieve significant results and create a business success story."

This orientation toward and track record in delivering results led Bain in the mid-1980s to experiment with approaches to share in the value created for clients. These approaches included the use of success fees, incentive compensation, and equity compensation. Such arrangements, judiciously applied, could better align Bain's incentives and the client's future success. While it was by no means universally applicable, some clients found these types of agreements extraordinarily attractive relative to the standard industry practice of fee-based compensation. This experience with value-sharing clearly differentiated Bain from its primary competitors (see Exhibit 4.7).

The most dramatic example of Bain's results orientation and value-sharing philosophy is Bain Capital. Founded in 1984 as a sister company, this venture capital/LBO group, predicated on Bain's ability to create business success stories, had been extraordinarily successful (see Exhibit 4.8).

BUILDING AN INTEGRATED GLOBAL NETWORK

Bill Bain was originally skeptical about the need for a plethora of offices. He felt it was easier to instill a common culture in staff if they shared the same "home base"—an important consideration for a rapidly growing firm that might otherwise fragment into divergent groups. Spreading people around a far-flung network of offices might also result in pockets of underutilized capacity. As a result, the U.S. business was driven from the company's Boston headquarters and international expansion was relatively slow in the early 1980s.

Following the Client

When Bain did begin to expand internationally, it adopted a "follow the client" strategy. It would open an office only when it had secured a

---

Exhibit 4.7 Value-sharing Approaches Used by Bain

- Tying fees to achieving results (and earning significant risk premium over standard fees). Examples include tying fees to:
  - sale of privatized companies in Poland
  - revenue growth in a retail business
  - cost reduction in a utility company
  - returns realized from the portfolio of a German LBO firm
- Taking stock in small to mid-sized companies in lieu of consulting fees
- Pursuing joint venture with clients to capitalize on business opportunities

Exhibit 4.8 Bain Capital Financial Performance

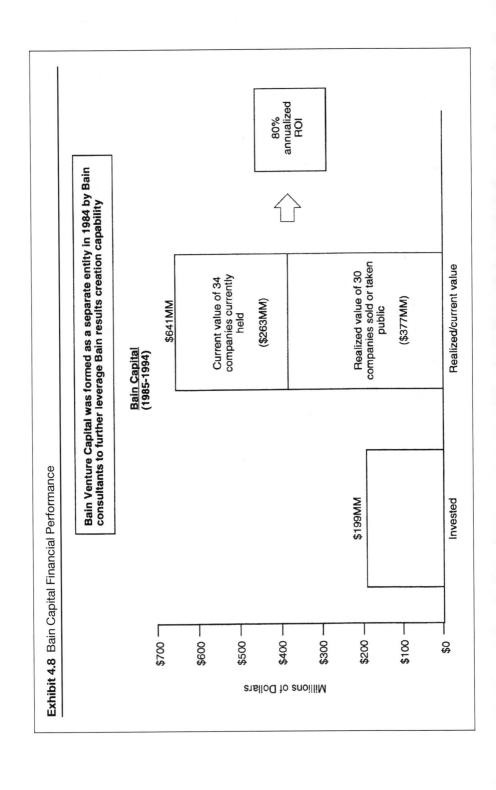

critical mass of client projects which it could expect would be sustained. London was opened in 1978 after, as the office head, Robin Buchanan put it: "we had established a solid base of businesses with U.S. multi-nationals based on people working out of flats." By the early 1980s, the London office had taken over the mantle of the main hub for serving the international (non-U.S.) markets. Work for multinational clients there "took Bain around the world," so London attracted a group of "internationally minded people" from within the company. Many of these people later went off to establish new, overseas offices so these outposts had a ready-made personal network based on relationships established working together in London.

The sole exception to the "follow the client strategy" was the opening of an office in Munich in 1982. The German market appeared to have enormous potential and so as Bain director Peter Tornquist put it: "It was put up your tent, lay out your wares, and hope somebody buys. . . ." In the early 1980s, revenue growth started slowly. By 1994, Bain had approximately 100 people in Munich, but it learned the lesson that building people capacity and selling cold at the same time is an uphill task. The advantages of centralization and international expansion only behind a base of clients were reaffirmed. But gaps in geographic coverage remained, limiting Bain's ability to mirror a multinational client's organization (see Exhibit 4.9).

Over the past three years, Bain had opened offices in Hong Kong, Beijing, Seoul, Singapore, Chicago, Costa Rica, Stockholm, Madrid,

---

Exhibit 4.9 Example Client-Bain Teams for Global Project (1987–89)

Location of the Client Project Team	Home Office of Bain Team Members
United States	Boston
Japan	Tokyo
Rest of Asia	Tokyo
Australia	San Francisco
Germany	Munich
Spain	London
France	Paris
Italy	London
Brazil	London
Venezuela	London
Mexico	San Francisco

Warsaw, and Rome. It had also undertaken major expansions in Sydney and Moscow (see Exhibit 4.10). One important lesson Bain had learned from this global expansion was the importance of champions. John Smith, who had a passion for Russia, was instrumental in the company's effort to build its highly successful Moscow office; Jim Hildebrandt had moved from Australia to Hong Kong to pioneer the firm's push into Asian markets; and Stan Miranda, a London-based American, had championed the firm's Madrid office, which he believed was essential if Bain was to both provide complete services to clients inter-

---

Exhibit 4.10 Sample of Bain's International Expansion (1991–1994)

- **Hong Kong:** Internal champions ("crusaders"); started business from Sydney office are recruited consultants from a number of other offices to build their team.

- **Seoul:** After three years, Bain's informal joint venture with InterConsulting became a standard Bain office when they "bought out" their partner. Seoul became a satellite operation of the Tokyo office in order to share human, intellectual, and administrative resources.

- **Costa Rica:** A senior Bain partner, born and raised in Central America, wants to return there to develop business and serve local companies. Bain supported this crusader with an eye toward future expansions into Mexico and Latin America. Costa Rica became a satellite of the rapidly growing Dallas office; some consultants are transferred to Costa Rica to support the initiative.

- **Stockholm:** A senior European partner was charted with expanding Bain's business in Scandinavia. He ultimately recruited a number of people from LEK. These individuals were trained and integrated in different Bain offices around Europe and were subsequently transferred to Stockholm (along with other Bain staff) to develop that business.

- **Madrid:** Bain hired a number of people from Gemini in Madrid — individuals who had been part of the MAC Consulting firm before Gemini acquired it a few years ago. A Bain partner in London was responsible for the start-up, including transferring people into and out of Madrid to facilitate integration.

- **Moscow:** Fully implemented Bain's 50/50 joint venture with Link, a local Russian firm. The business hired large numbers of Russians as well as expatriates. Many experienced Bain people were transferred in (temporarily and permanently) from other offices around the world.

ested in the European Union and compete in a market that had long been McKinsey's preserve.

As a result of this international expansion, Bain now had between 100 and 200 case teams working in 25 countries at any point in time and 15% (and growing) of its revenues coming from outside the G-7 countries. The ongoing management alone was a formidable task. At the same time, the firm needed to be able to marshall relevant resources and experience worldwide quickly to enable it to react to client requests at both the selling and execution stages of a case. There was also an increasing need for global coordination to meet the needs of emerging transnational clients.

Bain's global integration task was further complicated by the fact that expansion since the late 1980s, while driven by organic growth, had involved joint ventures in both Italy and Russia, a loose alliance in Korea and a number of "outside hires"—selected people attracted away from competitors. In the spring of 1989, for example, Bain had concluded a joint venture with Cuneo & Associates, a startup founded by a former director of McKinsey's Milan office. While this joint venture was regarded as a very successful move, it had taken considerable management time over a period of several years to achieve the expected level of integration into the system of Bain offices. Although the Russian joint venture was now largely managed by homegrown Bainies and was well integrated into the global operation, there had been some friction over the level of investment in early years, and decision making was "a little harder and a little slower," as one partner put it. On the other hand, John Smith believed that rapidly integrating local resources in Russia was critical to "marrying the best of Western analytical tools with an understanding of the local environment," and that back in 1990, the only legally and operationally feasible way to achieve this was through a joint venture. He added: "This required a considerable amount of learning on *both* sides, so we needed a strong Russian partner who could forcefully remind both Bain and the client that sometimes their frame of reference was simply wrong." Numerous partners believed that while these joint ventures had clearly paid off, the experience had taught them that joint ventures were a complicated mode of expansion and one that they would need to continue to be thoughtful about in the future.

Building Informal Networks

Historically, the international network was based on the simple, but powerful fact that all the senior partners knew each other well. As one of them put it, "We all grew up together." No one doubted that informal links would continue to be important, but it was also acknowledged that the firm could not rely solely on informal mechanisms that were bound to come under strain as the firm introduced new people, in new locations, with different backgrounds. A new partner who joined Bain in Sydney from another consulting firm spent quite a bit of time over his first six months flying around the world basically meeting people in the firm. But the opportunity costs of making this time available for new, senior hires to build a personal network were high.

Bain took many steps to reinforce its one-firm philosophy. Exchange of staff between offices for anything from six months to three years helped to build the one-firm culture and helped people to establish a personal network within the firm. Over the past two years, 12% of the professional staff had elected to transfer to other offices. Bain also had a culture (fully supported by the partner compensation system) that strongly encouraged cross-office "gang tackling" of potential new clients and building cross-office teams to serve clients. Finally, Bain ran its training program for all levels of professional on a worldwide basis. Bain saw these programs as fundamental to developing a common language and tools and creating the opportunity for an individual to expand their informal network.

The BRAVA System

As the company grew, however, it was becoming increasingly difficult to know who to approach in the firm to access information and experience on a particular subject. Historically, Bain had maintained a "Worldwide Experience Center" in Boston where full paper copies of all presentations were supposed to be collected and referenced. Once Bain developed substantial offices away from Boston, a number of problems began to arise. Not everyone got around to sending copies of their presentations. When the librarian identified three or four relevant presentations, formal release had to be obtained from the relevant vice-president. Even then, the consultant might be faced with hundreds of pages of slides in multiple languages (routine translation of more than a thousand foreign language presentations a year would have involved substantial cost). The system could no longer support a far-flung network of consultants working to tight deadlines.

In 1992, Bain partner Barry Harrington was asked to take on responsibility for heading up research and product development for Bain worldwide. One of the results was the BRAVA system. The concept was to create an information system that would identify a consultant anywhere in the world who had worked on a particular issue. Information on the system was kept to a minimum: a standardized format with some key information about the nature of the case (carefully disguised to protect client confidentiality), the main methodologies deployed and, most importantly, who had been involved in the work (see Exhibit 4.11). The idea was to enable individuals to quickly assess the overlap with their current problem and to identify who in the international network to call. The database could be accessed remotely or from a Bain office anywhere in the global network. No case would get a charge code until someone agreed to take responsibility for updating BRAVA after each phase of the work was complete.

Compensation and Performance Measurement

The Bain Partners agreed in 1990 to completely revamp their Partner compensation system. After studying a variety of service firms, including other consulting organizations, they designed an innovative system that balanced individual contributions with global and local teamwork. The new system, according to Tierney, placed heavy emphasis on asset building, which included developing long-term client results, enhancing Bain's human resources, and generating intellectual insights. All contributions were evaluated in the context of a multiyear meritocracy, where compensation was based upon actual contribution rather than tenure. Colin Anderson, Bain's finance director, elaborated on their system:

> Our Company is firmly rooted in the principals of meritocracy and global teamwork. We have a simple export credit system which doublecounts credit for client contribution if multiple offices and/or partners are involved (which is typically the case). Our systems are designed to capture data about individual contributions to the team across a variety of dimensions, both short- and long-term.

Compensation and promotion responsibilities rested with the line organization, with oversight from a central committee nominated by the Partners. This committee was ultimately responsible for ensuring high-quality global decisions which reinforced Bain's values and practices.

Exhibit 4.11 International Expansion Strategy

BRAVA NETWORKING

Title (Disguised)	International Expansion Strategy

Client Name (Actual)	

Presentation Date | 03/30/94

Study Types - Primary | Expansion/Growth Strategy
Study Types - Other | International Management
Market Assessment
Manufacturing Strategy
(Select up to Five from Table A)

Tools and Techniques	
Cost Management
Customer Segmentation
Benchmarking
Demand Forecasting
(Select up to Five from Table B)

Business Unit (Actual)	Containers

Case Code	XYZ

Industry - Primary	Industrial Materials
(for client) | (Select One from Table C)

Industry Sectors	Packaging and Containers
(for case)

Geographic Areas	China
CIS
Japan
Europe
South-East Asia
(Select up to Five from Table D)

	Network
Vice-Presidents	xxx-Boston
	xxx-Hong Kong
Managers	xxx-Tokyo
	xxx-Boston
Consultants	xxx-Boston
	xxx-Hong Kong
	xxx-Tokyo
CIT	xxx-Hong Kong
ACs	xxx-Tokyo
	xxx-Tokyo
	xxx-Boston

Summary Attached	
☐	Start-Up
☐	Interim
☑	Final
☐	Selling Presentation

Historian	
(Select up to Ten from Table E)

Date: 03/30/94

Summary Reviewed By	

Date: 03/30/94

SITUATION . . . .

A leading U.S. packaging manufacturer sees declining opportunity for growth in the United States—the only packaging market in which it currently participates. The client currently has 14% market share in the United States, which it expects to grow about 20% by 1995. Beyond 1995, however, volume and profit growth are expected to decline to the market growth rate of 2%–3%. Several major U.S. competitors have significant international operations, which, given the much higher expected growth rates overseas, could be a source of long-term disadvantage. Therefore, for both offensive (i.e., volume and profit growth potential) and defensive reasons, the client wants to develop a strategy and specific plans for international expansion.

OBJECTIVES . . . .

To develop a strategy to guide international expansion and to develop plans to enter two to three priority national packaging markets.

APPROACH . . . .

Construct initial screen to identify countries that should be studied in depth.

Gather key data (macro trends, market volume and growth trends, packaging penetration and drivers, packaging industry structure and key players) on each country passing the install screen.

Prioritize markets.

Develop entry options for the top two to three prioritized countries.

RESULTS . . . .

Client views international expansion as an imperative for three reasons: (1) Defend its low-cost competitiveness in the United States; (2) Opportunity to support key customer growth; (3) Only viable source of growth after year 2000. While where is no significant need for international presence in the short-term, the long lead time to set up packaging facilities requires the client to take immediate action. We selected markets of interest based on their long-term size potential and the client's ability to create a competitive advantage in these markets. As a result, the priority markets identified are Japan and Mexico.

TOWARDS 2000: SETTING THE DIRECTION FOR FUTURE INTERNATIONAL EXPANSION

Many firms in the consulting business had achieved spectacular growth for five or ten years, only to disappear without trace shortly thereafter. Having been through one financial cycle, Bain's management team knew the risks. Bain's objective had to be about enhancing a sustainable position as a global professional service firm where the overarching purpose was to help clients create business success stories rather than simply growth for growth's sake. It was against this purpose that investment of the firm's profits and resources needed to be evaluated. They also had to face the realities of a firm where capacity was already "sold out" and where, given the momentum in the business, people, not financial resources, would continue to be the constraining resource. At the same time, there were limits on the rate at which the firm could grow. Even individuals like partner Mark Daniell, a champion for high-growth in Asia, recognized that the global system's ability to train and integrate new people capped organic growth at somewhere between 25% and 30% per annum. If growth involved opening new offices, there was intense pressure on making senior resources available, since opening a new office took a great deal of partner time relative to revenues generated in the initial years. The rate at which Bain could absorb and integrate senior staff attracted from outside was also limited if the one-firm culture was to remain intact. Finally, there were financial considerations. Assuming that it began as a "satellite" of an established office, the incremental fixed costs associated with opening a new office averaged approximately $500,000. (See Exhibit 4.12 for the cost structure of a typical consulting firm.) Consistent with the economics of the industry, the profitability of a new office was highly dependent on consulting staff utilization rates.

It was against this background that the Bain partners were examining a large number of opportunities to expand in key international markets both organically and by acquisition/joint venture. Tierney offered three examples: the acquisition of a Europe-based consulting firm with 600 professionals, code-named "ECF," further expansion in Mexico, and a more aggressive push into the emerging markets of Asia.

Acquisition of ECF

ECF was among the top 30 consulting firms in the world, and one of the leaders in Germany and in the United Kingdom. It had 18 offices across 12 countries in Europe and North America, and a turnover of

Exhibit 4.12 Cost Structure of Consulting Firms

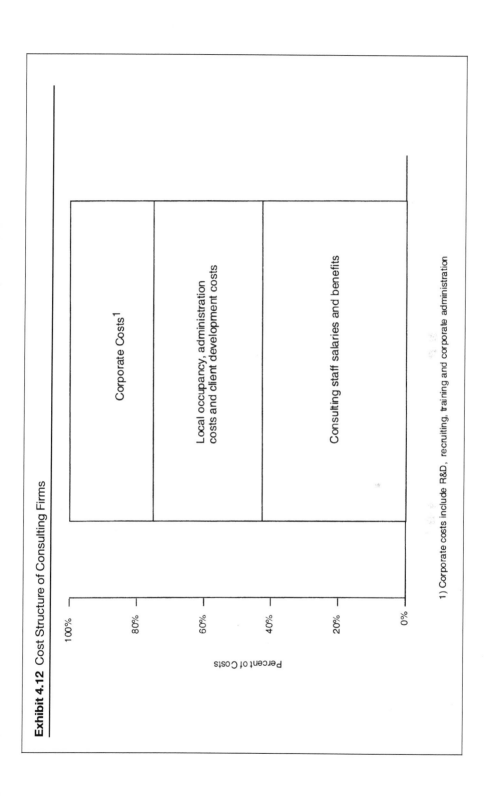

Percent of Costs

100%

80%

60%

40%

20%

0%

Corporate Costs[1]

Local occupancy, administration costs and client development costs

Consulting staff salaries and benefits

1) Corporate costs include R&D, recruiting, training and corporate administration

over $100 million. Twenty-five percent of ECF's business was with the public sector, with the remaining 75% in private-sector work that was almost equally split between clients in manufacturing and in service businesses. ECF described itself as "working for top firms and organizations on key issues in strategy, organization, human resources, and information systems" (see Exhibit 4.13).

Bain's profitability provided it access to the financial resources required to complete an acquisition of the scale of ECF. Although the profile of their staff was somewhat older than Bain's consultants, with fewer MBAs and more specialists, ECF believed the two firms were highly compatible. Senior partners defined their firm's core values as: professional excellence, no arrogance, solidarity, and a determination to see strategy through to implementation.

Bain had ample resources to complete an acquisition of the scale of ECF. The real question turned on how easy it would be to integrate ECF with Bain, and whether or not it would really enhance Bain's ability

---

Exhibit 4.13 Business Mix, E.C.F.

Strategy
- Global business and competitor analysis
- Corporate and business unit strategy
- Customer orientation
- Market entry strategy
- Partner search
- Strategic planning systems
- Benchmarking

Organization
- Cost cutting, productivity, lean management
- Corporate and business management
- Organization of the human resources function
- Manufacturing and logistics
- Marketing, sales efficiency
- Quality
- Training
- Re-engineering

Information Systems
- Cost control
- IS performance and effectiveness
- IS project management
- Organization of the IT function

to deliver client results. Pointing to Bain's past experience with joint ventures, some partners warned that cultural compatibility was extremely subtle. What looked good on paper might prove an impossible task in practice.

Further Expansion in Mexico

Few denied Mexico was a potentially interesting market, right on the doorstep on Bain's heartland. With the passage of NAFTA (the North American Free Trade Agreement), an increasing number of U.S. businesses were looking seriously at the role Mexico might play in their future strategies. Meanwhile, large Mexican businesses were interested in how consulting firms might help them access new opportunities in the U.S. market while coming to terms with more competition on their home turf.

It was perhaps paradoxical that Bain's Dallas office had been opened in 1990 to support a large Mexican client that had previously been served out of Boston. Mark Gottfredson, managing partner of the Dallas office, was frank about its history: "We were tired of making the trip from Boston to Mexico City and, in combination, we perceived opportunities in the southwestern U.S.—a Dallas office seemed like a good idea." The hunch proved right: what started with 8 people in 1990 had become almost 100 staff by 1994. Between one-third and one-half of its business was in Mexico, and 80% of this was for Mexican companies. One-quarter of Bain's Dallas staff were of Hispanic origin and another quarter spoke Spanish.

Gottfredson felt that in Dallas, Bain had been capitalizing on a window of opportunity created by the opening of the market and NAFTA. Mexican companies were looking for international experience. However, to continue to grow the business, local presence would be necessary. He also had grander designs for the future: "Our vision," said Gottfredson,

> is to let the Mexican office grow organically and expand south into Latin America. We don't see any immediate risk in this strategy. We are turning away business in Mexico now. We are building momentum and we have to take advantage of this, and we now have some professionals willing to move to Mexico City.

Looked at in isolation, Tierney was in favor of opening an office in Mexico. But it was part of his job to take a broader view: would opening an office in Mexico this year be too much of a "distraction" for the Dallas team? Gottfredson would have to be responsible for getting

Mexico off the ground for the first year at least. Would he still be able to manage the growth in Dallas? Ambitious managers and consultants might see the upside of moving to Mexico City, but were there any Mexican or even Spanish-speaking partners willing to go to Mexico for a period of years? Should Bain acquire (or joint venture with) small local consulting firms to get the people resources necessary to expand more aggressively in Mexico and the rest of Latin America? "Bain has many exciting opportunities," Tierney mused, "but we don't want to be spread a mile wide and an inch deep."

A Further Aggressive Push into the Emerging Markets of Asia

If Gottfredson was convinced of the virtues of Mexico, Greg Hutchinson, Jim Hildebrandt, Rick Yan, and Mark Daniell were equally certain that Asian expansion demanded Bain's full commitment. They put forward a powerful case for long-term, sustained investment in the region:

- Multinationals will increasingly be looking to Asia for growth. For many of these clients, the value created by bringing an existing product/system into a growth market is greater than that generated by investment in new product development.
- Successive expansion across Asia promises to keep up a flow of new challenges for people in the company—the chance to build an office for senior people, experience, and excitement for younger people.
- To serve clients around the world, Bain needs to have experience and insight into markets where the most interesting developments in economic activity are taking place. Today this means Asia—not just North America and Europe.
- Asia provided unique opportunities to leverage Bain Capital (the firm's venture capital arm) to enable Bain to share in value creation in a high-growth environment.

They were conscious of the need to avoid having "one man and a dog in 20 places in Asia." The long-term vision was to build a large operation there with "scale offices" of 30 to 40 people in a number of key countries and possible smaller satellites in Malaysia, Thailand, and Indonesia, as well as growing the existing operations in Hong Kong, Japan, and China. They were conscious that investment and accommodation by the global system would be essential to make this Asian expansion work: training people in a major office for subsequent deployment in Asia; bringing people in from major offices outside of

Asia—many with strong backgrounds in particular sectors (such as telecoms, banking, airlines, oil and gas) where experience was needed in Asia; and, releasing from other offices experienced staff with Asian roots. To the doubters they asked a simple question: "How serious are we about building Bain's global strength?"

DECISIONS ON INTERNATIONAL EXPANSION

For Bain the question was not so much "if" they would continue their aggressive geographic expansion, but "where and how?" Where would Bain need presence on the ground in the next three years? Regarding depth, in some markets there were significant local opportunities, but in others there were still virtually none. Were "vertically integrated," full-service offices necessary to serve a market anyway? After all, international manufacturing companies might have a comprehensive global distribution network, but that didn't necessitate cloning their headquarters and full-scale manufacturing everywhere they operated. Regarding timing, people constraints and opportunity costs had to be carefully factored in.

The long list of opportunities for international expansion was being evaluated within the context of the broader questions Bain was asking as it tried to plot a course to achieve the firm's objectives of doubling the value created for clients per dollar invested in Bain and making Bain, by far, the best strategy consulting firm with which to pursue a career. What new sources of competitive advantage should Bain be investing in? Should the company be rethinking the way it interacts with clients? For example, did further creativity in the way Bain added value and shared in value creation have the potential to significantly enhance the firm's economics and its attractiveness to potential clients and recruits? How aggressively did the firm need to expand geographically to maintain its stature as a "top tier" global strategy consulting firm? How should they choose between the acquisition and organic options to enter/further penetrate priority markets? What steps should they take to maintain their one-firm culture?

NOTES TO CASE

1. BBC Radio interview with Marvin Bower, "In Business," October 9, 1994.
2. Ibid.
3. Bain & Company is not technically a partnership, but its officers often refer to themselves as partners as a reflection of the way they operate the business.

Case 4.3

THE BRIDGESPAN GROUP

(John Kalafatas and Allen Grossman)

Bridgespan is off to a tremendous start. The Bridgespan-Bain partnership is truly unique and our early results with clients suggest we have the potential to make a significant contribution to the nonprofit sector. While we will have grown to nearly 30 people in our first year, when I look down the road, my concern is not that we will have grown too fast or have become overextended, but that we will have not taken full advantage of the opportunity our supporters have given us to achieve the greatest impact possible.

Jeff Bradach, Managing Partner, The Bridgespan Group

Based in Boston and San Francisco, The Bridgespan Group was an independent nonprofit consulting firm sponsored by the for-profit management consulting firm Bain & Company. The Bridgespan Group model was to offer "Bain-like" consulting capability that was customized to the distinctive needs and challenges of organizations in the nonprofit sector. In a February 2000, *New York Times* article, The Bridgespan-Bain partnership was referred to as an "entirely new thing," with Bain providing Bridgespan extensive access to its people, intellectual capital, and infrastructure.

In September 2000, nine months after The Bridgespan Group's launch, founding Managing Partner Jeff Bradach considered the firm's progress and prospects. Before Bridgespan opened its doors, Bradach and co-founding partner Paul Carttar had drafted a list of things that could go wrong. Nothing significant had. Although it had taken much hard work, the firm had successfully raised over $6 million in start-up funding, hired 27 staff, completed its first client projects, opened a West Coast office, and operated ahead of financial projections. Demand from clients far exceeded capacity. The *New York Times* article was just one example of the excitement generated by the new firm. Although past the start-up risks associated with new ventures, Bridgespan faced important strategic and operational challenges concerning how to grow effectively, accomplish its ambitious mission, and optimize its relationship with Bain.

BACKGROUND: CREATING THE BRIDGESPAN GROUP

While serving as Worldwide Managing Director of Bain and Company, Tom Tierney sought to extend and deepen the impact of Bain's pro bono work. Throughout his business career, Tierney had a "desire to serve" and make a contribution to society. As head of Bain's San Francisco office in the 1980s, he spearheaded some of Bain's first pro bono projects with the United Way and the Nature Conservancy. But Tierney increasingly questioned how the firm could do more in the nonprofit sector. In the wake of a major management and financial restructuring, Tierney moved to the Boston headquarters in 1992 to become Bain's worldwide managing director. By 1995, with more time and resources at his disposal, he began exploring the question: "How could Bain, with its talent and strategic expertise, be used as a platform to make a lasting impact in the social sector?" Over the next few years, he mobilized three Bain case teams to analyze the viability of creating a new nonprofit consulting practice and the best organizational approach for achieving that end.

Bain's Involvement with the Nonprofit Sector

Like many other major consulting firms, Bain was primarily engaged with the social sector through pro bono consulting. The firm was proud of its work and had over the years provided services to over one hundred nonprofits of various sizes, in industries such as human services, education and the environment. Because interest in nonprofits had increased among Bain employees and because demand from both past and new nonprofit clients was rising, pro bono activity had grown.

Bain's most common pro bono engagements originated and were managed locally, with local partners holding decision rights on client selection and resource allocation. Examples of pro bono work included the Boston office's long-term relationships with City Year and the Boston Public Schools; the Los Angeles office's work with the Museum of Contemporary Art; and the San Francisco office's consulting for the San Francisco Opera. Bain partner David Bechhofer had overseen much of the Boston office's pro bono work during the 1990s. He articulated five criteria for considering a case: (1) Would the project focus on one of the top three strategic issues facing the organization? (2) Is the client prepared to act on the results? (3) Is a Bain partner committed to leading the case? (4) Is staff capacity available at the firm? and (5) Is there sufficient interest among the ranks at Bain?

Tom Tierney discussed the pros and cons of Bain's traditional pro bono involvement:

Our pro bono work is very important to Bain and our clients. We do it because it reinforces our corporate values, encourages local community involvement, and it is simply the right thing to do. Nonprofits benefit from free, high quality service they might not otherwise get. We provide valuable resources and talented consultants interested in learning about and working with nonprofits. On the other hand, the scope and impact of our pro bono work is inherently self-limiting. Due to the economics, it is marginal and incremental at Bain, not mainstream, and thus will not grow to significant scale.

Developing the Concept

Beginning in 1996, Tierney directed Bain teams to research whether an unmet need existed in the non-profit market. Tierney enlisted Jeff Bradach, a former Bain consultant who was on the faculty at Harvard Business School and was involved with the school's Initiative on Social Enterprise, to serve as an advisor. Along with the analysis by the Bain teams, over the course of two years Tierney and Bradach conducted over 50 in-depth interviews with leaders of nonprofits and foundations about their needs. The research revealed that there was an insufficient supply of quality consulting, and in particular, there was a lack of the kind of data-driven, analytical strategy consulting services delivered by the top-tier consulting firms that had helped so many for-profit companies succeed. Bridgespan's business plan summarized the findings:

> There presently exists a major service gap with respect to the growing list of fundamental strategic issues facing nonprofit organizations. On one hand, consulting firms with sufficient nonprofit expertise and reasonable prices lack sufficient scale and strategic experience. On the other hand, large strategy consultants possess the requisite tools and scale but are expensive and tend to lack dedicated resources experienced in and sensitive to the needs of the nonprofit sector. Consequently, they tended to be available to non-profits only on an ad hoc basis, which limits the ability of these firms to generate lasting impact or build a body of experience and knowledge that can be of value to other nonprofits. As a result, there is a notable service gap, which could be addressed by a consulting firm able to deliver the desired strategic capabilities in a manner which is affordable, sustainable and attuned to the distinctive character of mission-driven organizations.

Exhibit 4.14 provides further data on the nonprofit consulting market.

Although a clear need existed in the sector, questions remained.

Exhibit 4.14 The Consulting to Nonprofits Industry

Bridgespan's research and a Harvard Business School study[a] indicated that although the non-profit consulting industry was complex, underdeveloped and fragmented, it was evolving.

Nonprofit Clients Of the sector's 1.4 million organizations, one million were "public-serving" nonprofits accounting for over $600 billion in annual revenue. Some 500,000 of these were direct service delivery organizations and 54,000 were foundations and financial intermediaries. Several characteristics, such as size, revenue mix, industry, life-cycle stage, geographic scope and management culture could influence an organization's management challenges and consulting needs. Demand for consulting in the sector had grown in response to increasing pressure on organizations to improve their management and performance, that included:

- scrutiny of nonprofit organizations and foundations about their use of public funds and the concomitant need to measure results
- concern about the capacity of nonprofits to effectively go to scale
- competition for funding among proliferating nonprofits and for market share from for-profits entering historical nonprofit industries
- demand for innovative revenue-generating and cost containment activities
- recognition among nonprofit managers, funders, and scholars that social impact requires both program and organizational effectiveness

Consulting Providers The nonprofit consulting industry's complexity reflected the array of industries and the diversity of organizations that constituted the nonprofit sector. Bain's research showed that some 3,000 providers delivered consulting services to U.S. nonprofits, generating $600 million in annual revenue. These consultants could be segmented along several dimensions, such as whether they charged fees, their size, industry served, tax status, type of services provided and geography. The most common provider of consulting services was the solo practitioner, followed by small boutique firms, both for-profit and nonprofit, employing several to 20 staff and serving mostly local markets. Large business consulting firms like Bain, for the most part, offered pro bono services. Other intermediaries, such as volunteer brokers and management support organizations, rounded out the industry. (See chart at end of this exhibit for a description of the basic attributes of each provider category.)

Differences from Business Consulting In comparison to business consulting, several factors complicated management consulting in the nonprofit sector. Together, these issues limited the efficiency of the nonprofit consulting market and posed challenges to the effectiveness of individual engagements. Consulting to nonprofits differed from business consulting the following ways:

1. Both client staff and consultants often had less education or training than business counterparts in either management skills or the use and provision of consulting.
2. Some in the nonprofit sector were leery that business concepts associated with management consulting would threaten the values of social-purpose organizations.
3. Multiple bottom lines and difficulty measuring performance of nonprofits made it hard for consultants to drive clients toward objective results or demonstrate project effectiveness.
4. The wider array of stakeholders in a nonprofit made it difficult to identify the real "client" or clearly diagnose and gain consensus on the problem consultants were engaged to solve.
5. The general lack of discretionary income among nonprofits made it hard for many organizations to afford consulting, or other professional services.

Continued

Exhibit 4.14 Continued

6. The lack of scale among both clients and providers in the nonprofit sector relative to those of the business sector limited the impact of the industry.
7. The industry could be characterized as an inefficient or under-developed market, exhibiting poor information about providers and their quality, a lack of extensive, competition for projects, unclear channels for connecting providers and clients, and low barriers to entry.
8. Lacking resources, nonprofits often did not pay for consulting, receiving pro bono work or asking third-parties to subsidize projects, potentially distorting consultant-client accountability.
9. Knowledge of best practices in the field of nonprofit management — among organizations, consultants, intermediaries, and academics — was less advanced than it was in business.

Consulting to Nonprofits: Provider Categories

Category	Attributes
Large Business Consulting Firms	For-profit firms, focused on business sector clients Ranging in scale from 25 to thousands of staff Most (Bain, BCG, McKinsey, Monitor) pro bono; some (AT Kearney, PwC) charged fees National presence Smallest segment (only 40 firms) but highest profile
Nonprofit Boutiques	Nonprofit tax status, dedicated to nonprofit clients only From several to 20 staff May charge full fees, discounted fees, no fees Local or regional presence
For-profit Boutiques	For-profit tax status, dedicated to nonprofit clients only From several to 20 staff Charge clients full fees Local or regional presence
Solo Practitioners	Typically for-profit status, nonprofit clients only One-person shop Most common provider type (over 2,000; 31% of market revenue) Local or regional presence
Volunteer Brokers	Nonprofit status, nonprofit clients only Groups organizing executive volunteers or business school student or alumni volunteers Local or regional presence

Management Support Organizations	Nonprofit intermediaries, focused on field building in a particular industry or sector-wide Nonprofit clients only Array of capacity-building resources: consulting, training, technical services, publications Local or regional presence

a Heiner Baumann, John Kalafatas, Stephanie Lowell, Shivam Mallick, & Ndidi Okonkwo, *Consulting to Nonprofits: An Industry Analysis* (Harvard Business School Field Study, advised by Bob Burakoff, April 1999).

Could Bain's pro bono work simply be expanded? Should a new non-profit consulting practice be created within Bain or should a separate firm be established? If so, should it be a for-profit or a nonprofit?

It became evident to Tierney that creating a new social enterprise practice within Bain was not a viable option. "Could we engage paying nonprofit clients on an ad hoc basis as part of Bain's mainstream consulting? Could we create a formal practice area, like health care or e-commerce? In both cases, there wasn't enough profitable business out there to make it worth it for Bain to dedicate resources. And, because of nonprofits' inability to pay full freight, the firm would have to subsidize the costs on an ongoing basis. A separate firm could devote resources to develop scale and focus." According to Bradach, "We quickly saw that the new firm had to be separate, but it was clear there was no way it could be created without a very strong connection to Bain. Neither I nor the other founders could have started or sustained a firm with the capability we desired without Bain's sponsorship."

With the broad concept in mind, in the summer of 1997, Tierney assembled a Bain case team out of the San Francisco office to develop the detailed business plan. The firm would be sponsored by Bain, but would be a separate independent organization with nonprofit tax status. No precedent could be found in professional services or other industries of a for-profit creating a separate nonprofit organization that served the social sector through the same core business functions as the parent. Bradach observed, "determining the relationship with Bain was critical. It was crucial that Bridgespan be able to deliver Bain-quality consulting to the nonprofit sector, and we had to figure out how to tap into the talent, ideas, and infrastructure of Bain so that we could do that." The parameters of the relationship between the new firm and Bain would need to be carefully defined and consistently tested without any analogous models to benchmark.

Founding the Firm

By late 1998, based on the strength of the business plan, Tom Tierney, Jeff Bradach and Paul Carttar joined together to co-found The Bridgespan Group. Carttar was a former Bain partner who had left the firm in 1990 to pursue other commercial interests: "I worked in the public and nonprofit sectors prior to business school and joining Bain, and I always expected to return. When Tom told me about the formation of Bridgespan, I knew this was an ideal opportunity to put my consulting and managerial experience to work towards a more rewarding social purpose." For Bradach, "After working on this project on the side for two years, I became convinced of the extraordinary potential of the idea. I had spent many years working with nonprofits and for-profits as a board member and consultant, but this stood out as a big idea, one with a chance to make a huge difference on important social issues. This enabled me to make my passion my job." Through the spring of 1999, the founders worked on three major issues: 1) obtaining support from Bain, 2) receiving IRS approval of Bridgespan's nonprofit status, and 3) raising initial funding.

During the fall and winter of 1998–1999, Tierney built consensus for the venture among the Bain partners. Tierney's pitch did not simply call on their altruism, but emphasized how the new firm would create value for Bain. At an April 1999 meeting of all seven Bain North American office heads, Bradach and Carttar presented the business model and asked for Bain's support. Bradach recalled that "We stopped on one particular slide which outlined the benefits to Bain. We told them that it was important to us that the benefits were real because we were not looking for a short-term contribution from them, but were looking for a long-term partnership that would last for decades. And that had to be built on mutual benefits."

The North American office heads voted unanimously to support the formation of The Bridgespan Group. Their support consisted of over one million dollars in start-up funding over three years, as well as nonmonetary support, including the ability to recruit Bain staff, access to the Bain knowledge base, and access to a variety of administrative systems at a discounted cost. In return, Bain expected three benefits, as described by Phyllis Yale, managing director of Bain's Boston office:

First, Bridgespan extends our opportunity for impact in the community, consistent with Bain's mission. Second, there is a "halo effect," which strengthens Bain's public image and reputation.

People think more highly of Bain because they associate Bridgespan with us. Third, and most important, Bridgespan helps Bain attract and retain top talent who may be looking to get exposure to the issues facing global 1000 companies and help the nonprofit sector. Our people want to work for a company that cares.

Because of Bridgespan's tight affiliation with a for-profit in the same line of business, the IRS closely examined the new organization's proposed nonprofit status. Carttar recalled:

The IRS wanted to assure itself of two main things. First, that we were serving a social purpose. Our commitment to serving clients regardless of ability to pay and to raise money from donors to do that helped to address that question. Second, the IRS wanted to make sure that the Bridgespan Group was not in some way inappropriately generating value for Bain. As the business plan clearly demonstrated, the preponderance of value ran from Bain to Bridgespan, not the reverse. To ensure independence from Bain, our eight person Board of Trustees is composed of five outside, non-Bain people and three representatives from Bain.

The IRS approved 501(c)(3) nonprofit status for Bridgespan in the spring of 1999.

Beyond Bain's start-up grant, Bridgespan raised $5.5 million in outside financing from several foundations, including Irvine, Surdna, Rockefeller Brothers Fund, and Edna McConnell Clark. This money was to be used primarily to subsidize projects for clients who could not afford the services. Other priorities in 1999 included signing on initial clients and building a governing board, which was chaired by Tom Tierney (Exhibit 4.15 includes biographies of Board members). As for attracting Bain staff, Tierney voice-mailed all Bain offices announcing the creation of The Bridgespan Group and encouraging interested staff to apply. The response exceeded expectations. Bridgespan planned to start consulting operations in January 2000.

BAIN & COMPANY

A private, for-profit company, Bain was known as one of the elite business management consulting firms, competing with the likes of McKinsey and Boston Consulting Group. Headquartered in Boston, Bain employed 2,400 professionals in 26 offices worldwide. Estimated revenues for 1998 exceeded $500 million, with recent annual growth exceeding 20%.[1] By 2000, Bain reported being virtually "sold out," with demand pushing capacity. Since its 1973 founding, the firm had served over 2,000 companies—from start-ups to large multinationals—in a range of industries. Bain tended to conduct large engagements with multiple teams and maintained long-term relationships with clients. Bain was reported to have an enthusiastic, social and entrepreneurial internal culture. It also had a history of launching ventures outside of its core management consulting business, such as Bain Capital, a private equity investment firm, and Bain Lab, an incubator for new economy start-ups.

Bain was considered an innovator of "strategy consulting," a subfield of the management consulting industry that the firm defined in the following way: "Bain was created around a vision of generating 'break-through' results that would enable clients to set new standards of success in their respective industries. Strategy consulting involves identifying and addressing the most critical issues affecting a company's ability to achieve its full potential. The hallmark of Bain's approach has been an unwavering emphasis on achieving dramatic, measurable improvements in a client's overall performance and success." Critical to Bain's approach was an emphasis on rigorous "data-driven" analysis, as well as "customizing recommendations and action plans to the particular needs, capabilities and circumstances of each client to ensure real change."

Bain's organization was structured in a staff pyramid typical of large consulting firms. Recent college graduates joined Bain as "associate consultants" for a fixed term of two years. Some stayed on for a third year as "senior associate consultants." After their stint at Bain, many pre-MBA's would attend business school, and a significant number would later return to Bain. At the post-MBA level, individuals joined the firm as "consultants" for an indefinite period. Consultants were responsible for a work stream within a project (a "case" at Bain), eventually supervising associate consultants. After several years of experience, some consultants advanced to "managers," responsible for the day-to-day management of case teams and project deliverables. The next and highest tier at Bain was "partner" or "director" who were responsible for managing the firm's business development and client relations.

THE BRIDGESPAN GROUP MODEL

Mission

Providing a "bridge" between the business and nonprofit sectors, the mission of The Bridgespan Group was to *enhance the capability of nonprofit organizations to achieve breakthrough results in their vital work of addressing society's most important challenges and opportunities.* Bradach summarized the organization's purpose:

We are about impact. It is our reason for being and the sole measure of our success. We are driven by the question, "Have we helped our clients achieve their missions and make a significant difference in the world?" To do that, we need to be able to tap into the best strategic thinking—which is greatly enhanced by our partnership with Bain—and be part of and deeply knowledgeable about the nonprofit sector. This is what makes Bridgespan unique and enables us to deliver impact for our clients.

Strategy

The firm would fulfill its mission through a three-pronged strategy: (1) consulting directly for nonprofit clients, (2) disseminating knowledge generated from its consulting to other leaders in the nonprofit sector, and (3) serving as a model for how other professional service firms could enhance their contribution to the sector. This strategy hinged on several key elements, including the firm's organizational structure, alliance with Bain, knowledge sharing, financial model and client focus.

Independent, Nonprofit Structure

The Bridgespan Group was organized as a separate nonprofit with an independent Board of Trustees. According to Bradach:

> Bridgespan is separate from Bain and structured as a nonprofit for one overarching reason: it enables us to pursue our mission most effectively. We are committed to working on the most important strategic challenges facing nonprofits. Sometimes that involves organizations that can afford to pay and sometimes it does not. We did not want our strategy driven by who could pay. In addition, we are committed to sharing what we learn with others. If we were a for-profit, we would have many more incentives to make proprietary use of what we are learning rather than use it to maximize our potential for social impact. Finally, being a nonprofit has given us the ability to obtain philanthropic support, and importantly, it is a clear signal to clients about what we are trying to do.

Bridgespan was governed by an independent Board of Trustees. An Advisory Board was also created to provide guidance on the selection of clients, the distribution of subsidies, and the agenda for developing and sharing knowledge (see Exhibit 4.16 for list of members).

Strategic Partnership with Bain

Along with financial support and affiliation with its brand identity, Bain provided several critical resources to Bridgespan. Most importantly, Bridgespan had permission to recruit experienced Bain consulting staff. Bain recruited top graduates of premier schools, then invested heavily in their training and development. By drawing from Bain, Bridgespan could obtain high-quality, experienced consulting talent

Exhibit 4.16 Board of Advisors

Greg Dees is the Peter and Miriam Haas Professor of Public Service, Stanford University. He is also director of the Center for Social Innovation, Stanford Graduate School of Business.

Jed Emerson is President of the Roberts Enterprise Development Fund. He is also the Bloomberg Senior Lecturer at Harvard Business School.

Jan Masaoka is Executive Director of CompassPoint Nonprofit Services, San Francisco, California. CompassPoint is one of the nation's leading nonprofit management consulting firms to nonprofit organizations.

Ed Skloot is Executive Director of the Surdna Foundation.

and avoid the costs of a recruitment and development infrastructure. Bain employees took a pay cut of 25–35% when they joined the Bridgespan Group. Bain employees could either leave Bain permanently to join the Bridgespan Group, or could rotate there for a six-month period after which they would return to Bain.

Additionally, Bain provided Bridgespan with full access to its knowledge resources that had been built up over 26 years of operation. Bridgespan employees participated in all Bain professional development activities, including extensive training programs. The Bridgespan office was connected to the Bain intranet and Bridgespan employees had full access to Bain's knowledge management system, which included the BVU (Bain Virtual University), an on-line training program that contained over 150 modules on tools and concepts, and the GXC (Global Experience Center), which captured the lessons and insights from Bain's work with its clients. Bain provided these services and other administrative support services at their incremental cost.

The Product

A Bridgespan consulting engagement involved the use of tools and concepts that were customized to the needs of the non-profit sector. Partners at Bridgespan believed that what differentiated their services was the mix of cutting-edge business strategy expertise and deep knowledge of the nonprofit sector. "Nonprofits face unique challenges," said Susan Colby, a Bridgespan partner. "You cannot take Bain tools off-the-shelf without considering how they might apply differently in the nonprofit sector."

A consulting engagement with Bridgespan typically encompassed two phases of work: an analytic phase and an advisory phase. The analytic phase was modeled on Bain: teams of consultants, led by a partner or manager, gathering data and conducting analyses on the strategic and operational issues facing the organization. In the advisory phase, a partner or manager would work with the leadership team in the client organization to implement the recommendations. The need for an advisory phase emerged from the exploratory interviews with nonprofit leaders. The leaders often commented that their biggest challenge was not identifying the needed course of action, but was instead figuring out how to implement the action.

Financial Strategy

There were two key elements of the firm's financial strategy. First, Bridgespan sought to build an organization that could deliver Bain-quality consulting at a substantially lower cost than top-tier for-profit firms. This lower cost structure was made possible because of its tax-exempt status, which eliminated the need for profit; lower compensation relative to the for-profit market; and the ability to utilize Bain infrastructure and services at a substantial discount. Second, Bridgespan sought to raise philanthropic support that could be used to subsidize projects with organizations that could not afford to pay. Over time, once Bridgespan demonstrated the value of its services, the strategy assumed that the bulk of the funding of projects would shift from subsidies granted by Bridgespan to fees paid by organizations who would either pay themselves or raise money from funders to support the work.

The overall cost to Bridgespan for a typical consulting project ranged from $100,000 to $400,000, and that represented the full price that Bridgespan would charge for the work, but the actual fee charged to the client would vary, depending on the client's ability to pay. Bridgespan had raised an initial pool of funding of over $5 million that enabled it to subsidize projects for clients. For comparable projects, Bridgespan charged substantially lower fees than Bain, with prices averaging between one-third to one-fourth of a Bain project.

Selective Client Focus

Bridgespan's client base included both direct service nonprofits and foundations. It expected to devote 60–70% of its work to non-profits, and 30–40% to foundations. Instead of focusing on particular segments of the nonprofit arena (e.g., education, arts, environment), Bridgespan sought to engage clients facing specific strategic challenges that were important and common to many nonprofits. The areas of focus included going-to-scale; nonprofit use of the internet; strategy for intermediaries (nonprofit training, technical assistance, consulting firms), and high-impact grant-making for foundations. The firm sought to serve clients of all sizes and ability to pay. Because health care and higher education had access to well developed consulting alternatives, Bridgespan decided to make these segments secondary priorities. The firm developed a set of criteria to prioritize potential clients:

- A compelling mission that if executed to its full potential would have significant social impact
- Strategic needs that reflect the fundamental challenges facing non-profits, fit well with Bridgespan's strengths, and support the goal of sharing valuable knowledge with the sector
- Lack of access to acceptable alternatives among existing consulting firms
- An organizational philosophy that embraces change, with a proven management team able and willing to push an organization toward its full potential
- A willingness to share its experience with other nonprofit organizations and otherwise leverage The Bridgespan Group's contribution for the betterment of the sector

Knowledge Sharing

Fundamental to the business model were Bridgespan's efforts to develop and disseminate knowledge about nonprofit management. Bradach observed, "There are over 770,000 nonprofits in the United States. If The Bridgespan Group wants to make a major difference, it will have to extend its reach beyond the relatively few clients it will be able to serve." The firm had two major sources of intellectual capital: capturing learning from consulting engagements and leveraging management tools and frameworks used with Bain's business clients that could be adapted to a nonprofit environment.

YEAR ONE OF OPERATIONS

Bridgespan was off to a fast start. Its staff had grown rapidly and it was still not able to keep pace with the demand for its services. The first year had also been a period of rapid learning and adaptation, as the leadership team identified new challenges and opportunities.

Operating Highlights

Clients

During the first nine months of operation, Bridgespan established consulting engagements with eight nonprofit clients. These included two of the 50 largest U.S. foundations and six service delivery nonprofits. Of the service delivery organizations, two were large institutions and four were community-based organizations. The latter four were all grantees of a foundation client. In that case, the work had begun with the strategy for the foundation and had evolved to include Bridgespan working in its portfolio with high potential grantees. For three clients, Bridgespan had completed the major analytical phases of work and had moved to implementation issues. As for new client development, demand far exceeded the firm's capacity to take on new work. The firm had received over 200 inquiries, 50 of which were considered to have serious potential. Bridgespan was in discussions with six prospective clients and expected to take on four new engagements in the fall of 2000.

Staff

By October 2000, Bridgespan had 27 people on staff—23 consultants and 4 support staff. Eighteen consultants worked in the Boston office, five in San Francisco. The firm had planned that consultants would be a mix of staff rotating from Bain and a core group of permanent managers and staff committed to Bridgespan in the long run. Seventeen were permanent hires and six were on rotation from Bain. Of the 23 consultants on staff, 17 had some tie to Bain and 6 had no past affiliation with Bain (Exhibit 4.17 includes biographies of the leadership team). This growth was well ahead of the business plan, which had called for 12 consultants in the first year, including 2 partners, 1 manager (usually with 3–5 years consulting experience), 5 consultants (post-MBA), and 4 associate consultants (pre-MBA).

San Francisco Office

In September 2000, Bridgespan opened a West Coast office eighteen months ahead of schedule to capitalize on regional client demand, support from funders, and significant support from Bain's west coast offices. The office was already serving a top-25 foundation and was in the process of selecting its second client. Six staff had committed to join the group, including two partners who were Bain alumni, Susan Colby and Seth Barad. In contrast to Boston and in response to an expensive real estate market, Bridgespan's San Francisco operation would be

Exhibit 4.17 Management Team

Jeffrey L. Bradach (Managing Partner) has been a professor at the Harvard Business School for the past seven years, where he has specialized in leadership and social enterprise. He has published a book, several articles, and many cases on franchising, human resource management, strategic alignment in organizations, and going-to-scale in the nonprofit sector. In addition to teaching numerous executive education programs for private-sector and nonprofit executives, he has consulted extensively in both sectors, and sits on the boards of directors of several for-profit and nonprofit organizations. He worked as a consultant at Bain before graduate school. He received his BA from Stanford University and his MA and Ph.D. from Harvard University.

Paul L. Carttar (Partner) is a former Vice–President at Bain & Company who prior to joining Bain served in both the public and nonprofit sectors. Noteworthy positions included special assistant to Ambassador Arthur F. Burns at the U.S. Embassy in Bonn, Germany, budget analyst for the U.S. Senate Budget Committe, and community liaison on the Brooklyn, NY staff of the late Allard K. Lowenstein. In recent years, he has held executive management positions in the healthcare industry, most lately as chief operating officer of a national physician practice management company. He received his BA from the University of Kansas and his MBA from Stanford University.

Susan J. Colby (Partner and San Francisco Office Head) recently left Pharmacia (previously Monsanto) as President of the Sustainable Development Sector, a for-profit business development initiative that developed economically, environmentally, and socially viable solutions for sustainable agriculture. Prior to Monsanto, Susan spent ten years at McKinsey & Company, where she co-founded the North American Environment Practice, serving clients in the areas of environmental management and strategy. She also served foundations and environmental NGOs on a pro bono basis and worked with clients in the financial, consumer goods, and energy industries. Susan is an advisor and board member for several nonprofits. She began her consulting career at Bain, prior to earning her MBA from Stanford University and is a graduate of The American University.

Seth A. Barad (Partner) recently left Providian Financial, where he was Executive Vice-President and was responsible for seven businesses. He grew the customer base from 200,000 to over 6 million, and managed all aspects of marketing, credit, operations, and systems with a staff of over 5,000. He was also instrumental in creating internal training programs that developed future leaders for the company. He has served on the boards of several for-profit and nonprofit organizations. Seth began his career as a consultant and manager at Bain. He is a graduate of Tufts University and earned his MBA from Harvard Business School.

Margaret Boasberg (Manager) recently left Homeportfolio.com, as the director of business development and strategic alliances. Prior to Homeportfolio.com, she worked at Bain for six years as a consultant. In graduate school, she co-founded and ran a non-profit organization to train and finance entrepreneurs in economically depressed East Palo Alto, California. She earned her BA from Yale University and MBA from Stanford University.

Kelly L. Campbell (Manager) was a Bain manager who served in Bain's Boston, Sydney, and Seoul offices, assisting clients in a variety of industries, including work on nonprofit strategy and government privitization. Prior to Bain, she worked with the public sector consulting division of Price Waterhouse in Washington, DC, advising public and private organizations on business strategy and process redesign. She earned her BS from Stanford University and her MBA in Finance from the Wharton Business School.

Stephan Bissig (Team Leader) was a Bain consultant who had worked in the London and Sydney offices. While at Bain, he worked with clients in the financial services, manufacturing, and entertainment sectors. After graduate school, he spent several months working with SOS Kinderdorf Children's Villages in Latin America on strategic issues. He earned his undergraduate degree at the University of Fribourg and an MBA from Harvard University.

Mara F. Wallace (Team Leader) was a Bain consultant from the San Francisco office. During her time at Bain she worked with clients in industries such as telecommunications, consumer products, and retail. For the past two years, her work has focused almost exclusively on the nonprofit sector, providing strategic consulting services to KQED, Inc.— the Bay Area's public radio and television station—and assisting in the development of the business plan for The Bridgespan Group. Prior to Bain, Mara spent six years as a manager in nonprofit organizations ranging from healthcare services to magazine publishing. She holds a BA from the University of Michigan and an MBA from Columbia Business School.

co-located in the Bain office. Colby observed, "The west coast presents distinctive challenges and opportunities for Bridgespan. The explosion of new wealth and the emergence of new forms of philanthropy—for example, venture philanthropy and e-philanthropy—along with a vibrant and innovative nonprofit sector make it important for us to have a west coast office."

Knowledge Sharing

The firm had just begun to develop and implement its knowledge capture and sharing strategy. Staff undertook activities in support of "knowledge capture," such as a weekly learning series that included internal reviews of ongoing work and guest speakers from the non-profit sector. The staff also conducted case team debriefs at the end of a project to evaluate the impact of their work and the strengths and weaknesses of their approach. Bridgespan received client feedback through interviews at the end of each project. An independent consultant had been engaged to interview Bridgespan clients about their experiences with the firm. The firm had recently contracted with the former editor and senior editor of the Harvard Business Review to advise on knowledge strategy and develop content for dissemination to nonprofit leaders. Early in 2001, Bridgespan planned to launch a website that would capture knowledge internally and serve as a platform for sharing information externally.

Reflecting on Year One

Reflecting on their experiences to date, Bridgespan staff, board members, and colleagues at Bain discussed issues related to client work, involvement with foundations, staffing and recruiting, the organization's culture, and Bridgespan's relationship with Bain.

Client Work

Bridgespan had begun to see its work produce major change in clients. One foundation had fundamentally changed its grant-making strategy with the help of Bridgespan. An executive from a community-based nonprofit commented that "there is no one else out there like Bridgespan. Its work is having a dramatic impact on our organization."

At the same time, Bridgespan had identified several key challenges to generating impact with clients. Carttar noted:

The complexities of nonprofit organizations make this work complicated. Because the Bain tool kit is ultimately designed to help clients maximize profit, it's not fully transferable to non-profits with dual bottom lines. In many cases, we have found that we need to break new ground in terms of developing concepts and frameworks that can help crack problems facing nonprofit organizations. We do not have off-the-shelf products right now.

Another important distinction from typical Bain work is that our clients are smaller and our teams are smaller. One might think that a small nonprofit is analogous to a small division of a for-profit company, and hence, a relatively junior consultant could run the project. But these nonprofit CEOs are facing big issues—they are dealing with multiple constitutencies, complex strategy questions, and difficult resource allocation decisions. We have found that to provide maximum value to these clients, our teams need the substantial involvement of senior consultants. It may be that our staffing structure needs to look more like an hourglass—a mix of senior people and relatively junior associates—than a pyramid.

While demand was high for Bridgespan services, the partners had heard from some client prospects that Bridgespan was relatively expensive. Bradach reflected on Bridgespan's pricing:

Bridgespan prices are deeply discounted from Bain's, approximately 20–30% of Bain's prices. Still, for some nonprofit organizations, we are relatively expensive. The price difference compared to other consultants is due to the labor-intensive nature of our work—we have teams gathering and analyzing data. In contrast, many nonprofit consultants rely on facilitative approaches—a weekend retreat and a white board—to build an organization's strategy. There is nothing wrong with facilitation; we just do something different. We are offering a new product that is hard to find in the sector. What is crucial is that we demonstrate that the value produced by our work far exceeds its price. If we can't do that, we shouldn't be in business.

Geoff Lieberthal, an outgoing Bridgespan senior associate consultant who had moved from Bain, discussed how consulting with Bridgespan differed from for-profit business consulting: "At Bridgespan, we have had to learn to communicate consulting concepts more effectively. As opposed to corporate clients, the nonprofit managers we work with at Bridgespan rarely have business training. So, we need to be teachers, first explaining management concepts, then presenting the analysis and its implications." Hadley Mullin, a Bain consultant who rotated to Bridgespan before business school, found that, "working with nonprofits requires a very different communication style. Bain presentations are typically 'answer first,' which nonprofits can perceive as arrogant and noncollaborative. When we offer an initial hypothesis to guide our analysis, we may be perceived as thinking we know 'the answer' too early in the process."

Consultant Joanne Clain, formerly with Bain, discussed how her experience at Bridgespan compared with her expectations: "I'm still doing the same job—I'm still a consultant. We're still using the Bain tool kit, doing analysis, and making presentations to clients. But, the work just feels different. There is a new intellectual component and a very different approach to the problems and the client. At Bain, our work with corporate clients revolved around concrete, measurable outcomes such as profitability. Here, we're helping clients balance financial outcomes with less quantifiable mission-driven outcomes. We're constantly talking about how business frameworks fit with nonprofit issues and how they can be adapted. Although some might perceive our nonprofit work as 'softer,' I think it can often be more complicated."

Kelly Campbell, a former Bain manager, described issues unique to nonprofit consulting:

> There are distinctive challenges with nonprofit clients that require us to work differently from Bain. There is simply less data available, which makes our data-driven approach more difficult. Data utilization is different as well—nonprofits are more apt to consider data in an academic way rather than use it for decision making. Because of the absence of clear financial incentives to change, client decisions often take longer and there is hesitancy to act. Pressure must come either from the internal ambition of managers or the demands of a funder. We have also found that we need to build on our own process skills because for many of our projects—especially those with small nonprofits—the work at the beginning is less about data analysis and more about helping the leadership team sort out what they are trying to accomplish.

The issue of implementation was an important one facing Bridgespan. Its focus on results placed a premium on helping clients implement new strategies. Bradach highlighted the challenge:

> It has become clear that our advisory phase is just a small part of the challenge of helping a nonprofit client implement a new strategy. Two other crucial ingredients are funding and new staff skills. I am concerned that we may work with a client to develop a compelling, high impact strategy, but then the Executive Director will have to spend the next several years trying to raise the money to fund the strategy. Increasingly, we are trying to look ahead from the outset to identify how the new strategy might be funded. Otherwise, what is the point? It is also clear that many of these organizations have operated in a world of resource scarcity, which is typical of non-profits. Often there has been a systematic under investment in the infrastructure of the organization. In

many cases, what is needed is not big strategic thinking but first an investment in basic infrastructure and growing and strengthening the staff.

Involvement with Foundations

The interest in Bridgespan's work among foundations—as clients and funders to both Bridgespan and of grantee projects—was greater than expected. Bridgespan felt that foundations represented an important point of leverage for generating impact in the nonprofit sector. Tierney observed that "in many ways, foundations set the rules of the game for nonprofits—they have a big impact on the flow of capital. It is important that Bridgespan help redefine those rules, especially at a time when so much new money is flowing into the sector."

Bridgespan's largest client was a major foundation. Bridgespan had completed a strategy project to assist the foundation in adopting a "venture philanthropy"-type approach to its grant-making—fewer grantees, bigger investments, and higher engagement with its grantees. As Bridgespan became involved in the implementation of this new strategy, the foundation had also agreed to a seven-figure engagement with Bridgespan to assist its high-potential grantees in developing their growth strategies.

Bridgespan partners were thinking through the implications of having an unexpectedly large proportion of projects funded by foundation partners. Currently five out of six service delivery nonprofit clients fell into this category. Carttar noted, "This kind of relationship enables us to serve the kind of community-based nonprofits that reside at the heart of the nonprofit sector. Furthermore, the consulting work is funded by the foundation and it is committed to making substantial grants to support implementation. This kind of relationship holds great promise for us." But, despite the benefits, the involvement of third-party payers added complications for Bridgespan. As Jeff Bradach commented, "managing the triangle of clients, funders, and the firm can be tricky. Questions arise, like 'who is the client?' To get the best outcomes, we need clients to be honest with us about their challenges. Sometimes having funders in the mix can make that difficult."

Staffing & Recruiting

Bridgespan had hired some of the strongest performers from Bain on a permanent and rotating basis, and had also added non-Bain staff with strong track records. Interest in Bridgespan among pre-MBAs staff at

Bain was particularly strong. Bridgespan consultant Joanne Clain had worked for Bain's Boston office and was considering leaving. Having studied public policy, she joined Bain hoping to obtain management skills that she could apply to the public or nonprofit sector. "When I heard Tom Tierney's voicemail," she said, "I thought, this is my dream job!" While at Bain, senior associate consultant Geoff Lieberthal founded a nonprofit that consulted to charter schools. He was thrilled about Bridgespan because, "now I could move from spending only 10% of my time with nonprofits as a volunteer to making it my full-time job and identity."

Bridgespan found aspects of staffing to be complex. Carttar observed:

Managing our staffing mix between people with and without Bain experience and people on a permanent vs. temporary basis has turned out to be a big challenge. Originally, we expected virtually all of our staff to come from Bain, either directly or indirectly, but that has changed. We now expect that, steady state, around 60–70% of our staff will have prior Bain experience and that at least 60% of the total will be here on a permanent basis. Of course, the mix of Bain vs. non-Bain and permanent vs. rotating will vary at each staff level and will probably change over time.

At Bain, the value proposition for a Bridgespan Group rotation has been strong for pre-MBAs but is perceived as more mixed for more senior staff. Because pre-MBAs are usually expecting to leave Bain and attend business school, they are more likely to be focused on expanding their own experience bases—or differentiating their resumes—rather than on their current income. In contrast, post-MBA consultants, managers and partners at Bain are typically focused on building their business consulting careers and may perceive that a rotation at Bridgespan will take them off track. Time at Bridgespan also involves a significant pay cut—tougher for the more senior people who may have a family and mortgage. The implication? We may need to fill these levels with more non-Bain people than planned.

It was unclear how potential imbalances would be sorted out. One concern was that the mix could evolve to the point where senior staff with no Bain experience were managing junior consultants from Bain with no nonprofit experience. The partners were concerned about whether Bridgespan would be able to deliver Bain-quality results if the mix shifted too far in this direction.

The rotation program also posed challenges for staffing cases and building knowledge. Managers could find it difficult to match project time frames with the rotating cohort from Bain. Bridgespan needed to capture knowledge from outgoing staff and transfer it to the new cohort. Because of the turnover, some considered formal knowledge management even more critical than at Bain. Carttar noted that "the rotation program is central to our relationship with Bain and it is the source of unparalleled people and fresh ideas. We need to keep working on how to manage the program in a way that fits the needs of our enterprise and the needs of Bain's."

The recruiting pipeline depended on delivering quality experiences for consultants from Bain. Kelly Campbell commented:

> The work we do is just as rigorous as at Bain. For a cultural institution, we built a financial model that was as complex as those Bain does for corporate clients. For a foundation client, we designed due diligence and business planning techniques as sophisticated as those used by Bain's private equity group. We need to combat the view that Bain staff coming to Bridgespan will be off the Bain career track. We can't afford to have staff go back to Bain and say that Bridgespan was not a good experience. To prove we offer as strong a professional opportunity as staying at Bain, we communicate the quality of our work to Bain in several ways. We conduct the same performance reviews as Bain and share the results. A Bain committee will review our actual case work, and our board includes three Bain directors. In the end, if our teams are involved in high-impact work—projects that really deliver results and make a difference—and people are challenged to learn new things, then we will get all the top-notch people we can handle.

Organizational Culture

Bridgespan's founders believed that creating a culture rooted in both the business and nonprofit sectors was extremely important. Bradach described the organization's culture and values:

> We have borrowed the best from Bain in terms of its values. We share its commitment to client results, its desire to redefine the consulting industry, its belief in the power of teamwork within the firm and with clients. We build on that. Our people often take a pay cut to join us and are committed to service and making a difference in the world. We tap into that idealism in the work we do. We also do service days regularly to both create an ethos of

service and to keep us connected to the realities of delivering services in non-profit organizations.

We value highly humility and respect for our clients. We believe we have a lot to offer, but we also recognize the complexity and enormity of the challenges faced by nonprofit leaders. We have a lot to learn from our clients. Finally, we are building a culture that is reflective, open to learning, and focused on developing new knowledge. Nonprofit management and nonprofit consulting are relatively new fields, at least compared to the for-profit world where bookstores are full of management books and a multi-billion dollar industry of consultants serve for-profits. We need to be able to produce new knowledge if we are to maximize our impact.

Bridgespan associate consultant Tamara Olsen, who came from a nonprofit organization, described her experience in the Bridgespan culture as a non-Bain hire: "Having people with nonprofit industry experience is important. We can help people from Bain understand the nonprofit context and how to adjust their language to fit that culture. I haven't felt like an outsider being a non-Bain person. As soon as I was hired, I was immediately immersed in the Bain way through the training program, which was valuable for learning both the analytical tools and the culture. Bain people have been welcoming and curious. The expertise of Bain colleagues and the Bain tool kit are great resources to draw upon."

The Bain Relationship

The partnership between Bain and Bridgespan was considered by both firms to be of critical importance. "Managing the Bain relationship is a big part of my job," said Jeff Bradach, "in fact, I keep a well-worn folder in my top desk drawer titled Contributions to Bain, to track the ongoing benefits we at Bridgespan deliver for Bain. Bain provides a tremendous amount to us, and we need to make sure we are helping them, too." At Bain, Boston Managing Director Phyllis Yale also considered the relationship a priority: "I'm working to institutionalize my enthusiasm and support for Bridgespan. In my communications to partners and staff, I celebrate Bridgespan's successes as if they were our own."

Phyllis Yale discussed administrative issues that the two firms tackled as the partnership began: "We had to work up front on the nitty-gritty policies to make Bain's human resource systems, knowledge base, and training opportunities seamless and accessible to Bridgespan people. We tried to anticipate questions that would come up. For example, in the area of compensation and benefits: should staff rotating outside Bain to Bridgespan have the same vesting in client equity that we provide to Bain consultants who remain here or rotate within Bain to the Sydney office?"

Tom Tierney discussed what Bain received for its investment:

> Bridgespan helps with Bain's recruiting. Like Bain Capital, Bridgespan differentiates Bain on campus and helps us attract consultants. Even if people never go there, the opportunity exists and they can take pride in its accomplishments. Bridgespan also helps with staff retention. To keep people at a professional service firm like Bain, we need to create a wide variety of interesting career options. Finally, Bridgespan reinforces Bain's core values of results, entrepreneurship and teamwork.

David Bechhofer found another benefit: "Bain does not do pro bono work or sponsor Bridgespan for business development purposes per se. But it does give us something interesting to talk about with our CEO clients, who are often involved with nonprofits. It doesn't sell business but can reinforce relationships."

Along with mutual benefits, the Bridgespan-Bain relationship held risks. Phyllis Yale commented: "When we started Bridgespan, we actually made a list of the potential tensions that could arise between us. Going in, we knew where our interests might not be aligned. So, the partners in both firms need to work together to manage through those problems." For example, she noted that Bridgespan could hire too many staff from Bain: "In Boston, some of our best people—some of our most capable SACs and one of our strongest managers—have joined Bridgespan. That can pose a short-term challenge for staffing our corporate clients when we're sold out." (As it was, top consulting firms faced major labor market competition, with desirable candidates increasingly opting for internet companies and other start-ups.) On the other hand, there was a risk to Bridgespan not taking enough Bain people, according to Yale: "If only SACs rotate to Bridgespan—but no consultants, managers or partners—then that will not be good for Bain either. As Bridgespan hires more non-Bain people, there will be less overlap between the firms in consultant's skills and culture."

Bridgespan associate consultant Tamara Olsen described the balance the firm needed to strike: "Each of our stakeholders—clients, Bain, our staff and funders—could potentially pull us in different directions if we don't set up a strong overarching mechanism to keep aligned. They are like four overlapping circles, and we need to hit and maintain the spot where all four line up with our mission. If we work it right, all can be aligned. But it will require a lot of energy and effort."

OPTIMIZING IMPACT

The partners at Bridgespan were encouraged by the accomplishments of the young firm—they were delivering. Considering the future of the Bridgespan Group, Bradach asked, "Given where we are now and what we've learned, how can we best fulfill our mission of creating impact in the nonprofit sector?" Bradach and the Bridgespan partners saw three areas where the firm faced decisions that could influence its ultimate impact. These areas were client mix, growth, and knowledge sharing.

Client Mix

Significant decisions lay before Bridgespan about what types of clients to serve. The firm had decided to serve both foundations and service delivery organizations in order to impact the sector at multiple levels and increase the rate of learning. As opposed to a firm that specialized in one segment, this client variety required Bridgespan to be versatile and maintain a wide range of capabilities. Choices about client mix and type of services provided had implications for the talent that Bridgespan needed to recruit and develop within the firm. Bradach pondered the question:

> What should our client portfolio look like? Should we be serving small nonprofits, large nonprofits, and foundations or should we focus on a particular segment? Our current thinking is that it is important to serve all three—because they are all interwoven. However, more than one person has said that if we wanted to maximize our impact we would focus just on foundations—a critical actor in the nonprofit capital market that dictates so much of what happens in the sector.
>
> Another important question is whether to try to replicate the relationship we have with our major foundation client where we are now working with its grantees. Perhaps we should only be in the "wholesale" business—identifying and working with clients through these foundation relationships—and not work with non-profits on a "retail" basis. It simplifies greatly the client selection process—foundations are in the flow of good opportunities—and it provides a compelling economic model for funding the consulting work and implementation.

Growth

Bridgespan faced decisions about what size and growth strategy would support their ability to achieve maximum impact. The firm was already larger than most nonprofit consulting firms. How big should Bridgespan be and how long should they take to get there? What would it take to build a strong organization and maintain high quality? What new challenges would surface as Bridgespan became a multi-site organization? Bradach discussed some of the issues:

> We are growing rapidly and have discussed the possibility of eventually growing to 100 or so total staff in Boston and San Francisco. We're committed to expanding no faster than the rate at which we can find high-caliber people to lead our teams and do our style of consulting. The key challenge is recruiting post-MBA consultants, particularly case team leaders and managers. Bain is struggling to attract and retain these people, so it is no surprise that we face that same challenge. I'm concerned that Bridgespan may be approaching the limit of how many people we can recruit from Bain. But what are the implications of shifting the mix toward more people without Bain experience? We've seen some very talented external candidates, but need to ensure they have Bain-like capability and deeply understand our approach. It takes years to develop a skilled Bain-quality consultant, so we cannot take lightly a shift from obtaining most of our people from Bain to "making" them ourselves. In addition, with less Bain overlap, there is some risk that we will drift apart, yet our core proposition depends on Bain. We'll need to be vigilant to maintain a strong relationship.

Tom Tierney commented on the challenges of growth:

> Bridgespan needs Bain in order to reach its potential. The goal is to provide a sustainable, high quality resource customized to the nonprofit sector. That resource is built on the best strategy consulting skills and tools around—Bain's—and Bridgespan's ability to go down Bain's learning curve rather than start its own. The access to Bain's people and knowledge is critical. A consulting firm is only as good as its people. There is a risk that the Bain-Bridgespan relationship could atrophy out of modest neglect, if the players on either side don't make it a priority. But the goodwill we've generated and the committed personalities involved will help avoid this. Perhaps a greater risk is the challenge of growth. Bridgespan is moving fast to be a leader and seize the

opportunity for impact emerging in the sector. But, we could be growing too fast. Bridgespan does not face financial risk now, but there is a risk that we become overextended given the breadth of opportunities.

Knowledge Sharing

The partners at Bridgespan were also concerned with elements of Bridgespan's mission that went beyond direct consulting work for clients. How extensive should the firm's other activities, like knowledge sharing, be? What other ways could the firm have impact in the non-profit sector? Bradach noted that:

> Based on our strategy, we need to consider complementary activities that will support change in the sector. One area we are committed to is knowledge sharing and dissemination. Building the knowledge base on nonprofit management issues and sharing it with people in the sector can have a huge impact. We've taken initial steps to launch this effort, but questions remain about the content, the vehicles and the target audiences. How much should we invest in this? How can we create a culture of reflection in our consulting operation and channel those insights into our knowledge sharing operation? Should we commit significant resources to publishing and training endeavors aimed to leaders in the sector? Are there other activities beyond knowledge sharing that we can provide to reduce barriers to performance in the sector? For example, many of our engagements have identified new skills that will be required to take their organizations to the next level. Should we develop an executive search capability to help find people with those skills?

There was a lot to think about. The Bridgespan partners realized that the decisions the team was making every day would have a significant influence on their ultimate ability to deliver on their mission. Bradach noted that "We don't want to find ourselves five years from now having missed opportunities to realize our full potential. We need to be creative and capitalize on opportunities to help leaders in the nonprofit sector achieve their dreams to make a difference and to pursue our desire to make as great a contribution to the sector as possible."

NOTE TO CASE

1. A source of revenue estimates: *Consultant News*, June 1998, p. 9.

Case 4.4a

DATAVISION (A)

(Gregory C. Rogers and Michael Beer)

ABOUT THE AUTHOR

Research Associate Gregory C. Rogers prepared this case under the supervision of Professor Michael Beer as the basis for class discussion rather than to illustrate either effective or ineffective handling of an administrative situation. It was made possible by a company that prefers to remain anonymous. Company data have been disguised. This case is based on an earlier version written by Research Assistant Emily Stein.

Datavision, a small computer company, had grown rapidly since its birth in 1985. By 1993, the organization was a leader in the process control monitoring industry. Despite the fact that Datavision's business was flourishing, its president, Dr. Larry Campbell, was concerned with some existing and potential problems inherent in rapid growth situations. He was particularly concerned about Datavision's high turnover rate, the lack of collaboration between functional areas, and "morale" problems within the organization. In general, Campbell was disturbed by a lack of vitality both in the executive wing of Datavision's office building and across the organization. To deal with these issues specifically and to improve their ability to manage organizational issues generally, Campbell and his vice president of finance, Matt Leona, enrolled in a two-week executive education program held in August 1993 at the Harvard Business School.

At the seminar, participants met in large classes as well as in small, 8- to 10-member action planning groups. By the end of the two weeks, Campbell and Leona had gained perspective on Datavision's needs and identified an appropriate course of action. The focus of their plan was to set in motion a process designed to get problems out on the table, increase the executive group's ability to communicate, and plan more effectively. They had no clear ideas about what particular changes in management, in managerial roles, or in organizational structure might result from this process. At the suggestion of other managers in their action planning group, they planned to use an organizational development consultant to play a catalytic role in their effort to identify and address issues.

DATAVISION'S BUSINESS

Datavision Incorporated is an organization involved in the design, development, manufacturing, and marketing of process control monitoring systems that provide real-time visual feedback of process type manufacturing operations. Datavision has pioneered the use of interactive graphic displays in process monitoring. Their advanced workstation-based systems replace older minicomputer-based monitoring methods.

Process control monitoring systems are used in a number of different industries. Datavision has directed its marketing and sales efforts toward large companies in the chemical processing, food processing, and utility plant industries. A Datavision system sells for approximately $250,000.

HISTORY OF DATAVISION

Datavision began in 1985 when Larry Campbell, Walter Jackson, Luther Beale, and Paul Winter—four engineers from Lincoln Labs at MIT—decided to go into business for themselves. Campbell became president; Jackson, Beale, and Winters became vice presidents; four other people were hired, and headquarters was set up in Campbell's living room.

Datavision's engineers worked closely that first year and in 1986 introduced the first workstation-based system with interactive graphic process monitoring ever to appear on the market. The systems were well received, particularly in the food processing industry, and by 1988, Datavision was growing at a rate of 50% per year. But by 1993, Datavision was a very different organization than it had been initially. Campbell and Jackson were still involved in company management; Beale, however, had returned to MIT in 1988, and Winters had gone to work for another computer company in 1992. In the spring of 1993, the company employed a total of 470 people.

Despite rapid growth and profitability, the company was not without problems. In an industry where the average turnover rate is from 12% to 15%, Datavision's turnover was 30% in 1991 and 1992, and in 1993 it was still a troubling 18%. Although the top management team was stable, engineers, programmers, technicians, and marketing people would come and go quickly.

Datavision's business is characterized by high technology that changes rapidly. Thus, turnover can be a serious problem because qualified people are in high demand but limited supply, so that recruiting, interviewing, and hiring them costs the company both time and money. The industry is also highly competitive. Datavision has a 31% share of the current workstation-based graphics processing market. Its five major competitors have 37%, 14%, 9%, 3%, and 6% of market share, respectively. To continue to grow, gain market share, or simply maintain its position in the marketplace, Datavision must actively market its product to generate sales. Active marketing is also important to build up order backlog. The organization aims for a steady $5 million backlog of orders. In addition, the company must constantly develop more efficient, more advanced, and less expensive products. According to one manager:

> This is a highly pressurized and competitive industry. To survive you have to be one step ahead of everyone else. Every six months there is a significant change in our marketplace. That kind of activity puts a lot of pressure on everyone, engineering, but particularly sales. People simply don't wait in line to buy a $250,000 computer.

BUSINESS STATUS

Since 1989, net sales at Datavision have grown at a compound rate of slightly less than 50% per year (see Exhibit 4.18, Consolidated

Exhibit 4.18 Datavision Incorporated and Subsidiary, Consolidated Statements of Income for the Years Ended April 30, 1989–1993 ($000s)

	1989	1990	1991	1992	1993
Net Sales	$3,457	$7,265	$9,461	$10,183	$16,640
Cost of Sales	1,976	4,236	5,759	5,661	9,471
Gross profit	$1,481	$3,029	$3,702	$4,522	$7,169
Operating Expenses:					
Engineering, marketing, general, administrative and other	$1,280	$2,609	$3,309	$4,254	$5,253
Income (loss) from operations	$201	$420	$393	$268	$1,916
Interest Expense, net of interest income	12	87	230	302	265
Income (loss) before provision for federal and state income taxes	$189	$333	$163	$(34)	$1,651
Provision for Income Taxes:					
Federal	$76	$123	$59	$(12)	$860
State	17	21	4	–	–
Income (loss) before extraordinary credit	$96	$189	$100	$(22)	$791
Extraordinary Credit—	–	–	–	–	
Federal income tax reduction resulting from net operating loss carry forward	76	123	–	53	–
Net income	$172	$312	$100	$31	$791
Net Income per Common Share:					
Before extraordinary credit	$.09	$.15	$.08	$(.02)	$.50
Extraordinary credit	.07	.09	–	.05	–
Net income (primary)	$.16	$.24	$.08	$.03	$.50

Statements of Income, 1989–1993). When Campbell and Leona left their offices to attend the executive seminar, results of the first quarter of fiscal 1993 were in. (See Exhibit 4.19, Consolidated Operations Report.) Actual total revenues were less than predicted. Income before taxes, however, was slightly higher than predicted for that time of year. By the time the seminar had ended and Leona and Campbell had returned to Datavision, there was decided concern about the financial situation. According to Finance V.P. Leona:

> In April 1993, we had just finished a very big year. By August, though, we were behind our predictions. We hadn't thought the summer doldrums would affect business that year but apparently they did. We had to readjust our thinking and cut down our forecasts for fiscal 1994. We had originally predicted a year with $25 million in sales at that point in time [August 1993]. We had to cut that forecast down to $22 million.

Datavision's managers were also concerned with company financials. According to a manager in the manufacturing department:

> We all know in an industry like this that we need a backlog. By the end of the summer of 1993, we had really eaten away and were continuing to eat away at the backlog we had. At that point, our backlog was only $2 million to $3 million and, from what I understood, we just weren't getting orders.

THE ORGANIZATION AND COMMUNICATIONS

Twenty-nine of the 470 employees at Datavision were executives and managerial staff. The organization was housed in six separate buildings in an area north of Boston, Massachusetts. Five of the six buildings were within walking distance of each other. The sixth (a manufacturing building) was only 15 minutes away by car. The president and vice presidents of finance, engineering, and marketing and their staffs were in one building; manufacturing was in three others; customer service was in the fifth; and sales, the sixth.

President Campbell was responsible to a 12-member board of directors of which he and the other vice presidents were members. Reporting to Campbell were five functional managers. (See organization chart and personnel profile, Exhibits 4.20 and 4.21.)

To maintain contact and disseminate information about departmental and company activities, Campbell's staff met weekly for several

Exhibit 4.19 Consolidated Operations Report—Quarterly Comparison

	First Quarter FY 1994			First Quarter FY 1993		
	Budget	Actual	Percent	Budget	Actual	Percent
Revenues						
System and Upgrade Shipments, Customer-Funded Engineering Shipments						
Less discounts:						
– System and Upgrade Shipments						
– Customer-Funded Engineering Net Shipments,						
Customer Services, Application Development and Other Revenue						
Total Revenue	$5,014,000	$4,721,764	100.0%	$3,324,857	$3,397,296	100.0%
Cost of Sales						
System and Upgrade at Standard, Manufacturing Variances, Color Plotter Development, Customer-Funded Engineering, Customer Services,						

Application Development						
Total Cost of Sales	2,797,932	2,503,704	53.0	2,019,429	1,980,898	58.3
Gross Profit	2,216,068	2,218,060	47.0	1,305,428	1,416,398	41.7
Operating Expenses						
Engineering, Marketing, Corporate Administration, and Other	1,621,770	1,602,761	33.9	1,115,161	1,143,888	33.7
Income from Operations	594,298	615,299	13.0	190,267	272,510	8.0
Interest Expense	60,000	37,305	0.8	78,000	83,677	2.5
Foreign Currency Exchange	—	2,768	—	—	—	—
Income Before Tax Provision	$534,298	$575,226	12.2%	$112,267	$188,833	5.5%
Provision for Income Taxes	283,000	335,000	7.1	60,000	85,000	2.5
Net Income	$251,298	$240,226	5.1%	$52,267	$103,833	3.0
Net Income per Share	$.14	$.14		$.04	$.08	

Exhibit 4.20 Organization Chart

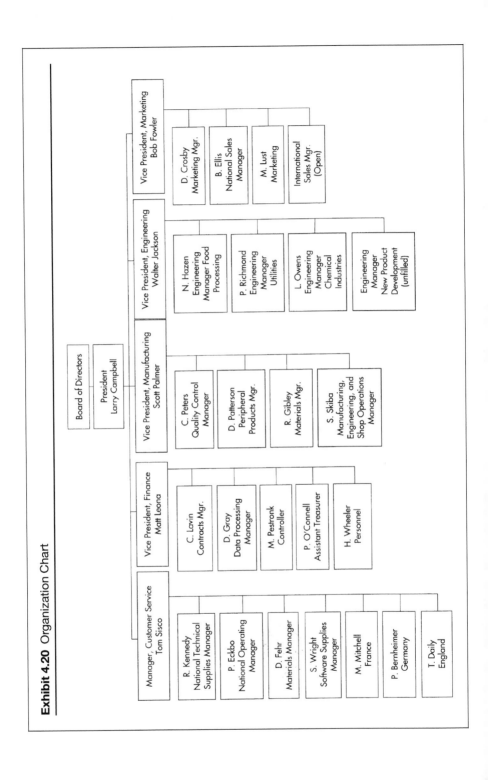

Exhibit 4.21 Personnel Profiles

Larry Campbell: President, 38 years old. Dr. Campbell received a BS, MS, and Ph.D in Engineering from the University of California at Berkeley. During his graduate studies, Dr. Campbell consulted for several organizations in the area of process control. After a brief period as a professor at Cal, he went to work in research at Lincoln Labs at MIT. He worked there for two years and founded Datavision in 1985. Dr. Campbell is a member of Datavision's Board of Directors.

Bob Fowler: V.P., Marketing, 37 years old. Fowler received an undergraduate degree from Fordham and an MBA from New York University. After his graduate education, he went to work for Exxon, then Pitney Bowes in Sales. He was recruited by a search firm and came to Datavision in 1988. Mr. Fowler is also a member of Datavision's Board of Directors.

Walter Jackson: V. P., Engineering, 36 years old. Jackson received a BS in Engineering at the University of Arkansas. He continued his education in engineering at the University of Illinois and received a Ph.D. After finishing his doctorate, Jackson went to work at MIT, stayed there for one year and left to begin Datavision in 1985. He is a member of Datavision's Board of Directors.

Scott Palmer: V.P., Manufacturing, 38 years old. Palmer received a BS in Engineering at the University of Rhode Island. He continued his education at Wharton and earned on MBA. After graduate school, Palmer worked for General Electric for 10 years in manufacturing before being recruited and joining Datavision in 1989. Palmer is also a member of the Board of Directors.

Matt Leona: V.P., Finance, 39 years old. Leona earned a BS in Electrical Engineering from Case Western Reserve and an MBA from Harvard. He went to work for IBM directly out of Harvard, in finance and pricing. He stayed with IBM for several years before working at an investment banking firm for one year. His next job involved venture capital work at General Electric. While at GE he invested GE's and his own money in Datavision. In 1991, he left GE to join Datavision and became a member of the Board of Directors.

Tom Sisco: Manager, Customer Service, 34 years old. Sisco earned a BA from St. Anselms College, went to work in the Peace Corps and then spent eight years as a manager at the United Parcel Service Company. Sisco and Dr. Campbell are neighbors and friends. Sisco was personally recruited to Datavision by Campbell.

hours. Typically, Campbell ran the meeting. He'd ask for informal reports of department activities and problems. Then he would present an idea and ask for input, which he would use to make decisions. According to Campbell:

> I generally make most of the organizational decisions around here. When we first started the company, I did everything. I made all the decisions and didn't really explain to anybody why I made them. I was in a position though to have a very complete picture of the organization and was the only one in a position to make good decisions. Things have changed since the beginning though, and there are just too many decisions to make. I've been adapting to our growing organization and trying to change. I let certain people make decisions but I don't feel right now that I can delegate all or even most of the decision making. I tend to be a bit of a perfectionist and expect an awful lot. I feel as though I'm a little ahead of the organization in terms of knowing or thinking about where we are going, where we ought to be, and what ought to be done. I have a tendency to figure things out, make assumptions, and make decisions. That confuses people sometimes but I think it's what we need right now. I use the information I'm given at executive meetings but really make final decisions mostly myself.

Following Monday staff meetings, each vice president met with his own department managers to communicate organizational plans, decisions, or discuss company or department activities. Such meetings gave managers the opportunity to meet formally and communicate with their area vice president and with each other.

The monthly written report was another important communication tool used at Datavision. Each vice president was responsible for preparing a monthly activity report for the president. Once the president received all five reports he consolidated the information into one report for the board of directors and each vice president. In order to best prepare such reports, Larry Campbell met with each vice president and his managerial staff for several hours during the week before the reports were to be written.

The atmosphere at Datavision was friendly, though at the same time a formality was emerging. In early days, doors were always open. Managers felt comfortable dropping in to chat with vice presidents and the president. As the organization grew, the atmosphere changed and, although managers usually met their vice presidents whenever necessary, Campbell was seen by appointment.

THE INTERVENTION

On September 16, 1993, approximately one month after completing their executive seminar, Campbell, Leona, and personnel manager Harold Wheeler had a luncheon meeting with Dave Brennan. Brennan was an organizational development consultant recommended to Campbell and Leona by both a seminar faculty member and fellow participant. (See his personnel profile, Exhibit 4.22.) Larry Campbell explained:

> We attended MOE [Managing Organization Effectiveness] generally because there was a feeling on the part of some people that our hang-ups (turnover, morale problems, people feeling overworked) were organizational, and somehow we weren't managing the organization to be effective. As a result of our seminar experience, we decided to hire an organizational development [OD] consultant to come in, do some work, and help us bridge the gap between many different parts of the organization. We expected he would do that by talking to different people, sensing feelings and attitudes, and bring them forth in a way that doesn't offend people. We had had a sense of this OD need before going to that program, about a year earlier, and in fact hired someone who came in for a day. Anyway, after the summer program, we, Matt and I in particular, were really motivated to do some OD work. Brennan seemed like the right guy.

Exhibit 4.22 Personnel Profile

R. David Brennan: Consultant, 38 years old. Dr. Brennan received a BA in psychology at the College of Wooster, an MS and a Ph.D from Case Institute of Technology. His Ph.D is in Organizational Behavior. In 1982, he began working as a self-employed consultant in the area of organizational training and development. He has worked in a variety of settings including large and small businesses, government and community agencies, and educational and health institutions. Simultaneously, since 1983, Dr. Brennan has been on the faculty of the Whittemore School of Business and Economics at the University of New Hampshire. He has taught a variety of courses in the organizational behavior area. In 1993, he was promoted to full professor. At that time he decided to work primarily as a consultant but is still affiliated with the university as an adjunct professor. Between 1989 and 1991, while on leave from UNH, Dr. Brennan was employed by Digital Equipment Corporation in Switzerland as the European personnel manager.

During their three-hour lunch, Brennan explained himself and his ideas to Campbell, Leona, and Wheeler. He outlined a possible action strategy for Datavision. Brennan recalled:

> I spoke with the three of them back then and told them that I was interested in new and developing organizations. I've done a lot of work with high technology in rapid-growth situations where there are very bright people, usually engineers. I thought that I could help the vice president group work together more effectively. Larry and Matt referred to that as "team building."

As a result of that meeting, Brennan was hired to help Campbell's staff work more effectively as a managerial team. Brennan planned to begin the "team building" effort in three phases. First, he would interview each member of Campbell's staff individually. Next, on November 3 and 4, he planned to meet with Campbell and the staff at a resort in Newport, Rhode Island, for an off-site session. Finally, Brennan suggested that after Rhode Island, he hold a meeting with company managers who reported to the staff. Brennan planned to meet with those managers, about 25 in all, by himself and then have Campbell and the vice presidents join the session for a question and answer period.

Interviews with Top Management Group

On October 18, Brennan spent the day at Datavision interviewing the top staff. These interviews served two major purposes: (1) By introducing himself to the staff, Brennan was able to explain his goals, Campbell's goals in hiring him, and his plans for carrying out the team-building task. (2) In addition, by questioning each manager, Brennan could learn more about the operating environment at Datavision. He reported:

> I started all my interviews by saying, "I'm Dave Brennan. I'm here to interview you but before we can do that I need to know what kind of expectations you have and what you've heard about me." I got five different stories from those five different guys. The theme was basically that Larry had gotten ahold of me because he went to Harvard, he [Larry] thought I could help them work together better, and that they needed it. Although initially people were a bit formal and stiff, I was received very well.

The idea of a consultant was not new to Datavision executives. About a year before Brennan, another OD consultant came to Datavision, interviewed executives and managers, and made some recommendations to

Campbell. Datavision executives were also used to off-site, two-day meetings. Each quarter the executives and their spouses went to a resort for a combined business meeting and social gathering. One vice president commented:

> We were relieved to meet Dave. We all felt that Datavision needed something. We'd probably all mentioned our interest in having outside help to Larry independently. We hoped Dave would give us what we needed. I wasn't so sure that anything would change, but I was willing to give it a try. If nothing else, I was sure he could act as referee when we started yelling at each other at the off-site meeting. We were in the habit of getting pretty excited at those sessions.

After introducing himself, Brennan asked questions about Datavision's strength and weaknesses and about Campbell and their fellow vice presidents. He was particularly interested in assessing problem areas that might be preventing the top management group from working together as a team. As a result of his interviews, Brennan identified six key issues:

1. Lack of trust among the top-level people and across the organization;
2. Confusion about company goals;
3. Poor decision-making policy and too much decision un-making;
4. Lack of clarity regarding organizational structure;
5. "Cronyism";
6. Conflicting management styles at the executive level.

Brennan drew up a flip chart presentation that included a list of the six problems and illustrative quotes gathered during the interviews. He planned to use the charts to introduce the issues and help promote discussion in the two-day session. His agenda included convening on Thursday the 3rd at 8 a.m., working until noon, and working again from 4 p.m. to 8 p.m. The purpose of the first day would be to raise problems and "clear the air." For Friday the 4th, Brennan scheduled meetings from 8 a.m. to noon and 3 p.m. to 6 p.m. He expected that on Friday the group would be ready to devise strategies for dealing with Datavision's weaknesses.

The Off-Site Meeting: Thursday

On Thursday morning, Brennan began the session by explaining his agenda and the ground rules for the two-day meeting. According to one vice president:

There were several rules Dave suggested we follow. First, he said that we should try to stay on the topic of conversation and not bring in other issues when we were concentrating on one issue. Next, he suggested that if we were discussing or criticizing the behavior or style of a particular person, then we had to look that person in the eye. Also, you had to give the person being discussed a chance to talk and respond. Finally, the receiver of criticism also had the power to control the flow of conversation. If he or she was upset, offended, or uncomfortable, he or she had the option to say "Stop—I'd like to discuss something else."

As part of the ground rules, Brennan also described the role he would play at the meeting: an unbiased outsider whose primary function was to help people listen, talk, and hear each other more effectively. According to another vice president:

> To be honest, when we were beginning that meeting in Rhode Island I was thinking to myself, we've been trying to get along for years, we've had a consultant, we've met together at off-site gatherings. I was discouraged and didn't think it would work. I was also convinced, though, that I would try, and because Dave had come across so straightforward and capable, I had a glimmer of hope. I trusted him and wanted this to work out for us. I felt willing to do what had to be done and even put myself on the line.

Another vice president recalled:

> I thought that we all really had a good feeling at the start of that session. Larry was behind the effort. I really thought it could work.

After setting up the rules, Brennan unveiled his flip chart presentation. The first chart included a list of all six problems and quotations illustrating each issue. He focused on each problem one by one, trying to elicit additional comments and discussion. Participants were hesitant initially, but began to contribute by clarifying the ideas on the list.

1. *Trust* was a major concern around Datavision. Nearly each vice president had criticized other executives. According to one vice president:

> We've developed strict territories around here; we stay out of each other's departments mostly because we don't trust or approve of what the other person is doing. I'd like to question someone on their department's activities but I'd have to let them do it to me and I'm not sure I want that.

Apparently, these feelings were particularly true between marketing and engineering. It was not unusual for Walter Jackson (vice president, engineering) and Bob Fowler (vice president, marketing) to argue and blame each other for missed deadlines. Fowler was quite vocal in blaming the slippage in orders on the inadequacies of the engineering department. Each vice president took great pride in his own department and seemed to feel that "things are operating well in my department. If everyone else took care of his or her area like I take care of mine, things would be terrific around here."

Another problem related to trust was that no vice president seemed to feel he or she could confront another vice president, or could discuss negative feelings about another vice president or manager openly to Campbell. In some ways, they didn't feel that Campbell would listen and in other ways they didn't want to diminish another's reputation.

2. *Confusion* about company goals was related to the trust issue. One commonly held feeling was that no one around Datavision was skillful enough to plan for the company's future. Each vice president had confidence in the organization's technical competence but felt that no one was really in touch with the marketplace and realistic enough to make some good planning decisions for the business. One vice president explained at the meeting:

> We are all, except Scott [vice president, manufacturing] relatively new at managing. We are probably all experts in our own areas, but because we don't really trust each other, we don't pool our information. That kind of coordination isn't the norm around here. Another reason for the confusion is that the company may have outgrown whatever managerial skills and planning skills some of us had.

One major criticism about planning was the marketing department. Participants recalled:

> There are many places our system can be used. We haven't figured out what's happening in the marketplace. Our competitors seem to know. We are, or have become, very weak in that area. Our sales are dropping and we've been eating away at the backlog. There are some real doubts about the skills in that department. The vice president in marketing had made some particular blunders we all knew about, blunders that especially affected the engineering and manufacturing departments. He'd talk to a customer, find out what the customer wanted, and promise a system. That would

have been a good move except sometimes the product wasn't designed or produced yet.

To a lesser extent, the engineering department was criticized for not developing products quickly enough or not effectively designing a less costly product. During the session, vice presidents initially became defensive when criticized this way, but learned, as the session went on, to listen to the criticism and try to deal with it constructively. Brennan commented:

> They were all putting a great deal of effort into working hard at listening and abiding by the ground rules. Bob Fowler, who took the most criticism, tried especially hard to sit quietly and respond rationally.

3. *Decision making and "unmaking"* was related to the goal issue and a source of complaint. Several vice presidents commented to Brennan, "It seems that no one is willing to take a stand on long-range goals." Not only did the vice presidents worry that no one, particularly Larry, was willing to take a stand on long-range goals, but sometimes when a stand was taken it would be reversed quickly. Several of the vice presidents had mentioned this during their interviews and again during the Thursday session:

> Sometimes these Monday staff meetings we had were more confusing than not having them at all. Sometimes we'd talk for eight hours straight and leave without having a real sense of what had gone on. Other times, Larry outlined some very definite plans and ideas. We left the meeting assuming our policy was one way. You'd tell your managers and make sure the policy was understood. Soon you'd get a memo that the policy was changed. Larry did that all himself. That kind of change of plans was very confusing and irritating for Datavision employees. It was also pretty embarrassing for the vice president who made a statement that was reversed or negated a week later.

During the meeting, several vice presidents were irritated, recalling how they could leave a meeting committed to implementing a marketing, engineering, or manufacturing plan that would then be changed when the finance department discovered a new piece of data. One vice president commented, "It is apparent when Matt [Leona] goes to Larry with some new information, because we are all told to stop what we are doing and proceed a different way." The vice presidents felt that this type of situation was frustrating and costly. Engineers who had to stop one activity and get geared up for another lost valuable thinking time. Manufacturing also became angry when they set up shop to proceed one way and then had to close down to restructure activities.

During Thursday's meeting, several vice presidents confronted Campbell with comments like "Sometimes it seems you make decisions for reasons of your own, unmake them for reasons of your own, and don't bother to communicate to us why or what is going on. You make decisions without involving people who have a right to be involved."

Voices became raised during these kinds of confrontations, though participants consciously tried to control their tempers. Brennan contributed only to add a comment like "Well, Larry, did you understand exactly what Bob was saying? Why don't you rephrase that?" "Does anyone else feel the same way? How about you, Scott?" Through such questions, Brennan helped Campbell, the vice presidents, and Customer Service Manager Tom Sisco better understand the criticism and avoid one-to-one hostile confrontations.

4. *Lack of clarity related to organizational structure* was also a problem. Participants recalled feeling angry as the group began to discuss this topic. The consensus among the vice presidents was that Campbell made all the organizational decisions and in many ways those decisions didn't make sense. "One day a certain service group is a member of one department, and the next day it's been moved and reports to another department." One particular irritant to several vice presidents was the fact that Sisco reported to Campbell. The vice presidents were angry because Sisco had been elevated to an executive level and had managers reporting to him. During their interviews, several vice presidents told Brennan that they felt Sisco didn't have the title or experience to be a member of the top staff. At the meeting, they confronted Sisco with these feelings. Sisco remembered that at the off-site meeting:

> I was really shocked to hear that people, Matt in particular, doubted my credibility. I had trouble relating to them, but I just thought that was because I was a friend of Larry's.

5. *Cronyism* was the fifth problem Brennan found to be recurrent. In thinking back about the meeting, one vice president expressed the sentiments of the rest when he reported: "Tom Sisco didn't belong there. We told him we tolerated him but didn't trust him in the company and didn't trust him to be there. He was a tennis buddy of Larry's, which is why he was there in the first place."

Active discussion took place around the cronyism issue. The vice presidents felt that the friendship between Campbell and Sisco stood in the way of business because around the company, people felt that you got promoted if you were Campbell's friend. Sisco recalled:

> Those kinds of feelings were surprising to me because I really thought we played down our friendship. It was good to get it out in the open though because I knew where I stood, we all did, and that was good.

When first discussing these five issues the group had been somewhat subdued. As the hours went by they grew more willing to participate. Leona, Jackson, Fowler, and Campbell were the most vocal participants. Sisco and Palmer were fairly reserved. Brennan attempted to include them and elicit their comments when they were "watchers" for too long. When introducing the sixth issue, however, Brennan had a difficult time getting anyone to comment right away.

6. *Conflicting management styles* was an issue that each staff member discussed with Brennan during their respective interviews. As a result, Brennan was keenly aware that Fowler's (vice president, marketing) management and decision-making style was completely different from those of the other vice presidents. Fowler himself was aware that he had a different approach and a different philosophy than his peers. Fowler described himself as "the kind of person who is caring, feeling, people oriented and intuitive. I have a gut feel for a project or procedure and am often right. No one else around here feels that way. Campbell and Sisco, in particular, are logical and analytical; it is a very different style."

Dave Brennan remembered that, after interviewing the staff:

> It became obvious that Bob was perceived as the center of many of Datavision's problems. Before the meeting on Thursday, I had breakfast with Bob. I wanted him to be aware before the session that his management style was seen, not only as different from, but in conflict with, the management styles characteristic of other Datavision executives. He was upset about that, didn't like it, but said that he wasn't surprised. When we got to the issue in the meeting, people started denying it. At that point, I had to confront them and said, "Bullshit, these are your quotes right there. I said let's not monkey around, we've only got two days and there's a lot of hard work to do. I really need your help." After being straightforward in that way, a couple of the guys admitted to their feelings

and their quotes. After that point, for the rest of that day the discussion centered around Bob.

At this point, Jackson and Sisco, in particular, became vocal. Even Palmer jumped into this part of the discussion. Each saw Fowler as having a caustic, hostile, angry approach. Palmer expressed the opinions of Jackson and Leona when he commented, "We all felt that Bob was into winning and losing. He was confrontational and angry. He raised his voice and was very aggressive. That was just not necessary to get the job done. It wasn't our style here."

At the session, Leona remembered expressing the idea that

Bob and I had a very different approach to decision making. I knew he was certainly aware of it. He just fought me on it all the time. I believe in reality; facing it, living with it, and making well-thought-out logical decisions based upon it. Bob couldn't give me data to back up his ideas, or wouldn't, and that annoyed me, and at the meeting I let him know how I felt.

Another serious criticism directed at Fowler related to his "empire building" and salesmanship attitude. More specifically, Fowler was seen as someone who needed to feel important and powerful and would approach customers as if he were in control of everything at Datavision. He promised customers products and then would ask engineering to develop them. He'd promise customers deadlines that were impossible for manufacturing to meet. Scott Palmer recalled:

It really boiled down to a lack of trust in Bob. At the meeting we all took turns and confronted him on these issues. He didn't seem to be getting the marketing job done. Our sales were down, we were eating away our backlog. He was probably feeling some pressure but as a result he'd take things out on Jackson, or try to put blame somehow on engineering or manufacturing.

Once issue number six had been raised, all subsequent discussion became focused on Fowler. Every other issue was related back to Fowler's inabilities and personality style. Although Brennan helped maintain calm, and the criticism was delivered constructively, Fowler was subjected to several hours of direct confrontation. Jackson commented:

For a long time, Bob and I had had problems. This was a forum for expressing my feelings about those problems and getting them out on the table. We all tried to explain ourselves pretty calmly. He may have perceived it as an attack.

Fowler said later that he had perceived the session to be an attack. At the time, he did not react defensively or with hostility. Although he admitted feeling initially that the whole session was a set-up to confront him, he listened to everyone's comments and tried to understand them. He also redirected some of the criticism if he thought he was being unfairly blamed for something or that others could benefit from similar criticism.

Scott Palmer stated:

> Because Dave was there, I guess we were able to voice complaints we had never voiced before. For the first time, I was able to tell Bob that it really irritated me that he never listened. That kind of honesty caught on and Bob and Larry went back and forth about individual management styles and things about each other that bothered them. Bob said Larry always turned around his [Bob's] decisions. Larry expressed the feeling that Bob was too dogmatic. It was refreshing in a way because people had things buried for five years and they were able to express them. As positive as it was, though, in some ways it was brutal. Bob sat there through criticism that was mostly directed at him and maintained his cool. I give him a lot of credit, we all did. He was open and made no attempt to stop the flow of conversation. We all learned a lot about each other during that time. We all wanted this thing to work and all appreciated Bob's willingness to listen and take criticism pretty calmly.

Larry commented:

> You could almost see the improvement. Bob was really trying. He did quiet down and acted much calmer. He tried not to raise his voice and seemed to really hear what everyone else was saying.

As the first day ended, people were both energetic and exhausted. Participants remember having positive and negative feelings about the day. They were relieved to get their feelings about issues, particularly Fowler, out into the open. However, it was upsetting for most of them to imagine what Fowler must have been going through during the day. All credited Dave Brennan for being an effective coach, moderator, and guide. They perceived Brennan as helping keep decibles down, fists from flying, and the conversation flowing. When the meeting adjourned, the group went to dinner feeling that they worked hard and made some good progress.

The Off-Site Meeting: Friday

Although the schedule for Thursday did include a four-hour break in the afternoon, the group had stopped only two hours for lunch. They were just as energetic Friday morning. Friday's meeting was to run from 8 a.m. to 6 p.m., with a quick break for lunch in the middle of the day. Campbell and his staff agreed that corporate planning would be the topic of discussion for day two. The group discussed how they planned to make efficient use of their meeting time, how to communicate individual department needs, what ground rules they would use for meetings.

Campbell ran most of the meeting on Friday and together the group developed a planning procedure for Datavision. The plan excited everyone because it seemed to integrate functional area needs. Overall, Palmer and Sisco remained less vocal than the rest of the group but seemed as enthusiastic about what they were accomplishing. Jackson recalled, "Our feelings were very different on Friday than they were on Thursday. We seemed more committed on Friday. Campbell was listening more carefully and Fowler was almost low key. He only spoke his fair share of the time."

They worked steadily, all day. They seemed committed to preparing planning strategies together. Brennan was less involved Friday than he had been Thursday but, apparently, his presence was a catalyst for discussion. One vice president recalled:

> On the second day, Brennan had the effect, even when he didn't say anything, of helping us talk without ignoring each other or becoming argumentative. He wasn't involved as an obvious leader but he did promote honesty and openness on our parts—the first day especially, but even the second day. Even when he was quiet we did need him in the room. That became obvious when he left to make some phone calls in the afternoon on Friday. After a few minutes, I guess when we realized he was gone, no one said a word. Apparently, we needed him there to really help us communicate, team build, or whatever.

At about 5:00 in the afternoon, Campbell suggested cocktails, which had not been served Thursday or before 5:00 on Friday, and started up a feedback session. He wanted to hear perceptions of his behavior for the two days and asked Leona, Jackson, Fowler, Sisco, and Palmer to take turns commenting. They mentioned strengths like "you seemed to be listening more," "you seemed to take our suggestions seriously," "you were trying hard to get our input." They also asked him to try to maintain some of these behaviors back at the office. Campbell enjoyed the feedback process and suggested they continue to comment on each participant. On the whole, the feedback was positive, applauding their listening skills and their honesty. The group seemed proud of itself. At 6 p.m. the meeting ended, and because he had plans Friday night, Campbell headed back to Boston. Those who stayed on had an informal post-meeting dinner.

After the session, participants thought about what had been accomplished and what might be accomplished as a result of their efforts. Feelings about the meeting ranged from very positive to very negative. Tom Sisco said:

> I came out of that meeting feeling very high. So many things came out in the open as a result of those two days. I felt we could all be much more open and honest with each other, and I had a very good idea about who the vice presidents were and where they stood on certain issues. I learned a lot about Walter and Matt. I felt I could work with both guys much more efficiently as a result of those sessions.

Another positive, though less enthusiastic, opinion shared by several staff members was:

> When we first heard about going to Newport, we all had a certain amount of skepticism about being able to work together well and about our planning capabilities. We had consultants before that; we were used to off-site meetings. I wasn't convinced that this guy [Dave] on this team thing would be any different for us. The first day was very encouraging though. We didn't have fistfights and didn't yell too much. We had all been so open that there was a collective feeling that things might really change. We were all hoping for it anyway.

There were a couple of participants who, despite overt enthusiasm, were doubtful that the session had changed anything or would act as a catalyst for future change. Their comments were:

> We have a pattern of leadership, decision making, and management style here that we are used to. We've had consultants before who pointed out the same problem issues to us that Dave did now. We didn't listen a year ago, why should we listen now?

The question now facing Campbell and Brennan was what steps to take next in moving change along. Brennan's original idea was to meet with the top 25 managers to discuss what had gone on in Newport and then to bring in Campbell and the vice presidents. Was this still a good idea? Their main objective was to carry ahead the movement begun at the two-day meeting into the company. What was the best way to do this?

Case 4.4b
DATAVISION (B)

(Gregory C. Rogers and Michael Beer)

ABOUT THE AUTHOR

Research Associate Gregory C. Rogers prepared this case under the supervision of Professor Michael Beer as the basis for class discussion rather than to illustrate either effective or ineffective handling of an administrative situation. It was made possible by a company that prefers to remain anonymous. Company data have been disguised. This case is based on an earlier version written by Research Assistant Emily Stein.

Brennan scheduled a meeting with company managers who reported to session participants for the week following the session. The meeting would let the managers know what had taken place in Newport and would run for about an hour. For the first half, Brennan would meet with the managers alone and after about 30 minutes the officers would join the session.

On Monday, November 7, 1993, Campbell sent a memo to the 25 managers that were to be included, announcing that a meeting would be held the next day at 11:00 in the conference room of Datavision's main building. Brennan stated:

> I wanted to do three main things at that meeting. I wanted to present an overview of the idea of team building, gain credibility, and give a brief description of the Newport meeting. I didn't plan on describing comments or anything like that, but I did want to explain the process, major issues raised, and the sense of excitement and commitment that came out of that meeting. I hoped that would promote questions that I could answer and that the officers could answer when they entered the room.

There was some confusion about the purpose of the November 8 meeting. Not all the managers were aware that any special off-site meeting had already taken place; some thought that this meeting was to be a typical managers' meeting at which Campbell would announce some kind of change in the organization. One manager recalled:

> Some of us were blasé, others curious, others pissed off. No one really knew what was up. Those of us who knew that the meeting was about consulting were, for the most part, unimpressed. We had spoken to consultants before and hadn't seen any results. There was no reason to think this would be different.

Campbell began the November 8 meeting. He explained briefly that the officers were "all fired up" about new corporate goals, strategies for planning, increasing market share and profits. Next he pointed to Brennan as the man who was going to help achieve those goals. Several managers remembered a tense moment in the session:

> Dave began his presentation by saying something like, "Well, I'm sure you're all curious about the weekend we spent in Newport." Someone spoke out at that point and said, "Frankly, we don't give a damn about what happened in Newport because lots of us don't even know they went to Newport." There was silence. Dave handled it well. He explained and proceeded as he had planned. He probably thought he had a better idea about what was going on than we did.

As the meeting progressed, Brennan talked about organizational development generally and about Newport specifically. He outlined general problems. Managers at the meeting agreed that Brennan seemed credible, likable, and genuinely committed to changing things at Datavision. They were less convinced, however, that things could, in fact, be changed and were hesitant to confront Brennan with those feelings. As he spoke, many managers felt doubtful and whispered among themselves. As recalled later by participants, the ideas going through people's minds and being exchanged were as follows:

> We don't have a team work problem in the company. The only problem is at the top. The rest of us work together fine because we know we have to. The troops communicate across departmental lines. It's just the generals that don't.

> We've heard all these promises before, nothing will change now.

> If they'd get together and take a stand maybe something would get done. Larry sends a memo to go ahead and proceed a certain way on a product, or something. The next thing you know he sends another memo that says with more information the project stops.

> It is going to take a lot for most of those guys to improve as managers because, first of all, they are all engineers and second of all, they never had to manage anyone before they managed us. They just were never taught how to do it.

> The officers go off to the woods for a couple of days and think they are a team now. It's just not true. It can't be. They can't be a team when they all have such strong personalities.

About 45 minutes into the meeting one manager asked Brennan a question. In doing so, he raised a volatile issue, one that every manager reported remembering and worrying about. The question was, "Don't you think that, at the top, there may be a couple of people who won't change because they don't really want to and, in fact, don't have the capacity?" Brennan responded with a flat "No." He explained that Newport convinced him that all the officers were committed to changing and were willing to work very hard at integrating, planning, and acting as a team. Until that point, Brennan was viewed as a competent ray of hope for Datavision. At that point, however, several managers became discouraged. They remembered:

> Dave really lost credibility points. It was no secret that there were attitude, capability, and personality differences and problems at the top. Bob Fowler was very different from the rest of them and there were bad feelings about that filtering through the company. We couldn't believe that Dave hadn't picked up on that or wouldn't tell us. If he didn't figure that out then he wasn't so skillful or had been lied to.

A wave of cynicism and doubt spread through the conference room after Brennan's response. Feelings of frustration, anger, and discomfort permeated the meeting. One manager commented on the perceptions of the group:

> We wanted things fixed very badly. We wanted Brennan to be able to give us solid evidence that things could improve. Instead his efforts seemed like they would almost have to be fruitless. It was almost like a joke after that. We were all very skeptical.

Another manager reflected:

> We all felt pretty awkward after that. When the officers came in, it got worse. People asked a couple of questions trying to assess their [the officers'] real commitment to organizational development, Dave Brennan, and team building, but the tone was disbelieving and doubtful. The people who were relatively new to the company were more hopeful than those who had been around for four years or so. Generally, although those of us who were new weren't convinced that it would change, I don't really think we expressed our doubts or questions very honestly during that meeting. We became even less open and honest, however, after the officers came in.

Case 4.4c
DATAVISION (C)

(Gregory C. Rogers and Michael Beer)

ABOUT THE AUTHOR

Research Associate Gregory C. Rogers prepared this case under the supervision of Professor Michael Beer as the basis for class discussion rather than to illustrate either effective or ineffective handling of an administrative situation. It was made possible by a company that prefers to remain anonymous. Company data have been disguised. This case is based on an earlier version written by Research Assistant Emily Stein.

After the officers' session in Newport, Campbell felt committed to OD work and team building at Datavision. He was enthusiastic and felt that his fellow officers were similarly excited. But his spirits fell after the managers' meeting. "It was really the first time I was aware of such wide-spread skepticism," he said. "That disappointed me and discouraged me."

He became even more discouraged when, after the meeting, he approached several of the managers individually. Such discussions convinced him that many managers at Datavision were certain that the officers could never work together as an effective team and that, given who they were, no OD consultant could help change things.

Other events also disturbed him. Financial results for the company's second quarter were in, and both revenue and income were well below prediction (see Exhibit 4.23). In addition, it was two weeks into November, sales were down, and the backlog was becoming smaller and smaller. Brennan reported,

> Larry called me with two major problems. He was upset by the amount of skepticism felt by the managers. It seemed to him that they didn't believe anything the officers said. He also mentioned that he had approached a couple informally and, it seemed to him, that the whole team-building and planning effort would fall by the wayside if he didn't come to grips with what he saw to be the major issues. He continued and reported that, he felt, there was no confidence in Bob. He was convinced that if he didn't deal with that, then "we can plan ourselves to death and nobody is going to believe the planning process."

Campbell was distressed and discouraged. He was not sure how to proceed. He recalled his eventual conclusion:

> It all of a sudden became obvious to me—Bob was an outsider in the organization—I don't think he was viewed as a competent marketing guy. His style was troublesome for some people too—I had a realization. Everyone was against Bob. Morale was very low. I wasn't 100% sure what to do. Whatever it was though, it had to be done quickly.

After talking with Brennan, Campbell spoke individually with Datavision's board members. By the third week in November 1993, Campbell decided upon a course of action. On November 29, 1993, he asked Bob Fowler to hand in his letter of resignation. Fowler agreed upon a monetary settlement and resigned with little argument.

Exhibit 4.23 Consolidated Operations Report—Quarterly Comparison

	Second Quarter FY 1994		Second Quarter FY 1993	
	Budget	**Actual**	**Budget**	**Actual**
Revenues				
System and upgrade revenue	$4,466,000	$3,986,298	$3,300,000	$3,294,611
Customer-funded engineering revenue	478,000	423,405	467,000	382,761
Total	$4,944,000	$4,409,703	$3,767,000	$3,677,372
Less discounts:				
● System and upgrade shipments	401,000	224,445	343,500	319,006
● Customer-funded engineering	43,000	21,659		
Net AGS revenue	$4,500,000	$4,163,599	$3,423,500	$3,358,366
Customer services	774,000	800,249	434,000	438,160
Application development	138,000	58,526	52,500	66,586
Color plotter	–	4,693	–	4,584
Total revenue	$5,449,000	$5,027,067	$3,910,000	$3,867,696
Cost of Sales				
System and upgrade at standard	$1,696,000	$1,677,761	$1,400,000	$1,441,325
Manufacturing variances	–	106,944	–	(53,933)
Customer-funded engineering	304,000	257,798	231,000	254,251
Customer services	810,568	764,647	423,918	422,995
Application development	103,352	32,375	52,987	57,562
Color plotter	97,503	111,299	–	–
Total cost of sales	$3,011,423	$2,950,824	$2,107,905	$2,122,200
Gross profit	$2,437,577	$2,076,243	$1,802,095	$1,745,496

Continued

Exhibit 4.23 Continued

| | Second Quarter FY 1994 | | Second Quarter FY 1993 | |
	Budget	Actual	Budget	Actual
Operating Expenses				
Engineering, marketing, corporate administration, and other	$1,797,620	$1,829,601	$1,223,754	$1,246,904
Income from operations	639,957	246,642	578,314	498,592
Interest expense	79,600	41,059	84,100	83,639
Foreign currency loss (gain)	–	8,445	–	(3,397)
Income before tax provision	$ 560,357	$ 197,138	$ 494,241	$ 418,350
Provision for income taxes	297,000	135,000	243,000	209,000
Net income	$ 263,357	$ 62,138	$ 251,241	$ 209,350
Net income per share	$ .14	$ .03	$ .18	$ .15

Case 4.5a

MERCER MANAGEMENT CONSULTING (A)

(Thomas J. DeLong and Michael W. Echenberg)

ABOUT THE AUTHORS

Professor Thomas J. DeLong and Michael W. Echenberg (MBA '02) prepared this case. HBS cases are developed solely as the basis for class discussion. Cases are not intended to serve as endorsements, sources of primary data, or illustrations of effective or ineffective management.

You can still tell them apart! Mercer's culture still reflects its two lineages. The Strategic Planning Associates people are still super-analytical and the Temple, Barker & Sloane folks are still more focused on relationships and industry expertise. It seems strange. I mean, the merger closed more than eight years ago.

Agnes Tang (HBS MBA '02)

"Are you with us or not?" asked Dean Silverman. Until two months ago, he and Dean Wilde had been firm leaders and top revenue generators at Mercer Management Consulting's 175-person Washington, D.C. office.

Now over breakfast at the city's Four Seasons Hotel they were trying to interest Ware Adams, a young star at Mercer, to join them in starting a firm of their own. He had been wrestling with the decision since receiving Wilde's first call two weeks before. Unbeknownst to Adams, George Overholser, a senior professional at Mercer who had had a close working relationship with Silverman, had already turned down a similar offer.

THE MANAGEMENT CONSULTING INDUSTRY

Writing in 1983, management and organization scholars Larry Greiner and Robert Metzger defined management consulting as follows: "An advisory service contracted for and provided to organizations by specially trained and qualified persons who assist, in an objective and independent manner, the client organization to identify management problems, analyze such problems, recommend solutions to these problems, and help, when requested, in the implementation of solutions."[1]

A statement primarily of objectives, this definition omitted the vastly different strategies that had been developed by management consulting firms, which differed from one another along multiple dimensions, including the degree to which they organized their problem-solving strategies into "products," the number of separate practice areas they maintained, and whether their services embraced implementation as well as diagnosis and problem solving. Choices around these dimensions determined a firm's annual revenue per professional, a key economic driver for professional services firms. Management consulting had become incredibly varied and exceedingly large over the past 20 years, accounting for more than $100 billion in annual revenue worldwide by the end of the 1990s.[2]

HISTORICAL PERSPECTIVE

In 1886, Massachusetts Institute of Technology Professor Arthur Dehon Little joined with fellow chemist Roger Griffin to found one of the first consulting firms. Named for Arthur D. Little, the firm focused initially on solving engineering problems for its clients. It developed for the U.S. Navy, for example, a fuel-efficient vapor-compression still to transform seawater into fresh water.[3]

This engineering focus was taken in a new direction by Harrington Emerson, who popularized "efficiency engineering" and in the process created the modern discipline of management consulting. From his

20s through his 40s, Emerson was a professor of modern languages at the University of Nebraska, a land speculator in western Nebraska, a surveyor for the Lincoln Land Company, and finally a campaigner for William Jennings Bryan. When Bryan lost his bid for the U.S. presidency, Emerson joined the Alaska Gold Rush. After a number of failed ventures, including the laying of a transpacific telegraph cable from Seattle to the Philippines via Alaska, Emerson endeavored to pay off his debts by consulting for glass factories and other industrial clients.[4]

Meetings of the Pennsylvania-based American Society of Mechanical Engineers acquainted Emerson with the work of Frederick W. Taylor, a former chief engineer at Pennsylvania's Midvale Steel Works who had conceived the theory of scientific management in response to the overwhelming inefficiency he perceived in American business. The management-worker relationship had grown increasingly adversarial, with managers paying workers as little as possible and workers doing as little as possible in return. Taylor advocated "close, intimate, personal cooperation between the management and the men."[5]

Taylor, who held that much more was required of managers—in terms of task design, project planning and oversight, and worker training, for example—than had previously been thought, assured workers that greater productivity would translate into higher compensation rather than job losses. Scientific management as a theory mandated the replacement of workers' rules of thumb with work processes that were standardized down to the last detail. "In order to have any hope of obtaining the initiative of his workmen," Taylor wrote:

> The manager must give some special incentive to his men beyond that which is given to the average of the trade. This incentive can be given in several different ways, as, for example, the hope of rapid promotion or advancement; higher wages, either in the form of generous piecework prices or of a premium or bonus of some kind for good and rapid work; shorter hours of labor; better surroundings and working conditions than are ordinarily given, etc.[6]

STRATEGY CONSULTING COMES OF AGE

Names that would come to define contemporary consulting entered the discipline in the first quarter of the 20th century. In 1914, Arthur A. Andersen and Edwin G. Booz, both entrepreneurs anxious to work for themselves, started consulting firms in Chicago, the former emphasizing accounting, the latter statistics. In 1926, James O. McKinsey, an accounting professor at Northwestern University, founded a Chicago-based firm to which he gave his name. A. "Tom" Kearney and Marvin Bower were among his first partners.

When the 48-year-old McKinsey died of pneumonia in 1937, Kearney and Bower disagreed about how the firm should be organized and operated. In 1939, the two parted ways, with Kearney keeping the firm's Chicago office and calling it A. T. Kearney and Bower heading up McKinsey & Company in New York. The disagreement was precipitated by the belief shared by Kearney and his Chicago partners that the firm should not operate multiple offices, likely resulting from a period during which the Chicago office had had to fund losses incurred in Boston and New York. The offices had split into separate firms with the understanding that they might one day be reunited. When Bower revisited this discussion in the wake of World War II, it was determined that the firms had progressed too far along different paths; Bower had raised fees beyond what would be tenable in Chicago and begun to focus recruiting efforts on "outstanding young people" rather than on the industry experts Kearney still sought.[7]

A graduate of Harvard Business School and Harvard Law School, Bower had started out as a Depression-era lawyer engaged primarily in helping companies navigate bankruptcy proceedings. He later decided that he preferred to help companies avoid bankruptcy as a business adviser than to help them through its aftermath as a legal adviser.[8]

Bower established practice areas at McKinsey & Company, refocused recruiting on the top schools' best graduate students, and insisted on putting clients' interests before the firm's in generating revenue. A memo sent to the firm's London office in 1967 shortly before he ended his tenure as managing director captures the essence of Bower's philosophy with respect to management consulting:

> My farewell hopes are these three: first, that down the years our directors and principals will provide formal training and on-the-job coaching in the professional approach. Two, that down the years our directors and principals will shout out whenever they feel we're doing anything that might impair the enduring values of the professional approach or just letting those values erode through inattention. And the third, that down the years our directors and principals will speak up whenever these principles that make up our philosophy are not being followed.[9]

According to McKinsey professionals, the "values of the professional approach" to which Bower referred had existed in various forms since the beginning of his tenure. "In addition to serving the client in a superior manner" he wrote in *Supplementing Successful Management*, a booklet he penned for prospective clients in 1940, "We must consistently put client interests ahead of firm interests, adhere to high ethical standards, preserve confidences and maintain an independent position—we must be ready to differ with client managers and tell them the truth as we see it even though it may adversely affect our income or endanger continuance of the relationship."[10]

The Boston Consulting Group (BCG) and Bain & Company, which were to become McKinsey's chief rivals in the competition for talent and clients, were founded in the 1960s and 1970s, respectively. In 1963, Bruce Henderson founded BCG, which was the first firm to focus exclusively on business strategy from its inception. Ten years later, when BCG had grown to 142 professionals, William W. Bain, Jr., a BCG partner, left to found Bain & Company.

MARSH & McLENNAN

In 1905, Henry W. Marsh and Donald McLennan, pioneers in the field of risk management, founded what was at its inception the world's largest insurance brokerage agency, with $3 million in premiums.[11, 12] In 1923, the firm was incorporated as Marsh & McLennan, with Marsh as its first chairman. Reinsurance broker Guy Carpenter & Company was acquired the same year.[13] Another of Marsh & McLennan's many acquisitions across a range of professional service industries was William M. Mercer Limited, purchased in 1959. The Vancouver-based employee benefits consulting firm, founded in 1945 to serve Canadian clients, constituted Marsh & McLennan's entry into the consulting industry. (See Exhibits 4.24 and 4.25 for details on Marsh & McLennan's acquisitions.)

STRATEGIC PLANNING ASSOCIATES[14]

Walker Lewis, a relatively junior professional at BCG in the early 1970s, jokingly refers to Strategic Planning Associates (SPA) as the "second-largest BCG spin-off after Bain."[15] Bruce Henderson, BCG's founder, had divided his firm into professional groups named for colors. The "Blue Group," into which Lewis had been placed, was headed by Bill Bain and later became the nucleus of Bain & Company. Uncomfortable

Exhibit 4.24 Timeline

Date	Event
1905	Marsh & McLennan is founded in Chicago, Illinois.
1945	William M. Mercer Limited is founded in Vancouver, British Columbia.
1959	Marsh & McLennan acquires William M. Mercer Limited.
1970	Temple, Barker & Sloane is founded in Wellesley Hills, Massachusetts.
1972	Strategic Planning Associates is founded in Washington, D.C.
1984	Marsh & McLennan acquires U.S. firm Meidinger Inc. and U.K. firm MPA Limited.
1986	Marsh & McLennan acquires U.K. firm Duncan C. Fraser & Company.
1987	Marsh & McLennan acquires U.S. firm A. S. Hansen.
1987	Richard Fairbank and Nigel Morris leave Strategic Planning Associates to launch an initiative that leads to Capital One.
1987	Strategic Planning Associates goes public.
1987	Marsh & McLennan acquires Temple, Barker & Sloane.
September 1989	Ware Adams joins Strategic Planning Associates as an analyst.
November 1989	Marsh & McLennan acquisition plan is announced at all-hands meeting at SPA the day before Thanksgiving.
February 1990	The deal uniting Strategic Planning Associates and Temple, Barker & Sloane is closed.
June 1991	TBS-SPA officially changes its name to Mercer Management Consulting (MMC).
January 1992	MMC's senior partners kick off the Vision 95 process, which defines the firm's three-year strategic plan.
April 1993	Senior vice presidents Dean Wilde and Dean Silverman leave the firm to start Dean & Company. Washington, D.C. office head Roy Barbie leaves.
July 1993	Wilde and Silverman ask Overholser and Adams to join Dean & Company. Overholser declines.
August 1993	Jim Down asks Overholser to become the "culture czar." He accepts.

Source: "Evolution," Mercer Management Consulting Web page, http://www.mercermc.com, accessed November 6, 2001.

Exhibit 4.25 Mercer's Corporate Family Tree

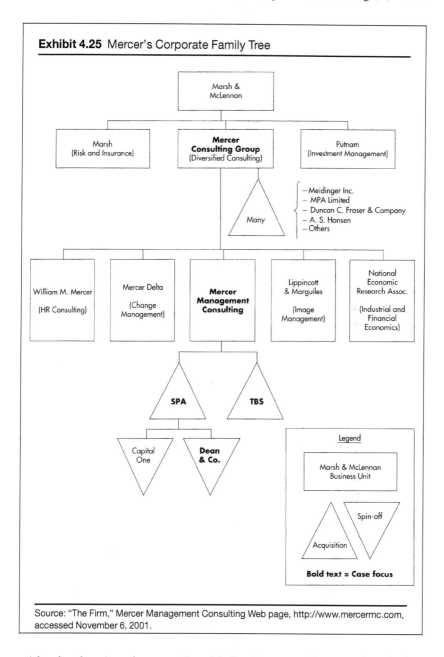

Source: "The Firm," Mercer Management Consulting Web page, http://www.mercermc.com, accessed November 6, 2001.

with what he viewed as questionable business practices, Lewis asked to be transferred to another group. When his request was denied, he left the firm. "The only thing I knew how to do at that point was consult," recalled Lewis, so in early 1972 he began to consult on his own.

In reference to the birth of SPA, he remarked that the firm "was never founded; it just happened."[16]

Lewis's choice of the name "Strategic Planning Associates" reflected his new firm's focus on developing a computer-based strategic planning tool to sell to clients. Throughout much of the 1970s, Lewis's team worked on a software application called The Profile Program. When he realized in the early 1980s that it was "nothing more than a very large, very expensive version of Lotus 1-2-3," the company wrote the project off for $5 million.[17]

SPA's guiding principle that "technology could be used to enhance analysis,"[18] however, remained strong; it simply took a new form. Rather than build a new software package, SPA would use existing software to build sophisticated models for clients. A major oil company, for example, paid $25 million over five years for a model that simulated the operations of 100 refineries worldwide. "Clients hired SPA," explained Lewis, "in the hopes that we would generate new insights with data that they had in hand, but that they knew they couldn't analyze like we could." SPA guaranteed from these analyses (called "killer ideas" within the firm) 15-fold returns on clients' consulting fees.

Washington, D.C.-based SPA had, by the time of its February 1990 merger with Temple, Barker & Sloane (TBS), opened offices in New York, Paris, London, Singapore, and Geneva. A 1986 article in the *Journal of Business Strategy* entitled "New Trends in the Strategy Consulting Industry" put SPA in the "strategy specialist" category with BCG and Bain, distinguishing it from "large general consulting firms" such as McKinsey, Booz-Allen & Hamilton, and A. T. Kearney.[19]

Believing that they would require new capital to continue to grow, Lewis and his partners had taken SPA public in 1987. But they neither used nor needed the capital to which the public markets provided access. SPA's challenge, according to Lewis, was that its skill set, not its capital, was limited. Clients valued the firm's highly specific set of sophisticated mathematical modeling capabilities. SPA had emphasized "depth over breadth" and was now overly focused.[20]

Faced with the choice of "rebuilding the firm in a very different way" or "becoming part of something much larger,"[21] Lewis and his partners chose the latter course. With the help of their investment bank, they initiated a process to sell the company. That Marsh & McLennan emerged as the high bidder pleased Lewis, who appreciated the degree to which that firm had committed itself to building a thriving consulting enterprise through acquisitions.

SPA had prided itself on being data driven and entrepreneurial. SPA professionals preferred to emphasize objectively verifiable facts over opinion and shunned what they called "cookie-cutter solutions." They wanted to "crack the code" of each new industry they found themselves analyzing. The firm's guiding principle was that extremely smart people thinking analytically could solve clients' most pressing problems with little or no experience in the respective industries.[22]

SPA's emphasis on smart people as its key differentiator was manifested in a rigorous recruiting process and up-or-out policy for professional development. SPA focused on hiring undergraduates and, unlike most competitors, allowed outstanding professionals with only college degrees to progress beyond the analyst level without returning to business school. (See Exhibit 4.26 for details on seniority levels.) To be promoted, a professional had to be in the top quintile of his or her current level within the firm. "If you were in the second quintile," explained Lewis, "we were happy to have you; you just wouldn't be promoted." Many who could not break out of the second quintile, though, chose eventually to leave on their own. Those who remained in the lower quintiles could eventually be asked to leave.

Most professionals, given the rhetoric surrounding SPA's recruiting process, considered themselves to be analytical superstars soon after they joined the firm. But promotion patterns varied markedly. That some professionals became partners in as little as 18 months and others in as many as 11 years reflected the firm's focus on the "speedometer, rather than the odometer."[23] Compensation at all levels was competitive with the rest of the industry. However, it grew more rapidly for employees with demonstrated analytical ability than at most other firms, including TBS.

SPA was filled with relatively young, self-described analytical superstars when it was acquired and merged with TBS in 1990. Brought together with a mix of older MBAs and former industry managers whose consulting approach emphasized industry experience, these professionals were loath to embrace their new parent, Marsh & McLennan. Their approach to dealing with Marsh & McLennan and with TBS, recounted one former partner, was best summarized in a single question: "How do we keep them out of our hair?"[24] Ironically, SPA had written a report on mergers and acquisitions that maintained that two-thirds of such transactions "either fail or do not add value."[25]

Exhibit 4.26 Seniority Levels at Mercer Management Consulting and Predecessor Firms

Level	Description
Analyst	– Hired with undergraduate or graduate non-MBA degree – Carry out essential research and data collection – Conduct complex quantitative, strategic, and financial business analyses – Work directly with client teams to solve client business problems
Consultant	– Promoted from analyst or hired with graduate non-MBA degree and experience – Generate ideas and structure problems and work plans – Structure and present results and client implications of advanced financial/business analyses – Assume leadership role in interactions with clients and development of less experienced Mercer staff
Associate	– Promoted from analyst or hired with an MBA – Prepare, package, and present recommendations and results of complex research and analysis – Assume case leadership and client responsibilities – Work with clients on implementation; manage and develop other case teams
Senior Associate	– Promoted from associate or hired with an MBA and significant experience – Serve as case manager, managing people, work plans, and quality of deliverables – Provide thought leadership on cases and contribute to the firm's intellectual capital – Build effective relationships with clients and help sell new work to grow the firm
Principal	– Promoted from senior associate or hired with industry experience and expertise – Manage large projects with ultimate responsibility for quality of delivery to clients; serve as day-to-day client advisors, strengthening client relationships, and actively sell work – Manage, coach, and develop non-partner consultants at Mercer
Vice President	– Promoted from principal or hired with significant senior industry experience – Serve as strategic advisor to senior clients; sell work and develop Mercer's intellectual capital – Set direction and strategy for Mercer; drive its continued growth and success

Source: "Careers," Mercer Management Consulting Web page, http://www.mercermc.com/, accessed November 6, 2001.

TEMPLE, BARKER & SLOANE[26]

Lexington, Massachusetts-based Temple, Barker & Sloane (TBS) had been founded in 1970 by Harvard Business School graduates Peter Temple, Jim Barker, and Carl Sloane and Harvard Business School Professor Paul Cherington. The partners built their firm based on two guiding principles. The first was that, contrary to the prevailing thinking at consulting firms at the time, the best way to serve clients was to develop deep industry-specific expertise.[27] The second principle was that clients were interested in tangible results rather than studies or reports that only described strategies. From these two principles flowed all of the decisions that managing partner Sloane and his team made in building their firm.

First, the partners built practice areas that they called "centers of excellence" and set out to populate them with world-class experts. The practice areas included transportation, energy, telecommunications, and financial services.[28] Each center of excellence constituted a separate business with its own profit and loss (P&L) responsibility and hiring procedures. To manage the P&L and develop the hiring procedures, each practice area also had its own managing partner.

This overall business strategy, built around world-class experts in specific domains organized into practice areas, led the firm to its distinctive recruiting strategy. The founders believed that it would take eight to twelve years on average for a newly hired MBA to become a world-class expert. This meant that, unlike competing firms that hired graduates with the explicit expectation that most would treat their consulting experience as a "stepping stone" lasting no longer than two to five years, TBS made clear that it was interested in hiring professionals who were interested in building a career with the firm.

In exchange for the time commitment that the firm asked its professionals to make, it made certain commitments to them. First, the firm offered multiple general management opportunities. At most firms, P&L responsibility resided exclusively with the managing partner or a small managing group at the top of the firm. At TBS, each center of excellence had its own general manager. This meant that a professional who might otherwise leave the firm to seek a general management position outside the consulting industry no longer needed to do so.

Next, to reduce the likelihood of burnout and early departure among its career consultants, the firm sought to make life "tolerable" for them.[29] Through a heavy orientation toward research, the firm minimized travel requirements. TBS professionals were trained to gather tremendous amounts of data on brief visits to client sites, data that they could then analyze back at the office. During one representative quarter in the late 1970s, the average TBS professional spent 1.8 nights per week away from home; professionals at many competing firms spent three or four nights per week away. In addition, the firm chose to locate its offices in a suburban location surrounded by residential neighborhoods that were especially attractive to young families. This was key to attracting MBAs who, in addition to developing content expertise, were interested in balancing work and family.

TBS was able to retain its professionals at higher-than-average rates. For most of the 17 years of its independent existence, its annual turn-over among consultants was 6% to 8%, less than half the industry average. This was one factor contributing to the firm's steady annual revenue growth, which hovered around 30% for most of the 1970s and 1980s.

TBS's revenue came in smaller increments than SPA's, however. Individuals hired into one practice group rarely crossed into others. Even when one practice area had professionals to spare and another was in need of help, the partners in charge of the first were loath to give people up. Because partners selling projects could commit only the resources they directly controlled, the majority of projects TBS sold were small relative to those sold by SPA. Whereas SPA pursued relatively few clients, each accounting for several million dollars per year, TBS had longer and deeper relationships with more clients. TBS's smaller projects translated into comparatively short sales cycles and high utilization rates, the opposite of SPA's experience.[30]

Every two years or so, a suitor would approach Sloane and his partners to ask about acquiring the firm. They would react by asking three questions of the interested party: (1) Did they have a well thought-out strategy for the future? (2) Did the chemistry feel right? (3) Was the offer attractive? According to Sloane, they rarely got past the first two questions.

Sloane and his partners met every five years to discuss possible modifications to the firm's strategy. In the first two of these meetings—in 1975 and 1980—they decided that no change was necessary. In 1985, they came to a different conclusion. They decided that with their main office in Lexington and their handful of small satellite offices, they simply did not have the distribution network necessary to join the ranks of the major industry players.[31] They calculated that, by 2000, they would need offices in 20 cities—eight of them international—to build such a network. To establish and maintain for the first year, each domestic office would cost $500,000; each international office would cost twice as much.

With $14 million in cash and access to at least that much in debt, TBS had more than enough resources to implement this new plan. (However, Sloane and others harbored concerns over whether or not the firm's partners, by then numbering 70, were willing to put all of that capital at risk with an expansion strategy.) Then Marsh & McLennan became the latest in the series of suitors to approach Sloane asking about a potential acquisition. Marsh & McLennan had a strategy that was consistent with the TBS vision. After acquiring William M. Mercer, as discussed previously, it had gone on to purchase the corporate identity consulting firm Lippincott & Marguiles and the economic consulting firm National Economic Research Associates (NERA).[32] Based on the recommendation of its bankers, Marsh & McLennan was now in the market for a corporate consulting firm. And, because TBS was organized by industry just as Marsh & McLennan was in its core insurance business, it rose to the top of Marsh & McLennan's short list of acquisition candidates.

In addition to this clear strategic fit, there was good chemistry between the senior management at TBS and Marsh & McLennan. And the purchase price was right. All three of TBS's questions had been answered to its satisfaction. The deal was closed in October of 1987.

WARE ADAMS, GEORGE OVERHOLSER, AND THE MERGER

Ware Adams joined the Washington, D.C. office of SPA on September 11, 1989, having graduated from Dartmouth College with a bachelor's degree in engineering a few months earlier. Eleven other analysts had joined with him. (Exhibit 4.26 defines the analyst role and other seniority levels.) Possessing an analytical way of thinking about business problems, a legacy, in part, of his undergraduate training in engineering, Adams relished SPA's approach and had been known to deride the "gray-haired middle managers" at other firms whose wisdom reflected experience rather than data.[33]

Steady year-over-year profitability growth punctuated by occasional bad years of zero or negative growth was the norm for SPA from its inception. The year 1988, had been the worst for SPA, which subscribed to the idea that the best way to grow and become increasingly competitive was "to get big clients," an approach not without merit but extremely risky. In 1988, SPA lost Equitable and British Telecom, two clients that together represented 40% of its sales. Although both had assured SPA that their decisions had nothing to do with its performance—British Telecom's decision had been prompted by a change in corporate direction, Equitable's by a change in senior personnel—this information was little comfort to a firm that had just increased the size of its professional staff by 20% to support what had been solid growth in the preceding five years. To deal with its lost business, SPA laid off 15% of its professionals in September of 1988.

Adams's career had started auspiciously when he proved his analytical mettle in a cost-reduction project for a Baby Bell. Two months after he started at SPA, rumors of an acquisition began to spread, followed by heavy trading in the firm's stock. Senior partners Wilde, Silverman, and Roy Barbie and founder Lewis were said to be in active negotiation with at least one suitor. The day before Thanksgiving, 1989, they announced to 175 assembled employees and another 175 by phone that the rumors were true; an acquisition was in the works. Although unable to share details of the plan, save to certify that the acquirer was not to be Deutsche Bank as the rumor mill had suggested, they assured those present that it was in the best interests of the firm and its people.[34]

When the deal closed in February of 1990, Marsh & McLennan, which had acquired TBS in October of 1987, owned SPA as well and intended to merge the two firms. No one from either firm had been involved with an integration of this type before, so there was trepidation on both sides. To mitigate the sense of uncertainty, the two firms' partners decided to move slowly. They held joint partners' meetings and brought consultants with common interests together. They even jointly won a bid for a transportation industry project for which they had competed prior to the merger. Firm names and management structures (Sloane was named chairman and CEO, Lewis vice chairman) were also combined.

Beyond these "quick hits," however, little was done through 1991 to achieve true integration. For instance, although the official firm name had become "TBS-SPA," receptionists in the former SPA headquarters in Washington had been instructed to answer phones: "SPA-TBS, can I help you?" "Frankly," recalled one partner of that time, "there wasn't a vision as to how the merger would play out over time."[35]

A transition phase began in 1991. Sloane, who felt "burned out after 30 years in consulting and two years trying to harmonize TBS and SPA," left the firm in response to an offer to join the Harvard Business School faculty.[36] Lewis, who succeeded Sloane as CEO of TBS-SPA, left the firm a year later to join Avon, a TBS-SPA client, as a senior executive. Lewis would later become Avon's president.[37]

The two leaders' departures and an economic contraction that had begun in mid-1990 and had hit the consulting industry hard, led the remaining partners to conclude that they needed to act quickly to prevent a large-scale loss of people and capital. Consequently, they crafted a strategic plan called Vision 95 (so named because it defined a set of goals to be achieved by 1995). Senior partners on both sides remember the January 1992 Vision 95 meeting as having been marked by cooperation, camaraderie, and broad consensus. Decisions were made concerning the firm's target growth rate (annual revenue growth of at least 15%), investments in new offices (Germany and France were key priorities), and compensation system (which was to be linked to both individual and firm performance). Leadership roles were assigned to key individuals. The combined entity appeared to be living up to the promise of its new name, chosen six months before in June of 1991. Given the firm's new commitment to an acquisition-intensive strategy, the partners had abandoned the practice of combining predecessor firm names. They chose to name the firm "Mercer Management Consulting" in order to identify it more closely with its sister firm, William M. Mercer.

LEAVING IN THE NIGHT

Silverman and Wilde had been among SPA's biggest revenue generators and continued to be so for Mercer. As they oversaw many of the firm's most important client relationships, it made sense to put them in charge of key areas. Consequently, Silverman was made head of firm research and Wilde head of the worldwide telecommunications practice. Less than six months into their tenures, the two packed up their Mercer offices in the middle of the night and left. They had given their partners no forewarning.[38] "I just have no darned idea why they left," remarked Lewis, who was already at Avon at the time. "I think they're great guys, smart guys, and I can't help but think that Mercer would have been much better off had they stayed."[39]

In July, Silverman and Wilde, at a clandestine breakfast meeting at Washington, D.C.'s Four Seasons Hotel, had tried to woo Adams, who had risen quickly to the level of senior associate by that time, away from Mercer. Adams knew that their new firm, Dean & Company, had barely secured office space, but he also knew that Silverman and Wilde had excellent client track records and that they would promote him from senior associate to principal if he joined them.[40]

Overholser, already a principal at Mercer, although well aware that Silverman and Wilde had been the Washington office's two key revenue generators and notwithstanding that he had been one of Silverman's top lieutenants for more than a year, had earlier declined the same invitation.[41]

Roughly concurrently with Silverman's and Wilde's departures, Barbie, who had been heading the Washington office, left. (He had shared his departure plans with the firm before the Vision 95 kick-off meeting.) Jim Down, head of the general consulting practice and therefore the executive to whom most of Mercer's North American office heads reported, had no obvious choice to lead the Washington office.[42] For nine months, beginning in April 1993, Down himself stepped in and began spending one or two days per week in Washington. (He spent the rest of the week in Boston, as he was office head there as well.) With "everybody moping around" in response to the rash of high-level departures, Down's first priority was to settle the 175-person office down.[43] This proved to be particularly challenging because there were many whom he knew only in passing, having previously spent relatively little time in Washington. Moreover, he was a former TBS partner, and the office was composed largely of former SPA professionals.

Within a few months of assuming direct oversight of the Washington office, Down, perceiving Overholser to be talented, well respected, and creative and to care deeply about the office, had asked him to lead an initiative to integrate the office's disparate cultures. Having just turned down Wilde and Silverman's offer, Overholser, who had been on a leave of absence when the merger was planned, accepted the challenge. Dubbed "culture czar" by Down, to whom it was evident that cultural differences between the firms were the most significant impediments to successful integration, Overholser realized that the initiative he was to lead would affect the lives and careers not only of his fellow principals and the associates, consultants, and analysts below them, but also of partners who were senior to him and over whom he had no formal authority.

Other offices, being composed entirely of professionals belonging to either TBS or SPA and involved in few interoffice projects at the time, had escaped post-merger culture clash. An exception was the New York office, which was split evenly between TBS and SPA professionals. But because both firms' New York offices had been operating for less than a year at the time of the merger, the newly combined office was too focused on a successful launch to become mired in culture problems. Only the Washington office was dealing with culture-related merger challenges daily.

MAKING DECISIONS

Adams and Overholser were both faced with significant decisions. Adams, sipping his third cup of black coffee at the Four Seasons Hotel, had to decide whether to forsake Mercer Management Consulting for the newly established Dean & Company. Overholser, having already made that decision and then having been entrusted by Down with the leadership of the new integration effort, had to decide what to change in Mercer's Washington office, how to change it, and how quickly to change it. The futures of careers and of firms hung in the balance.

NOTES TO CASE

1. Larry Greiner and Robert Metzger, *Consulting to Management* (Englewood Cliffs, NJ: Prentice-Hall, 1983), p. 7.
2. Worldwide consulting revenue was $102 billion in 1999 and $114 billion (projected) in 2000 and was expected to surpass $200 billion by 2005 (Kennedy Information Group, *The Global Management Consulting Market-place: Key Data, Forecasts and Trends*). Roughly half of the $114 billion projected for 2000 was attributed to the U.S. market, up from less than $1 billion in 1960, $2 billion in 1970, and $3 billion in 1983 (Greiner and Metzger, p. 3).
3. "About ADL," Arthur D. Little Web page, http://www.adl.com/about/index.htm, accessed November 28, 2001.
4. *Harrington Emerson Papers*, 1848–1931, Pennsylvania State University Web page, http://www.libraries.psu.edu/crsweb/speccol/FindingAids/emerson4.html, accessed November 28, 2001.
5. Frederick Winslow Taylor, "The Principles of Scientific Management" (1911), http://www.socsci.mcmaster.ca/~econ/ugcm/3ll3/taylor/sciman, accessed November 28, 2001.
6. Taylor.
7. Amar V. Bhide, "Building the Professional Firm: McKinsey & Co., 1939–1968," HBS No. 393-066 (Boston: Harvard Business School Publishing, 1992).
8. Portions of the description of McKinsey & Company are based on "Five Days at McKinsey," a paper written by Michael W. Echenberg following a summer internship with the company.
9. "Marvin Bower—The Soul of McKinsey," McKinsey & Company Web page,

http://www.mckinsey.com/firm/values/marvinbower/index.asp, accessed November 5, 2001.

10. As quoted in Katharina Pick and Jay W. Lorsch, "McKinsey & Co.," HBS Case No. 402-014 (Boston: Harvard Business School Publishing, 2001), p. 6.

11. Risk management is the evaluation and selection of appropriate insurance policies for companies.

12. Three million in 1905 dollars was equivalent to roughly $60 million in 2001.

13. Reinsurance is "a contract under which an originating insurer (called the 'ceding' insurer) procures insurance for itself in another insurer (called the 'assuming' insurer or the 'reinsurer') with respect to part or all of an insurance risk of the originating insurer." (From http://www.lrc.state.ky.us.)

14. Walker Lewis, telephone interview with author, December 10, 2001.

15. Ibid.

16. Lewis interview.

17. Ibid.

18. Ibid.

19. Adrian F. T. Payne, "New Trends in the Strategy Consulting Industry," *Journal of Business Strategy*, Volume 7, Issue 1 (Summer 1986): 43–55.

20. Lewis interview.

21. Ibid.

22. The proprietary information-based strategy (IBS) developed by SPA alumni Richard Fairbank and Nigel Morris was evidence of the ability of the firm's professionals to create new, analytically rigorous intellectual capital and to be entrepreneurial. Fairbank and Morris left the firm in 1987 to join Signet Bank and subsequently founded Capital One. Their IBS was very much in the analytical tradition of SPA and won them dozens of awards and millions of customers worldwide. By 2001, they had more than 40 million customers, in excess of $39 billion in managed loans, and 17,000-plus employees. Many SPA professionals who left after the merger joined Capital One.

23. George Overholser, telephone interview with author, September 28, 2001.

24. Ibid.

25. See "William Hickey on all the things that are necessary to make a merger work," *Business News New Jersey*, Volume 11, Issue 12 (March 23, 1998): 15.

26. Carl Sloane, interview with author, Boston, March 25, 2002.

27. While TBS had practice groups that focused on specific functions (like strategy) or specific issues (like environmental regulation), most of its practice groups were organized by industry.

28. The firm's original expertise had derived from experience dealing with the collapse of the Pennsylvania Railroad, and transportation had remained its most lucrative practice.

29. Carl Sloane, written correspondence with author, Boston, April 29, 2002.

30. Phil Giudice, telephone interview with author, November 9, 2001.
31. In the words of one former TBS principal, the firm's European presence had consisted of "one or two consultants wasting time in London for a few years." (Phil Giudice, telephone interview with author, November 9, 2001.)
32. Lippincott & Marguiles had created the corporate logos of American Express, Chrysler, and Continental Airlines, among others.
33. Ware Adams, telephone interview with author, September 27, 2001.
34. Deutsche Bank was genuinely interested in acquiring the firm, but federal law prohibited a foreign-owned bank from owning U.S.-based businesses.
35. Jim Down, telephone interview with author, November 9, 2001.
36. Carl Sloane, written correspondence with author, Boston, April 29, 2002.
37. Carl Sloane became the Ernest L. Arbuckle Professor of Business Administration at Harvard Business School and served as a director of Ionics, Rayonier, Pittston, and Sapient; an advisory board member of the Center for Science and International Affairs at the John F. Kennedy School of Government; and chairman of the Harvard-Radcliffe Hillel Foundation. Walker Lewis, in addition to serving as president of Avon, served as a member of the management committee at Kidder, Peabody; a director of American Management Systems, Owens Corning, and Mrs. Fields, Inc.; and a member of the Council on Foreign Relations in New York. Both were honors graduates of Harvard College and served on Harvard's Committee on University Resources.
38. Later, Mercer initiated a successful lawsuit against Wilde and Silverman because of the manner in which they left the firm.
39. Walker Lewis, telephone interview with author, December 10, 2001.
40. Ware Adams, telephone interview with author, September 27, 2001.
41. George Overholser, telephone interview with author, September 28, 2001.
42. Jim Down, telephone interview with author, November 9, 2001. Down was a TBS veteran (having joined the firm in 1980) and was former head of its transportation practice.
43. Ibid.

Case 4.5b

MERCER MANAGEMENT CONSULTING (B)

(Thomas J. DeLong and Michael W. Echenberg)

On the first Tuesday in October of 1989, Ware Adams decided to leave Mercer Management Consulting and join the Deans. His first stop was the office of Jeff Totten, the human resources manager for the firm's Washington, D.C. office. Adams explained his decision to Totten and gave his two weeks' notice. Totten tried unsuccessfully to convince Adams to stay; he then declined the two weeks Adams had offered. Unfazed, Adams decided to take Wednesday and Thursday off and then return on Friday to clean out his desk. Monday was to be his first day at Dean & Company.

When he returned on Friday, Adams found that a parade had been planned in his honor. It was not, however, a parade to wish him well and send him off to his new challenges on a positive note. Rather, it was a parade of senior professionals marching into his office to try to entice him to stay. Adams was assured a quick promotion to principal if he chose to stay. But the Deans had already promised Ware an immediate promotion to principal—and they had also promised him something that he was sure Mercer could not match: the opportunity to help build a new firm from the ground up. Ironically, as the list of enticements offered by Mercer's leaders grew longer, Adams grew less interested.

Adams's final discussion was with office head Bill Bain, on whose case team he had been working before deciding to leave. Bain had developed an affinity for Adams based on the young consultant's demonstrated abilities and their shared New Orleans roots. He hoped he could convince him to stay. Bain reminded Adams of how successful he believed he could be at Mercer. He also reminded Adams that Mercer had launched a lawsuit that might threaten the financial viability of the young Dean & Company. Unbeknownst to Adams, Bain had gone through an experience similar to his. In 1977, his former BCG colleague Mitt Romney had tried to convince Bain to follow him to Bain & Company. Bain had refused and had gone on to lead BCG's worldwide recruiting efforts to new levels of success. Adams stood firm in his decision to leave.

At Dean & Company, Adams did remarkably well. He managed key client relationships and was instrumental in growing the firm from a handful of professionals to over 75. By 1997, before his 30th birthday, he had been elected partner. By 1999, he was on the firm's management committee, a committee to which human resources manager Jeff Totten reported after he joined Dean & Company himself in 1998.

The firm was on a roll as well. Dean & Company grew steadily in terms of revenue, number of clients, and number of professionals. By 1995, the firm had grown to 40 professionals while maintaining yearly revenue per professional of $400,000, which was near the top of the industry. It also maintained average employee tenure close to double the industry average. It staffed its new hires on projects sold to a range of clients, including three of the 20 largest companies in the United States. In 2000, Dean Silverman left the firm to spend more time with his family and to become president of WashingtonCapitals.com, the online division of the Washington Capitals National Hockey League franchise.

At Mercer, George Overholser succeeded as culture czar. "George provided spirit for everyone," remembered Jim Down, "even the people senior to him."[1] He used a combination of good humor and inclusive brainstorming to lead everyone toward full integration. At the first meeting he called as culture czar, he insisted that all attendees wear clown wigs. Later, he set aside a room in the office dedicated to integration-related problem solving. All members of the firm were required to spend time in the room either putting forth suggestions or commenting on the suggestions of others. The ideas generated in the room were taken to a series of off-site meetings and transformed into a detailed plan that won broad support from all.

Afterwards, Mercer's consulting businesses continued to blossom. The creation of the Mercer Consulting Group in 1992 brought together six major and a host of smaller consulting firms.[2] By 1995, the Mercer Consulting Group was generating annual revenues of $1 billion. By 2000, with 13,500 employees (9,000 professionals) in 30 countries, its annual revenues exceeded $2 billion. Marsh & McLennan, which comprised the insurance businesses of Marsh, investment businesses of Putnam, and consulting businesses of Mercer, had 57,000 employees and $10.2 billion in revenues in 2000.[3]

Exhibit 4.27 Timeline

1993	Mercer Management Consulting merges with Unternehmensberatung Munchen GmbH (UBM) to form its Munich and Zurich offices.
1995	Mercer Management Consulting merges with the French firm MID S.A.
1997	Mercer Management Consulting merges with the U.S. firm Corporate Decisions, Inc. (CDI).
1998	Mercer Management Consulting merges with the German firm Dr. Seebauer & Partner.
2000	Mercer Management Consulting merges with the Mexican firm Análisis y Desarrollo de Proyectos (ADP) to form its Mexico City office and with St. Gallen Consulting Group (SCG) to form its Frankfurt and Geneva offices.

Source: "Evolution," Mercer Management Consulting Web page, http://www.mercermc.com/, accessed November 6, 2001.

The Mercer Consulting Group's consulting businesses were organized into five divisions. In 1990, SPA and TBS had been combined to form the management consulting division. Other mergers followed. (See Exhibit 4.27.) By 2001, Mercer Management Consulting had 1,400 employees (including 280 partners and 1,000 professionals) in 23 offices in 12 countries on four continents.

NOTES TO CASE

1. Jim Down, telephone interview with author, November 9, 2001.
2. The major firms were Meidinger Inc., MPA Limited, Duncan C. Fraser & Company, A. S. Hansen, Temple, Barker & Sloane, and Strategic Planning Associates. "Evolution," Mercer Management Consulting Web page, http://www.mercermc.com/, accessed November 6, 2001.
3. "Welcome," Marsh & McLennan Web page, http://www.marshmac.com, accessed November 5, 2001.

Part 5

Managing the Consulting Firm

Introduction

Case 5.1

Diamond in the Rough (A, B)
(Catherine Conneely and Thomas DeLong)

Case 5.2

Tim Hertach at GL Consulting (A, B, C, D)
(Scot Landry, Ashish Nanda, and Thomas DeLong)

Case 5.3

Integral Consulting
(P.J. Guinan, Valerie Mulhern, and David Wylie)

INTRODUCTION

It is often said that, "professional service firms are managed in one of two ways—badly or not at all"[1]. Most consultants choose to go into consulting because of the attractiveness of working with clients and building an experience base across a variety of industries. They initially shun pursuing management positions in their firms, though later they often take senior jobs with clients. They prefer a high degree of autonomy and express a strong distaste for close supervision. As a consequence, the priority given to management expertise within consulting firms has typically been limited or downplayed.

However, the competitive landscape for consulting has changed dramatically over recent years, and now there is clearly a need for advanced professionalism in the management of consulting firms.

While many firms have recently upgraded their management efforts and resources, still others have fallen victim to many of the same management ills that they have cautioned their clients to avoid. The importance of managing consulting firms effectively is the subject of Part 5 in Greiner and Poulfelt's book[2], which covers numerous issues, from strategic planning to operational efficiency to growth management and leadership problems.

This part includes three cases concerning the management of consulting firms. The *Diamond in the Rough (A)* case represents a strategy consultancy firm that focuses on digital technology assessment issues. Diamond's management suddenly finds that the firm's rapid growth has turned sour and they must make some difficult decisions about either reneging on new hire offers or asking their partners to take a pay cut. The *Tim Hertach at GL Consulting (A), (B), (C)* and *(D)* cases describe how a young partner, Tim Hertach, protests about unethical behavior in the firm's billing practices, and then how the firm's management responds to him. It is a useful case series for students to learn about professionalism in consulting as they make decisions in class in response to the unfolding cases. The *Integral Consulting* case addresses issues of knowledge management within the firm. It shows how the firm develops an innovative knowledge management system but then encounters problems with its staff in their recording and sharing information generated by the system.

What we learn from these cases is that good management of the consulting firm does indeed matter, from exercising leadership to improve motivation of consultants, to installing systems that leverage knowledge across the staff, to developing a coherent business strategy, to improving the quality of work produced for clients. The future will undoubtedly require even more effective management in growing the firm, becoming involved in alliances, expanding globally and diversifying into non-consulting services."

NOTES

1. Maister, D. (1987). *Firm Management*. Public Relations Journal. August.
2. Greiner, L. & Poulfelt, F. 2009. *Management Consulting Today and Tomorrow*, Taylor & Francis.

Case 5.1a

DIAMOND IN THE ROUGH (A)

(Catherine Conneely and Thomas Delong)

One evening in July 1996, Mel Bergstein and Chris Moffitt sat talking, smoking, and worrying in a glass-walled office 30 stories above Lake Michigan. Bergstein was CEO of Diamond Technology Partners, a two-year-old strategy and technology consultancy, Moffitt his co-founder. Old colleagues and friends, they had doubled Diamond in each of its first two years from nothing to $12.8 million in 1994 to $26.3 in 1995. Earlier in 1996 they had planned to double again. The information technology consulting and systems integration market was huge and rapidly growing. Industry analysts estimated it at $100 billion and growing at 25% to 35% per year. The largest firms in this industry, such as Andersen Consulting, IBM, and so on, were about $1 billion to $2 billion in size and growing at the rate of the market or faster. Bergstein and Moffitt, having been part of this industry for decades, believed there was a need for an independent and objective voice that could assess the needs of a digital strategy without being biased toward trying to sell a big outsourcing or systems integration job. They estimated that this independent advice market was approximately 10% of the total market, or $10 billion. Furthermore, this market was growing faster and had higher margins than the total market, thus providing an enormous opportunity for Diamond.

In April, at the beginning of Diamond's third fiscal year, two major clients, representing 50% of the prior quarter's revenues, had pulled out of deals. All of the partners had hunted up projects to cover these losses, but their heroic efforts produced only damage control. Having lost $0.7 million in the past quarter, Diamond was now operating below break-even. To add to the seriousness of the situation, a long-planned IPO was imminent; Diamond had recently offered jobs with signing bonuses of $20,000 to $30,000 each to 50 MBAs, 28 of whom had accepted; and staff and employees were expecting their standard year-end bonuses (which were budgeted between $1.5 million and $2 million). Now, all this was on hold, and tomorrow Bergstein would have to host the monthly All Hands Meeting—a gathering of the whole firm, known as an occasion for open communication and collegiality. Most of these meetings had been high-spirited events. Bergstein and Moffitt had dressed up as The Blues Brothers to kick off the first one in early 1994. Now celebration was far from their minds. The question was how to break the bad news to their talented, hard-working staff. Bergstein exhaled a big puff of smoke and stubbed out his cigarette.

MEL BERGSTEIN

Bergstein's business experience extended back to 1968, when he started in the consulting division of Arthur Andersen & Co. (now Andersen Consulting). After rising through the ranks to partner (1977–1989), managing director of worldwide technology, and member of the board (1985–1989), he also chaired the firm's Consulting Oversight Committee. Then he left Andersen to become senior vice president of Computer Sciences Corporation and made another move, in 1991, to become president, co-CEO, and a member of the board of directors of Technology Solutions Company (TSC), a publicly traded Chicago-based systems integrator. At TSC, his function was to balance the founder-CEO's creative influence. When TSC went through a period of internal strife in 1993, the board forced the founder-CEO to leave. As part of a compromise between the board and the founder's family, Bergstein also lost his job.

Bergstein commented: "One of the lessons I learned from being fired was that I never again wanted to be in a position where outsiders controlled the firm."

CHRIS MOFFITT

Chris Moffitt met Mel Bergstein at TSC, which Moffitt had helped found in 1988. When Bergstein left, Moffitt resigned in protest against the board's treatment of the CEO. Moffitt had a strong background in information systems. In 1974, he began as a systems engineer and account manager at Electronic Data Systems. Then he became director of information systems for Neiman Marcus (1981–1986), and moved to the Management Consulting Group of Arthur Young (now Ernst & Young). There he advanced to principal and, later, partner (1986–1988), before leaving to help establish TSC. He served as TSC's senior vice president until his departure in protest in 1993.

Moffitt, too, learned from the experience at TSC:

Starting TSC had shown me that I really enjoyed the thrill of establishing and running my own business. I said to Mel, "We have to write a plan together or I'm going to go start a company on my own." I was convinced [our] new company would be four times the size of anything I could do personally if I could persuade Mel to take a stake in the foundation. With over 20 years' experience in the IT/consulting business, Mel had a name in the industry. I also thought that Mel had a clearer notion of where the market was going.

THE BUSINESS PLAN

Bergstein recollected:

After I left TSC, Chris would not stop badgering me to start a company. I was still licking my wounds and trying to decide what I wanted to do—talking to friends in the industry and listening to potential job offers at big companies and so on. Eventually I concluded that Chris was right. We could have started a company with our own money. We had enough to do it. But we concluded that we needed outside funding for several reasons. First, we did not think we could do really important work for our clients if we could not show financial stability. Second, we did not think we could attract real talent if there was very significant financial risk. Third, we did not want to do work simply to pay the payroll, as we had a very specific scope of practice and a very specific client base in mind. Lastly, we decided that sleeping at night was a good thing.

They found potential investors reluctant to provide capital for a proposed business with no concrete outline or detailed financial forecasts. Moffitt told Bergstein, "We have to have a business plan." Bergstein decided to work on one while searching for a new position. In October 1993, they both started work on what Bergstein called the "blue book."

Bergstein reported:

We put together a business plan in an empty office borrowed from our attorneys. A lot of cigarettes and a lot of late nights went into it. It seems to me that it came together at the beginning of November 1993. A lot of what we did was in reaction to our experiences at different companies. For example, we wanted to prevent any possibility of "founderitis." My son, an analyst at Morgan Stanley, helped us put together the financial models, and Chris's father, a retired editor, flew to Chicago to polish the final document. We ended up with a business plan that many folks considered one of the best they had seen. (See Exhibit 5.1.)

Bergstein and Moffitt agreed to call the venture Diamond Technology Partners because of the "diamond" team and partnership structures

---

Exhibit 5.1 Diamond Technology Partners, Financial Projections for Fiscal Years 1994–1998 ($ millions)

	1994	1995	1996	1997	1998
Net revenue	$10.7	$28.7	$43.3	$53.2	$63.8
Gross margin	0.8	10.9	18.2	22.3	26.5
Gross margin	5.6%	40.0%	42.0%	42.0%	41.5%
PBT	(3.3)	4.0	10.1	12.5	15.1
PBT margin	(30.8%)	13.9%	23.3%	23.5%	23.7%
Net income	$(3.3)	$2.4	$6.0	$7.5	$9.1
Net income margin	(30.8%)	8.4%	13.9%	14.1%	14.3%

Source: Diamond Technology Partners Business Plan, November 1993.

they planned to use.[1] They both wanted a particular kind of corporate culture, driven by a set of guiding principles:

- to deliver for clients the highest quality economic results achievable through the creative application of technology;
- to place clients' interests ahead of their own;
- to hold clients' confidences sacred;
- to communicate the truth to clients, even if it challenged their own positions;
- to agree to do only work that would achieve superior economic benefits for clients.

Instead of keeping ownership for themselves, they decided to require partners to put in personal funds—as Bergstein and Moffitt would—at the same price as external investors. They agreed that the firm would deploy small, multidisciplinary teams on which business strategists and technologists worked in concert. And they allowed for a steady pace of growth. (In initial discussions with investors, the founders predicted an eventual growth rate between 25% and 35% per annum. Growth rates were built from general expectations about the growth of the client/ server and reengineering markets coupled with Bergstein's and Moffitt's judgments about the firm's capacity to absorb and assimilate new staff.)

Early in the design process they decided to plan for Diamond to go public. Bergstein explained, "We felt the wealth creation opportunity in public firms was much greater than in private firms. By going public we could attract and reward higher-quality people." By sharing equity in the new company, Bergstein ensured talented professional staff whose interests, as shareholders, would be aligned with the market.

OTHER FOUNDING PARTNERS JOIN

Mike Mikolajczyk (*Mik-o-lay-chick*) met Bergstein and Moffitt at TSC. There, Mikolajczyk was senior vice president of finance and adminis-tration and CFO from 1993–1994. A Harvard MBA, he had previously worked with MCI Telecommunications Corporation as vice president of various departments. He joined Bergstein and Moffitt because of his interest in the kind of company they were building and enthusiasm about the financial projections in their business plan.

Another founding partner commented, "To me, the critical thing we did early on was to assemble a nucleus of people who shared the core

Exhibit 5.2 "The Diamond Approach" Service Delivery Model

Diamond's services are delivered in teams of one partner, four principals, and two associates.

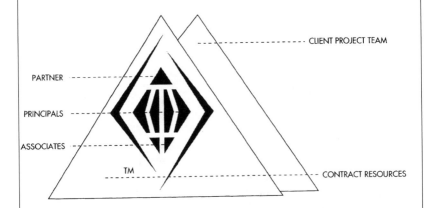

. . . Conventional systems implementation teams resemble a pyramid with an experienced leader plus a few capable specialists at the top, supervising a large number of relatively less experienced staff. The Diamond service model, in contrast, delivers a greater concentration of experience and greater depth of specialized skills. If a project requires general purpose programmer or analyst skills—typically the lower levels of implementation—Diamond will complement the team with lower cost contract resources to maintain the overall cost effectiveness of the solution. . . .

—From: *Managing Complexity Strategy, Process, Technology, and Organization. Contemporary Solutions for Contemporary Problems*

Diamond delivers its services in small, experienced and focused teams. We build trust in our clients by demonstrating—and more importantly, by sharing—our industry, program management and technical experience. With Diamond, [staff] work closely with clients to help them set the right goals, initiate the right programs and make the appropriate investments to translate their strategy into concrete business solutions.

Active involvement by our clients helps them build the foundation for lasting organizational change. For our people, this collaborative method means we are continuously teaching our clients what we know. This, in turn, offers—in fact, demands—continual professional growth and development as we force ourselves to stay ahead of the curve.

—From: *Diamond: Breaking the Traditional Barriers, Experience Consulting with a Personal Focus*

Source: Company documents

principles and values of the business plan." (See Exhibit 5.3 for more founders' and partners' information.)

POSITIONING THE COMPANY

In discussions with other founding partners, Bergstein saw a real opportunity to fill a gap in the consulting industry by uniting information technology (IT) with business strategy. (See Exhibit 5.4.)

He and Moffitt estimated the domestic (U.S.) market in which Diamond would compete at $37 billion in 1993. Some forecasts for the total U.S. consulting and systems integration market suggested that it could reach $60 billion by 2000.[2] Diamond had the potential to become a player in a market with annual growth of nearly 15%.[3]

Exhibit 5.3 Diamond's Founding Professionals (ages in February 1994)

Founding Partners:
- Mel Bergstein (51), formerly TSC, Andersen Consulting.
- Chris Moffitt (39), formerly TSC.
- Mike Mikolajczyk (43), formerly TSC, MCI.
- Jim McGee (40), formerly Andersen Consulting. Knowledge Architect.
- Kirk Siefkas (37), formerly TSC. Strength in program/project management, IT strategy.
- Mike Palmer (41), formerly TSC, James Martin Associates, Andersen Consulting. Strength in program management, data warehouse.
- Woody Forsythe (46), formerly TSC, CIO of Fingerhut. Strength in program management, IT management.
- Adam Gutstein (31), formerly TSC, Andersen Consulting. Strength in program management.
- Karl Bupp (31), formerly TSC, MCI. Head of internal planning.
- Bruce Quade (36), formerly Booz Allen, Andersen Consulting. Strength in reengineering, operations improvement.

Founders who were later promoted to partner:
- Alan Matsumura (36), formerly TSC, industry. Knowledge leader in data warehouse, data management.
- Mark Sieferston (34), formerly TSC, EDS. Knowledge leader in technology architecture, Head of Technology group.
- Brent Lohrmann (38), formerly TSC, industry. Strength in program management, IT operations, management.

Source: Company documents

Exhibit 5.4 Diamond's Market Positioning in the Consulting Industry: Digital Strategy

a) The Consulting Industry

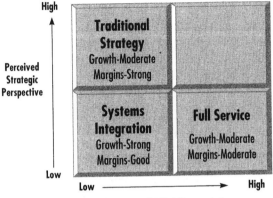

Emphasis on multi-disciplinary solutions

b) Digital Strategy Market Attributes

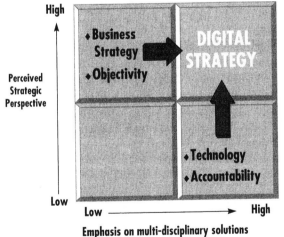

Emphasis on multi-disciplinary solutions

(Continued)

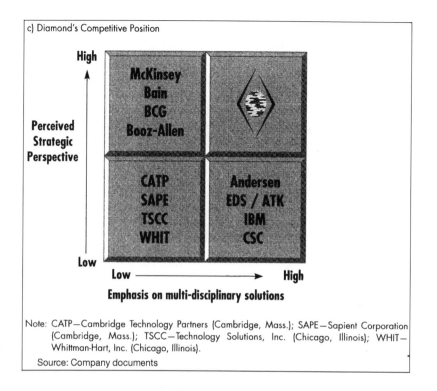

c) Diamond's Competitive Position

Note: CATP—Cambridge Technology Partners (Cambridge, Mass.); SAPE—Sapient Corporation (Cambridge, Mass.); TSCC—Technology Solutions, Inc. (Chicago, Illinois); WHIT—Whitman-Hart, Inc. (Chicago, Illinois).

Source: Company documents

GETTING START-UP FUNDING

With business plan in hand, Bergstein and Moffitt began to meet with potential investors. A headhunter friend told Bergstein about a Pennsylvania-based firm that invested in high-tech start-ups and brought firms public through a rights-offering process.[4] The firm was called Safeguard Scientifics, Inc.

Bergstein remembered:

At first I was reluctant to meet the Safeguard team because one of their investments was a Massachusetts-based systems integrator, which had just completed an IPO. I thought they were going to see a conflict there and I didn't really want to waste their time or mine. When I talked to Pete Musser, the CEO of Safeguard, in early December 1993, he assured me that an industry that would eventually be worth one hundred billion dollars would have room for Diamond and another firm.

Bergstein went on:

Chris and I met with the Safeguard team the following week and were invited back to the table on January 6, 1994. They offered us a term sheet over dinner that night. They had brought along Safeguard sweatshirts to give us if we signed the deal. We were very disappointed in the deal for three reasons. We thought the standstill period could be shorter for Diamond. We did not like outside investors having too much equity—the maximum we wanted to give them was 50%. And . . . I can't remember the third reason now.

Bergstein and Moffitt rejected Safeguard's terms but took the sweatshirts anyway. They expected to fly out of Philadelphia the next day, but an ice storm hit the city overnight. Over breakfast the next morning they decided to call the Safeguard team again. They contacted the president, Don Caldwell, and arranged to meet him at the Safeguard offices.

Bergstein recounted what happened next:

Over dinner the previous night, the Safeguard team told a story about a watchman in one of their facilities hitting a guy in the head with an ax—and the guy showing up for work two days later. We wore the Safeguard sweatshirts the CEO had given us, and, on the way to the Safeguard offices, we bought a big ax. The offices were dark because of the ice storm. Nobody was there but the president. We showed up wearing the shirts, carrying the ax, and saying, "We've come to make the deal." Then we sat down and made the deal. It wouldn't have happened if there hadn't been an ice storm.

THE START-UP (FEBRUARY–MAY, 1994)

Bergstein and Moffitt each put $250,000 into the company and started work with 11 employees, including 5 partners, in February 1994. Their first client was a former TSC client. (Bergstein observed that clients and employees initially came to Diamond because of prior business connections.) Mike Mikolajczyk, who decided to join Diamond after working as a consultant in his tranche early in March. Safeguard's $3 million investment in Diamond was completed on March 22, 1994. The other founding partners, 13 in all, put in their investment in May 1994. By June, there were 37 people on the payroll.[5]

Bergstein and Moffitt established a system of governance meant to see the company through the IPO and beyond.

Bergstein said:

We sat down and wrote a governance agreement, which we now call the Partners' Operating Agreement. We had some basic rules about how we were going to run the place. One was that we, the partners, were going to manage internally as a group of partners. At the same time, as majority shareholders we wanted a clear boundary between internal operations and our responsibilities as a public entity. At TSC, we had seen the troubles that happened when that boundary wasn't clear. Our solution was the CEO proxy. All partners grant a proxy to the incumbent CEO for their shares. That gives us a single voice in the market as majority shareholders. Our internal governance processes then ensure that the CEO has the support of the partners as a group.

Second, we shared the equity broadly. When the partners started coming up with money, I did not have any more cash, so Chris said to me, "Take options. You're the franchise here. We'll give you a ton of options." But we had employees coming in who had an opportunity to buy into the firm, and I was concerned about taking options. We agreed that no one in the firm would take options—everyone would buy in at the same price. If people want to be here, they must buy shares. But only a limited amount of stock could be held by any one person. We gave Safeguard 40% and of the remaining 60%, I took 6%, Chris took 5%, and Mike took 4%. The employees held 45% of the company.

Third, the firm was organized around four committees: management, nomination, compensation, and CEO succession. The management committee is appointed at the discretion of the CEO and consists of four members. The nomination committee and compensation committee are elected by the partners and partners on these committees are limited to three-year terms. The nominating committee identifies and performs due diligence for internal or external candidates to become partners at Diamond. The compensation committee prepares the compensation plan for the organization as a whole including partner compensation. Seventy percent of the partnership must approve the plan for it to pass. If the partners vote down the plan, then the CEO succession process is triggered. In that event a new CEO would be elected and the CEO proxy transfers to the CEO-elect. The CEO thus undergoes an annual vote of confidence in his or her leadership.

As the firm operated, Bergstein and the other partners tried to create a unique culture. This goal included everything, from communication and training policies to the office layout. They offered employees attractive benefits, such as equity and widespread ownership of the company; downtime between assignments; and light work loads on weekends.

DIAMOND'S SERVICE MODEL

Bergstein and Moffitt saw other consulting firms using project teams that resembled a pyramid, with an experienced leader supervising numerous relatively inexperienced consulting associates. At Diamond, partners managed projects as well as client relationships.

Principals were responsible for helping partners complete engagements successfully. Senior principals worked on client engagements, extended client relationships to get extra work, and mentored new staff members. Associates and Analysts supported teams during the client engagement. Promotion to senior principal, and then partner, went relatively fast at Diamond.

According to Bergstein:

> The strength of Diamond's service model is that clients see the partners as the most senior team members and a very important part of each team. Having partners involved day-to-day, on the ground, three to five days a week adds to the quality of our results for clients. It also gives younger consultants interactive time with very senior people and opportunities to learn from them. This is important to our current capabilities and long term health.

Diamond kept consulting teams small for practical reasons. Bergstein explained:

> Part of the value of a collaboration lies in not disrupting the client. Small teams can collaborate smoothly with clients and enhance the client's knowledge base, particularly about issues of long-term economic value to the client.

Diamond's projects included an informal transfer of knowledge throughout the whole process of finding and implementing strategies. The goal was to make clients self-reliant.

Diamond's teams were interdisciplinary because Bergstein and Moffitt felt that no individual could have all the skills necessary for consulting—there is no such thing as the "renaissance consultant." There was no bias at Diamond in favor of either the business strategy or technology side of consulting. Salary rates were the same for all partners and staff at particular levels, and all projects had the same billing

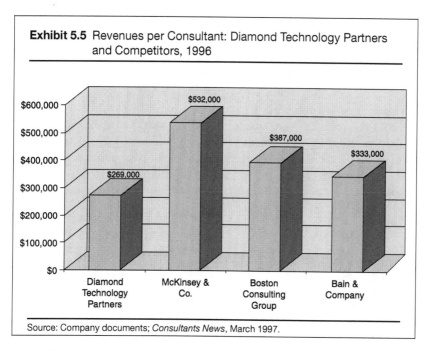

Exhibit 5.5 Revenues per Consultant: Diamond Technology Partners and Competitors, 1996

Source: Company documents; *Consultants News*, March 1997.

rates. (See Exhibit 5.5 for a comparison of revenues per consultant at Diamond and its main competitors.)

CLIENT RELATIONSHIPS

To Diamond's staff, Bergstein emphasized the great importance of staying focused on the client's needs—even if this should mean ignoring what was best for Diamond. He also believed that the company should take on projects only if a Diamond team could genuinely add value to the client's business. If not, he considered it important to have the courage to turn down a project.

EARLY GROWTH

By June 1994, four months after going into business, Diamond had eight clients. (Seven had developed from the partners' previous business relationships.) By this time there were 37 employees. The partners put minimal effort into marketing because they did not want to risk generating demand they could not fill. Also they feared that Bergstein and Moffitt's reputations would tag Diamond as a technology firm, and they intended to be known as much more than an IT/systems integration company.

Bergstein instituted the tradition of monthly All Hands Meetings as a way for Diamond's staff to stay connected by coming in from client sites to meet and discuss issues with peers. His policy of openness with staff led to wide-ranging discussions at the meetings. Even the office layout at Diamond headquarters, in the Hancock Tower in Chicago, was designed to promote a feeling of equality. Teams, not partners, had the corner offices. All partners' offices were the same size, and all had glass walls so that private meetings could be seen, if not heard. Outside walls included as much glass as possible. Everyone walking around the office could enjoy the spectacular 30-story views of Lake Michigan.

THE INVESTMENT PHASE: YEAR TWO, 1995, TWENTY-THREE-AND-A-HALF-YEAR PLAN

Bergstein and Moffitt had seen too many companies fail after a successful IPO for the simple reason that they had not adequately prepared to go public. Late in 1994, they drew a graph to represent a 23½-year plan that included an IPO. (See Exhibit 5.6.) The point of the diagram was to emphasize that Diamond's goal was to create an organization that could grow sustainably for 20 years, not to do an IPO. They accompanied the graph with a short list of goals to explain what the partners were trying to accomplish over time. Their original business plan had not explicitly

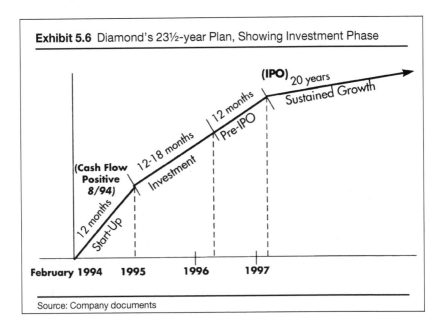

Exhibit 5.6 Diamond's 23½-year Plan, Showing Investment Phase

Source: Company documents

identified an investment stage. Bergstein and Moffitt articulated this stage to clarify priorities as Diamond entered its second year of business. They showed their graph to recruits and potential clients to underscore Diamond's long-term aspirations and perspective.

According to the plan, once the investment stage was complete, management would look for four or more quarters of good growth, with positive cash-flow, and then embark on the IPO. Early investment in human resources, training, development, and operations policies were meant to build an infrastructure that would not need constant reworking as the company grew and went public.

YEAR THREE: 1996

In April 1996, after completing two years of operation, Diamond had a staff of 138, with projects running for 17 clients. The firm's consultants were now becoming known for "digital strategy" and consulting teams whose members understood both technology and business strategy in depth (as the founders had hoped). Diamond's projects ended not only with strategy reports, but also with tangible assurance that the client had achieved beneficial results.

In order to create equality within the partnership, Bergstein and Moffitt went to great lengths to avoid dominating junior partners. For example, the first time partners were elected, a process was put in place whereby partners spoke in order of reverse seniority, with Bergstein and Moffitt speaking last, so as not to influence junior partners' decisions.

The organizational structure of Diamond had also now reached some stability. Diamond's management committee consisted of Bergstein, Moffitt, Mikolajczyk, and a fourth partner, James Spira. Each member of the management committee had specific responsibilities. Mikolajczyk, as CFO, owned the back office. Moffitt was in charge of the bulk of the organization—line consultants and clients. Bergstein spent the majority of his time externally and Spira was in charge of marketing the company. (See Exhibit 5.7.) This was the company the partners now felt ready to start marketing.

The consultants were organized by industry, in a series of groups vertically aligned within the organization. The partners and senior principals each belonged to one of four market and industry focused vertical teams: banking and finance; product-oriented businesses; services; or telecommunications and insurance. In addition, the company included staff teams—groups of 12 to 15 associates and principals, each

Exhibit 5.7 Organizational Chart of Diamond Technology Partners

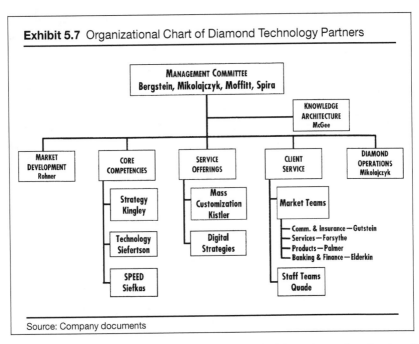

Source: Company documents

managed by a partner. Staff teams were filled with an intentional mix of individuals from each core competency. Staff team partners managed the staffing process and employees' career development.

By now the partners had identified a further core competency—speed—to accompany technology and strategy. On the down side, in this two-year-old company, most of the staff were relatively new and not everyone knew where they fit in the industry groups or the competencies. On the positive side, Diamond's attractiveness for talented recruits increased. New employees felt encouraged to develop skills and talents in many areas. The multidisciplinary structure did not force them into rigid categories.

Diamond was now growing at more than 100% per annum. The partners had just developed a plan based on the assumption that the firm was ready to do over $50 million worth of business in the next twelve months. Bergstein and the partners set the plan at $50 million to achieve a critical mass for the company as quickly as possible. All were concerned about revenue concentration with a few major clients and wanted to grow to a point where no project team, or "diamond," represented more than 5% of revenues. (This worked out to around $100 million in revenue assuming 20 diamonds of seven professionals generating $5 million in fees each.) The company's revenues had doubled in each of the first two years; the partners were convinced that they could do it again.

By April, staff compensation plans had been decided; people were looking forward to substantial year-end bonuses. In the previous six months, Diamond had offered positions to 50 MBAs, 28 of whom expected to join the company over the summer. Diamond had also expanded physically: its Cleveland office was scheduled to open at the beginning of August.

In April 1996, the partners were pondering a number of issues. Marketing had now become a major priority. Two initiatives formed the core of the initial marketing plans. Diamond Network was designed to be "a 'virtual organization' of world-class experts that can provide clients with a broad range of perspectives during an engagement." Members of the network were granted stock options, and consulting arrangements were defined in advance. Exhibit 5.8 identifies the

---

Exhibit 5.8 Members of the Diamond Network

John Perry Barlow	Co-Founder and Vice Chairman, Electronic Frontier Foundation
Gordon Bell	Senior Researcher, Microsoft Bay Area Research Center
Leonard L. Berry	Professor of Marketing at Lowry Mays College and Graduate School of Business
Larry Downes	Consultant and Author, Digital Strategies
Tim Gallwey	Author and Consultant on Learning
James H. Gilmore	Co-Founder, Strategic Horizons LLP
Alan Kay	Disney Fellow and VP of Research and Development, Walt Disney Imagineering
Andrew Lippman	Associate Director and Founding Member, MIT Media Lab
B. Joseph Pine II	Founder, Strategic Horizons LLP
David P. Reed	Information Architect and Independent Entrepreneur
John J. Sviokla	Associate Professor, Harvard Business School
Richard Y. Wang	Associate Professor, MIT Sloan School of Management
Marvin Zonis	Professor, International Economics, University of Chicago Graduate School of Business

Source: Company documents

members of the Diamond Network. Diamond Exchange was planned as a forum to bring together senior executives from clients and prospective clients, the Diamond Network, and consultants from Diamond. Deliberately designed to be a small group of less than 50, the Exchange intended to focus on helping organizations cope with the changes brought on by a digital world.

The company's growth meant that many new employees were operating in a structure initially created for only 50. Bergstein worried about keeping staff feeling connected to the firm. Another issue was keeping Diamond's professionals abreast of technological advances; in this culture, knowledge and intellectual capital development were as important as training for client engagements. In addition, the long-range plan called for beginning the IPO within 12 months. (See Exhibits 5.9 and 5.10 for financial information.)

Exhibit 5.9 Balance Sheet of Diamond Technology Partners for Fiscal Years Ended March 31, 1995 and 1996 ($000s except share data)

	1995	1996
ASSETS		
Current Assets:		
Cash and cash equivalents	$4,690	$4,635
Cash in escrow from subscribed stock		
Accounts receivable, net of allowance of $512, $270 and $566 as of March 31, 1995, 1996 and 1997, respectively	1,435	3,304
Prepaid expenses	320	1,180
Notes receivable from stockholder	163	226
Deferred income taxes	119	99
Total current assets	$6,727	$9,444
Computers, equipment, and training software, net	573	2,010
Other Assets:		
Deferred organization costs, net	213	161
Total Assets	$7,513	$11,615
LIABILITIES AND STOCKHOLDERS' EQUITY		
Current Liabilities:		
Notes payable	$150	$125
Accounts payable	557	1,155
Accrued compensation	160	1,089
Deferred compensation	622	1,452

Income taxes payable	119	83
Deferred revenue	612	
Accrued stock issuance costs	106	
Other accrued liabilities		1,143
Total current liabilities	$2,326	$5,047

Stockholders' Equity:

Preferred Stock, $1.00 par value, 2,000,000 shares authorized, no shares issued		
Class A common stock, $.001 par value, 40,000,000 shares authorized, 3,320,625 issued in 1995, 3,370,125 issued in 1996 and 4,594 issued in 1997	3	3
Class B common stock, $.001 par value, 20,000,000 shares authorized, 4,392,092 issued in 1995, 4,505, 119 issued in 1996 and 4,967 issued in 1997	4	4
Class A common stock subscribed, 1,755 shares		
Additional paid-in capital	6,533	6,844
Notes receivable from sale of common stock	(91)	(257)
Retain earnings (deficit)	(1,263)	(26)
Total stockholders' equity	$5,187	$6,568
Total liabilities and stockholders' equity	$7,513	$11,615

Source: Company documents

BAD NEWS IN APRIL

Two clients canceled projects in April 1996, the beginning of the first quarter of fiscal 1997. One canceled because of the acquisition of a business that eliminated the need for Diamond's services. The other canceled the business initiative for which it had retained Diamond. These two clients represented 50% of revenues in the January-March quarter of 1996, i.e., the last quarter of the fiscal year.

Bergstein's immediate response was to ensure that all professionals had something to work on. Diamond put staff on projects for free to keep them employed. The partners went into high gear to find extra business and managed to bring in the first quarter at just over the previous quarter's revenue. Many of the partners believed they could turn things around without cutting any expenditures for the year. Diamond's second quarter, however, had been one of the slowest for closing new work. The partners were running out of untapped names in their rolodexes.

Bergstein and his management committee held intense discussions as they tried to form a plan of action. The issue of hiring so many

Exhibit 5.10 Statement of Operations, Fiscal Years Ended March 31, 1994, 1995, and 1996 ($000s except per share data)

	1994	1995	1996
NET REVENUES	**$261**	**$12,843**	**$26,339**
Operating Expenses:			
Project personnel and related expenses	633	8,351	15,312
Professional development and recruiting	106	1,395	4,587
Marketing and sales	94	451	606
Management and administrative support	317	3,108	4,460
Total Operating Expenses	$1,150	$13,305	$24,965
Income (loss) from operations	$(889)	$(462)	$1,374
Interest income	3	136	251
Interest expense		(51)	(87)
Income (loss) before taxes	$(886)	$(377)	$1,538
Income taxes			(302)
Net Income (loss)	$(886)	$(377)	1,236
Net Income (loss) per share of common stock	(0.35)	(0.05)	0.13
Shares used in computing net (income) loss per share of common stock	2,511	8,272	9,824

Source: Company documents

MBAs was divisive. Some partners questioned the practice of paying competitive signing bonuses to new recruits and pointed out that the total amount of these bonuses could have covered employee bonuses at year-end. Some worried about reneging on commitments. Others pointed out that the MBAs came from Kellogg, Wharton, and Chicago, so the firm could withdraw on its offers to them and recruit at new business schools the following year.

Fundamental questions were raised: How would Diamond deal with the loss of revenue in light of its espoused long-term strategy? How would Diamond grow without more contacts? Would lack of growth change the basic philosophies on which Diamond was built? Most important, would Diamond still exist in a year?

Eventually the management committee came up with two options. Either the partners would take a significant pay cut or Diamond would have to renege on its job offers to MBAs. The partners had all invested financial and sweat equity in growing Diamond to $26.3 million in revenue in two years. It would be painful to tell them their bonuses were gone. Even more galling would be announcing that the long-anticipated IPO was now on hold. Bergstein and Moffitt agonized over how to present the news to the partners and the rest of the organization. The fate of Diamond—and, ultimately, its founders' professional and economic futures—rode on what Bergstein would say at the next day's All Hands Meeting.

NOTES TO CASE

1. The "Diamond approach" consisted of a team of 5 to 10 people who held the key positions in implementing the project. A partner headed up the team of 5 to 6 principals and associates, and 1 to 2 analysts, in contrast to other consulting firms which used pyramid-like team structures and kept most systems building in-house. (See Exhibit 5.2.)
2. IDC Research, 1996.
3. Tucker Anthony Equity Research, April 29, 1997.
4. A rights-offering allowed holders of Safeguard Scientifics stock to acquire shares of the company going public, relative to the amount of Safeguard stock they held. The rights usually traded on NASDAQ and could be bought or sold during the offering period.
5. According to Jim McGee: "The initial shares were priced at $1.50/share. The company authorized a total of 5,000,000 shares of which Safeguard bought 2,000,000 shares for their initial $3 million investment. Bergstein, Moffitt, and Mikolajczyk each put in an initial $250,000 for the Spring 1994 launch. Bergstein, in common with many other early partners, got his cash by taking a second mortgage on his house. Bergstein and the others put in additional amounts (which account for the differences in their holdings) when the initial round of financing closed in May."

Case 5.1b

DIAMOND IN THE ROUGH (B)

(Catherine Conneely and Thomas DeLong)

ABOUT THE AUTHOR

Research Associate Catherine Conneely prepared this case under the supervision of Professor Thomas DeLong as the basis for class discussion rather than to illustrate either effective or ineffective handling of an administrative situation.

Bergstein discussed facing the crisis:

We decided pretty quickly that we weren't going to lay off professionals in the line or withdraw any offers. We'd seen what effect that had elsewhere and concluded it would set us back five years at best.

The partners agreed to take a one month pay cut, which we spread out over the next fiscal year. The founding partners forgave about a million dollars in prior years' deferred compensation. We scrubbed the budget, looking for discretionary expenditures we could cut or postpone. We stopped some training and cut the number of All Hands Meetings to eight a year. We also let go four or five people in the back office. At the All Hands meeting when we announced these decisions, several of the staff who had been here from early on volunteered that they should give up their bonuses as well, which we also did.

What's interesting is that we replaced the lost clients fairly quickly. We actually ended up doing slightly better than the preceding quarter and we replaced all the lost business within a quarter.

For fiscal year-end March 31	1994[1]	1995	1996	1997	1998
Sales ($000s)	$261	$12,843	$26,339	$37,557	$58,369
Net Income ($000s)	(886)	(377)	1,236	633	6,008
Client-serving Professionals	–	69	115	146	175
Clients	–	16	24	45	65

[1] This represents only one quarter of business for Diamond.

Barely eight months after announcing the crisis to employees, Bergstein and his partners took Diamond public. The company successfully completed an IPO on March 31, 1997, in the form of a "rights" offering to shareholders of Safeguard Scientifics. Diamond went public at $5.50 per share and, in little under a year, closed at $23.63 on March 24, 1998.

Case 5.2a

TIM HERTACH AT GL CONSULTING (A)

(Scot Landry, Ashish Nanda, and Thomas DeLong)

Walking to his car outside the Chicago headquarters of GL Consulting, Tim Hertach was looking forward, after a hectic couple of weeks at work, to spending the three-day Memorial Day holiday with his wife. Hertach's career and stature at GL Consulting LLP (GLC) had progressed rapidly; he was viewed as a leader among the cohort of recently promoted partners and was routinely praised by clients. But something was troubling him. "I was pondering over a dilemma while leaving the office that Friday night," recalled Hertach.

I had just helped win a large project at Parks Food. It meant a lot for the firm and obviously for my career. But I couldn't get out of my mind a comment my colleague had made. He had described a billing practice at another client that, on the surface, appeared to be questionable. I had squelched any possibility of following such questionable practices in the Parks Food project. But I was left wondering whether it was my responsibility to probe deeper into our firm's billing practices with other clients.

TIM HERTACH

Early Childhood and Schooling

Hertach had grown up just outside Reston, Virginia. An introverted child, he struggled in school and at forming friendships. He had almost failed first grade and was required to attend remedial education programs until the fourth grade. "I was overweight as a kid and was mocked by my classmates," Hertach recollected.

> Often they would call me "professor" or "egghead." I guess they thought I was smart even if my teachers did not. I remember once, in the fourth grade, giving away money I had saved from my modest weekly allowance and earned doing extra chores to some of the kids that were nice to me at school. At times my parents made the problems I faced at school worse by expressing their frustration with my mediocre academic performance. Owners of a small, local, and highly successful accounting firm, they were consumed by the demanding needs of their clients.

In seventh and eighth grades, Hertach's academic performance improved dramatically once he was placed in some advanced classes that he enjoyed, though he still had difficulties socially. In 1974, at age 13, Hertach left home to attend Deerfield Academy, a private boarding school in Massachusetts. Although his social and academic experiences continued to be uneven, his participation, in the summer of 1977, in the Colorado Outward Bound School, a wilderness-based personal development program, did boost his self-confidence.

Upon graduation from school, Hertach, rejected by a number of universities because of his spotty academic record at Deerfield, was finally accepted at Oklahoma State University in Stillwater, Oklahoma. Finding the transition from a small, private, elite, East Coast boarding school to a large midwestern public university difficult, Hertach followed his 1978–1979 freshman year with a year in Volunteers In Service to America (VISTA), a government-run program that employed volunteers to assist the economically disadvantaged. "It was one of the most rewarding and important experiences of my life," he recalled. "I worked with a neighborhood association in Baltimore, Maryland, formed many close relationships, and felt, for the first time in my life, accepted by a community." Upon returning to Oklahoma State in 1980 Hertach flourished, achieving high grades, becoming president of his fraternity, and leading several other major campus organizations.

Hertach's First Job: Weston Consulting

Upon graduating from Oklahoma State in 1983 with a B.S. in Chemistry and a minor in business, Hertach joined Weston Consulting. Among the world's largest consulting firms, Weston set aggressive sales targets and asked its managers and partners who failed to meet their targets to leave. The firm's competitive, high-pressure environment took its toll on professionals; morale was low and turnover among consultants averaged 25%. In the course of working on a wide range of projects, Hertach encountered situations that made him feel increasingly uneasy. "On my first project," he recalled,

> I was on a team that designed and implemented a large computer system that we knew, in the later stages of the project, wouldn't work, but we never told the client. On another team we violated the client's bidding guidelines. In the second instance, I confronted the partner in charge and we were able to reach a compromise that I felt resolved the issue. After these two experiences I came to the conclusion that Weston's high-pressure environment to generate revenue caused "good people to do bad things."

Working for a Nonprofit

Hertach entered Harvard Business School's MBA program in the fall of 1986. Upon graduating in 1988, unlike most of his classmates who sought jobs in corporations, investment banks, or consulting firms, he joined Habitat for Humanity, a nonprofit organization that built housing for economically disadvantaged families.

Hertach enjoyed the experience. "The people in the organization were dedicated and compassionate individuals," he observed. "I made many great friendships, learned a tremendous amount about managing projects and teams and had a lot of fun. It seemed that we were making a real, meaningful impact in the lives of others." (Exhibit 5.11 summarizes

Exhibit 5.11 Tim Hertach's Career Values

Desired Job Characteristics Feedback for Timothy Steven Hertach

This chart summarizes what you seek in terms of an ideal job, with the most important characteristics higher in the chart. Additionally, the chart tells you what relative weight you attach to each characteristic. For example, a bar that is twice as long as another bar tells you that you consider the former factor to be twice as important as the latter.

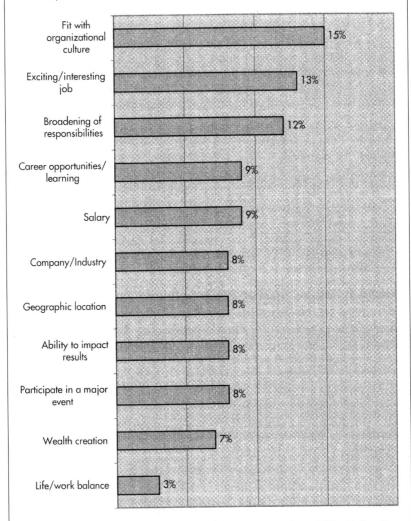

The chart was developed by Hertach's taking a self-assessment test in August 1999 with Korn/Ferry Futurestep.

Hertach's career values.) In April 1991, Hertach married Linda Howard; his wife was an artist and shared many of his interests.

After working with Habitat for three years, Hertach decided to seek a change. "I felt as though I was no longer as challenged as when I had started," he reasoned.

My next promotion would take me into administration rather than running the projects I so enjoyed doing. The compensation I was receiving was low, as to be expected at a nonprofit, and would remain so for as long as I stayed with the organization. Since my only source of wealth was what I earned working, I was concerned that I would not be able to support my family if I stayed at Habitat. And I missed some of the challenges and faster pace of the for-profit world.

Hertach Rejoins the For-Profit Sector

Hertach left Habitat in August 1991 to join The Bec Company, a medium-size consumer products company, as director of strategic planning. He was soon promoted to vice president of production planning and customer service and made responsible for managing an 18-person department that controlled the production of 5,700 products at 7 manufacturing facilities, managed inventories, and resolved problems with retail customers such as Wal*Mart, Kmart, Sears, and JC Penney. "It was a tough job," recalled Hertach. "I learned a tremendous amount. Fortunately I had a department filled with dedicated and experienced people."

But the firm, having experienced a leveraged buy-out in the mid-1980s, was suffocating under a mountain of debt. "I thought that Bec's future might be limited," Hertach recollected, "and I did not have a high regard for most of the senior management team." In August 1993, Hertach moved from Bec to Consultants Limited (CL), a small consulting firm that had been conducting a business process re-engineering project at Bec.

At CL, Hertach sold and delivered business process re-engineering projects to governmental agencies and consumer products companies. But the firm was having financial problems and decided to exit a number of businesses, including Hertach's area, re-engineering, and focus exclusively on packaged software implementation. Although he could have stayed on at CL by relocating, Hertach chose to leave the firm since he did not want to focus only on implementing software. "At the time CL was going through merger negotiations with a much larger firm, GL Consulting," Hertach recalled. "CL partners introduced me to some of the senior partners there. Although CL did not eventually merge with GL Consulting, I received an offer from them and decided to join the firm in January 1996."

TIM HERTACH AT GL CONSULTING

GL Consulting

An established, respected, fast-growing consulting partnership, GL Consulting had more than 40 years' experience executing strategy, process improvement, information technology, operations, and logistics projects for some of the largest and best-known companies in the world. Reflecting its emphasis on delivering high-quality, results-oriented consulting services, GLC's work came mostly from repeat clients. Unlike many large firms that frequently staffed projects with people with little or no relevant experience, GLC was reputed in the industry for maintaining a high ratio of experienced to inexperienced staff on projects. Remarked a senior GLC partner: "One of the few ways to get fired from GLC is to screw up a client engagement."

In addition to client focus, tight control of compensation, administrative and other overhead expenses helped make the firm highly profitable. Competitors and industry analysts alike generally viewed GLC positively. Many considered it a "sleeping giant," believing that it could greatly increase its market share if it were to become more aggressive in seeking new clients. A frequent acquisition target of other consulting firms, GLC routinely rejected such overtures, since the senior partners at GLC wanted to remain independent.

A Friendly Culture

GLC was perceived by outsiders to have solid, experienced people who delivered tangible results to clients. One industry analyst characterized it as the kind of place anyone would be proud to work at. Hertach felt that GLC had a friendly, congenial atmosphere. Cooperation was emphasized and individuals enjoyed considerable latitude in determining their career focus. "I was surprised at how little direction I was given when I joined the firm," he recalled. "Basically it was up to me to decide what I wanted to do."

Consultant turnover at GLC averaged 10% to 12% per year, about half what other large consulting firms experienced. Hertach felt that one reason for the low turnover was that capable people remained at

GLC (even though they knew that they could make more money elsewhere) for cultural and lifestyle reasons. He had heard several stories of GLC partners and consultants rebuffing executive recruiters offering job opportunities with compensation increases of 30% to 50%.

Sales targets for managers and partners that were lower than at most other major consulting firms fostered a less-intense work environment. Compensation, including bonuses, was tied more closely to seniority than to individual performance. Working on weekends was the exception; most consultants worked 40 to 60 hours per week.

Traditionally, GLC had promoted from within, but as the firm grew in the mid-1990s, it became necessary to hire outside professionals (from other consulting firms and from industry). Bringing in outsiders occasioned no discernible internal dissension, most long-time employees seeming to realize that outside hiring was necessary to continue growing the business. GLC, like most consulting firms, struggled to find qualified people who fit its culture; some of its outside hires were successful, others not.

Hertach's Debut at GLC

Hertach was one of the experienced hires. In January 1996, Hertach joined GLC as a senior manager in a newly formed practice area that was responsible for selling and delivering multi-functional consulting projects that required a mix of strategy, systems, and process improvement services.

In late 1996, Hertach was appointed manager for a fairly large project reporting to two partners, GLC chairman Mark Williamson and senior partner Bob Morton, who was relatively new to the firm. Hertach quickly became friends with Morton, 10 years Hertach's senior. Hertach admired Morton's positive attitude. Realizing that he could learn a lot from him, he became Morton's confidant and sought to work with him as often as possible. Morton reciprocated by bringing Hertach into major sales efforts and creating opportunities for Hertach to lead large projects and firmwide management initiatives. "By late 1997," Hertach recalled,

> my career at GLC was going very well, thanks largely to Bob Morton. I had helped him sell several large engagements, was starting to be quoted in the press, delivered a presentation at a major trade show, and served on several internal GLC committees. Additionally, I was asked to lead a consulting project I had helped

to sell: to create and launch a new business unit for a large company. It was definitely the most interesting, successful, and enjoyable stage of my career and I was very enthusiastic about my work. The firm recognized my accomplishments in these areas and promoted me to the partnership in January 1998.

In 1998 Hertach spent most of his efforts developing a new practice area. Although his investment in the new business line adversely affected Hertach's sales, management continued to reward him with more responsibility. "I enjoyed working at GLC and continued to build experience, contacts, and knowledge," recalled Hertach.

Early in the year I was appointed, through Bob Morton's support, to head a committee of senior GLC partners responsible for coordinating marketing efforts throughout the firm. I was quoted in about 20 articles in the general, business, and trade press on a wide range of business and consulting issues. And I was selected to travel to Europe to deliver a presentation at an industry conference. Overall it was a successful year.

Taking Stock

As 1998 drew to a close, Hertach reflected on his impressions of GLC and his plans for the future. Although he believed that the day would eventually come when he would seek to do something else, Hertach nevertheless saw himself working for GLC for the foreseeable future. "On the positive side," he explained,

GLC was a profitable and growing firm. It placed high, but not unreasonable demands on its employees. It tried to treat everyone fairly, taking into account individual circumstances when making staffing assignments and treating people with respect. The firm tried to do what was right for the client rather than simply maximize firm revenue. I felt that the firm was very well managed and wrote personal notes to both chairman Mark Williamson and president Lester Simpson of GLC thanking them for their efforts.

But GLC, like any organization, was far from perfect. I didn't think Mark and Lester provided a clear or inspiring vision for how to grow the firm. They would periodically send memos to all the partners extolling them to sell more and raise hourly rates. Many of the partners ridiculed these memos. I felt these memos were basically pointless, equivalent to telling a basketball team to score more points than its opponents, an obvious goal everyone understands, when the real problem was figuring out how to do so. I discussed this with Mark and Lester, but they, even when pressed, could not explain how to grow the business other than to say, "we need to work harder selling larger projects."

GLC had not built Internet or Enterprise Resource Planning software practices early enough, thereby ceding leadership in these important growth areas to other firms. The firm was also not investing enough in infrastructure. Our accounting system was hopelessly outdated and inflexible; and we lacked method-ologies. I felt that we were way behind our competition in these and other infrastructure areas and simply not spending enough to catch up.

Hertach believed that he was generally viewed positively. On several occasions senior partners had told him that they needed "more people like you at GLC in order to grow the firm." In 1998, he was presented an award for outstanding firmwide performance. Phil Mabree, the strategy practice head who was Hertach's direct supervisor, stated in Hertach's 1998 year-end annual performance review:

Tim performs well in creative situations and in managing and coordinating others. His verbal skills are strong. He builds very strong relationships both with clients and other GLC personnel. He enjoys business development and will be strong in this area as he builds his experience, network of contacts, and skills.

Tim is very much a team player, willing to sub-optimize his position or performance if it benefits the client or the firm. He is also a natural entrepreneur, taking great satisfaction out of creat-ing something new such as the firmwide marketing campaign for food, drug, and consumer-packaged goods.

In terms of areas for improvement, Mabree offered the following feed-back:

Tim needs to continue to learn more about GLC culture, policies, and procedures. Sometimes in his effort to get something done, Tim violates the norms, culture, and procedures of the firm. He does, however, learn from these instances and rarely makes the same mistake twice.

Tim is, at times, more blunt in expressing his opinions than is the norm at GLC. He needs to continue to be sensitive in his communication with others.

Hertach agreed with Mabree's feedback. Yet, he believed that his communication style, characterized as blunt in the review, was an asset when dealing with clients. "I rarely had conflicts with my clients over my communication style," he reflected.

I frequently received commendations and thank-you notes from them and they usually gave my projects very high ratings on the evaluation forms that they periodically filled out. They appreciated my honesty and it helped me form many close friendships. In fact, often times my only regret was that I was not being honest enough with them. On occasions I foresaw problems developing, but did not, out of respect and friendship, address them with sufficient force. As a result, in some cases, I was not effective in helping them confront and solve some significant problems that, in turn, harmed their organizations and careers.

THE REVALUATION PROPOSAL

"Proposal to Enhance Value"

Preparing to attend GLC's annual worldwide partners meeting in February 1999, Hertach was intrigued by a two-hour block of time earmarked for a session cryptically titled "Proposal to Enhance Value." The first 90 minutes of the session were devoted to a presentation of the proposal by two senior GLC partners. "The longer I listened, the more annoyed I became," recalled Hertach.

They kept presenting slides and talking about the benefits of their proposal without describing the proposal itself. I started to have a bad feeling regarding what we were about to hear. Finally, an hour into the presentation, the partners described their proposal. They recommended quadrupling the valuation of a partnership unit. The units that each partner held would vest at their new valuation after five years.

The partners making the presentation stated that the new valuation would be a more accurate estimate of the true value of the partners' equity in GLC and would help the firm minimize dilution when acquiring other firms. They said that the firm's financial advisors had put together numerous cash flow projections using various assumptions that showed the revaluation would be advantageous for the firm. They said that the firm's bankers, lawyers, and accountants had all provided favorable opinions and recommended implementing it, and GLC's board of partners supported the plan.

The last half-hour was devoted to questions and answers. The first was a request to get a copy of the presentation that had just been delivered. The presenters answered that they would not distribute it because "the proposal might change." As the question period proceeded, Hertach, too, raised his hand. Once recognized, he said:

Maybe I don't understand something about this proposal but it appears to me that the 20% of the senior partners that own 80% of the firm will get a huge windfall from this whereas the remaining 80% of the partners will be left trying to pay for it.

The silence that suddenly enveloped the room was broken by one of the presenting partners responding with a long, somewhat rambling explanation. After the meeting was adjourned, several partners came up to Hertach and told him that they shared his concerns. One senior partner slapped him on the back and said with a smile, "I see that they taught you a few things at the Harvard Business School." Hertach smiled back weakly, sick with anger over a proposal that he felt mortgaged the future of the firm.

Later that evening Hertach met his mentor Morton. They got into an intense argument over the relative merits of the revaluation. It soon became apparent to Hertach that Morton strongly supported the proposal.

After the partnership meeting, GLC's board of directors named a committee of senior partners to take input, answer questions, and make a final recommendation to the board. Although several mid-level and new partners privately expressed their concerns to Hertach, he remained one of a handful of people that publicly objected to the committee regarding the proposal. His requests for copies of the cash flows, comments other partners had submitted, and the opinions provided by the firm's financial advisors were denied, making Hertach "angrier, frustrated, and more concerned."

Adoption of the Revaluation Proposal

A slightly revised proposal was put to partnership vote in May 1999 and passed with about 80% of the units voting in favor. When asked, the senior partners would not reveal how many of the actual partners, rather than units, voted in favor of the proposal. Hertach remembered his reaction:

It was over. On paper I was instantly $250,000 richer, or would be if I stayed with the firm for five more years. And this amount could increase, perhaps substantially, over that time. But, even though Bob Morton relentlessly championed the new valuation approach, extolling its virtues whenever he had the chance, I remained unconvinced about the proposal's merits. I believed that the senior partners had set up a system that would allow them to cash out with a huge windfall, draining capital from the firm, leaving the younger partners in the lurch. I especially disliked the way the proposal was presented and the way in which the senior partners withheld information. On top of everything else, Bob Morton and I were no longer on speaking terms.

Several junior partners that he barely knew voiced their concerns privately to him. Many expressed frustration that, henceforth, they would have to invest significantly more money, about 80% of their annual bonus, to buy the new more expensive units whereas, in the past, they typically had to invest roughly 30% of their bonus to make their annual unit purchases. One mid-level partner told Hertach that he did not support the proposal but felt it forced him to stay at GLC another five years till his new units vested. Several younger partners acknowledged to Hertach that they were exploring exit strategies "in case things do not work out" and had begun listening to the pitches from executive recruiters (whose intensity of calls had increased dramatically because they "smelled blood in the water").

In mid-1999, the senior partners publicly announced that the change had been successful. They had expected about seven partners to leave because of the change, but so far, none had. However, revenue at the firm had been sliding over the past six months and so the managing partners began, once again, to push partners to raise hourly rates and sell larger projects.

THE BILLING CONTROVERSY

As the revaluation process unfolded over the first half of 1999, Hertach, despite his disappointment, continued to sell work and deliver consulting services. He was even given additional responsibilities when Mabree put him in charge of the firm's food, drug, and consumer packaged goods strategy practice. Hertach soon found himself in the middle of a new controversy. He was part of a team proposing a multimillion-dollar consulting project for Parks Food, a leading but troubled company. The firm's chief financial officer inquired whether GLC would be willing to defer a portion of its fees until its recommendations were implemented and tangible results achieved, a type of billing arrangement GLC usually sought to avoid.

GLC's Billing Practices

GLC customarily billed clients for three categories of expenses: consulting fees referred to as fees for professional services, travel expenses, and administrative expenses. Fees for professional services were calculated by multiplying the number of hours consultants worked by their respective hourly billing rates. Airfare, lodging, and meals expenses were passed through to clients at cost; GLC did not share with clients the substantial rebates it received from airlines, hotels, credit card companies, and its corporate travel agent.[1] The last category of expenses was administrative.

Fees for professional services typically accounted for 75% to 80% of a project's cost. Although GLC preferred to bill clients fees as incurred with no maximum amount, which placed the risk of a project requiring more effort or running longer than expected squarely with the client, few consulting projects were sold in this manner. Many companies, desiring consultants to share some of the risk for completing work on time and on budget and needing to know approximate project costs in advance for budgeting purposes, preferred a billing approach of fees as incurred up to a maximum amount.[2]

Performance-linked payment schemes, such as the one being requested by Parks Food, also referred to as "contingent" fees" in the consulting industry, were not used widely. Under an arrangement termed "gain sharing," one of the two major variations of this approach, GLC billed clients an amount based on a percentage of the financial improvement attributed to the project (e.g., a percentage of savings resulting from an inventory reduction project). The other approach typically added a bonus to a fixed fee if specified performance or quality criteria were met or exceeded. Although it did not actively pursue performance-linked payments, GLC did, albeit infrequently, agree to such arrangements. Its experience with such arrangements had been generally bad. In a number of cases, even with long-term clients, disagreements arose over whether results were realized and amounts to be paid. Almost invariably, clients ended up paying more for the work than they would have otherwise because GLC charged more to compensate for the additional risk it incurred and the time consumed in closely monitoring results.

Administrative expenses charges were supposed to cover GLC's support and administrative expenses. These expenses being a mix of different items, billing was quite complicated. This category included client-related administrative expenses such as courier services and outside commercial printing. By far the largest component was an overhead charge equaling roughly 7% of total fees.

Although calculated almost entirely on a percentage basis, administrative expenses were shown on the invoice in dollars. As fees went up and down, so did administrative expenses. The few clients that eventually figured out that they were paying a percentage-based overhead charge rather than a direct expense objected verbally and often refused to pay it. GLC did not require clients that challenged the overhead charge to pay it. (Exhibit 5.12 provides a sample invoice.)

GLC Responds to Parks Food

GLC's response to Parks Food's request for a performance-linked scheme was complicated by two factors. The GLC team, aware that a competitor also bidding on the work had agreed to the request, feared that if it did not offer to make some comparable concession it would lose the bid. But aware also of Parks Food's reputation for being contentious and litigious with its vendors, the GLC team worried that if it agreed to the deferral and won the bid it might never get fully paid for its work.

One partner on the team suggested that GLC "instead offer them a discount like we did Bolton Machine [a long-time, multimillion-dollar GLC client], then increase our rates to make up the difference." Hertach remarked to the group that this did not sound ethical and the option was discussed no further.

Ultimately, GLC offered no fee concessions to Parks Food. Fees and expenses were to be billed as incurred with a fee maximum of $2.2 million. Expenses were estimated to be about 25% of the fees. The client was to be invoiced monthly, payment due within 90 days. Even though a competing consulting firm had agreed to a fee deferral, GLC was selected, in large part owing to the strong relationship the GLC team had established with the Parks Food executive team. The Parks Food team was particularly impressed with the experience, empathy, and understanding the GLC team had demonstrated for the pressures and issues Parks Food faced and with the GLC team's action bias in proposing to launch pilot tests after only six weeks of analysis.

Exhibit 5.12 GLC Sample Invoice

GL Consulting LLP[a]
Invoice
Through December 13, 1997

Attention of:

Jeff Higgins
Chief Financial Officer
Bolton Machine
54 Western Avenue
North Saddlebrook NJ 04712

Client: 12555
Project: 26453
Invoice: 97-62345
Project description: Implementation of redesigned product development processes and systems

Fees for professional services:	$265,780.00
Travel expenses:	43,345.11
Administrative expenses:	70.38
Interest charges:	0.00
Total due:	$309,195.49

Questions regarding this invoice or payments should be directed to Accounts Receivable department at 212-555-8332. Terms: Net in 90 days, thereafter 1.5% monthly interest is charged. All forms of payment should be made payable to: GL Consulting LLP.

---

a GLC also offered alternative invoice formats that were more detailed, although most clients received the version shown above. In the more detailed versions "fees for professional services" were broken down by individual consultant, and/or "travel expenses" were shown by category (e.g., airfare). More detail regarding "administrative expenses" was not available on any invoice format. Bolton Machine, on December 13, 1997, was not paying the 7% overhead charges normally included under "administrative expenses."

HERTACH PONDERS FURTHER INVESTIGATION

"I was thrilled that we were able to win the Parks Food account *and* do it above board," recalled Hertach,

but the comment made by my colleague about how billing had been handled on the Bolton account began to gnaw on me. That partner implied that GLC had done something questionable. Did I have a responsibility to bring the issue up? If so, who should I talk with? And how?

NOTES TO CASE

1. Some clients requested that travel expenses incurred by GLC on their projects follow their own more restrictive corporate guidelines or that GLC establish a maximum cap, either a set dollar amount or a percentage of fees. In most instances, GLC agreed to do so.

2. These were two of the five types of billing approaches used by GLC and most other large consulting firms: (1) fees as incurred (no maximum); (2) fees as incurred (up to a maximum amount); (3) fixed fee; (4) performance-linked fees (contingent upon some quantifiable milestone or result achieved); and (5) value billing (charging clients for a portion of the expected value created through provision of the consulting service).

Case 5.2b

TIM HERTACH AT GL CONSULTING (B)

(Scot Landry, Ashish Nanda, and Thomas DeLong)

ABOUT THE AUTHOR

Dean's Research Fellow Scot Landry prepared this note under the supervision of Professors Ashish Nanda and Thomas DeLong as the basis for class discussion rather than to illustrate either effective or ineffective handling of an administrative situation. This case is a rewritten version of an earlier case by the same authors.

INQUIRING INTO THE BOLTON MACHINE BILLING ARRANGEMENT

As the thrill of winning the Parks Food account wore off, Hertach began to wonder about the comment made by his colleague. What had really happened at Bolton Machine? Reasoning that "GLC should be transparent with its clients regarding its processes to protect the long-term interests of the firm," Hertach sent an email to the three senior partners responsible for running GLC: chairman Mark Williamson, president Lester Simpson, and chief executive officer Reg Anderbend. "Someone recently told me," Hertach's email read,

> that sometime in the recent past, Bolton Machine asked for a 20% reduction in our fees. They went on to say that we agreed, but, in order to make up the difference, increased our hourly rates by 20%. Do you know if this is true? And, if it is, do you agree with it?

A few days later Hertach received the following email back from Simpson: "What is the context of the question? We have had many people ask for reductions and we have taken many different tacks to try to work with their requests and still be fair to GLC."

In order to try to understand better what had happened at Bolton Machine, Hertach asked two other partners in the firm what they knew about the situation. Both said that GLC had, in fact, raised rates to offset a reduction in fees.

CONFRONTING MANAGEMENT

Hertach sent the following reply email to Simpson, with copies to the other two senior executives.

> The context for my question is as follows. As all of you are aware, Parks Food asked us for a fee holdback, which we ultimately refused. In a conference call to determine what would be an appropriate response after Parks Food had made their request, one partner on the GLC team suggested that we offer them, as an alternative, a discount, but then increase our hourly rates. That person then went on to explain in some detail how that had been done at Bolton Machine. I mentioned that I did not think that was ethical and no further discussion of the option ensued. Subsequently, I decided to contact you to see if you had heard this story and what your opinion would be in this regard.
>
> Since my email I have spoken with two additional partners familiar with Bolton Machine and they confirm the account I heard during the Parks Food conference call.
>
> I believe the next step is to review the billing and hourly rates to determine if, as has been related to me by three partners, the 20% "discount" coincided with a 20% increase in hourly fees on the Bolton Machine project. Would you please give me permission to review the billing records held by the accounting department for Bolton Machine?

A few days later, Williamson pulled Hertach aside at a client site. He began, in a clearly agitated state, asking Hertach why he was looking into the issue. Williamson scolded Hertach that if every partner were to review billing records there would be complete "chaos." He chided Hertach that he should have notified immediately senior management of what he had heard, passed along any relevant information, and then rest assured that they would look into it. Williamson proceeded to pepper Hertach with questions about precisely what he had been told and by whom. Williamson wanted to talk with everyone who had spoken with Hertach on the matter to "set the record straight." Hertach told him the names of the three GLC partners who had related the story to him. To Hertach's questions as to whether any impropriety had occurred, he responded that there had been no increase in hourly rates to recover the discount, that he had personally reviewed the billing records in accounting, and that everything had been done "according to GLC policies."

Later that same day Hertach received the following terse email from Simpson: "I don't think this is any issue for you. Use your time more productively." Over the next several days Williamson copied Hertach on voice mails he had sent and received on the issue. A number of the messages maintained that the Bolton Machine billing had been handled according to "GLC policies."

Case 5.2c

TIM HERTACH AT GL CONSULTING (C)

(Scot Landry, Ashish Nanda, and Thomas DeLong)

HERTACH DIGS DEEPER

Lester Simpson's email and Mark Williamson's conversation and follow-up seemed excessively hostile to Tim Hertach. He recalled:

> I was suspicious that both Mark and Lester were personally involved in this matter and, as a result, their reactions represented a personal rather than a firmwide perspective. Mark was a relatively "hands-on" chairman and had been the lead partner in charge of Bolton Machine. In addition, I suspected that both

Mark and Lester might have been directly involved in any fee discounting because, based upon my experience, a decision to reduce fees on a project of this size would have required the approval of them both. I wondered if both knew and approved of this discount that was not really a discount.

Feeling compelled to find out what had really happened at Bolton Machine, Hertach asked Ravi Gupta, one of the junior partners who had reported to Williamson on the project, to explain in detail what had transpired. Gupta informed Hertach that Bolton Machine was one of several clients not paying the 7% administrative overhead charges. When a Bolton Machine executive had asked GLC for a 20% fee reduction, GLC had initially agreed to provide a 10% reduction and discuss a further 10% reduction at a future date. To make up for the 10% loss, GLC had started charging the 7% overhead charges.

But if the 7% overhead charge had been handled according to normal GLC billing procedures, Gupta explained, the administrative expense category on the invoice would have increased dramatically and surely been noticed by the Bolton Machine executive who had requested the discount. Gupta had made numerous, difficult adjustments to the accounting system to load the 7% into hours worked so that the expenses would show up on the invoice under "fees for professional services" rather than as "administrative expenses." At the end of the discussion, as Hertach started to walk away, Gupta remarked that he did not see "anything unethical in it."

THE CONTROVERSY ESCALATES

Hertach felt that he now understood why the official story was that everything had been done "according to GLC policies" at Bolton Machine since technically it was within those policies to bill the client for the 7% overhead charges. He subsequently sent the following email to GLC's three senior executives.

Apparently my questions and/or request to look into the Bolton Machine situation violated a GLC norm since you are questioning my interest in the subject. Let me try to explain.

As a partner at GLC I believe it is my duty and obligation to understand our philosophy and practices regarding our interaction with clients. For one, I want to ensure that what I am doing is in compliance with the policy and philosophy of the firm. As a new member of the firm, I still have much to learn. Secondly, as a partner, I have legal and economic reasons for ensuring that our policies and actions are consistent, support the long-term health of the firm, and set the highest possible standards of integrity and honesty. In terms of spending my time, and I mean this sincerely, I cannot think of a better use than to help maintain, and possibly improve, the business practices within GLC.

In regards to Bolton Machine, this is my current understanding of what happened. I apologize in advance if I have this wrong. Someone at Bolton Machine asked GLC for a 10% fee reduction that we agreed to. We then began charging Bolton Machine for administrative overhead, which was loaded into "fees for professional services," resulting in a net reduction of about 3%. Charging them for administrative overhead was within GLC policies. The questions I have for you are: Is this correct? Did the person(s) at Bolton Machine that asked and were told that they would get a 10% reduction, in fact, realize that it was only 3%? If so, do you agree with this approach? Does it conform to current GLC policies? Is it ethical?

I would like to request the following—that a special three-person committee be formed to look into this matter, address these questions, and report back to all GLC partners their findings and conclusions. One person on the committee should be an outsider with no prior financial or personal relationship to the firm or with individuals active in the management of the firm. I also request that none of us serve on the committee since our relationships seem somewhat strained at this time over this issue.

Hertach received the following reply from Simpson.

Thanks for the explanation. I think that your request is completely out of line. It is a waste of time and money. Every project has negotiations and then results; going back and dissecting every situation would not be productive. Tim, as a partner, you have the responsibility to assure that you act ethically and consistently with GLC values. Every other partner has the same responsibility. It is management's responsibility to assure that other partners operate correctly. We don't operate as a police state where everyone tries to second guess everyone else and be "holier than thou."

Stung by Simpson's reply, Hertach began to wonder if he had made a mistake by becoming too deeply involved in the issue. "I could lose my job over this," thought an increasingly worried Hertach. Although

Linda had been supportive throughout, he recognized that "the reality was that we had only about $30,000 in savings and depended on my income to cover our mortgage, car payments, and living expenses. I knew she was beginning to worry too." That evening, over dinner with a number of GLC colleagues, he described his situation. "I was pretty upset at the time," he recalled,

> but everyone seemed to be shocked with the way GLC handled the billing at Bolton Machine and felt it was unethical. There was surprise at the negative reaction I was getting from GLC management after raising the issue. Many said that GLC's billing practice conflicted with one of our frequently stated firm values: "Always place the client interest first." Others remarked that GLC should eliminate the administrative expense category entirely because many clients had objected to it and simply raise hourly rates by 7% to make up the difference. A few were discouraged to hear that management reacted negatively to my inquiries. No one suggested I was wrong in pursuing the matter.

HERTACH CONSIDERS HIS NEXT MOVE

Two weeks after these events, seated in an airplane on his way to visit a client after attending a strategy conference, Hertach reflected on his feelings of growing frustration, unhappiness, and uncertainty. His efforts to get a clear answer to the billing controversy had been futile thus far. "I suspect," he reflected,

> that the senior management of GLC is misleading me by hiding behind the excuse that everything was done "according to GLC policies." They will not answer my questions directly, preferring instead to stonewall me with their self-righteous indignation.

> I want to know the truth; I want to see management held accountable if necessary; and I want the firm to standardize a billing approach that everyone feels is correct. But I am no longer sure that I should pursue the matter further.

> Should I do what I consider to be the right thing? I have a duty to the firm and to the other partners to pursue the issue. If clients realize we have been unethical in our billing practices we would experience a severe backlash and GLC's reputation could be destroyed. Everyone in the firm would suffer.

> Or, should I drop the issue and protect my career? The odds of success are slim and pushing this crusade further certainly will not help my career.

Case 5.2d

TIM HERTACH AT GL CONSULTING (D)

(Scot Landry, Ashish Nanda, and Thomas DeLong)

Sitting in an airplane en-route to a client on a warm June evening in 1999, Tim Hertach had been reflecting on his future at GL Consulting (GLC). By the time the flight landed he had come to a tentative conclusion. His first meeting the next morning was with Tom Harvey, the partner with overall responsibility for the engagement. Hertach mentioned to Harvey that he was thinking about leaving GLC. "Yeah, we thought you might be thinking about leaving the firm," Harvey replied, "so we have lined up a replacement for you on this project. There is no reason for you to stay here beyond this afternoon."

"I was surprised," Hertach described his reaction,

by his "suggestion" that I leave the project immediately. Although I had said that I was thinking about leaving GLC, I had not made up my mind yet. I expected this to start a dialogue with him and others that might last for several weeks. But my contribution and role were apparently seen as so negligible that I could be removed immediately!

The next day, upon returning to the office, Hertach spoke with his former mentor Bob Morton. The two discussed for approximately 10 minutes the possibility of Hertach leaving GLC. Morton advised Hertach that he should leave GLC as quickly as possible because it would be difficult to staff him on projects if he were considering leaving and, thus, he would become a financial drain on the company. "I was surprised by how much and how quickly everyone in the firm wanted me to leave," Hertach recalled. "Once I raised the issue of leaving, the whole thing seemed to take on a momentum of its own and the discussion quickly switched from 'if I was leaving' to 'when I should leave'."

The following day he spoke with his direct superior, Phil Mabree. Mabree also suggested that Hertach leave the firm. Mabree said that he had spoken with the senior management team and that "too large a gulf, both personal and philosophical, has been created to be bridged." After a bit more discussion, they agreed that Hertach's last day would be in two weeks.

During his remaining two weeks at GLC, Hertach told friends and clients that he was leaving primarily because he did not agree with the revaluation of the ownership units. Only to some close friends did he mention that another factor was his disagreement with some of the firm's billing practices. During his last week, Hertach was summoned to the office of Williamson, who reiterated that he had personally checked Bolton Machine's billing records and found no irregularities. Williamson also told Hertach that questioning the actions of others, not trusting their word, was not, in his experience, the way to run a successful professional services firm. Hertach remained non-committal in his responses, stating that he had simply needed to see the facts.

As he contemplated his final days at GLC, Hertach realized that, although technically he had quit, he had in fact been pushed out, the first time this had ever happened in his career. He reflected:

A part of me wishes I could have been less vocal in my opposition to the revaluation proposal and had not gotten myself involved in the billing controversy. The cost has been enormous—I have lost my job and my mentor and probably damaged my career. Another part of me feels mad at having lost both the revaluation and billing controversy battles and frustrated that those leading GLC appear accountable to no one but themselves. And yet another part of me feels relieved to no longer be a part of a firm like GLC, and proud that I have taken a principled stand.

Immediately after leaving GLC, Hertach and his wife left for a two-week trip to Montana to relax and to visit old family friends. "I need the space and beauty of the region," he said, "to gain some perspective on all that has transpired—to reflect on the lessons I have learned from this experience, and to determine how they will impact my search for a new job and perhaps even a new career."

Case 5.3

INTEGRAL CONSULTING

(P. J. Guinan, Valerie Mulhern, and David Wylie)

Jeff Elton and Eric Mankin, both principals at Integral, Inc., were pleased with the progress since they had introduced Team Room to the consulting firm almost a year before. They were, however, concerned about the new initiative called Knowledge Management[1] (KM).

Mankin questioned whether the momentum was sustainable: "Is it realistic to assume that our people will just populate our corporate knowledge base? It was one thing to enforce Team Room but KM will take a lot more time if it's to be done right. And right now, we can't bill for this service."

Elton was also concerned: "I realize it's a problem but we've got to take a chance with this one. If we're able to reward people for using the system initially, they will eventually become hooked on it just like Team Room. I think the bigger issue is how to determine if it fits with our current product offerings. I feel our clients would like this type of product but where do we get the resources from to do this, what will the systems look like—on the Internet and off—and at what cost?"

As the two pondered different alternatives, Alex Costanzo, a senior associate at the firm and one of the leads on KM reminded them both that the time to make these decisions was yesterday. "Let's face it— we've made a commitment to this thing, let's just do it!"

INTEGRAL, INC.

Integral, Inc. was a rapidly growing management consulting and research firm that specialized in the management of innovation. Head-quartered in Cambridge, Massachusetts, Integral was founded in 1988 by Harvard Business School professors Kim Clark and Steven Wheelwright and by economist Bruce Stangle. Growing at a rate of over 30% per year, by 1997 Integral had over 80 employees and branch offices in California, New York, and Cambridge, England.

Integral maintained close relationships with a network of well-respected academic affiliates at leading business schools. Its consultants helped clients apply the latest best thinking practices to achieve break-through solutions in the areas of product development, manufacturing, operations, and strategic planning.

Clients came from a broad range of industries including health care, electronics, automotive, chemical, utility, construction equipment, computer, pharmaceutical, telecommunications and consumer products. They were based in countries all around the world.

Integral consultants were multidisciplinary, with expertise in a variety of business and technical fields. Senior staff members had advanced degrees from top business schools and possessed an average of nine years of management consulting experience. Newly hired consultants started as associates and, based on skill and experience, rose to become managers and principals. Consultants frequently worked with one to two client engagements at a time, many involving similar issues.

Principals had overall responsibility for each project and for maintaining close client relationships. Case managers coordinated the daily activities of project teams while associates concentrated on the details of each engagement such as fact gathering, analysis, development of recommendations, implementation of solutions, and making client presentations. Project teams were generally comprised of Integral consultants, client representatives, and academic affiliates.

Communications and a smooth flow of information between team members and between different project teams were critical to this collaborative effort. Often geographically dispersed, team members had to be able both to coordinate their activities and to leverage the collective knowledge of the firm.

The current communications system was clearly inadequate. E-mail and voice mail systems had comprised the backbone of the communication system at Integral. The e-mail capabilities (CC Mail[2]), however, had been extremely inflexible. Users could scroll down and see messages but attaching documents and having conversations was difficult. One consultant commented: "It took hours just to read your mail in this format, let alone respond." Team members could not follow the "flow" of e-mail conversations since there was no easy way to create discussions. Similar problems existed with the voice mail system. Individuals would leave messages that were not always forwarded to the right people. Team members were inadvertently excluded from some of the mailing lists. It was difficult to respond to other team members while on the road because information was not always current.

Meanwhile, access to information was uneven. Along with actually saving time on a particular project, consultants wanted to level the playing field to ensure that everyone had equal access to information that could make their work easier and better. As Kevin Hugh, one of the more senior consultants, stated: "It had gotten to the point of tribal sharing. Depending on who your case team members were, some people would get a lot of good information while others wouldn't. A new system was needed to guarantee better and more equal access to everyone."

The partners at Integral prided themselves on maintaining very low overhead, but they had been forced to allow an administrative infrastructure to grow to support the burgeoning ranks of consultants. This option, however, promised to be expensive and unwieldly. The principals at Integral, therefore, decided to invest in a technological infrastructure to make the consulting teams more effective and productive and to weave people together.

The senior partners of the firm had tried to quantify the possible impact of the investment in the technology. As Jeff Elton explained: "In a consulting firm, it's not unusual to track work time in order to project possible new revenue streams. We actually started to track the amount of time it took us and the amount of resources that were required to do certain types of work. We hire new professionals at thirty percent annually. So if we're more productive and have a higher quality of work product, we can charge more, do it faster, make more money." The partners believed that a new system would help in several of these dimensions by enabling communication between teams and promoting the sharing of new ideas. They thought that Integral as a company, each team member, and especially newly hired consultants would just naturally be more productive.

TEAM ROOM

In the Spring of 1996, the principals at Integral decided after considerable research to invest in Team Room. Team Room was an application created by a team of researchers at the Lotus Institute that operated on a Lotus Notes platform. It was designed to provide team members with electronic space in which to manage objectives and commitments, to collaborate with colleagues, and to store work output. Team Room acted as a space for virtual team discussions, facilitated accountability among team members by managing and tracking work flow and performance, and served as a shared repository for all documents (see Exhibits 5.13 and 5.14). Team Room seemed to be the perfect solution for Integral.

The senior partners remained concerned, however, about Lotus' response to the Internet. It was evident that the Web was going to play an increasingly important role in communications and knowledge accessibility. They knew of Lotus' efforts in developing Dominoe, a program that would allow access to Web applications as well as to internal applications using Team Room. While they were unsure how these platforms were going to come together, they had faith in Lotus' commitment to the best possible software and Notes had one thing that no other technology could offer—replication.[3]

As Eric Mankin stated: "Replication is the thing that really has linked us to Notes—it's just a wonderful thing for people to take their offices with them. It allows us to have the most current information at our finger-tips at all times."

Exhibit 5.13 Team Room Elements

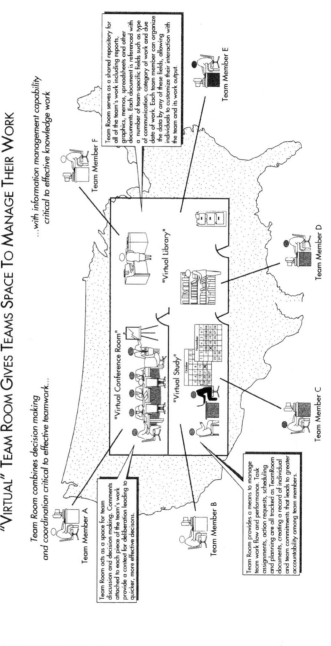

─────── INTRODUCTION ───────

Team Room provides team members with electronic space in which to manage objectives and commitments, to collaborate with colleagues and to store work output.

"VIRTUAL" TEAM ROOM GIVES TEAMS SPACE TO MANAGE THEIR WORK

Team Room combines decision making and coordination critical to effective teamwork...

...with information management capability critical to effective knowledge work

Team Room acts as a space for team discussion and decision making. Comments attached to each piece of the team's work provide a context for deliberation leading to quicker, more effective decisions.

Team Member A

Team Member B

Team Room provides a means to manage team work flow and performance. Task assignments, action requests, scheduling and planning are all tracked as TeamRoom documents, creating a record of individual and team commitments that leads to greater accountability among team members.

"Virtual Conference Room"

"Virtual Study"

"Virtual Library"

Team Member F

Team Room serves as a shared repository for all of the team's work including reports, graphics, spreadsheets and other documents. Each document is referenced with a number of team-specific fields such as type of communication, category of work and due date of work. Each team member can organize the data by any of these fields, allowing individuals to customize their interaction with the team and its work output.

Team Member E

Team Member D

Team Member C

Exhibit 5.14 Lotus Notes

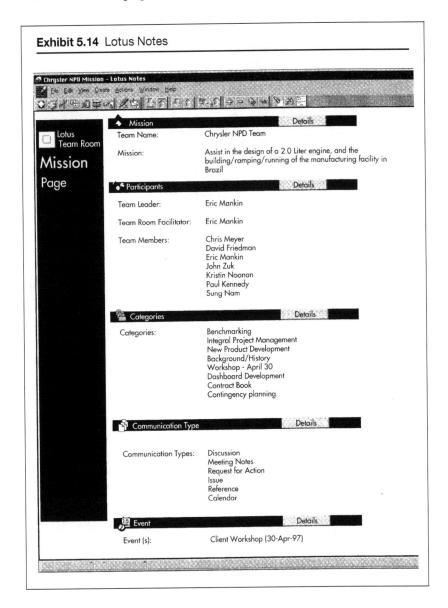

Implementation

Senior management was decisive about the pace and character of the introduction of Team Room to the firm and how it was to be used on projects. Using Team Room simply was made mandatory. Elton described the introduction: "The first thing we did was unplug CC mail and everyone had to use Notes mail. No one had a choice about using

Notes or Team Room. We then launched our first Notes application—expense and professional forecasting."

Along with brute force, Mankin and Elton also became "cheerleaders" for the technology. Mankin noted: "I find that I have to encourage people to use it regularly. I find myself saying: 'you need to use this because I need to see it.'" Such senior management endorsement was critical. Elton reiterated: "Eric and I are users. The reason why people are going to use it is because of our endorsement. This is number one and far and away above anything else. Number two is that there's an intuitive quality to using the tool. It's probably one of the first things around here that actually has a probability of working."

It was clear from discussions around Integral that senior support would carry the initiative forward but there was some concern that "champions" could go only so far in their flag waving and eventually classic reward systems would have to be employed. Integral rewarded consultants on three dimensions in addition to the more traditional metric of billable hours. The first was how effectively they worked with clients and added value to the engagement. The second was based on overall contribution to the firm's knowledge. The third dimension was how well s/he functioned as part of a collective. Since Team Room would help every consultant be more effective on all three levels, using Team Room had a natural linkage with existing reward systems.

The Jacobson Group, a professional consulting firm, was hired to train employees in the tools applications. Richard Weissberg, a principal at Jacobson, commented on Integral's adoption practices: "Integral has a real shot at making Team Room work. They have a vision, a real need for the technology. What they can't forget is that it is not always easy to train people to effectively use Groupware. That's where we come in. Integral has to take the time to train their people—otherwise, it simply won't work."

Results

Given the substantial financial and organizational commitment to adopting Team Room, Integral management had high expectations for its successful implementation and diffusion. Although Integral had no formal ways to evaluate the return on the investment in Team Room, Mankin thought that he would recognize success: "I'll know when it is part of the fabric of the ways things get done. We knew CC-Mail was successful because it was key to how people communicate. It'll be the same thing with Team Room."

Typical of any new technology venture, Team Room had its growing pains. On one international project, for example, a client had manufacturing centers in Sweden and its corporate headquarters in California. Integral's work teams were made up of consultants from offices in California and England. First, there were significant communication problems between the teams. People were unclear about what should go into the Team Room. Consultants in the United Kingdom were not expecting to see so much information about best practices and details about the engagement in the Team Room. They were reluctant to post such detailed or confidential information there, feeling more comfortable communicating about such matters in person. Second, this particular team had little training in the protocols of using the technology. How to find, categorize, and communicate in Team Room was not clear to novices. Finally, there was poor communication between teams. For example, there were times when consultants in the United States would meet to discuss an issue and neglect to post the discussion to the Team Room for their British counterparts.

Those who used the system did not always think that it was worthwhile spending extra time to put information into the system. One consultant commented: "Right now in the work that we do, you've got a Team Room that closes down with a deliverable that's sitting there. That final draft never gets out to the larger knowledge bank. The chance of anybody wanting that particular presentation is small. . . . If there's no incentive for me to post it, I'm not going to. You can tell me it's a great thing to do and you can tell me the culture supports this, but I need an incentive."

Despite possible limitations, Team Room proved to be especially helpful to new hires. As Integral grew exponentially, there was very little time to bring a new person up to speed. In a culture where time was critical, Integral was extremely hopeful about this capability. Instead of spending hours, days, or weeks with junior people explaining the "ropes," the novices were sent to active Team Rooms first to "muck around" in the information before joining a real team. The point was that employees could re-experience in hours what otherwise may have taken days or weeks. If the information in the Team Room was good, the new consultant could benefit from the collective experience of the entire group of individuals working on the project. In this way, s/he could hit the ground running on an otherwise unfamiliar project. Mankin stated: "The junior person can see the blind alleys that people entered; they can see the presentations and get a feel for the work that we do. From my perspective, that is an incredible advantage. I want to emphasize that they don't have a choice. The new hires must use the Team Room.

Elton also pointed out that practically: "When you are growing at 30% per year and you've got a hundred, two hundred new people, I can't talk to them individually. I don't even know who all of them are. How do you make sure that all these people get access to the same quality and state of knowledge that's out there?"

One of the new consultants stated: "In some ways, I feel as if I'm being mentored through the process. For example, I recently joined a team that had been formed the previous year and Team Room provided a lot of relevant information. There were, however, some problems. One of the features in Team Room is that it will archive anything after a certain period of non-use. The archiving system does not have the threading[4] capability so I have a difficult time sifting through the information. A number of people comment that without threading, the discussion databases are of much less value. There were questions around training in the use of the tool and the general difficulties with finding the "right" information as opposed to wading through lots of unstructured data." Although Team Room had certainly met with success at Integral, there was a resounding feeling that a good deal of valuable information was lost in the Lotus database black hole. This was particularly evident after a project ended and the related information was archived and became more difficult to find.

At about this same time, consultants all over the country were talking about the new management buzz word: Knowledge Management. The principals at Integral realized that their adoption of Team Room had created a springboard for introducing KM to Integral. This could become one of the most exciting initiatives in years. As Notes had been the platform for Team Room, so would Team Room become the foundation for a KM system.

KNOWLEDGE MANAGEMENT

KM was designed to capture information about the best practices from each engagement to form a body of knowledge from which each consultant could draw the best of the best rather than have to wade through the detailed threads of each part of the Team Room. The key was to create a system to pull the "nuggets" out of the data and for assigning responsibility for defining nuggets, insuring that they were captured in the system, and managing their use.

Strategy

The KM initiative began with a small group of senior consultants headed by Elton in the summer of 1996. He envisioned a "knowledge database" which would be a repository that held "the vessel of our knowledge." His original view of KM ultimately evolved into a company strategy.

With all of the surrounding excitement about KM in the consulting industry, Integral managers thought that KM could both add to the efficiency of the consulting practice and be adopted as an additional product offering. Integral had experience in innovation management and understood some of the major goals and limitations of knowledge transfer. Hugh made a point of explaining the relationship between KM and Integral's core competency of consulting on innovation management issues: "Innovation management is just an application of KM. We see it as a natural dovetail to innovation products that we sell to their clients. One of our directives is to match the strategic opportunities of the company with their capabilities. Questions that need to be answered by the client are what are you good at? What do you want to be good at in the future? What are the opportunities in the market with respect to what you are good at and what you want to be good at? Setting such standards of performance is what, in KM terms, we call "establishing the bar." The goal of Integral is to help its clients surpass that bar."

Alex Constanzo, senior managing consultant and a leader in the KM initiative, articulated Integral's pragmatic approach: "We essentially have three pieces to our approach. First, defining the bar—or the best practice for Integral's key products that we service. Second, the steps that need to be taken to bring everyone up to the bar—to the level of performance where everyone is implementing best practice approaches. And third, there's an innovation piece—or those value-added creative deliverables which are not predetermined at the beginning of an engagement but which hopefully occur as a team develops certain innovative synergies with the client."

Not surprisingly, developing the technology to enable KM was a difficult process. Consultant Kishore Dhupati described the challenge: "It is not a database. It is not a chat room. It is not an idea exchange in the same vein as a faculty smoke room. It's all of those and a lot more. It is a group of databases which have to systematize knowledge-sharing throughout the company." Making these lofty ambitions a reality remained a challenge, similar to implementing any new change that required both process and technology engineering. The management team knew this. After all, they were "innovation experts" and knew first-hand how difficult it was to effect change of any sort in an established organization. A number of individuals had pondered some of these problems and had identified three major issues: reward, culture, and technology.

Reward

At Integral, the consultant reward system was based on both case-project success (noted above) as well as individual contribution. As in most consulting firms, however, the impact on billable hours was the ultimate measure of success. Nancy Confrey, senior IT consultant, explained: "You don't want to do anything that could get in the way of billable time. Anything that you put into this effort is regarded as overhead. People get yanked off this project (working on KM). . . . If we can make KM somehow billable to the client, that's terrific and everyone will be doing it."

The "rub" for KM was how to motivate employees to contribute to the knowledge bank when the client could not yet be billed for these types of activities. So one of the questions that had to be addressed was what incentives were needed to motivate contributions to the knowledge bank. Whatever the solution, it would have to overcome the prevailing opinion: "If I'm rewarded based on new knowledge that I create, why should I use someone else's knowledge?"

Culture

The culture at Integral promoted sharing knowledge between case teams. Hugh noted: "Knowledge is valuable for consulting. In consulting by definition, what we sell is knowledge." And yet there was a real concern that teams might not want to endorse whole-heartedly an approach which suggested that standardization be practiced whenever possible. People might begin to question their own value-added to a case team. Costanzo commented: "There may be a number of different forces here working against this approach, not the least of which is 'Not Invented Here.' "

Confrey reiterated the problem: "People definitely need to be able to feel that they personally are adding value. In a culture like ours, that's very important. You need to show that you solved the problem your own way as though no one has ever done it before." Indeed, many of the consultants were hesitant to admit that much of their work could be reduced to standardized methods. Confrey was, however, reasonably pragmatic when she said that: "As both dollar value and innovativeness in the open market as well as the internal market decreases, then that's when you find that people are less possessive. It's not the hottest idea anymore and people are more likely to standardize these initiatives."

On the other hand, too much reliance on standardized and dependable solutions could discourage innovation and creativity. It meant walking a fine line between knowing when to be creative and innovative and when to use standard approaches.

Elton highlighted another problem: "To get knowledge into the knowledge base requires you to sit back, think about what you really learned, put it in there in a cogent way and attach the right things to it. At the same time, thinking takes time away from billable hours, too." (Exhibit 5.15.)

A number of initiatives were under way at Integral to address these problems. The most interesting by far was the notion of developing a "virtual idea trading zone." The notion was to develop a "knowledge currency" where individuals would be rewarded for the value of the contributions made to the knowledge base. In this type of market, an individual would be rewarded for creating and sharing knowledge and discouraged from keeping information a secret from colleagues. This "currency" would foster concurrently an atmosphere of both competiton and cooperation. Efforts to implement this plan were underway. No one really knew how the exchange would work or if indeed it would work at all.

Technology

A number of issues had to do with balancing human requirements with the technical capabilities of the system. Computer-based systems should, for example, formalize knowledge-gathering rather than allow the process to remain as "tribal hunting." Technology should enable everyone to hunt more effectively and to get a kill every time.

Although creating and managing such automated processes were difficult, a number of consulting firms were using them, including KPMG, Arthur Andersen, and Ernst and Young. They had all made substantial investments in such systems so that Integral was not alone in its efforts to computerize what was usually considered to be an extremely unstructured problem. Technology firms such as Lotus were racing to create systems to fill this important niche. Integral was not,

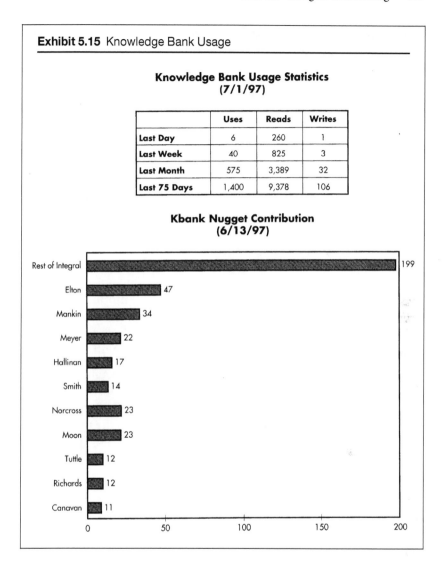

Exhibit 5.15 Knowledge Bank Usage

Knowledge Bank Usage Statistics
(7/1/97)

	Uses	Reads	Writes
Last Day	6	260	1
Last Week	40	825	3
Last Month	575	3,389	32
Last 75 Days	1,400	9,378	106

Kbank Nugget Contribution
(6/13/97)

Rest of Integral	199
Elton	47
Mankin	34
Meyer	22
Hallinan	17
Smith	14
Norcross	23
Moon	23
Tuttle	12
Richards	12
Canavan	11

however, interested in buying off the shelf software for KM. Instead, it created its own system based on Team Room applications and within the Lotus Notes infrastructure. Because of this, Lotus was very interested in seeing the final product to determine if other companies might be interested in using Team Room and Notes in a similar fashion.

Due to the technical nature of creating a homegrown product, limitations of the piloted KM system were becoming clear. Confrey visualized the problems to be in two major areas. The first was quality of information. At this time, there were different perspectives about what types of knowledge should be included and what should not.

Hugh had considered this problem and suggested that a new role of a "knowledge czar" might evolve at Integral: "We've got an inherent problem with how best to filter and transfer information from the Team Rooms into the knowledge bank. Each case team could make the decision what to post in the knowledge bank. From that point, the knowledge czar would acknowledge the value of the contribution with a "little smiley face."

Second, there was an issue over quality control once the information got into the database. "What happens is that people just put in what they have and that doesn't require a lot of extra work. There really needs to be more filtering, some more structure around what goes in there, some more instruction about the purpose of the material and the appropriateness to a particular type of client." Interestingly enough, Confry pointed out that the knowledge that goes into the knowledge bank must have a marketing quality. Realistically, since people have different concepts of what it takes to arouse their interests, tailoring a system to meet everyone's needs might prove to be daunting.

The most critical problem seemed to rest with the absence of an overarching framework, a front interface to the knowledge bank as it existed. Developing a common understanding of that framework and how everyone should use it would take time. Even the most sophisticated search engines couldn't capture what's in an industry specific PowerPoint presentation that had simply been dropped into the knowledge bank.

Steps were being taken to create one such framework (Exhibit 5.16). It was a graphical depiction of the different segments of Integral's work. This search engine could locate better "nuggets" with subtle industry specific nuances because it offered a filter on the knowledge. Senior management had not yet approved this approach but various factions within the organization were supportive of this structure. As Confrey stated: "Right now, they are really unable to develop tools on the Internet of the same quality as we have in the client/server world. So all of the tools that they're trying to bring to the Internet world are not truly cross-platform. There's still a long way to go on this. Where information is stored should be transparent to those doing the actual work"

Exhibit 5.16 Knowledge Framework

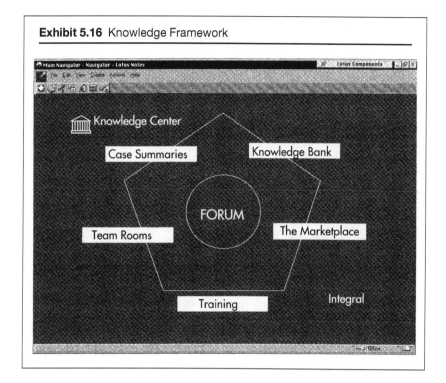

An Opportunity to Redefine the Role of Consulting

As the group at Integral pondered the possible ramifications of throwing themselves into the KM revolution, it became clear that it could transform the entire consulting practice. First, internal processes could drastically improve. As Elton recalled, "It should take a lot less time to do basic, routine tasks and we should be able to measure the difference." In senior managers' minds, it took a specific amount of time for a junior associate to create what they call a "resource analysis." If the associate could structure the activity of data gathering and compilation in a way that the same types of questions were standardized, then performance gains could be measured by calculating the billing rate of the associate. If the standardized material could be made available quickly to the consultant then s/he could spend more time developing the truly unique and innovative aspects of deliverables.

Integral's role with client offerings could also change because of KM and Team Room. Specifically, there were examples of active Team Rooms where the client could see and enter material into the Team Room along with Integral consultants. Alpha Company was a large organization who ensured fair housing to moderate and middle income consumers. It had been working with Integral for some time on how to manage innovation and to improve product development. Steve Morgan was the lead manager from Alpha and had been invited into the Team Room by Costanzo. As Steve commented: "We're using the Team Room to capture all of our documents about this project. It's an interesting way to manage the project. I liked the idea of being able to get my hand on any document that I wanted at any time. I don't think the full potential has been realized yet because Notes is not well understood here. We have an excellent relationship with Integral. We have put a lot of trust in them." Team Room was thus another vehicle around which Integral could build trust with its clients.

There was some concern, however, that bringing clients into the knowledge transfer business might cause more significant problems. Developing a complete guide to "knowledge transfer" might cannibalize future efforts with clients who learned to do some of the work which Integral previously had done for them. To paraphrase one of the consultants: "It's like going to the doctor. If you do your job too well and no one gets sick—no one ever returns."

It was clear that since effectively using a KM system necessitated adopting new habits, the connection between the reward structure at Integral and how consultants were measured would need to be reexamined. To this point, however, there was no consensus. As one of the principals suggested: "We have no accurate way of tracking and enforcing accuracy in the knowledge base." Elton described an example from a recent trip from California. He looked in the knowledge bank for one senior consultant and two managers who had created a specific solution that he knew. "When I pulled it up in the knowledge base, it had just one name on it, with no attribution to the others." Elton observed that it may in fact have been just an oversight but he admitted that he did not like the way it made him feel about the entire process. "We're almost setting this up. It's kind of like a social issue now about who has access to the technology and who doesn't. It's almost like this tyranny of knowledge origination. We are creating a class society of folks who have and haven't contributed to the intellectual capital of the firm."

Emerging Challenges

With Team Room behind them and KM just ahead, Elton, Mankin, and Costanzo knew that they needed to move quickly but not how or where? A number of unanswered questions needed to be resolved. For example, where should they spend their time—on developing in-house capabilities or software capabilities for their clients? If this was a new product offering, how much effort should go into it? After all, they had seen reengineering come and go—what if KM is just a fad as well? Should they shrink-wrap their own system to sell to other consulting firms or was it too sensitive to share? And what about the reward system? It was fine to say that people would be rewarded for using the Knowledge Base but what would really make this happen? Who could evaluate the quality of the "nuggets" adequately and fairly? These were but a few of the challenges that lay ahead for Costanzo as she attempted to implement a pilot version of the KM system. Costanzo was up to the challenge, however, as she reiterated the Nike motto: **"Let's just do it!"**

NOTES TO CASE

1. Knowledge Management is an initiative that promotes an integrated approach to identifying, capturing, retrieving, sharing and evaluating business information assets. These include: databases, documents, policies, procedures as well as the uncaptured, tacit expertise and experience resident in individual workers. (The Gartner Group)
2. CC Mail was an electronic mail system.
3. Replication was the process of updating the data in its most current form so that an end-user had access to the best possible information.
4. Threading was the concept incorporated into Team Room that allowed users to follow the progress, or "thread," of each discussion group.

Part 6

The Future of Consulting

Introduction

Case 6.1a

Agency.com (A): Launching an Interactive Service Agency
(Scot Landry, Ashish Nanda, and Thomas DeLong)

Case 6.1b

Agency.com (B): Managing Rapid Growth
(Scot Landry, Thomas DeLong and Ashish Nanda)

INTRODUCTION

Given our tendency to become preoccupied with current events, we often fail to consider and anticipate the future. In fact, many "today-oriented" executives shun futuristic thinking because they do not trust it. Clearly, the future rarely occurs as we predict; the world is moving faster with greater uncertainty than we can understand or control. Nevertheless, because of major changes now occurring in the industry, we think it useful to consider current trends and some possible scenarios for the future.

Our own view is that management consulting is facing a promising though highly challenging and uncertain future. Only those firms that respond quickly to new opportunities, accompanied by sound management, are likely to thrive. Competition for clients will be fierce, and sophisticated clients will be even more demanding. Alliances between consulting firms will probably accelerate, as will mergers and acquisitions, to build new service offerings and attain greater global scope. The Internet and information technology will increasingly cause a profound effect on the development of new consulting services, especially with regard to outsourcing and Web-based retailing.

The *Agency.com (A)* case describes a startup firm growing from its initial Web design and marketing capabilities to become a multiservice consulting firm. Here we read not only about the excitement of fast growth, but also about the difficulties of *Agency.com*'s managers in keeping pace with change. This case can also be used to launch a broader discussion about the uses of the Internet and online consulting, which are clearly huge opportunities in the future for consulting firms. Ironically, just about anyone, even nonconsultants, can now hang out a shingle in the Internet consulting business.

The future of consulting is obviously hard to predict, suggesting more questions than answers. What will the industry look like in 5 and 10 years? Will the scope and scale of the industry continue to evolve with new services? Will the consolidation of firms in the industry continue? Will information technology maintain its dominant position? Will consulting still be an attractive industry for new graduates and for experienced people who want to enter consulting? What type of ownership structures will be prevalent? These and other questions can be raised and discussed not only with respect to the *Agency.com* case but also extended back to the other cases in this book.

A final issue concerns the need for further research on management consulting. It is interesting that so much consulting is sold and purchased when so little is actually known as "fact" about effects of consulting on client performance. Too much is taken on faith by clients. We need to know much more about not only the results accruing from consulting, but also about the conditions surrounding successful and unsuccessful interventions. Further research is also needed to investigate how consulting firms are managed for better or worse, and to determine best practices. The future promises that these questions will be increasingly asked by demanding clients, as well as by scholars, critics, and the leaders of consulting firms.

Case 6.1a

AGENCY.COM (A): LAUNCHING AN INTERACTIVE SERVICE AGENCY

(Scot Landry, Ashish Nanda, and Thomas DeLong)

Chan Suh checked his watch and saw that it was two a.m. Suh and Kyle Shannon, co-founders of Agency.com, were working together into the early hours of that June morning in 1995 to prepare a response to a request-for-proposal (RFP) for General Electric. Suh was surprised not so much by the hour of the morning—late hours were very much a part of Agency.com's "spirit of getting things done"—as by the speed at which the past several hours had flown by. Other than his watch, he had no measure of the passage of time, as Agency.com's headquarters was a windowless inner office above the loading dock at *Time's* midtown Manhattan headquarters.

Although tired, Suh and Shannon were exultant about Agency.com's early success; they had won four of their five pitches in May, their third month of operations. "Because of our success in May," remarked Suh:

> we were confident in our chances and excited about the opportunity of winning the GE account. GE would be the biggest account ever in the industry—most previous jobs had budgets around $100 thousand. The GE contract was worth about $4 million. Winning an account that size definitely would solidify our positioning as a leading player in the industry.

As they prepared to finalize the GE RFP before the 8 a.m. submission deadline, Suh, focusing on the one question they still needed to address, called across the room: "Kyle, GE has a question on what we think the future of the Internet is. Can you whip up a little something?" Shannon surprised Suh with his response:

> I'm not sure if I want to do that, Chan. I'm tapped out and it's two a.m. in the morning. If we win this account we'll likely have years more of these two a.m. nights. I'm starting to be more concerned that we'll win this account versus lose it. Are we ready to win this account now? Chan, are you sure that we want to submit this RFP?

THE FOUNDERS

Kyle Shannon: From Yo-yos to Urban Desires

Upon graduating from Penn State in 1987, Kyle Shannon went directly to New York to become a professional actor and screenwriter. (Exhibit 6.1 provides biographical information on the key protagonists.) "I found it necessary to work at odd jobs," he recalled,

> such as selling yo-yos at FAO Schwartz and bartending to make ends meet. In 1990, sick of bartending, I switched to desktop publishing. I liked the work much more because it engaged both sides of my brain, allowing me to use both logical and creative skills. After freelancing for two years, I realized that I probably worked much harder and many more hours as a freelancer, because I also had to drum up work, than I would in a full-time position. So, in 1992, I took a full-time job doing desktop publishing at an advertising agency.

Exhibit 6.1 Background of Key Agency.com Personnel

Chan Suh
- Co-founder of Agency.com, February 1995.
- Marketing director of *Vibe* in 1994. Helped launch Time's Pathfinder site and was eventually charged with bringing *Vibe* online.
- Led marketing efforts for various magazines including *Details, Life,* and *Vibe*.
- Nine years in marketing positions at Conde Nast and NewsCorp.
- Studied creative writing at Sarah Lawrence College in New York.

Kyle Shannon
- Co-founder of Agency.com, February 1995.
- Created *Urban Desires* (first Web culture e-magazine) in 1994 (www.desires.com).
- Founder and president of World Wide Web Artists Consortium, 1994–1998 (www.wwwac.org).
- Director, image processing, YAR Communications, 1993–1995.
- Co-founder, artistic director, New Voice Theater Company, 1991–1998.
- Professional actor and screenwriter, 1987–1994.
- BFA in acting, Penn State, 1987.

Ken Trush
- Founded and operated independent accounting practice specializing in growing enterpreneurial companies, 1984–1997. Contributor to first Agency.com business plan.
- Ernst & Young, 1981–1984.
- Goldstein, Golub, and Kessler, 1980.
- Eugene V. Rose & Co., 1978–1979.
- Certified Public Accountant, 1981.
- BBA in accounting from Baruch College, 1978.

About a year later, I started to get interested in interactive stuff and I recommended to my boss that the company explore interactivity. When he responded "show me the bottom line" I got fed up and left. Actors are always looking for an excuse to quit our day jobs! I took another job as a manager at YAR Communications in early 1994. At this point, new media was starting to catch on. Later that year, while I was giving an impassioned speech to all the account executives, saying that "we *must* get on the Internet," my boss interrupted and asked me to "show him the bottom line." Frustrated, I quit two weeks later.

While at YAR Communications, Shannon received a flyer promoting a friend's band concert. He started investigating the possibility of saving the printing and distribution charges by posting the flyer on the Internet. Shannon considered starting an agency to represent and promote unsigned bands on the Internet. Working with a friend, he calculated that he would need about 150 bands to break even. Considering this a difficult proposition, he asked his friend to run an analysis to determine whether he could transform the idea into a webzine (an online magazine). Because of the potential for advertising revenue, the idea seemed as if it could be profitable. In November 1994, Shannon launched *Urban Desires*, a webzine devoted to promoting events and discussing artists' issues. A month later, he learned that the Parisian newspaper *Libération*, after accessing the site, had raved about *Urban Desires* in a full-page article. Recalled Shannon:

> At that moment I experienced an epiphany and realized how powerful the Internet was. The effort and time involved in creating websites was similar to staging artistic productions, but the impact was far larger. I couldn't believe that I could program HTML in my living room in Brooklyn, put it on a server in Los Angeles, and then have people access the site in Paris!

Chan Suh: Recognizing the Internet as a Great Equalizer
Chan Suh was born in Korea and spent much of his childhood in Paris. He arrived in New York City in 1980 to study creative writing at Sarah Lawrence College with the goal of becoming a fiction writer. "After graduating from Sarah Lawrence in 1984," Suh recalled,

> I spent a few years finding myself. I worked for a year as a bouncer and night manager at the Reggae Lounge in New York. Then I spent a year fishing for shrimp and crabs in Georgia. After that, I came back to New York and worked as an accounting assistant for a year. At the end of that job, in 1988, I still had a strong desire to enter publishing. To get my foot in the door at a publishing house, I decided to temp at *New York Magazine*. My task was to enter addresses into a database. When I realized that the magazine had at least five months worth of names, I suggested to them that it would be cheaper to hire me full-time for a year than to pay the temp agency for five months. They agreed and I was hired into the marketing department.
>
> I was dirt poor at the time. On my second day as an employee I had only $5 in my pocket, which I spent on a pint of ice cream. Desperate to get out of this financial hole, I worked incredibly hard. I found a great boss to work for and became a general gofer

for him. Most of the other folks in the department disliked him because he was moody at times, but I loved working for him because he was fair, completely transparent, and always let people know where they stood with him.

After about three years in the marketing department I was promoted to manager. My time there was short, though, as after my boss was fired in 1991, the new director cleaned house and let me go. I took a job as a manager of the startup magazine *Details*. Because it was not well funded I remained there only a short time and then moved on to Time Inc. to work on *Life* magazine. At this point I started to settle into thinking that my career would be in publishing though I hoped to do some writing eventually.

After a year at *Life*, Suh was promoted to marketing director of *Vibe*, a music magazine with a hip-hop and R&B urban youth focus. Suh thought one way to steal readers from competitors *Rolling Stone* and *Spin* would be to launch an online version of *Vibe*. Suh recalled:

I looked at who was on the Web and it was all colleges and college students. They took it up really quickly, as soon as Mosaic, the first graphical browser, came out; first the tech people, but then everyone else. I thought: "This is the perfect market for *Vibe*— young, urban—the kinds of people we want to take away from *Rolling Stone*."

However, nobody could tell me how to get on the Web so I had to learn the technology myself. I found that among the best sources of information were online bulletin boards that had dedicated areas to discuss the Web. As soon as I understood how to communicate online, I immediately fell in love with the medium. It was a forum to exchange ideas without their being colored by perceptions of race, gender, or appearance. The Internet had the potential to transcend the way people treated each other and overcome biases. It could serve as a great societal equalizer.

One of the first graphical publishing sites, the *Vibe* site generated substantial traffic. Recalled Suh: "Thousands of people visited the site, which back then meant it was hugely successful, and we got a ton of subscriptions out of it. Fortunately, it was also profitable from day one because I got advertisers to sponsor sections." Suh was soon working 16 hours per day—8 hours at his marketing director's job and another 8 hours on his Web projects. But he was thrilled: "I felt like a master of the universe, because I could change what was on the Web."

A Meeting of Minds

Shannon and Suh met through *Echo*, an online discussion group both had joined to learn more about the Web. Suh became a key source of answers to Shannon's questions regarding the launch of *Urban Desires*. Meeting to discuss a particularly difficult query from Shannon, the two found that they shared many similar passions. One of these was the video game *Myst*, which they found "compelling," according to Shannon, because

> it worked well within its constraints. At that time most other games were incredibly slow because their flashy graphics didn't work within the constraints of the technology. Upon reflection, Chan and I agreed that most Web designers similarly functioned without taking into account the Web's constraints. The consequence was many websites that functioned poorly or were too slow.

In October 1994, Shannon—"for selfish reasons, so that I could surround myself with people who knew more than I did about the Web"—founded a focused discussion group for Internet issues, the World Wide Web Artists Consortium (WWWAC). Network members, including Suh, began to work together on freelance projects. Shannon loved the work so much that he quit his job at YAR and began working full-time on the Internet. "Kyle is an anarchist at heart," Suh remarked. "He said, 'To hell with my day job, we can go start something.'"

In December 1994, Shannon prodded Suh to join him in "starting a company doing Internet stuff." Suh and Shannon joined a few friends at a planning meeting over beer at TGI Fridays to discuss starting a company to produce Web content. "If we don't suck," argued Shannon, "then we'll be leaps and bounds ahead of everyone else." But Suh wanted to ensure that their ideas went beyond "just doing Internet stuff" and real clients were attracted to their business concept before he would consider leaving Time. Recalled Suh:

> Everyone wanted to do content because they all came from artistic backgrounds. At one point I said, "Nobody's going to pay us for content. I know because I'm working on *Pathfinder*, Time's Internet project. So, either we're going to build content as a hobby, or we're going to do something else." The one thing we all knew was that the Internet was going to be big, I mean *huge*; this was going to take over everything . . . and the consultants and the advertising agencies and the IBMs of the world didn't know anything about it. So we decided that we would be a group of people who could help companies do stuff on the Internet. Then we

could use some of the proceeds to fund our creative interests, like Kyle's *Urban Desires.*

THE BIRTH OF AGENCY.COM

The Sports Illustrated *Swimsuit Site*

Suh's wait for breakthrough clients was short. In January 1995, two Time divisions familiar with his success with *VibeOnline* and his involvement in Time's development of its *Pathfinder* website, sought Suh's help with Internet related projects. The consumer marketing division wanted to study how it might increase subscriptions via the Internet, while *Sports Illustrated* (SI) sought to develop a website to promote its pay-per-view broadcast of the *Sports Illustrated Swimsuit Video* in mid-February. Suh negotiated a $20,000 fee from Time, half to be paid up-front and hired Shannon to help with these projects. "The number was very much of a guess," recalled Suh. "I had no real idea how much this work would cost and I just suggested $20,000 when they asked me for a price. With no delay or negotiation, they accepted it! Kyle and I thought that the profit from these gigs might be more than our combined savings from all of our years working!"

Shannon quickly set up three ethernet-connected computers in his Brooklyn living room, an arrangement affectionately referred to as their LRAN (living room area network). "My wife helped us out with the meals," he recalled, "and our dog helped keep us down to earth by continually tripping over our ethernet cables." Shannon began working full-time on the project; Suh joined him after his full days of work on *Vibe.* "We worked until about 4 a.m. each morning," Shannon described the experience, "particularly after the *Sports Illustrated* folks gave us a video on the first of February and told us to do whatever we thought would look good. With only two weeks before site launch, it was a big challenge to turn the video into pictures and then build the site."

As a result of viral marketing—intense word-of-mouth marketing that spread quickly, like a virus, with those exposed to the site "infecting" friends with information about it—the *Sports Illustrated* site became so popular that it crashed two servers within its first 12 hours of operation. Swimsuit models drew traffic, but the site's pinwheel design and extensive use of QuickTime video clips impressed prospective clients. The buzz created by the site and the news of the crashed servers generated tremendous publicity for the pay-per-view broadcast and for Suh and Shannon.

Incorporation

While working on the *Sports Illustrated* site, Suh and Shannon engaged certified public accountant Ken Trush, with whom Shannon had worked at YAR Communications, to begin the process of incorporation. "To get paid for our work at Time, we needed to set up processes for invoices, obtain permits, and name our company," recalled Suh.

> Ken told us to set up two checking accounts, one for payroll and one for general expenses. So we went to the bank in the bottom of the Time building. They said that there was no minimum balance for the accounts so I looked into my wallet, found $80, and put $40 into each account. Our company was founded with $80!
>
> We also needed a name for the company. Our first choice was "The Agency." I liked it because in publishing we worked with many different agencies that had a variety of talented people to help out businesses. Kyle liked the name because it would imply that we were a "Central Intelligence Agency type of operation that would send in agents to fix corporate problems." Unfortunately, though, a Boston company had already registered the domain name theagency.com. But, in the process of discovering that, we found that the domain name Agency.com was available. When I heard it, I liked it immediately because it was exactly what we did; we were an agency that helped companies get on the Internet. Our domain name became our company name. Kyle suggested that we make the name all capital letters to stand out in press releases and news articles.
>
> We were one of the first dot.com companies ever, because when we tried to register the company name with the state of New York, they didn't know what to do with the period in the middle! After the paperwork cleared, I quit my position at Time.

THE FIRST THREE MONTHS

Capitalizing on Initial Success

Thrilled with the results of the *Sports Illustrated* site, Time executives approached Suh about researching issues and developing websites for other Time properties. Shannon recalled Suh's response.

> Chan insisted that to make this work for us Time would need to swap office space in exchange for our work and he demanded that Time provide space in their building and lease us computers by

the following Monday [it was a Thursday]. When Time's director of consumer marketing, Marjorie Rich, replied that it would take longer than a few days to make that happen, Chan pounded his fist on the wall, angrily asked her, "Then where do you want us to work, on benches in Central Park?" and bolted out of the room. But Marjorie chased him down and promised us that she "would make it happen somehow."

By the middle of the next week, Time came through with ten computers and a space above the loading dock that formerly was Time's travel office. Although the space was dark and cavernous, we were psyched to be on the Avenue of the Americas, an address that we knew would help business.

After witnessing these negotiations, Shannon came to appreciate "Chan's awesome business instinct, particularly his guts to lay the company on the line in order to exert pressure. Chan was able to look people in the eyes and not break down. In the big leagues, people sense weakness. Chan's display of confidence led companies to have confidence in us." "Agency.com was able to avoid bank or private financing," noted Trush, "because they did not have to buy expensive computers or pay high monthly rent and a hefty rent deposit."

Building Momentum

Agency.com was hired as a subcontractor in March 1995 to build parts of the Zima and Mastercard websites. Impressed with its work, the firm to which it had subcontracted recommended Agency.com when MetLife sought help with a small budget project. "The MetLife account," recalled Suh,

allowed us to establish a foothold in the *Fortune* 500 by giving us credibility with other *Fortune* 500 companies. These were the types of companies we wanted to work with. I knew that $50,000 for website development was not a big deal for these large companies and I felt really comfortable working with them, since I myself had worked in a few.

Also, winning business on our own allowed us to say no to more subcontracting work. The firm we initially subcontracted for had asked us to partner with them long term to do subcontracting. But we didn't want to become factory workers for another firm and build up their reputation instead of our own. We knew our work was good, and we vowed that we would never subcontract again if we could build a site as good or better.

Agency.com began aggressively pitching business. Although Shannon felt "like David versus Goliath going in to pitch large companies," Suh did not consider the selling process particularly difficult. "Most sales were aspirational in nature," he recalled. "We just went in, presented slides of our previous work, and listened as clients asked us to 'do that for them, too.'" In April 1995, Agency.com won four of five pitches, adding Hitachi, American Express, GTE, and Columbia House to its client list. "The domino effect really helped us," Shannon recalled. "Once we got in the *Fortune* 500 club it was easy for big companies to trust that we could deliver strong results for them, too."

Shannon and Suh did not concern themselves with competition. "We had enough work to keep us busy seven days per week, 14 hours per day," recalled Suh. "There was plenty of business to go around. Most web-design firms just decided which business they wanted and they were successful at getting it."

By requiring clients to pay half the total fee up front, Agency.com achieved positive cash flow early (see Exhibit 6.2). Moreover, recalled Trush: "Chan, unlike some of his competitors, refused to take on business at a loss to land major accounts. After listening to him, most of Agency.com's potential clients were persuaded by his logic that they wanted us to make money so that we'd still be around to serve them in six months."

Exhibit 6.2 Agency.com 1995 Forecast Income Statement

	$'000	%
Revenue	2,162	100.0
Less: **Direct expenses**		
Labor	789	36.5
Gross Margin	1,373	63.5
Less: **Indirect expenses**		
Labor	86	4.0
Depreciation & amortization	6	0.3
Other operating expenses	413	19.1
Total indirect expenses	**505**	**23.4**
Operating profit	868	40.1
Less: **Other expenses**	0	
Profit before taxes	868	40.1

Although prepaid fees and reinvested profits assured Agency.com a steady cash inflow that facilitated staffing and avoided incurring heavy debt to finance growth, problems continued to crop up. "We were sleeping in the office, on the couch, and that's all we were doing besides working," explained Suh.

> My investment in a co-op was foreclosed because I couldn't afford to pay the mortgage, as all my money went into the company. The day they foreclosed, the marshals were coming to move me out. I packed all my stuff in a van and came to work. I had no place to go. One of our clients, who had a brownstone in Manhattan, lent me her basement so I could live there until I found a place to live. Apparently it didn't undermine her confidence in our company!

Trush, who worked with Suh together on business administration while the rest of the team focused on delivering client work, became a trusted advisor to the founders. Shannon called him "the secret ingredient behind our success in the early days."

A Team of Pioneers

"We learned virtually everything on the fly," recalled Shannon, "not only how to build certain tricks into websites, but even business fundamentals such as scoping out projects, billing, and recruiting. A mantra that was echoed frequently when we tried new things was 'this just might work.' Fortunately for us, it often *did* work." "We were in a survival mode all the time," recalled Suh.

> Yet it was exhilarating because we were doing things nobody else in the world was doing. We probably felt the same way that Steve Jobs and Steve Wozniak did while they launched Apple computer. And, like Apple, the process was fun because people didn't "wear hats" here. We pitched in where we were needed and tried to learn from one another.

Suh and Shannon hired friends, former colleagues, members of WWWAC, and friends of current employees. "There was only a small community of people who knew how to do this stuff, so we brought on everyone we could," explained Suh.

> But people we hired quickly self-selected into our organization or opted out of it. We tended to attract "doers," those with a "can-do" attitude who really sought to make things happen. "Manager-types" tended not to last long because of their frustration with the ambiguity of tasks and roles. A few times, we chose

to let them go. We had to fire a guy in our first month. There were only five of us then, including Kyle and me, and the first thing this guy wanted to do was draw up on org chart. There were only five of us!

Agency.com added 10 employees during its first three months. By the end of May its office above Time's loading dock was becoming crowded and cluttered. The spider web of cables that comprised the company's Intranet, taped helter-skelter to the walls and ceilings of the office, was termed its "tape-net." This makeshift headquarters contributed to Agency.com's "wartime mentality" whereby everyone pitched in and did whatever it took to deliver projects on time.

"The pay was terrible," recalled one of Agency.com's earliest hires, "much less than publishing. Nor was there an IPO hysteria or huge desire for stock ownership. But I didn't come here for the money. I just wanted to do something exciting." Most of the employees were quite young, many having recently graduated from college. One recent graduate recalled that "the Internet was becoming the rage in computer science programs and many of us thought it would turn everything upside down. Its potential was exponential. We knew that we were literally creating an industry." "I felt like a pioneer at Agency.com," remarked another early employee.

I remember the first time I saw an innovation that I developed appear on *somebody else's* website—what a compliment to see your creativity copied elsewhere! I knew that type of experience was enriching my soul, even if it wasn't building my checking account. It made the long hours and the intense time pressure worth it.

Suh pointed out that being located in New York was a major positive for the firm. "New York is the center of talent," he explained,

not only for business and communications, but also for creative folks. If you're a true thespian, you'll be here. If you're a playwright or graphic artist, you want to be here. If you're a financial wizard, you want to be in New York. There are a lot of people like that pursuing those kind of dreams in New York.

Similar personalities and interests supported Agency.com teamwork. "Almost everyone who liked working here," reflected Shannon,

tended to be beer drinkers, not martini lovers. We also were night owls and we all tended to dislike "big talkers": consultants, MBAs, or anyone who wanted to get their hand on the Agency.com joystick, thinking that they could run our firm better than we could. We enjoyed knowing that we controlled our own destiny. That in itself was great fun and an awesome motivator.

One of the internal programs that reflected the spirit that Shannon and Suh infused in Agency.com was "dress-up Fridays." CNN covered this novel concept and the *New York Times* wrote a feature article about it. "Agency.com team worked much longer hours than our Time counterparts," said Suh, describing the origins of the "dress-up Fridays,"

> and we all joked that because of our long hours we were often the ones who tended to stink in the elevator. When Time decided to make a big deal about introducing casual Fridays, we thought it would be funny for us to introduce dress-up Fridays. Then perhaps we could somewhat approach our Time neighbors in dress and looks.

THE GENERAL ELECTRIC DEAL

General Electric, one of the first companies to want to establish an interactive agency of record, asked Agency.com and other companies to reply to its RFP in the first week of June 1995.[1] GE wanted to build 88 interconnected websites in only eight months.[2] The opportunity was very attractive; winning the GE account would go a long way toward establishing Agency.com as an industry leader.

To win the account, Shannon and Suh would first have to complete and submit the RFP within the next six hours, including an answer to the "future of the Internet" question. Although he wondered whether "slicker" companies might be more capable and comfortable answering such a question and servicing the GE account, Shannon was "enthusiastic and confident about our chances of winning." He asked Suh: "If we pitch this business, we'll likely win it. Chan, are we ready to win this account now?" "GE is the biggest contract ever in the industry," reflected Suh, pondering Shannon's question.

> We can increase our revenues tenfold overnight and likely gain the reputation as the biggest player in this space. On the other hand, I wonder whether we really can staff up quickly enough to service both GE and our current clients with the quality of service that they expect. We have only 12 full-time employees now. We still haven't figured out how much work is needed to service the four accounts that we just won. Also, since GE would be at least 90% of our revenues, won't that take away our independence?

The clock was ticking. As Suh wondered whether the concerns expressed by the normally enthusiastic Shannon were simply the result of many nights' sleep deprivation or warranted careful consideration, Shannon asked again: "Chan, are you *sure* we want to submit the RFP?"

NOTES TO CASE

1. An "agency of record" relationship is much like the relationships that most advertising agencies establish with *Fortune* 500 companies, whereby the agency is expected to partner with a client for the long term and develop a deep understanding of the client's business. Agencies of record are normally placed on retainer and expected to not work with competing firms.

2. Katherine Cavanaugh, "The Wizards of Web Site Design," *Newark Star-Ledger*, 13 January, 1997, page 1.

Case 6.1b

AGENCY.COM (B): MANAGING RAPID GROWTH

(Scot Landry, Thomas Delong and Ashish Nanda)

ABOUT THE AUTHOR

Dean's Research Fellow Scot Landry prepared this case under the supervision of Professors Thomas DeLong and Ashish Nanda as the basis for class discussion rather than to illustrate either effective or ineffective handling of an administrative situation.

We chose to not submit the request-for-proposal to General Electric because we believed it was the kind of "win" that could have killed us. We had only twelve full-time people. Although GE would have been a great client, they would have required us to perform tricks before we were ready. We would have become their prisoners because they would have been nearly 100% of our business. The company that won the GE account, Meta4, eventually went out of business and had to sell to a competitor.[1]

Chan Suh, CEO, Agency.com

Agency.com experienced rapid growth despite foregoing a shot at the GE account in June 1995 (see Exhibit 6.3 for revenues, Exhibit 6.4 for a client list). In the four years since the GE decision, Agency.com grew from 12 people to 750 and from a few hundred thousand dollars in revenue to more than $30 million in the first six months of 1999. It had acquired nine companies and established its brand name as one of the strongest in the industry. (Exhibit 6.5 briefly describes the industry's evolution.)

Agency.com faced many new challenges in June 1999. "Our largest challenge going forward," remarked Suh,

will be attracting enough talented leaders to allow us to grow quickly and in a healthy way. Also, we need to finance this growth

---

Exhibit 6.3 Agency.com Income Statements, 1995–1998

	1995		1996		1997		1998[a]	
	$ 000	%	$ 000	%	$ 000	%	$ 000	%
Revenue	2,162	100.0	6,095	100.0	13,114	100.0	65,418	100.0
Less: **Direct cost** (Labor)	789	36.5	2,217	36.4	6,187	47.2	35,955	55.0
Gross Margin	1,373	63.5	3,878	63.6	6,927	52.8	29,463	45.0
Less: **Indirect costs**								
Labor	86	4.0	554	9.1	1,495	11.4	11,231	17.2
Depreciation & Amortization	6	0.3	61	1.0	311	2.4	2,048	3.1
Other operating expenses	413	19.1	372	6.1	2,850	21.7	14,167	22.1
Total indirect costs	505	23.4	987	16.2	4,656	35.5	27,746	42.4
Operating profit	868	40.1	2,891	47.4	2,271	17.3	1,717	2.6
Less: **Other expenses**[b]					(10)	0.0	13,058	19.9
Profit before tax and minority interest	868	40.1	2,891	47.4	2,281	17.4	(11,341)	(17.3)

[a] 1998 results are pro-forma, based on integration of the acquired firms results.
[b] One time charges in 1998 include early lease terminations in New York and San Francisco, employee retention payments, and employee vacation payments.

Exhibit 6.4 Agency.com Clients as of June 1999

Automotive	Financial	Retail
General Motors	ACE	Altec Lansing
Consumer Products	Allstate	American Express
Benetton	Answer Financial	Boots
Colgate	AXA	Kmart
Gucci	Blue Cross/Blue Shield	**Technology**
Johnson & Johnson	Comerica	Adaptec
Heineken	Deutsche Bank	Compaq
Malden Mills	Fidelity	Hewlett-Packard
Nike	Guy Carpenter	Intel
Unilever	Lazard Freres	Motorola
Electronics	Nationwide	Netscape
Hitachi	Met Life	Sun Microsystems
Honeywell	Oppenheimer	Quantum
Nortel	Prudential	Seagate Software
Pioneer	Putnam	Tektronix
Sharp	Salomon SB	
	State Farm	**Telecom**
Entertainment		AT&T
ABC Sports	**Media**	BT
Billboard	CUC	Digex
Disney Europe	Excite	GTE
Ministry of Sound	FT Group	Lucent
Showtime	The Economist	US West
Sony		Sprint
USSB	**Pharmaceuticals**	
	Eli Lilly	**Other**
Energy	Novartis	Armstrong
Pacific Gas & Bell	Pfizer	GTEC
Texaco	SmithKlineBeecham	Pitney Bowes
	Travel	
	British Airways	
	Hyatt	

in a way that we do not put Agency.com at significant risk. Finally, as more talented firms begin to compete against us we need to continue to keep raising our performance to maintain our reputation as a leading global provider of Internet professional services.

RAPID GROWTH FROM 1995 TO 1998

Agency.com grew its revenues and client list organically until mid-1997, when it commenced a string of acquisitions. Revenues more than

Exhibit 6.5 Agency.com's Perspective on Industry Evolution as of September 1999

The Internet is becoming an integral part of many people's lives. Individuals and businesses are increasingly using it to find information, communicate, and conduct business. International Data Corporation (IDC) estimates that the number of Internet users worldwide to grow from an estimated 142 million at the end of 1998 to approximately 500 million by the end of 2003 and worldwide commerce conducted over the Internet to grow from approximately $50 billion in 1998 (of which business to business market accounted for $35 billion and the consumer market $15 billion) to more than $1.3 trillion by the end of 2003.

Increasing acceptance of the Internet has created numerous opportunities for companies that seek to grow and are challenged by highly competitive and rapidly changing markets, geographically dispersed operations and demands for increased efficiencies. Already, companies are taking advantage of the Internet's opportunities to strengthen customer relationships, improve operational efficiency and spur product innovation. Initially, to lower marketing and service costs and increase customer awareness, companies developed "read-only," or brochure-ware, websites. Companies later added to their online resources transaction and commerce capabilities to enable consumers, business partners, suppliers, and employees to transact on a one-to-one basis at any time and from any location. These capabilities have changed the business landscape by introducing new channels, catalyzing competition and prompting new customer needs.

Companies that realize that the Internet is no longer an adjunct to their operations have begun to redefine all aspects of their businesses, including the way they interact with customers. These companies have found that merely enabling online transactions and commerce does not ensure a successful Internet business. Consumers have begun to want more than the mechanical ability to transact with companies online; they want partners. They want to interact with companies that not only market to them but are also responsive to their needs. Interactive Internet-based relationships uniquely meet customers' demands for customized, real-time information, products, and services. Satisfying these demands can foster customer loyalty, increase margins, and enable new markets.

To develop successful Internet businesses that promote interactive relationships requires a special set of capabilities. Businesses need to (1) understand customers' needs and how to fulfill them, and (2) possess integrated strategy, creative, and technology services. Few companies possess this multi-disciplinary expertise; it tends to be spread across disparate information technology, marketing, and planning groups. Moreover, many companies lack the management and technical infrastructure required to develop and support Internet-based solutions.

> Therefore, companies seeking to do business on the Internet are increasingly engaging Internet professional services firms. We believe that companies are best served by firms that have overcome the cultural and operational challenges of integrating strategy, creative, and technology services into a single offering and have developed a proven delivery methodology centered on customer needs.
>
> ---
>
> Source: Agency.com.

doubled each year, from $2.1 million in 1995 to $6.1 million, $13.1 million, and $65.4 million in 1996, 1997, and 1998, respectively.

Still a "Small Company" through 1996

Agency.com's staff size steadily expanded, reaching 60 professionals by the end of 1996. It had become the company of choice for many young creative artists and web programmers. "I came here," remarked one account executive, "because together we have a chance here to build something, to create a new industry, to be a pioneer like Henry Ford." Added a graphic designer: "It's a rush working here, despite the quick pace, because I get to work on so many cool projects over the course of a year." A programmer remarked that working at Agency.com presented a chance "to work in a glamour industry and create things that I can show all my friends." A project manager averred that he came to Agency.com "because of its culture and down-to-earth people. I had job offers for two-to-three times more money," he explained, "but I came to Agency.com because I can be eccentric here. Chan and Kyle are not your typical executives and they truly have an appreciation for diversity. They let us be ourselves."

The close working culture spawned unorthodox initiatives. During lunchtime "Geek-and-Tells" employees would share tricks and tools they had recently learned. Shannon formalized the program later that year with the launch of *Inspire-U,* a peer taught "university" within Agency.com that afforded employees the opportunity to learn business and personal skills at the firm's expense. Courses ranged from running meetings, to cooking, to musical instruction. (Exhibit 6.6 describes *Inspire-U.*) Shannon emphasized:

Inspire-U has helped enhance the type of teamwork that is critical in our business, bringing together creative, project management, and technical folks in the spirit of helping each other. Similar to architecture and the development of theme-park rides, we need a

Exhibit 6.6 Agency.com's Inspire-U Program

Mission Statement

Inspire-U *is a framework for discovery, inspiration, freedom and fun — in which ideas, knowledge and experiences are exchanged, generated and rewarded. It has been constructed to rejuvenate and inspire the people who make up this company, and to create leaders and scholars amongst us, all in the spirit of excellence.*

Sample Programs

- *Agency.com Stats Program* — Learn Agency.com's statistics program so you can help sell it to your clients.
- *Advanced Web Design* — Simple concepts that will blow your mind!
- *Book Club* — Meet with fellow employees in a very laid back setting and discuss a cool book like the "The God of Small Things" or "Into the Wild."
- *Brand 101* — What does the word "brand" mean? How does a brand work? How do you manage its expressions?
- *Demystifying Wall Street* — Overcome the unbelievable amount of jargon Wall Street has developed to confuse the average Joe. Get a plain English explanation of how Wall Street and investment banking work.
- *French Faux Pas, No More* — Appreciate the differences between French and American cultures: French wines, cheeses, breads, pastries, and table manners!
- *Prosaic Poetry, the Art of Writing Great Copy* — Writing copy is one part poetry, one part strategy, one part pure distillation (and about three parts flowers from manure). Ride the edge of cliché into the mystical, magic realm of great copy!
- *Project Management* — Classes will show you the best practices for running projects.
- *Running Brilliant Meetings and Discussions* — The road to the meeting from hell was paved with good intentions. Learn the gentle art of effective chairing.
- *Think You Know PowerPoint?* — Think again. Learn real skills and tricks to create awe-inspiring slides.
- *Visual Storytelling* — From early cave paintings to the current concepts of sequential art, juxtaposed still images have been used to create stories that can evoke different interactions and responses than film, television, and photography. Come see how these techniques can help tell stories on the web.
- *Web Site Usability* — Back by popular demand. Understand behavior patterns of website users and how to use data to create dynamic sites automatically.

Source: Agency.com *Inspire-U* brochure for fall 1998.

true collaboration of creative and technical expertise on our teams for us to be successful.

Aaron Sugarman, president of Agency.com's New York Office and an employee since 1996, recalled that landing the British Airways (BA) account in July 1996 was a crucial point in the firm's transition from being a small company.

> We were scared yet excited putting together that pitch. We knew the odds were stacked against us and we were thrilled that we beat out 30 other American companies to be the only American firm in the finals against three British firms. Given that BA was formerly a quasi-governmental agency, we sensed that there would be sentiment against hiring an American firm. However, Chan gave us confidence that we could win and helped us overcome internal doubts about whether we could staff the job.
>
> "We were completely sleep deprived when we went in to pitch BA," recalled Suh.
>
> I felt good about how our presentation went. Three weeks later I received a call from the BA client. With a deadpan voice he said "I'm calling because. ... um. ... we liked your presentation and. ... um. ... we'd like to work with you." I thought, *"Yeah and now comes the 'but.' "* After a few moments of silence, the BA client then said: "We'd like to hire you." There was no "but." I called everyone into the room and I announced the win in deadpan fashion myself. The room exploded.

"It was a huge win and a defining moment for us," recalled Sugarman. "We now felt as if we were a global player. The firm grew so quickly after that win that the BA deal was the last time the whole firm worked together on a pitch."

Partnering with Omnicom[2]

Omnicom, one of the world's largest communications conglomerates, approached Agency.com with an offer to buy a stake in the firm. "They came calling about January of 1996," recalled Suh.

> This lady, Felice Kincannon, calls up and says, "I represent a very large company looking to get into this field," and I was like, "So?" We had just come off of making $500,000 in our first year of business, and we were like, "So, what do you want?" She said, "I'd like to come talk to you and find out what you do." I said, "Well, are you going to pay for it?" But we saw her anyway, and she came

back five months later with Omnicom and they wanted to invest in the company.

They said, "We want to take a minority piece of your company for which we will pay you money. In addition, we can talk about what else you want." They offered to get clients for us, but I was leery of giving a large old media company any involvement in business operations. So we said, "Okay, here's what we want. We want you to pay us fair value for our shares, but we don't want any of your stinkin' clients because we've done that before, where we work for an agency who works for a client. And further, we're not an advertising agency. We want you to stay out of our business; we want you to give us a credit line; and if that's acceptable to you guys it's cool with us."

Omnicom president John Wren, whom I have tremendous respect for, then said to me: "We don't know what you do, and we're not going to meddle with something we don't know. It's a horse race in the interactive services world, and if seven horses are running, and I've got my money on six, I know I'll at least place, if not win."

The Omnicom offer left us with a choice between a profitable status quo and much more well-capitalized high growth strategy. We knew that if we want to grow quickly, we need the help of a strong partner. We accepted Omnicom's deal.

In September 1996, Omnicom purchased 40% of Agency.com for $11.7 million. Omnicom agreed to lend Agency.com $1.0 million on a revolving basis to meet working capital needs and finance Omnicom-approved "new media" acquisitions.

"I really had no idea negotiations with Omnicom were going on," acknowledged one Agency.com employee. "I'm glad we maintained control and that we gained resources to grow. It was a confidence booster and another reality check that we were on a winning team."

Wren stated his rationale for the purchase thus: "Interactive media is emerging as a viable marketing communications vehicle and with this move Omnicom is staking a claim in the long-term commercial possibilities of this field."[3] Omnicom also acquired stakes in Razorfish, Think New Ideas, Interactive Solutions, and Red Sky Interactive which Omnicom consultant Kincannon had identified, together with Agency.com as the five most promising players in the interactive advertising field. Omnicom subsequently acquired a stake in Organic Online and purchased Eagle River in its entirety. These seven companies became known as the Communicade Group.

Trush Joins the Team

For accountant Ken Trush, the closeness within the firm was brought home in March 1997 when his 12-year-old son, Daniel, was hospitalized for an extended period to treat a brain aneurysm. Recalled Trush:

> Chan and Kyle visited Daniel's bedside regularly, set up a webpage to provide updates on his condition, and just really supported the entire family. I had always had great respect for their business instincts and had enjoyed working with them, but this experience really taught me the type of people they were. Despite their incredibly busy lives, they were consistently there for Daniel and our entire family.

In July 1997, Suh, realizing that Agency.com needed a full-time chief financial officer, asked Trush to take the job. "I really enjoyed working with entrepreneurs and running my own accounting firm" recalled Trush, "but I decided I wanted to become part of Agency.com's team. It wasn't a financial play, I just wanted to do more to help them succeed— I wanted to create rather than just consult."

GROWING THROUGH ACQUISITIONS

Agency.com began immediately, with Communicade's help, to identify acquisition candidates both inside and outside Communicade's stable of companies (Exhibit 6.7 enumerates acquisition criteria). The principal drivers of the acquisition strategy were the desires to grow geographically to serve international clients, to expand service offerings through acquired companies possessing complementary skill sets, and to rapidly build a base of talented executives in a tight labor market for experienced technical and creative professionals. Reflected Trush:

> It would have been incredibly difficult to find independent executives who knew the interactive marketspace well, and if we found these free agents we would have had to pay them top dollar. Would they have been worth it? Probably not. In taking the acquisition route we paid a fair price for the executives, their client lists, and the dedicated employees of their firms.

In July 1997, Agency.com initiated a series of acquisitions (Exhibit 6.8 identifies the acquired firms and timing of the acquisitions). With

---

Exhibit 6.7 Agency.com Acquisition Criteria and Integration Philosophy

---

Acquisition Evaluation Criteria

Agency.com evaluates potential acquisition candidates on:

- cultural fit with a belief in a common mission and desire to help define the interactive future;
- quality management who are excited to work within a larger company;
- highly motivated and skilled staff;
- market-leadership position or potential for leadership in complementary skills and geographic location;
- ability to provide long-term service to a strong client base;
- opportunity to increase revenue based on the ability to offer additional services to existing clients;
- profitability and strong future revenue growth; and
- key success factors of target being similar to Agency.com's model.

Integration Philosophy

Integration is critical to the success of any of our acquisitions:

- senior management of acquired companies is integrated into our management structure, wherever feasible, based on experience, skills, and needs;
- we train all employees on common development practices, methodology, reporting, and new combined best practices;
- we ensure continuity of client relationships;
- one company-wide process for sharing resources across offices enables us to quickly take advantage of the entire company;
- our centralized business development department works with acquired companies to generate new business and sell additional services;
- integration into existing global financial system supports timely billing and reporting; and
- merging of IT platforms protects system integrity and ensures compatibility.

Source: Agency.com internal documents.

Agency.com's acquisition of Eagle River and Ketchum Interactive, both wholly owned subsidiaries of Omnicom's Communicade group, and Interactive Solutions, in which Omnicom held a significant interest, Omnicom's ownership stake in Agency.com became 49.9%.

Exhibit 6.8 Agency.com Acquisition History

Date	Company	Location	Revenue ($ m)	Employees	Agency.com Ownership Share	Payment in Shares (000)	Cash ($ 000)[a]
7/97	Spiral Media[b]	New York	1.5	20	51%[b]	481 (at $1.12)	5,630
10/97	Online Magic[b]	New York, London	4.8	60	42.5%[b]	498 (at $1.12)	1,641
4/98	Ketchum Interactive	San Francisco	1.5	10	100%		643
7/98	Interactive Solutions	Boston	7.0	75	100%	1,576 (at $1.21)	12,691
	Quadris Consulting	Boston, New Jersey	10.0	80	100%	Subsidiary of Interactive Solutions	
7/98	Eagle River Interactive	Multiple, Chicago HQ	22.6	170	100%	7,988[c] (at $1.22)	17,407
8/98	The Primary Group	New York	0.2	2	100%	–	53
1/99	The Edge Consultants	Singapore	N/A	N/A	30%[d]	–	3,027
5/99	Digital Vision	Chicago	N/A	N/A	100%	–	1,100
7/99	Pictoris Interactive SA	Paris	N/A	55	5%[e]	N/A	N/A
8/99	Twinspark Interactive People	Amsterdam	N/A	100	100%	1,057 (at $4.06)	700

[a] Most of the cash paid by Agency.com was borrowed from Omnicom; some was from debt.

[b] In July 1998, Agency.com purchased the remaining shares of Spiral Media and Online Magic. The amount paid shown against these firms accounts for the total price paid for acquiring these firms.

[c] Omnicom (which owned 100% of Eagle River Interactive) received 3,659,548 shares of Agency.com common stock and a 20-year warrant to purchase 4,328,752 shares of Agency.com common stock at an exercise price of $0.005 per share. The transaction was valued at approximately $9.79 million when the transaction was announced in July 1998.

[d] Agency.com held an option to purchase an additional 30%. The initial 30% was purchased in two stages. 12% was purchased in December 1998 for $1,572,203. An additional 18% was purchased in July 1999 for approximately $1,500,000.

[e] Agency.com held an option to purchase the remaining 95% stake in the firm.

Integration Challenges

Blending Several into One

Integrating the operations, processes, and cultures of the disparate acquired firms was a major challenge for Agency.com. In July 1998, Kevin Rowe, former CEO of Eagle River Interactive, now Agency.com's president of North American operations, was charged with overseeing the integration of Agency.com's domestic offices. "Each of the formerly separate firms and offices needed to improve in different areas to become one firm," observed Rowe. "For example, Agency needed to enhance its project management capability, Eagle River and Interactive Solutions to build up their creative capabilities."

Believing that a common culture would emerge from shared processes since "culture is really everything about the way a company does business," Rowe focused on establishing common processes among the offices. He wanted the Agency.com culture to emphasize "career growth, job satisfaction, training, clear roles, clear milestones, and a pride of being with the market leader."

Owing, in particular to the previously different operating philosophies of Agency.com and Eagle River Interactive, the adjustment process proved difficult at times. Agency.com's success criteria tended to be qualitative—"do great work and the business will come"—Eagle River's more quantitative (e.g., utilization, project profitability, and so forth). "Everyone at Agency.com realized that as we grew we needed the type of systems and structures that Eagle River had," recalled Suh. "But we also wanted to maintain the *soul* and feeling of Agency.com, which historically was a main driver of our success."

Managing Turnover

An additional challenge facing the firm during the integration process was increased turnover. Previously, turnover at Agency.com had hovered around 15%, well below the industry average. But in early 1999, turnover rose to the industry average of 30%, problematic in a tight labor market. As Agency.com became larger, some employees left for smaller startup firms. "There were incredible opportunities for our people elsewhere," remarked Rosemary Haefner, VP of human resources, "either to freelance in New York or to earn more money with consulting firms that were trying to enter the market." Some of the turnover was initiated by management. "We wanted to ensure consistency of service delivery and we needed to raise the bar for performance in some jobs, particularly project management and client services," explained Haefner.

Some executives attributed the increased turnover to demographic rather than firm-specific reasons. One vice-president pointed to the personal demands the industry placed on the employees:

This is a market that was built on the backs of 20 year-olds, and those 20 year-olds now are marrying and starting families. They don't get the same rush they used to get about staying up night after night finishing client projects. As the industry matures, some of our people feel that the work just isn't as fun as it used to be because the clients are becoming more demanding and some of the processes feel a little stifling at first.

High employee turnover and rapid growth in staffing needs led, according to Sugarman, to a situation, during the summer of 1999, in which "50% of our employees in New York have been with us less than six months. With all these new faces," he observed, "it is difficult to get to know everyone and to maintain the connection of small companies. But we try."

Integrating Senior Management

At senior levels, Agency.com experienced virtually no turnover as a result of the acquisitions, notwithstanding that many of the acquired firms' leaders were entrepreneurs and used to being *the* chief executive. CFO Trush explained: "Chan was a master at recruiting the top executives. He allowed them the freedom to express their broad knowledge while at the same time, being responsible for a very focused discipline. Seventeen of the eighteen senior executives of the acquired firms decided to stay on with us after the acquisitions." (Exhibit 6.9 presents an organizational chart for Agency.com as of June 1999.)

However, one senior executive, who emphasized that turnover at senior levels often takes awhile to materialize, observed: "Some executives accepted roles that may have been out of their comfort zones. Everyone has worked hard at their new positions, but I suspect that within a year a few members of our executive team will choose to leave the company to take on roles that better fit their skills and interests. Many of us were happy to be smaller fishes in a much bigger pond, but there are some that will always prefer to be the big fish."

Exhibit 6.9 Agency.com Organizational Chart (as of May 19, 1999)

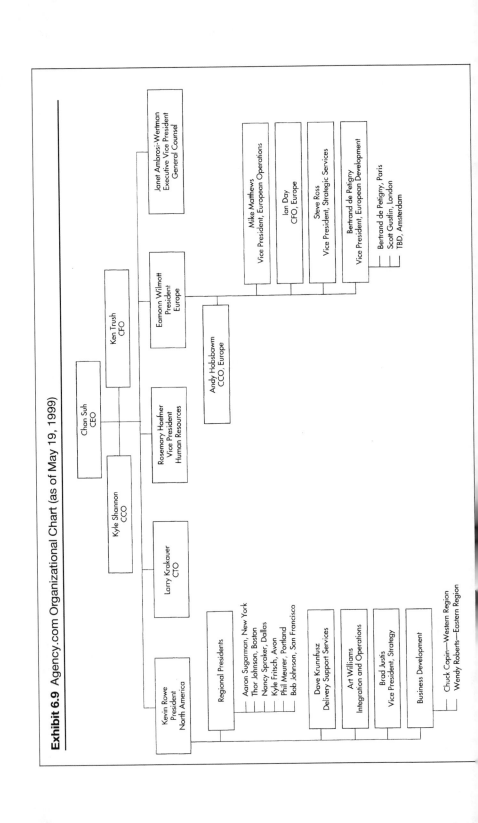

Chan Suh
CEO

Ken Trush
CFO

Kyle Shannon
CCO

Larry Krakauer
CTO

Rosemary Haefner
Vice President
Human Resources

Janet Ambrosi-Wertman
Executive Vice President
General Counsel

Kevin Rowe
President
North America

Eamonn Wilmott
President
Europe

Regional Presidents
├─ Aaron Sugarman, New York
├─ Thor Johnson, Boston
├─ Nancy Spraker, Dallas
├─ Kyle Fritsch, Avon
├─ Phil Meurer, Portland
└─ Bob Johnson, San Francisco

Dave Krunnfusz
Delivery Support Services

Art Williams
Integration and Operations

Brad Justis
Vice President, Strategy

Business Development
├─ Chuck Capin—Western Region
└─ Wendy Roberts—Eastern Region

Andy Hobsbawm
CCO, Europe

Mike Matthews
Vice President, European Operations

Ian Day
CFO, Europe

Steve Ross
Vice President, Strategic Services

Bertrand de Petigny
Vice President, European Development
├─ Bertrand de Petigny, Paris
├─ Scott Gustin, London
└─ TBD, Amsterdam

CHALLENGES IN 1999 AND BEYOND

Heavyweight Competition

Demands on Internet professional services companies were growing rapidly. Big companies were increasingly demanding global Internet service. "We need to get much bigger," Rowe explained, "because clients in 1999 simultaneously want *scale*, enough person-power to meet their needs, *scope*, broad enough skills—that is, strategy, marketing, and production—to service them, and *reach*, the ability to serve them globally.

With Forrester and other research organizations predicting explosive global growth for the Internet professional services market, new competitors entered the market seeking to capitalize on their established global presence (see Exhibit 6.10 for Forrester's projections, Exhibit 6.11 for a list of competitors). System integrators such as IBM believed that they could compete effectively by adding creative departments, management consultants such as McKinsey and Andersen by exploiting their breadth of services and global scale, and advertising agencies by supplementing their consumer knowledge, strategic thinking, and

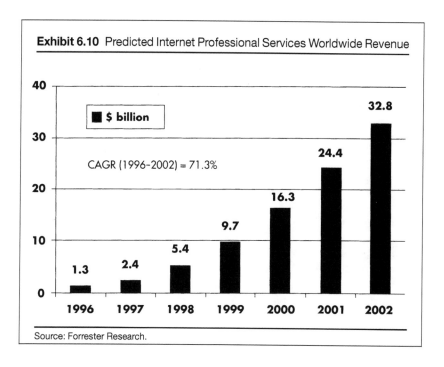

Exhibit 6.10 Predicted Internet Professional Services Worldwide Revenue

$ billion

CAGR (1996-2002) = 71.3%

1996	1997	1998	1999	2000	2001	2002
1.3	2.4	5.4	9.7	16.3	24.4	32.8

Source: Forrester Research.

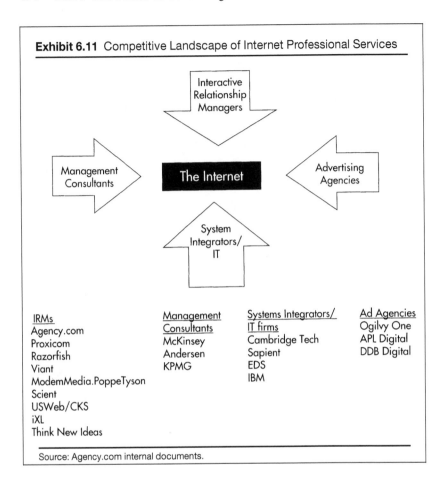

Exhibit 6.11 Competitive Landscape of Internet Professional Services

Interactive Relationship Managers

Management Consultants

The Internet

Advertising Agencies

System Integrators/ IT

IRMs	Management Consultants	Systems Integrators/ IT firms	Ad Agencies
Agency.com	McKinsey	Cambridge Tech	Ogilvy One
Proxicom	Andersen	Sapient	APL Digital
Razorfish	KPMG	EDS	DDB Digital
Viant		IBM	
ModemMedia.PoppeTyson			
Scient			
USWeb/CKS			
iXL			
Think New Ideas			

Source: Agency.com internal documents.

branding expertise with programmers. Competition from other interactive agencies would remain a threat.

Organizationally, Agency.com was in some respects beginning to resemble aspects of management consulting firms. It developed a strategic services consulting practice to help clients decide how the Internet can be used to grow their businesses *before* commencing design work on their websites. Agency.com also established a business development organization and implemented formal training programs. Rowe, a former consultant at Andersen Consulting, observed that "consulting firms hire incredibly smart people and have organizations to train them quickly and effectively; we need the same to compete effectively with them."

Exhibit 6.12 Silicon Alley's Public Interactive Firms as of July 1999

Name	Ticker marker	Description	Filing Date	Opening Day[a]	Monthly Index May 15–June 15	52 Weeks
K2 Design	KTWO Nasdaq	Web design and integration company; one of the earliest alley companies to go public	May 22, 1996	7/26/96 P:$6; A:$6;O:$6; C:$7°	5–15: 41 3/8 6–15: 29 ¾	N/A
Think New Ideas	THNK Nasdaq	Internet marketing company augmented by proprietary software for tracking Web statistics	Dec. 26, 1996	12/26/97 P:$5; A:$7; O:$7; C:$7	5–15: 11 13/16 6–15: 14	High: 37 3/8 Low: 3
DoubleClick	DCLK Nasdaq	Ad creation, placement, management, tracking, and reporting services for online advertisers	Dec. 16, 1997	2/20/98 P:$16; A:$17; O:$29; C:$27	5–15: 118 11/16 6–15: 70 1/8	High: 176 Low: 6 3/4
RareMedium	RRRR Nasdaq	Online full service agency including design and integration	Apr. 15, 1998	NA	5–15: 15 1/16 6–15: 11 ½	High: 20 1/8 Low: 1 5/8
Frontline Communications	FCCN Nasdaq	Internet services primarily for individual and small business subscribers in NY & NJ	Aug. 21, 1997	5/14/98 P:$4; A:$4; O:$5; C:$4.88	5–15: 12 3/8 6–15: 9 7/16	N/A
IBS Interactive	IBSX Nasdaq	Provider of outsourced computer networking, programming, applications development, and internet services	Mar. 11, 1998	5/15/98 P:$6; A:$6; O:$8.5; C:$8.13	5–15: 20 ¾ 6–15: 20	N/A
24/7 Media	TFSM Nasdaq	Operates a full scale advertising and marketing network working with both major portals and niche ad placement	Dec. 19, 1997	8/14/98 P:$12–14; A:$14; O:$18.5; C:$20.25	5–15: 44 6–15: 24	High: 69 5/8 Low: 5
Modern Media. Poppe Tyson	MMPT Nasdaq	Interactive agency provides Web design, integration, and marketing strategies	Nov.27, 1998	2/5/99 P:$13–15; A:$16; O:$55.63; C:$45	5–15: 25 1/16 6–15: 24 11/15	High: 55 1/8 Low: 22 3/16
Razorfish	RAZF Nasdaq	One-stop-shop for Web integration, design, consulting, and implementation	April 27, 1999	4/26/99 P:$13–15; A:$16; O:$35; C:$33.50	5–15: 33 ¾ 6–15: 29	High: 31 3/8 Low: 28

Source: *AlleyCat News*, volume 3.7/8, July–August 1999, pp. 30–34.

[a] P: proposed, A: actual,; O: open; C: close.

Financing Growth

In the wake of Agency.com's 1998 acquisition spree and several of its Silicon Alley competitors having had already gone public (Exhibit 6.12 lists these firms), the stock market had been anticipating an IPO by Agency.com. "An IPO," according to Suh,

> would have many benefits. First, it would provide the significant financial resources needed to reach critical mass quickly while simultaneously limiting our dependence on Omnicom. Our relationship with Omnicom has provided the capital for us to grow up until this point. But we don't want to over-rely on Omnicom for our growth. Secondly, it would allow us liquid stock to recruit, retain, and compensate key employees. Finally, it would allow us an acquisition currency as we grow.

In terms of potential downsides, there would be no more restrictions on stock ownership. The stock price would be subject to many things beyond our control, such as interest rates or

---

Exhibit 6.13 Percentage of Agency.com Common Stock Beneficially Owned (as of 6/30/99)

Name	Role	Shares (000)	% Ownership
Chan Suh	CEO, co-founder	4,756	19.0%
Kyle Shannon	CCO, co-founder	4,580	18.3%
Ken Trush	CFO	600	2.4%
Kevin Rowe	President, North America; *former president of Eagle River Interactive.*	115	0.5%
Eamonn Wilmott	President, Europe; *former director of Online Magic.*	331	1.3%
Larry Krakauer	CTO, *former president of Quadris Consulting.*	940	3.7%
Omnicom		12,566	49.9%
Others		1,207	4.8%
Total	**Total**	**25,095**	**100.0%**

Source: Agency.com S-1 Filing.
There were 71 stockholders of record.

investor sentiment. An IPO might also lead to internal changes, as many of our employees could earn a windfall. This might make retention more difficult because they could leave and become entrepreneurs themselves.

My major concern, however, is that an IPO might eventually lead to a loss of control over Agency.com. Omnicom owns 49.9% of the stock with many warrants. If they sold a huge block of shares it would put us in play. Also, by buying shares on the open market, Omnicom theoretically could become the majority shareholder. (Exhibit 6.13 details the ownership structure as of 6/30/99.)

NOTES TO CASE

1. Meta4 (1997 revenues of approximately $2.3 million) was purchased in July 1998 by fine.com for $1.1 million in common stock (*Business Wire*, July 30, 1998).

2. Omnicom Group Inc. consisted of the advertising agency networks BBDO Worldwide, DDB Needham Worldwide, and TBWA Chiat/Day International as well as Diversified Agency Services (which operated a number of leading, independently branded agencies in marketing services, advertising, and public relations) and Goodby, Silverstein & Partners. Omnicom subsidiary Communicade oversaw acquisitions in new media.

3. "Omnicom Group Acquires Significant Minority Participation in Five Interactive Agencies," *PR Newswire*, 22 September, 1996.

APPENDIX

Recent Books on Management Consulting

Argyris, C. (2001). *Flawed Advice and the Management Trap*. New York: Oxford University Press.

Ashford, Martin (1998). *Con Tricks—The Shadow World of Management Consultancy and How to Make It Work for You*. New York: Simon & Schuster.

Beer, M. & Nohria, N. (2000). *Consultants Role in Change*. Section VI in *Breaking the Code of Change*, p. 337–338. Boston: Harvard Business School Press.

Bellman, Geoffrey M. (2002). *The Consultant's Calling*. San Francisco: Jossey-Bass.

Biech, Elaine (1999). *The Business Of Consulting—The Basics and Beyond*. San Francisco: Jossey-Bass/Pfeiffer.

Biech, Elaine (2002). *The Consultant's Quick Start Guide*. San Francisco: Jossey-Bass/Pfeiffer.

Biswas, Sugata & Daryl Twitchell (2002). *Management Consulting—A Complete Guide to the Industry*. 2nd ed. New York: John Wiley and Sons Ltd.

Buono, Anthony F. (ed.) (2001). *Current Trends in Management Consulting*. Greenwich: Information Age Publishing.

Buono, Anthony F. (ed.) (2002). *Developing Knowledge and Value in Management Consulting*. Research in Management Consulting, vol. 2. Greenwich: Information Age Publishing.

Carucci, Ron A. & Toby J. Tetenbaum (2000). *The Value-creating Consultant—How to Build and Sustain Lasting Client Relationships*. New York: Amacom.

Cockman, P., Evans, B. & Reynolds, P. (1999). *Consulting for Real People: a Client-Centered Approach for Change Agents and Leaders*. New York: McGraw-Hill.

Cody, Thomas G. (2001). *Management Consulting—A Game Without Chips.* Fitzwilliam: N.H.

Cohen, William A. (2001). *How to Make it Big as a Consultant.* 3rd ed. New York: Amacom.

Cope, Mick (2000). *The Seven Cs of Consulting—Your Complete Blueprint for any Consultancy Assignment.* London: Prentice Hall.

Curnow, Barry & Jonathan Reuvid (eds.) (2001). *The International Guide to Management Consultancy—The Evolution, Practice and Structure of Management Consultancy Worldwide.* London: Kogan Page.

Czerniawska, Fiona (1999). *Management Consultancy in the 21st Century.* London: McMillan Business.

Czerniawska, Fiona (2002). *Management Consultancy—What Next?* London/ Basingstoke: Palgrave Macmillan Press.

Czerniawska, Fiona (2002). *The Intelligent Client—Managing Your Management Consultant.* London: Hodder & Stoughton Educational Division.

Czerniawska, Fiona (2002). *Value-based Consulting.* London/Basingstoke: Palgrave Macmillan.

Engwall, L. & C. B. Eriksson (1999). *Advising Corporate Superstars.* London: Kings College.

Fombrun, Charles J. & Nevins, Mark (eds.) (2003). *The Advice Business.* Upper Saddle River, New Jersey: Pearson Education, Inc.

Freedman, Rick (2001). *The eConsultant—Guiding Clients to Net Success.* San Francisco: Jossey-Bass/Pfeiffer.

Fuller, Gordon W. (1999). *Getting Most Out of Your Consultants.* New York. CRC Press.

Haslebo, Gitte & Kit Sanne Nielsen (2000). *Systems and Meaning—Consulting in Organizations.* London: Karnac Books.

Hilburt-Davis, Jane & W. Gibb Dyer (2003). *Consulting to Family Businesses—A Practical Guide to Contracting, Assessment, and Implementation.* Chichester: John Wiley and Sons Ltd.

Kipping, M. & Engwall, L. (eds.) (2002). *Management Consulting. Emergence and Dynamics of a Knowledge Industry.* Oxford: Oxford University Press.

Holtz, Herman (1999). *The Concise Guide to Becoming an Independent Consultant.* New York: Wiley.

Holtz, Herman (2000). *Getting Started in Sales Consulting.* New York: John Wiley and Sons.

Kara, H. & Muir, P. (2003). *Commissioning Consultancy—Managing Outside Expertise to Improve Your Services.* Dorset: Russel House Publishing.

Kubr, Milan (ed.) (1998). *Management Consulting—A Guide to the Profession.* Geneva: ILO.

Lilja, K. & Poulfelt, F. (2001). *The Anatomy of Networks in Management Consulting.* In Anthony F. Buono (ed.) *Current Trends in Management Consulting.* Research on Consulting Series 1. Greenwich, CT: Information Age Publications Inc.

Nelson, Bob & Economy, Peter (1997). *Consulting for Dummies.* New York: IDG Books Worldwide.

O'Shea, J. & Madigan, C. (1997). *Dangerous Company—The Consulting Powerhouses and the Business They Save and Ruin.* London: NB Publishing.

Mooney, Paul (1999). *The Effective Consultant—How to Develop the High Performance Organisation.* Dublin: Oak Tree.

Paris, L. (2003). *Behind the Façade—The Consulting Profession in Focus: Cautionary Words for the Wise.* New York: Writer's Showcase.

Petersen, Nicoline Jacoby & Poulfelt, Flemming (2002). *Knowledge Management in Action: A Study of Knowledge Management in Management Consultancies.* In Anthony F. Buono (ed.) *Knowledge and Value Development in Management Consulting.* Research on Consulting Series 1. Greenwich, CT: Information Age Publications Inc.

Pinault, Lewis (2000). *Consulting Demons—Inside the Unscrupulous World of Global Corporate Consulting.* Chichester: Harper Business.

Sadler, Philip (ed.) (1998). *Management Consultancy—A Handbook for Best Practice.* London: Kogan Page.

Schaffer R.H. (1997). *High-Impact Consulting.* San Francisco: Jossey-Bass.

Schein, Edgar H. (1999). *Process Consultation Revisited—Building the Helping Relationship.* Reading, Mass.: Addison Wesley.

Scott, M.C. (1998). *The Intellect Industry. Profiting and Learning from Professional Services Firms.* New York: Wiley.

Sveiby, K.E. (1997). *The New Organizational Wealth—Managing and Measuring Knowledge-based Assets.* San Francisco: Berrett-Koehler.

Weiss, Alan (2002). *How to Acquire Clients—Powerful Techniques for the Successful Practitioner.* San Francisco: Jossey-Bass/Pfeiffer.

Weiss, Alan (2002). *Value-based Fees.* San Francisco: Jossey-Bass/Pfeiffer.

Werr, A. (1999). *The Language of Change—The Roles of Methods in the Work of Management Consultants.* Stockholm: The Economic Research Institute, Stockholm School of Economics.

Weiss, A. (2001). *The Ultimate Consultant.* San Francisco: Jossey-Bass/Pfeiffer.

Wickhan, Philip A. (1999). *Management Consulting.* London: Financial Times—Pitman Publishing.

INDEX